Shojo Beat

Godchild™

Earl Cain Series 5

Vol. 1

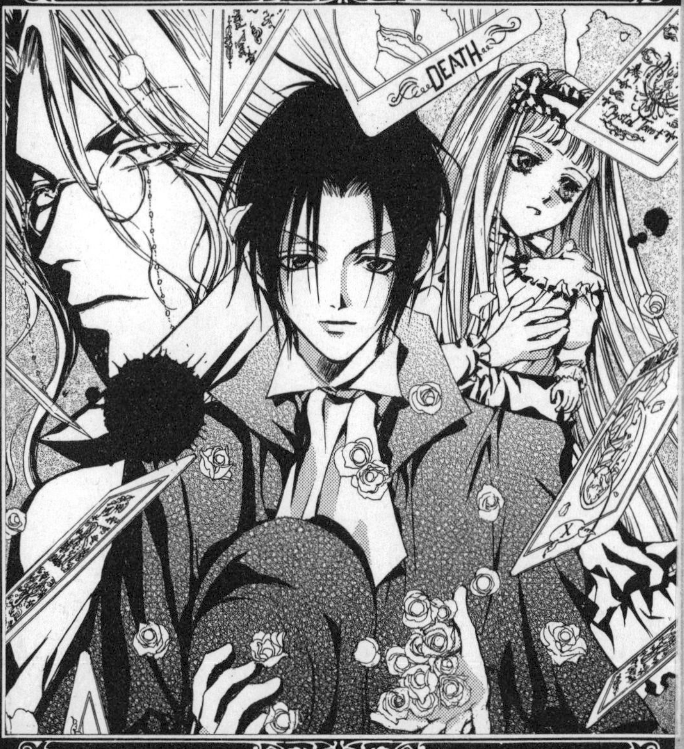
DEATH

Story & Art by Kaori Yuki

Contents

Godchild 1 ·············· 4

Postscript ·············· 197

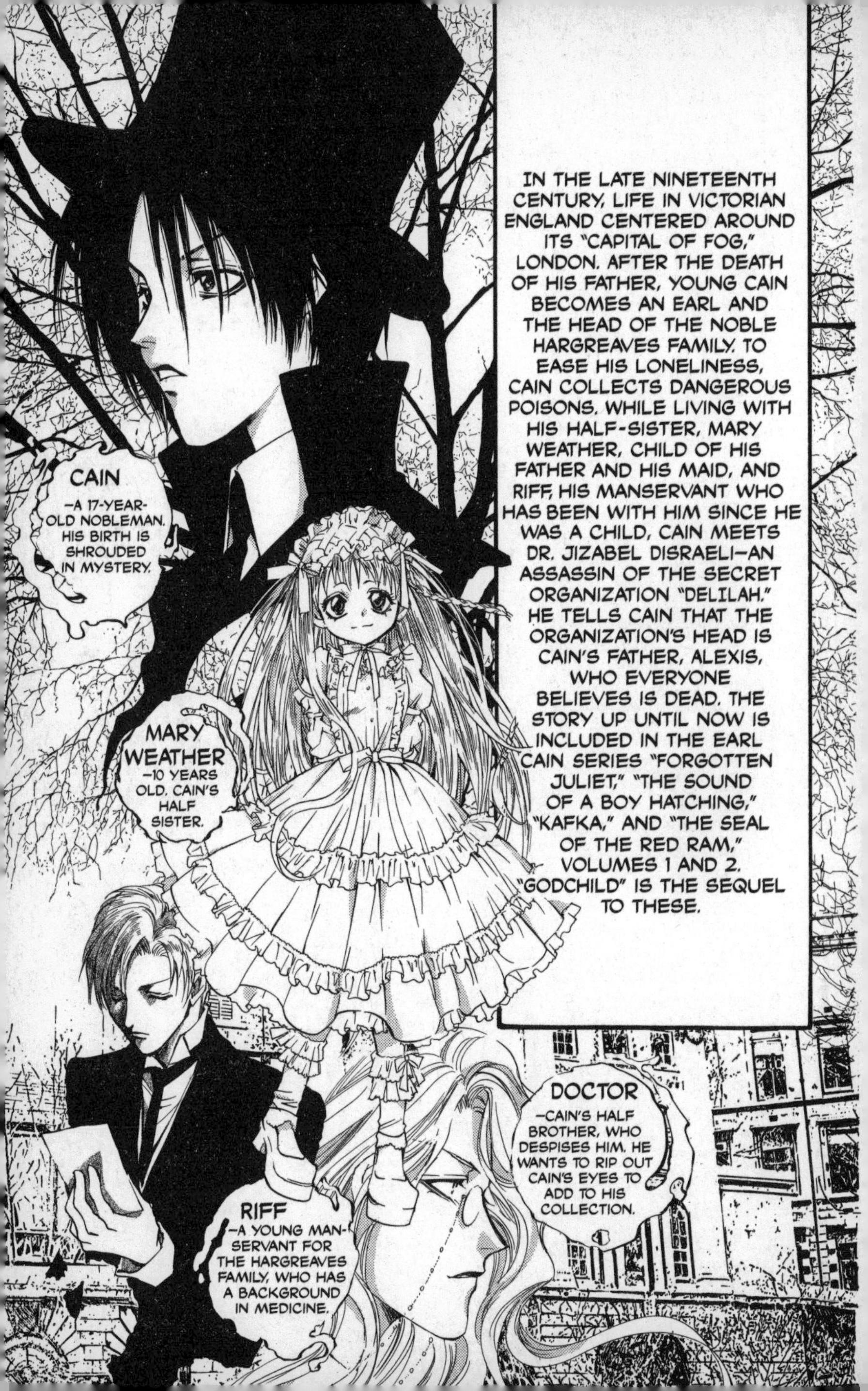
IN THE LATE NINETEENTH CENTURY, LIFE IN VICTORIAN ENGLAND CENTERED AROUND ITS "CAPITAL OF FOG," LONDON. AFTER THE DEATH OF HIS FATHER, YOUNG CAIN BECOMES AN EARL AND THE HEAD OF THE NOBLE HARGREAVES FAMILY. TO EASE HIS LONELINESS, CAIN COLLECTS DANGEROUS POISONS. WHILE LIVING WITH HIS HALF-SISTER, MARY WEATHER, CHILD OF HIS FATHER AND HIS MAID, AND RIFF, HIS MANSERVANT WHO HAS BEEN WITH HIM SINCE HE WAS A CHILD, CAIN MEETS DR. JIZABEL DISRAELI—AN ASSASSIN OF THE SECRET ORGANIZATION "DELILAH." HE TELLS CAIN THAT THE ORGANIZATION'S HEAD IS CAIN'S FATHER, ALEXIS, WHO EVERYONE BELIEVES IS DEAD. THE STORY UP UNTIL NOW IS INCLUDED IN THE EARL CAIN SERIES "FORGOTTEN JULIET," "THE SOUND OF A BOY HATCHING," "KAFKA," AND "THE SEAL OF THE RED RAM," VOLUMES 1 AND 2. "GODCHILD" IS THE SEQUEL TO THESE.
CAIN —A 17-YEAR-OLD NOBLEMAN. HIS BIRTH IS SHROUDED IN MYSTERY.
MARY WEATHER —10 YEARS OLD. CAIN'S HALF SISTER.
DOCTOR —CAIN'S HALF BROTHER, WHO DESPISES HIM. HE WANTS TO RIP OUT CAIN'S EYES TO ADD TO HIS COLLECTION.
RIFF —A YOUNG MAN-SERVANT FOR THE HARGREAVES FAMILY, WHO HAS A BACKGROUND IN MEDICINE.

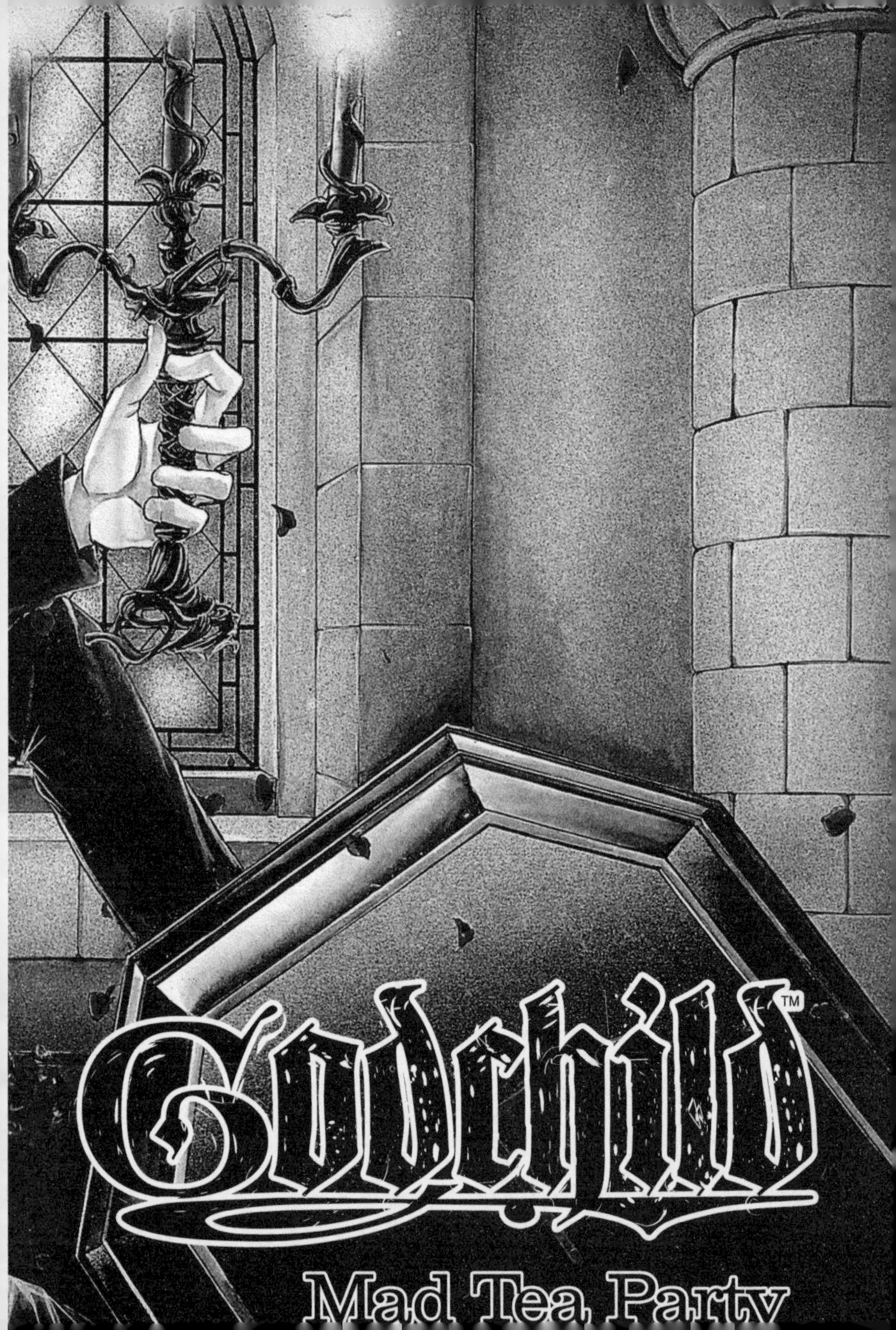
Godchild™
Mad Tea Party

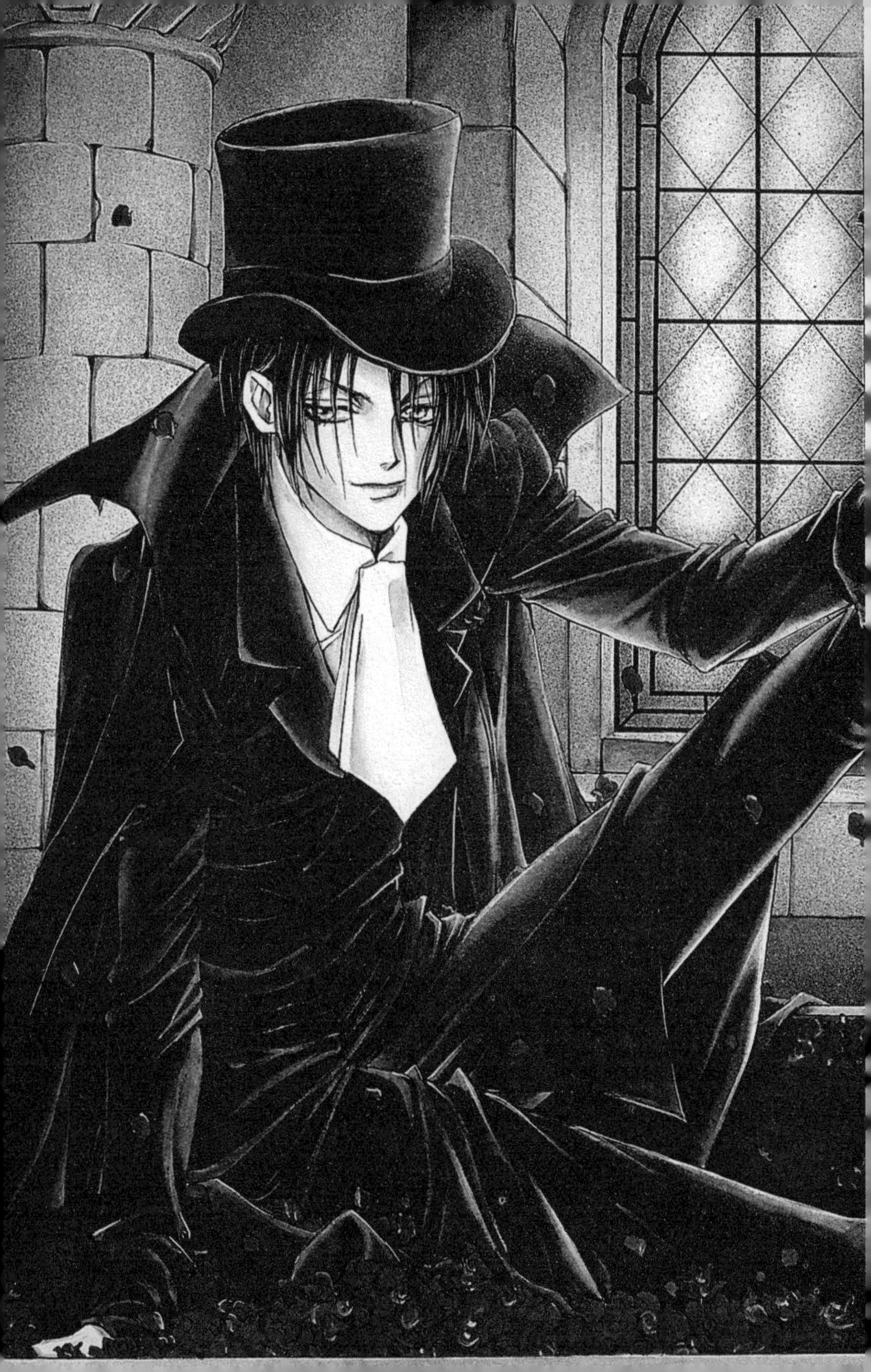

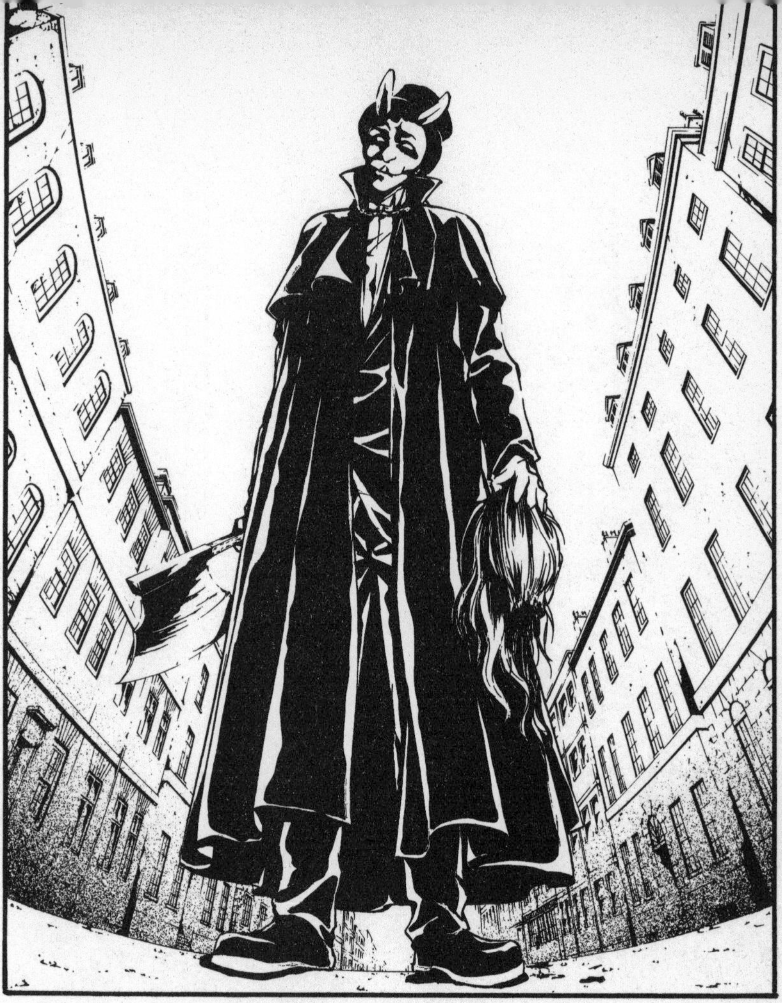

Mysterious Murders in London!

A man in a rabbit mask is cutting off the heads of young girls in the Regent district. Witnesses call this eerie killer the "White Rabbit."

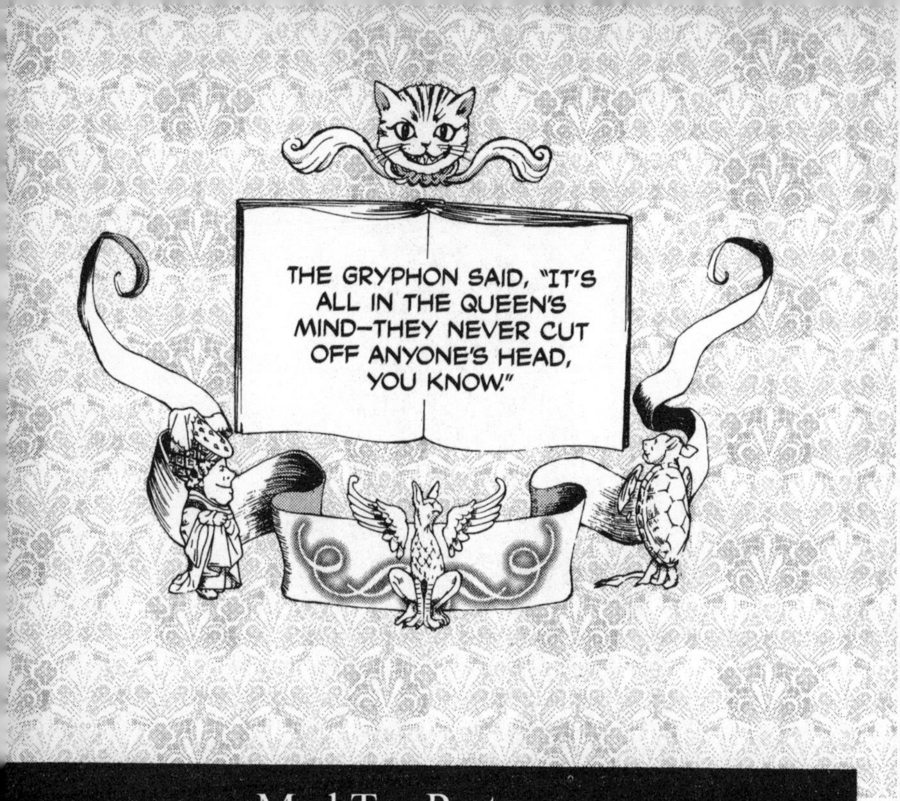
THE GRYPHON SAID, "IT'S ALL IN THE QUEEN'S MIND—THEY NEVER CUT OFF ANYONE'S HEAD, YOU KNOW."

Mad Tea Party

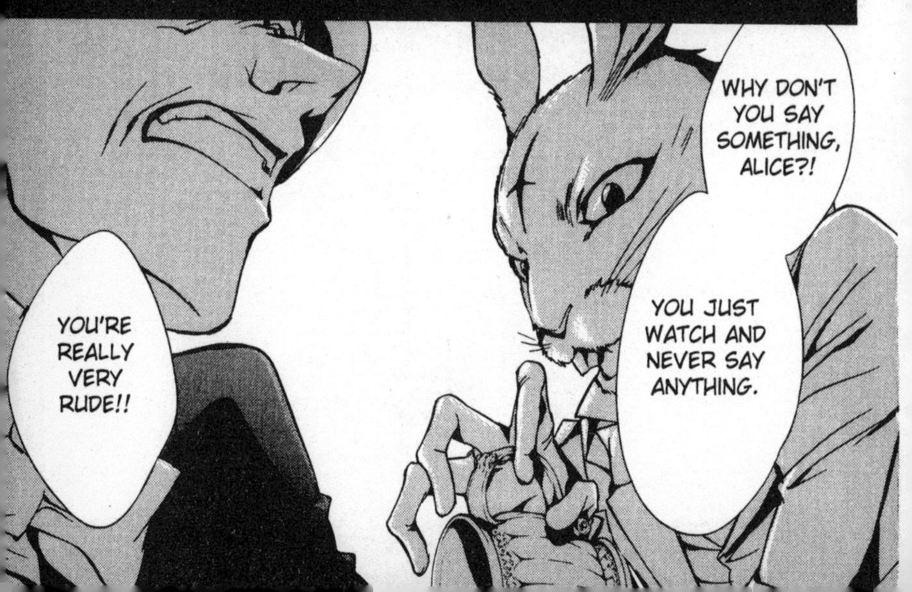
WHY DON'T YOU SAY SOMETHING, ALICE?!
YOU JUST WATCH AND NEVER SAY ANYTHING.
YOU'RE REALLY VERY RUDE!!

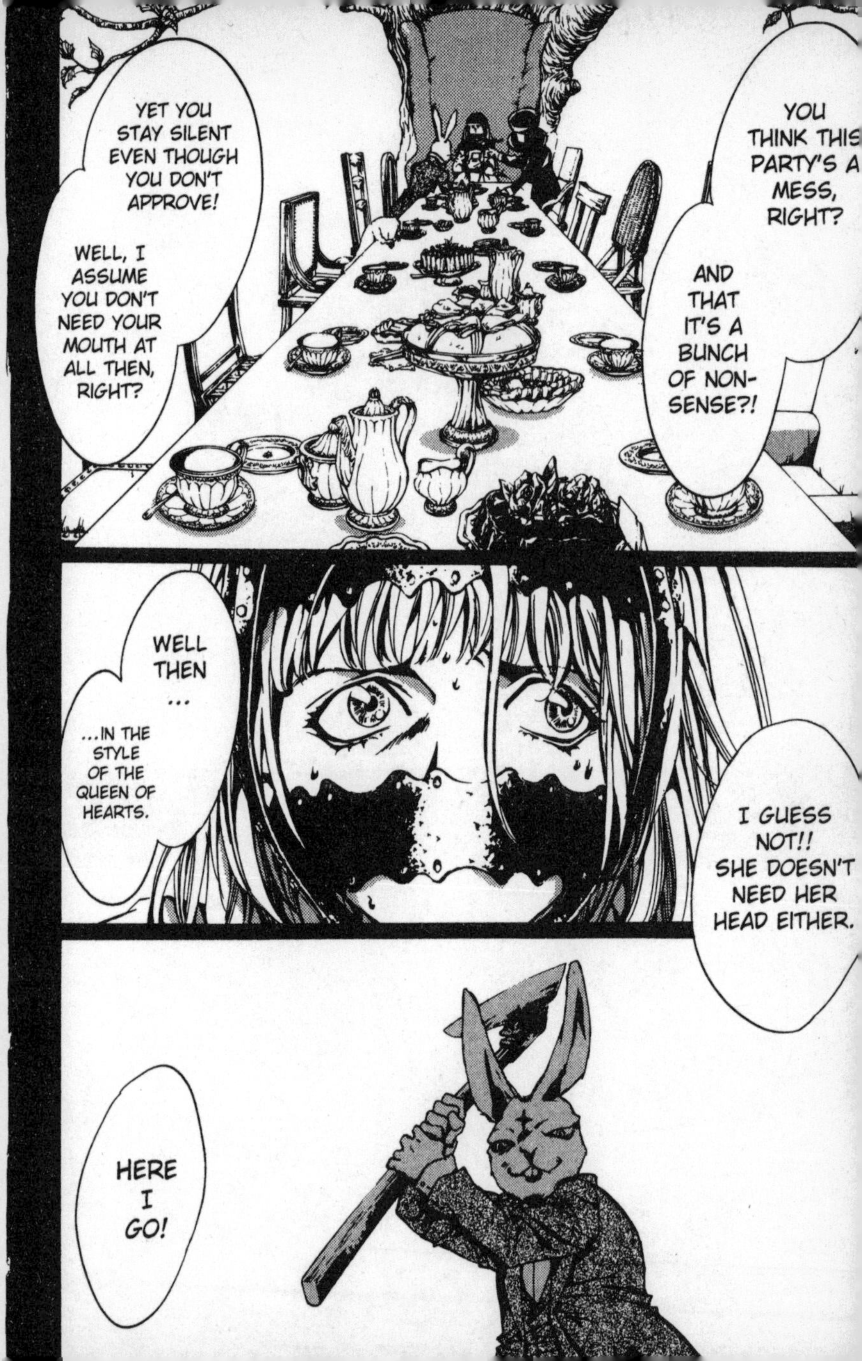
YOU THINK THIS PARTY'S A MESS, RIGHT?
AND THAT IT'S A BUNCH OF NON-SENSE?!
YET YOU STAY SILENT EVEN THOUGH YOU DON'T APPROVE!
WELL, I ASSUME YOU DON'T NEED YOUR MOUTH AT ALL THEN, RIGHT?
I GUESS NOT!! SHE DOESN'T NEED HER HEAD EITHER.
WELL THEN ...
...IN THE STYLE OF THE QUEEN OF HEARTS.
HERE I GO!

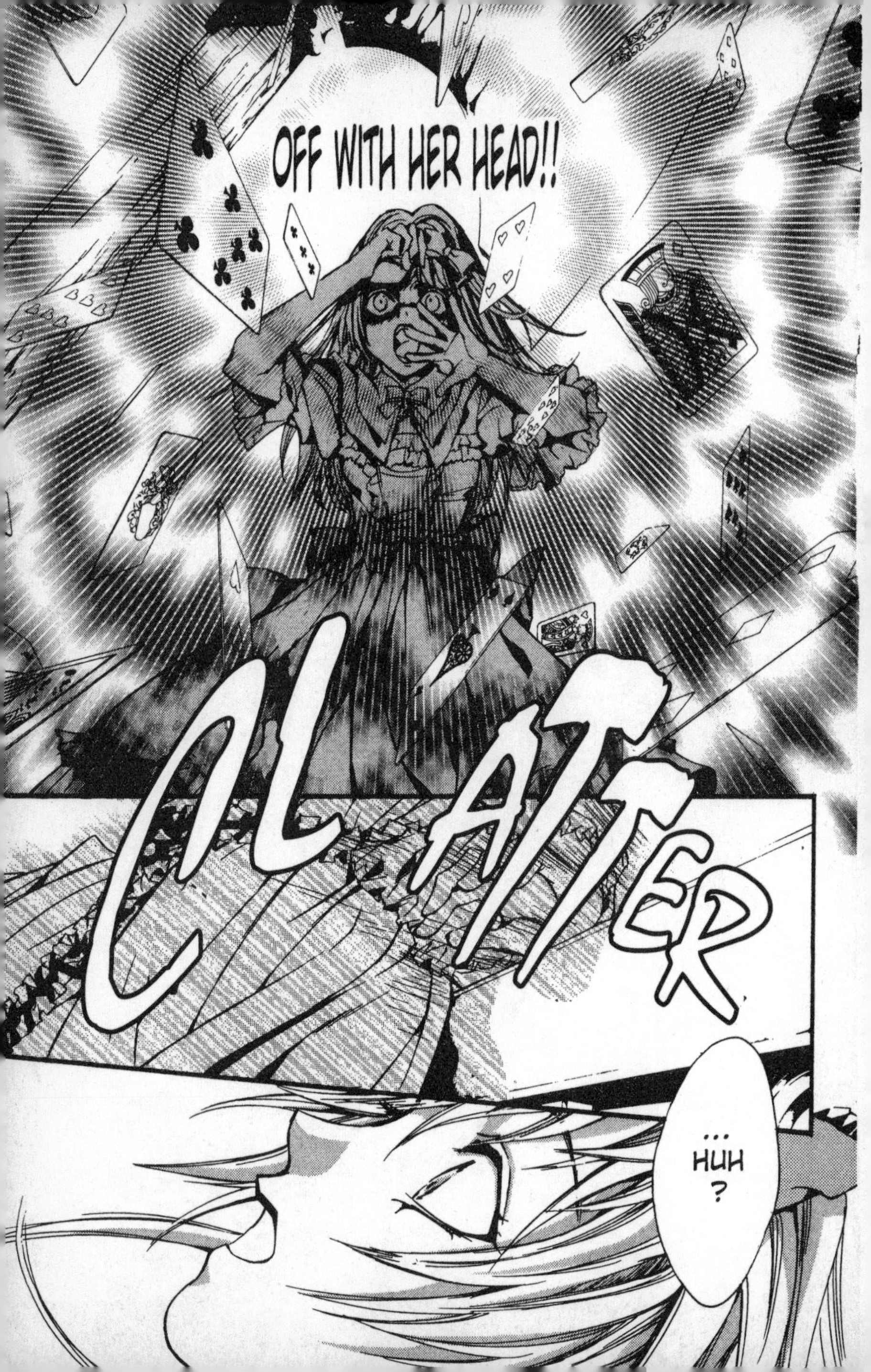
OFF WITH HER HEAD!!
CLATTER
...HUH?

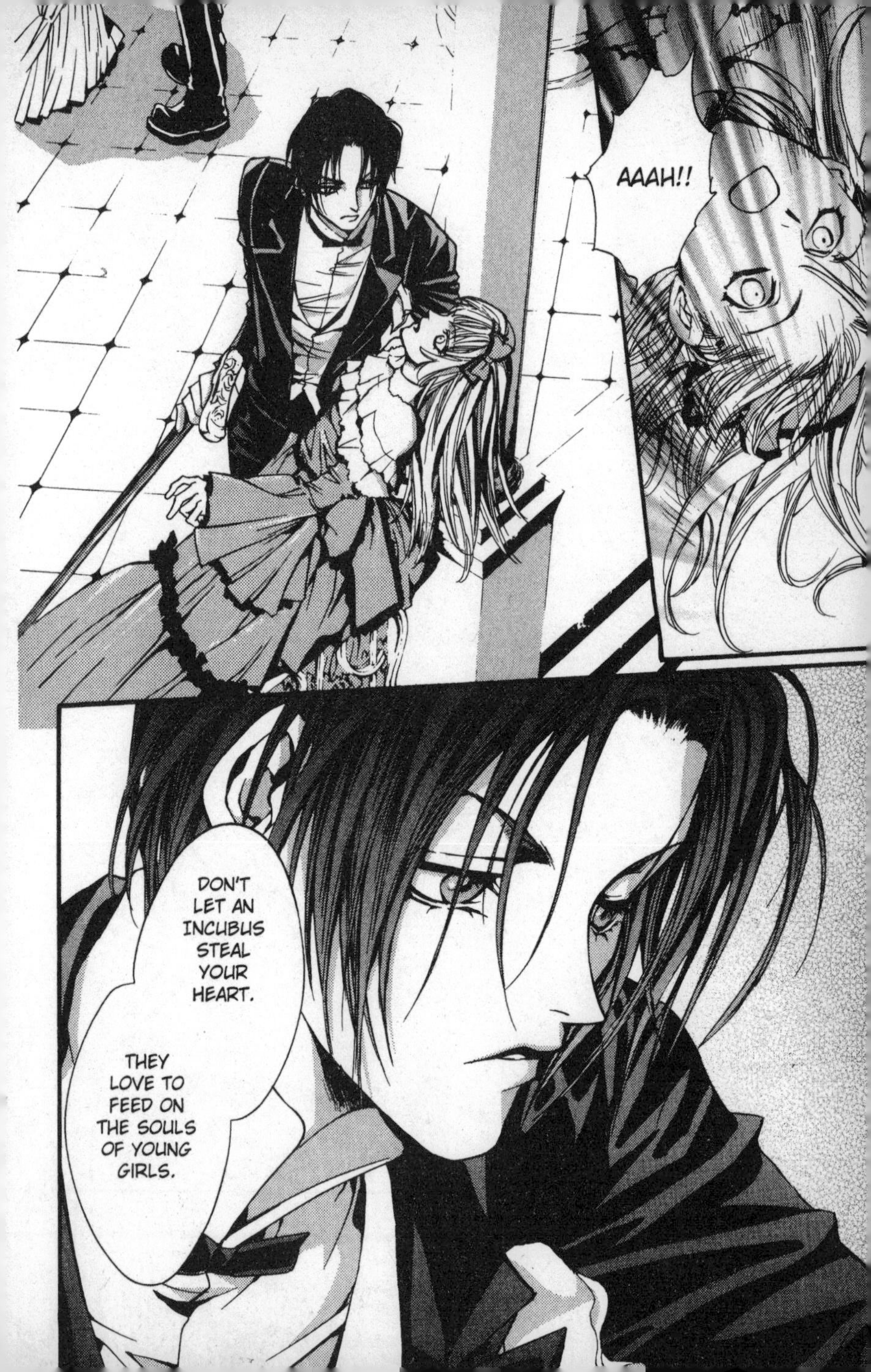
AAAH!!
DON'T LET AN INCUBUS STEAL YOUR HEART.
THEY LOVE TO FEED ON THE SOULS OF YOUNG GIRLS.

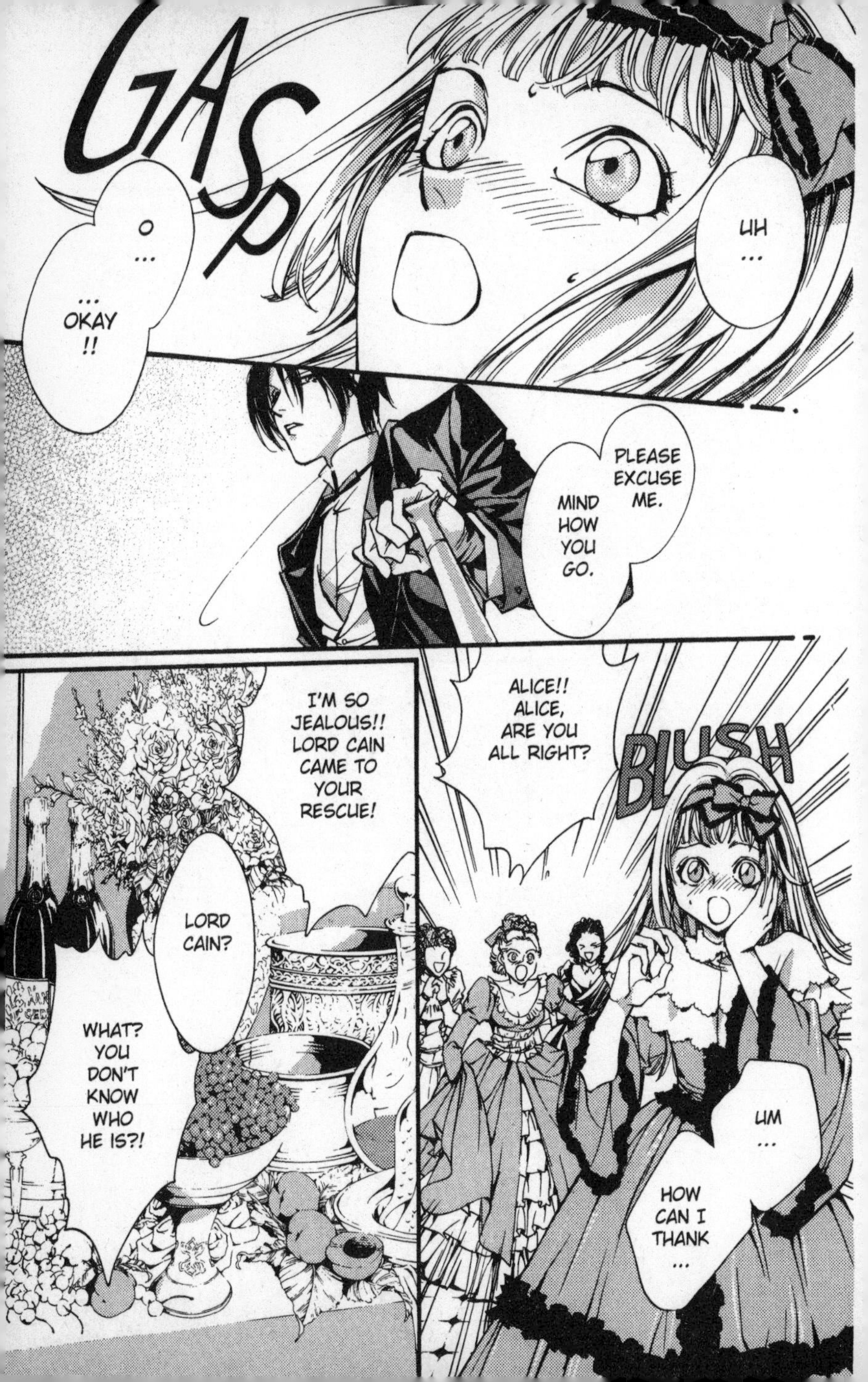
UH ...
GASP
O ... ... OKAY !!
PLEASE EXCUSE ME.
MIND HOW YOU GO.
ALICE!! ALICE, ARE YOU ALL RIGHT?
BLUSH
UM ...
HOW CAN I THANK ...
I'M SO JEALOUS!! LORD CAIN CAME TO YOUR RESCUE!
LORD CAIN?
WHAT? YOU DON'T KNOW WHO HE IS?!

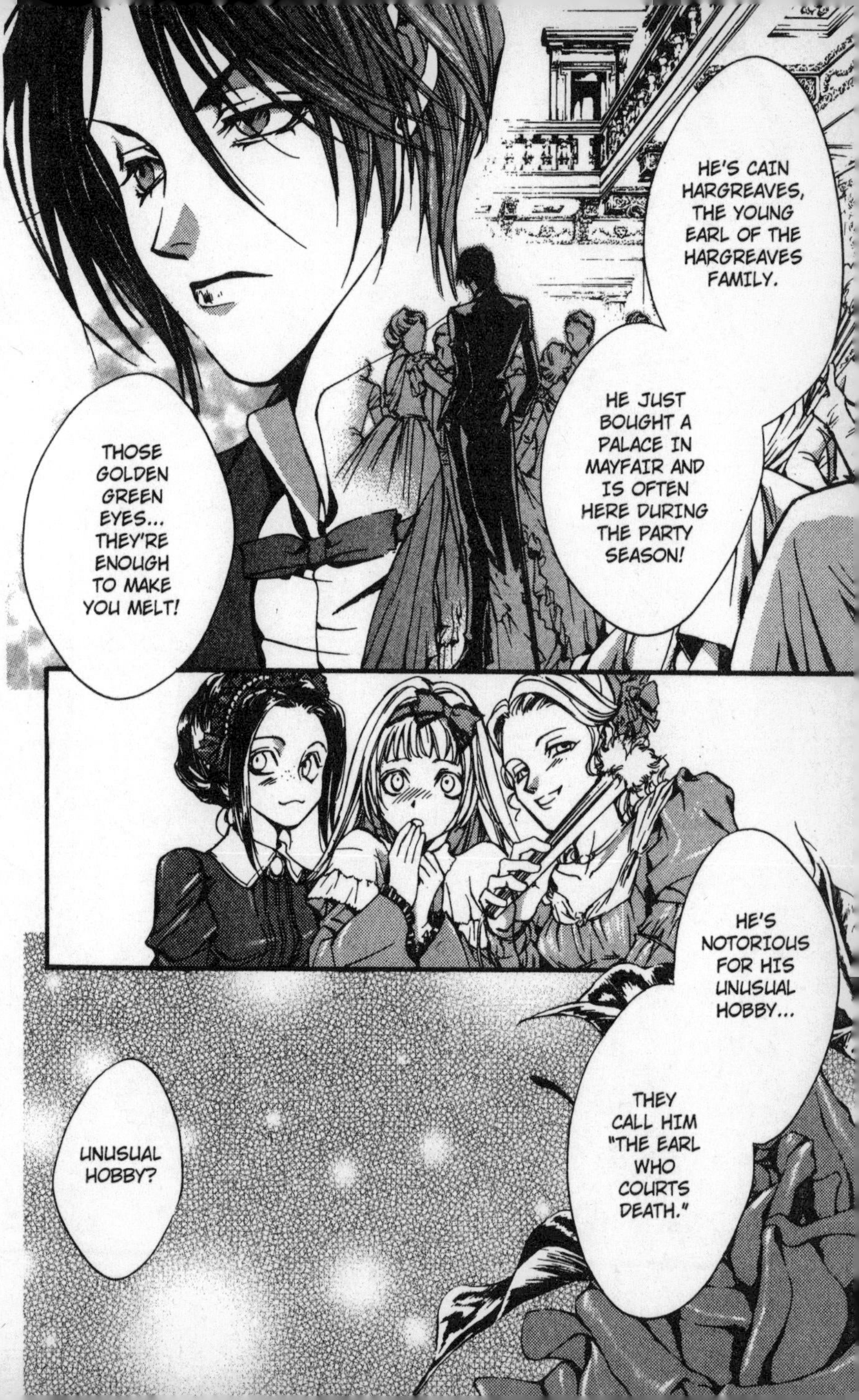
HE'S CAIN HARGREAVES, THE YOUNG EARL OF THE HARGREAVES FAMILY.
HE JUST BOUGHT A PALACE IN MAYFAIR AND IS OFTEN HERE DURING THE PARTY SEASON!
THOSE GOLDEN GREEN EYES... THEY'RE ENOUGH TO MAKE YOU MELT!
HE'S NOTORIOUS FOR HIS UNUSUAL HOBBY...
THEY CALL HIM "THE EARL WHO COURTS DEATH."
UNUSUAL HOBBY?

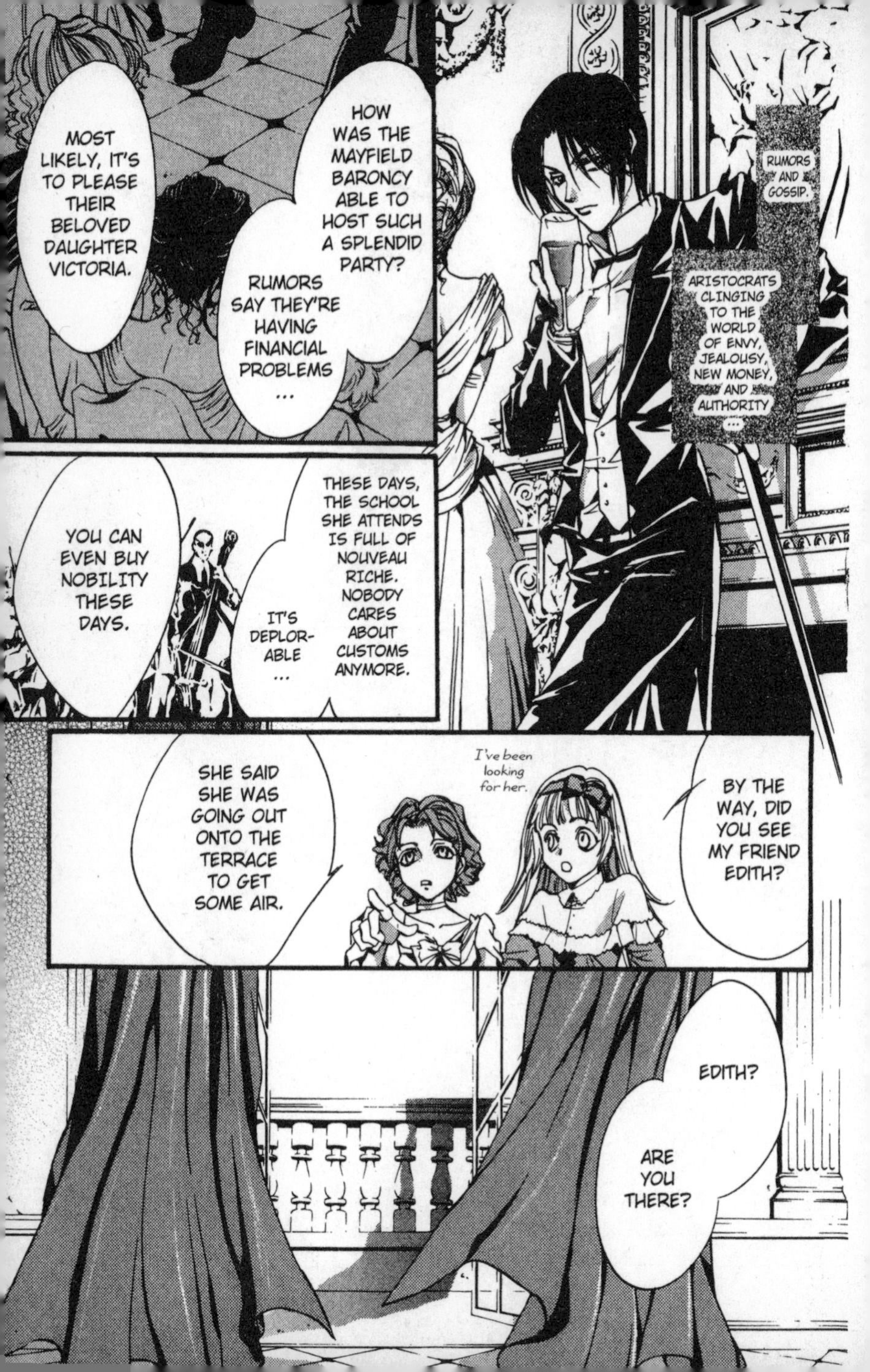

RUMORS AND GOSSIP.
ARISTOCRATS CLINGING TO THE WORLD OF ENVY, JEALOUSY, NEW MONEY, AND AUTHORITY ...
HOW WAS THE MAYFIELD BARONCY ABLE TO HOST SUCH A SPLENDID PARTY?
RUMORS SAY THEY'RE HAVING FINANCIAL PROBLEMS ...
MOST LIKELY, IT'S TO PLEASE THEIR BELOVED DAUGHTER VICTORIA.
THESE DAYS, THE SCHOOL SHE ATTENDS IS FULL OF NOUVEAU RICHE. NOBODY CARES ABOUT CUSTOMS ANYMORE.
IT'S DEPLOR-ABLE ...
YOU CAN EVEN BUY NOBILITY THESE DAYS.
BY THE WAY, DID YOU SEE MY FRIEND EDITH?
I've been looking for her.
SHE SAID SHE WAS GOING OUT ONTO THE TERRACE TO GET SOME AIR.
EDITH?
ARE YOU THERE?

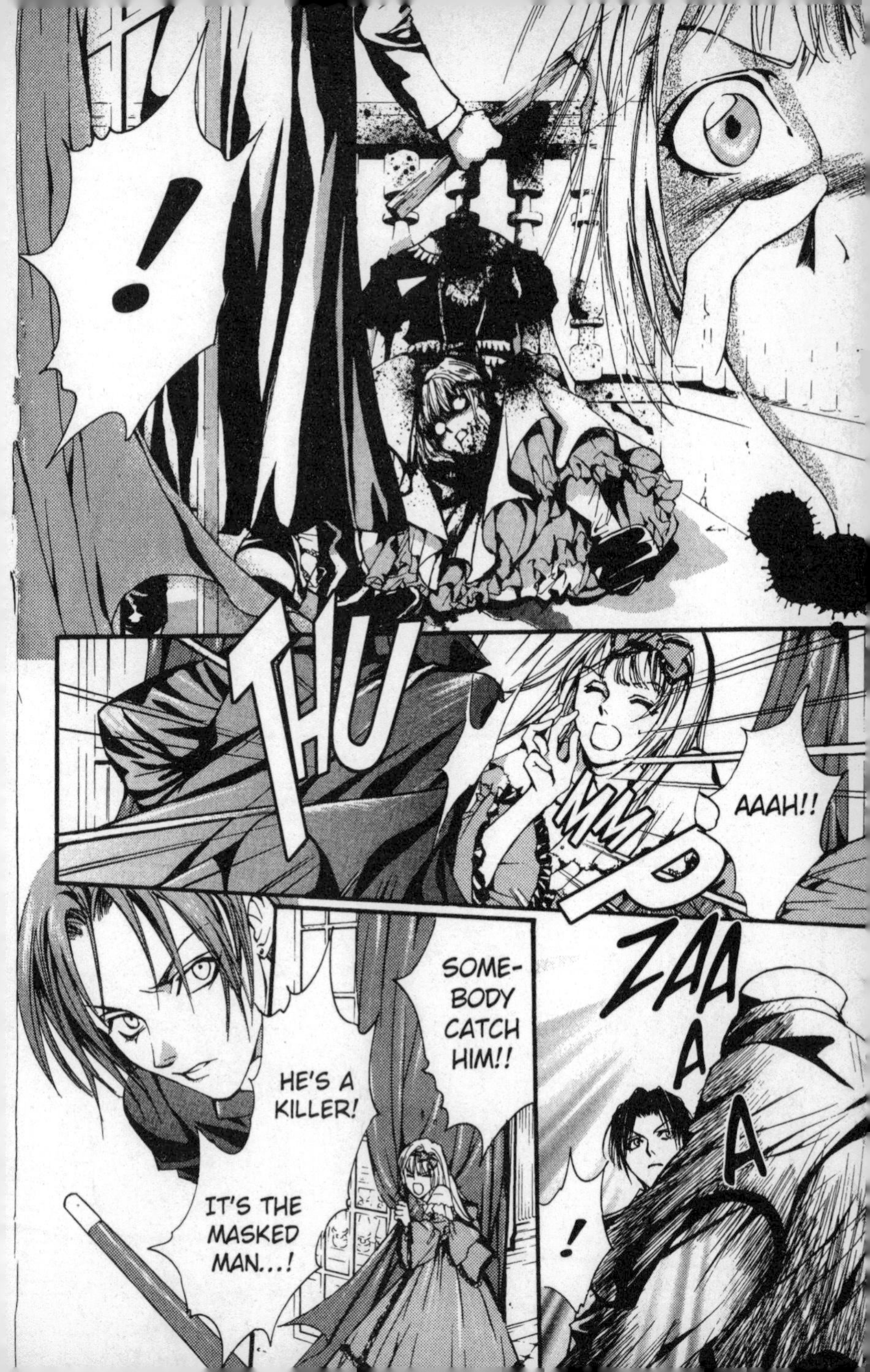
!
AAAH!!
THUMMP
ZAAAA
!
SOME-BODY CATCH HIM!!
HE'S A KILLER!
IT'S THE MASKED MAN...!

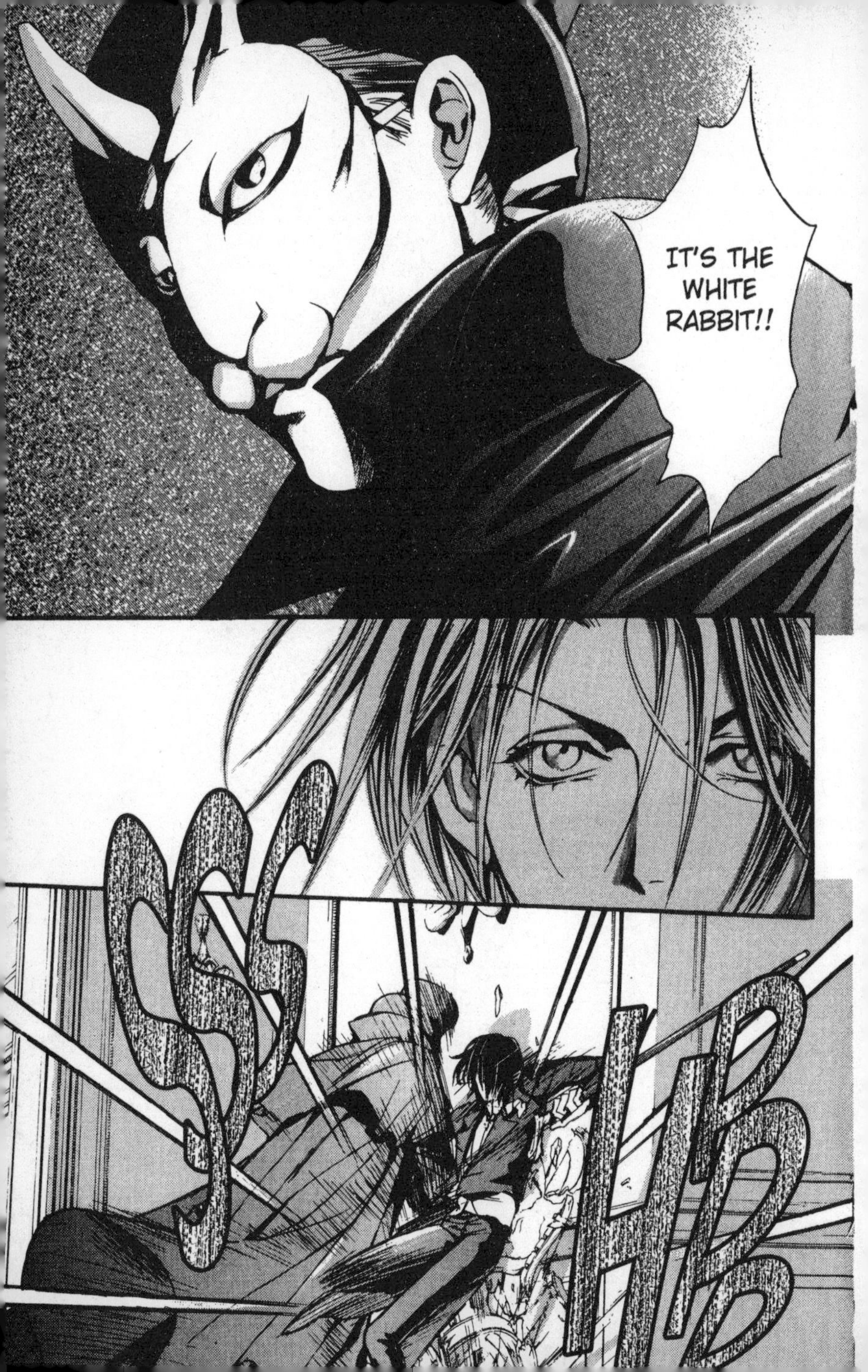
IT'S THE WHITE RABBIT!!
SSSHB

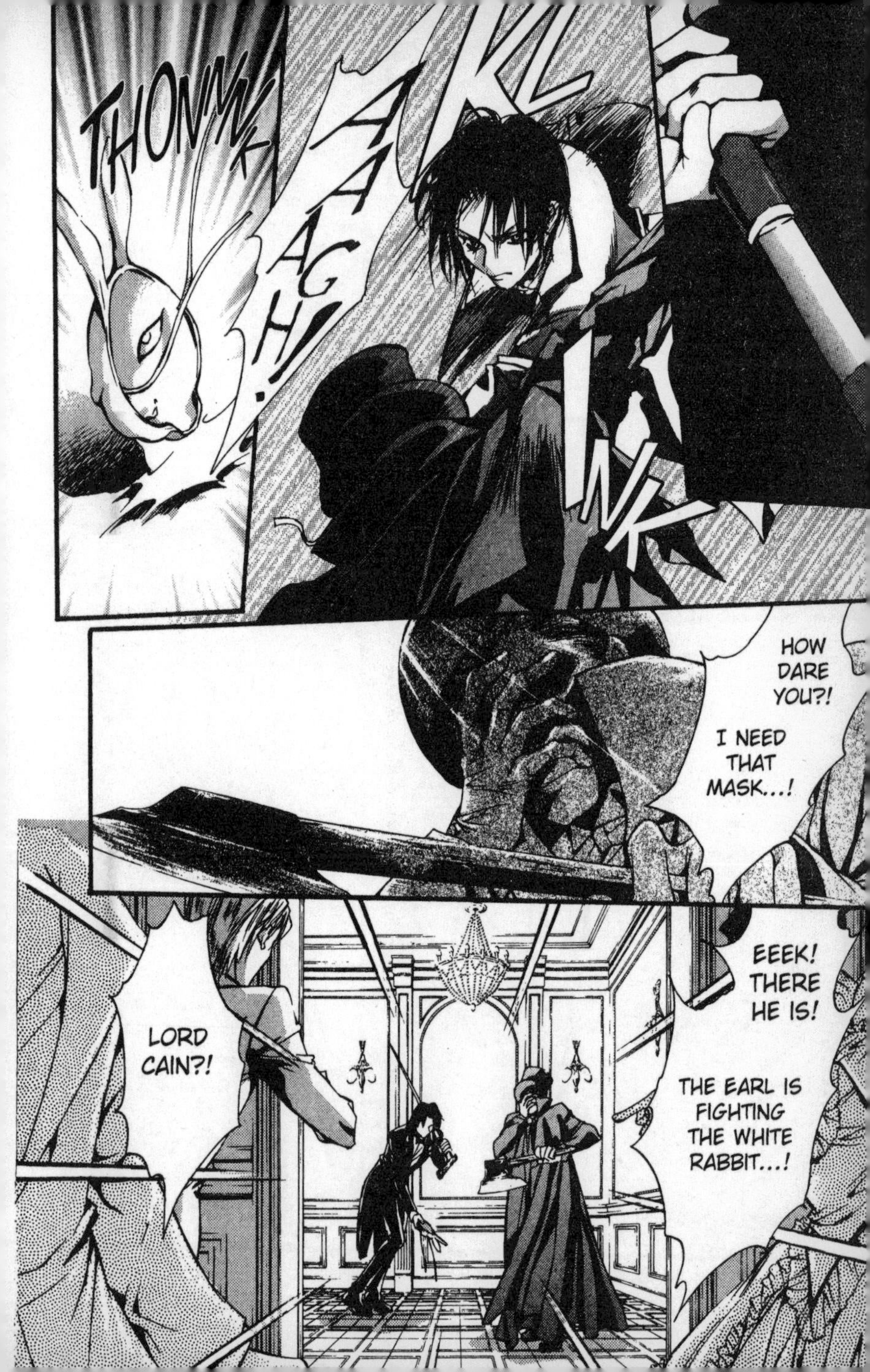
KLINK
AAAGH!!
THONK
HOW DARE YOU?!
I NEED THAT MASK...!
EEEK! THERE HE IS!
THE EARL IS FIGHTING THE WHITE RABBIT...!
LORD CAIN?!

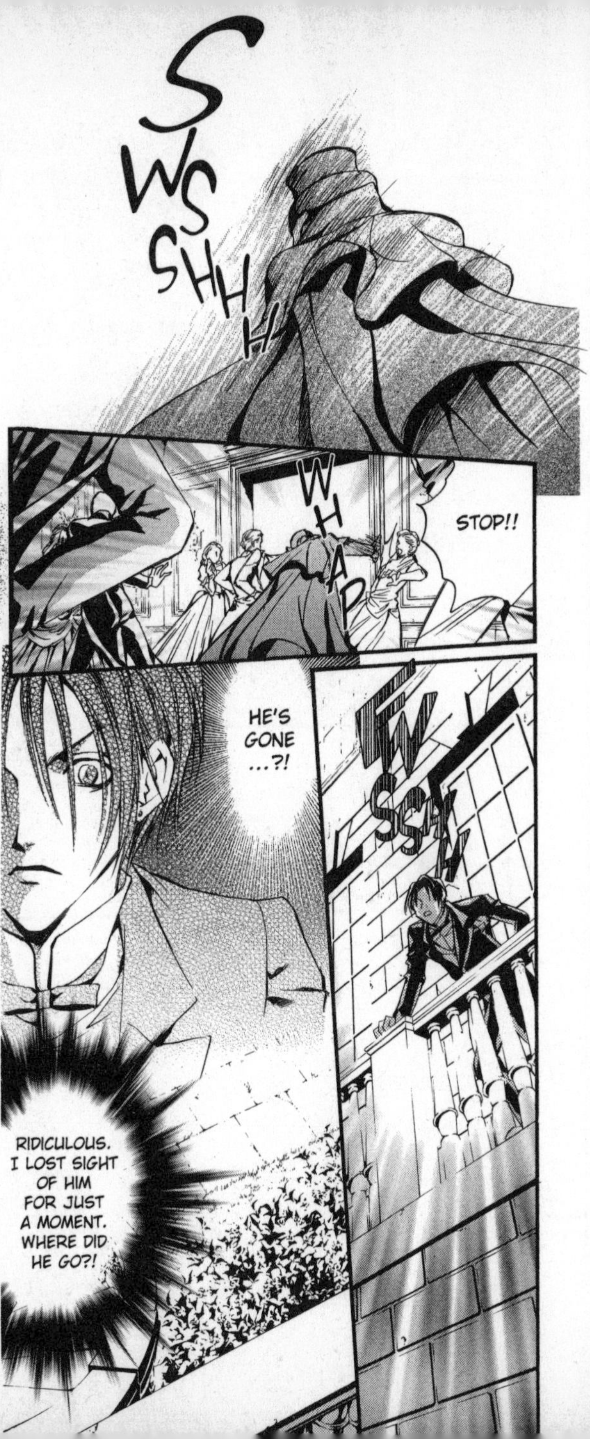
SWSSHH
WHAP
STOP!!
HE'S GONE ...?!
RIDICULOUS. I LOST SIGHT OF HIM FOR JUST A MOMENT. WHERE DID HE GO?!

ALICE IN WONDERLAND.

◆

When I was a child I never really liked this story. Actually I felt more like "???" toward it.

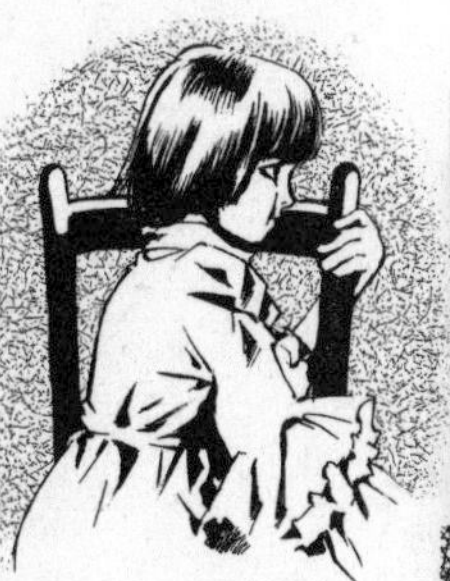

Alice Liddell's real life.

As most of you probably know, the story is based on one that author Lewis Carroll made up during a rowboat outing for the three Liddell sisters. (The young Liddell sisters were Alice, Lorina and Edith.) There was an older brother there, too. Apparently, that event was called, "The Golden Afternoon."

◆

As I was writing this, I got my inspiration for "Victoria" from "The Queen." Because I used Elizabeth before......

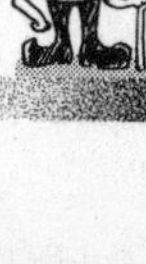
Humpty Dumpty and the Jabberwocky are from "The Silver City," too......

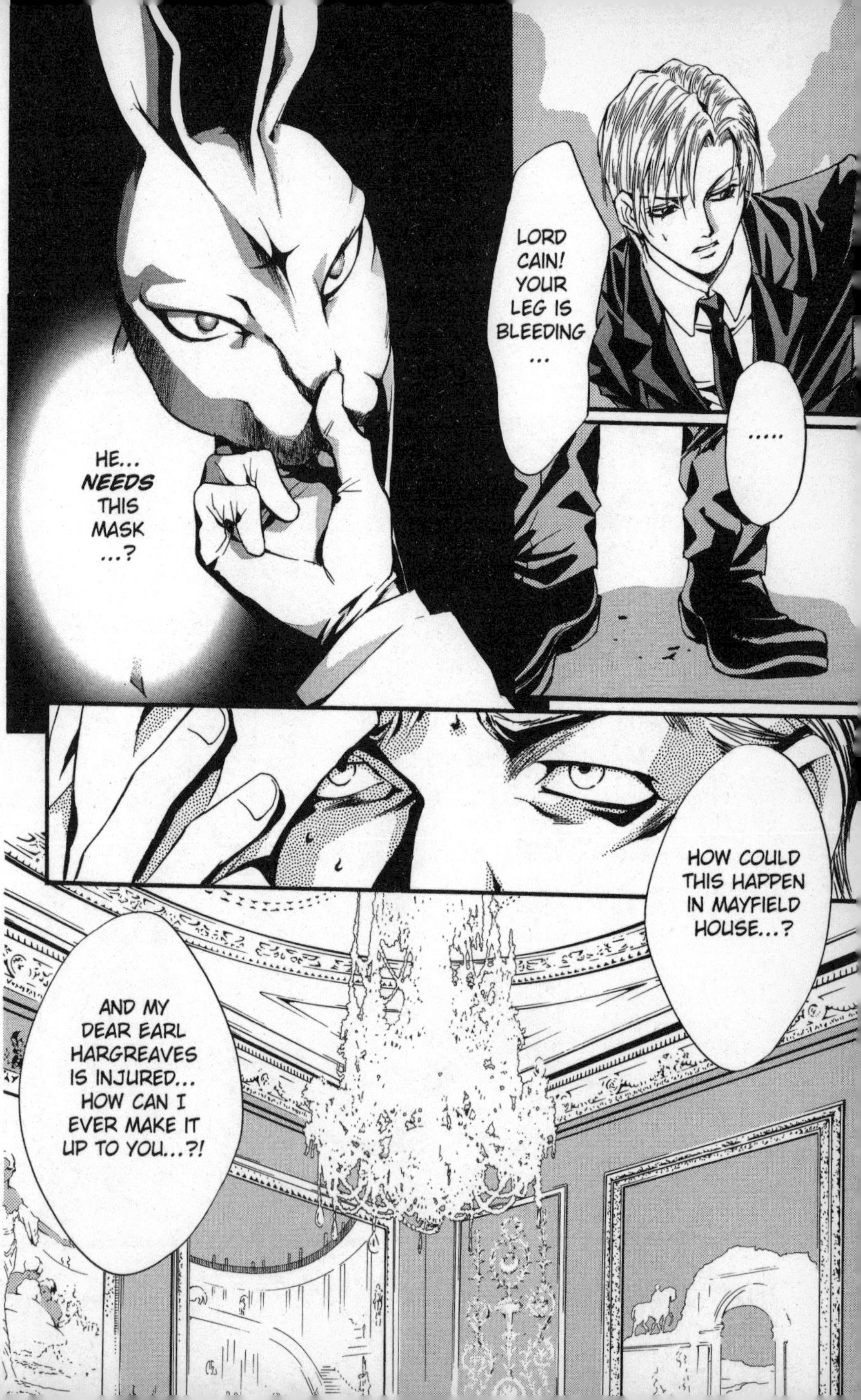
LORD CAIN! YOUR LEG IS BLEEDING ...
.....
HE... *NEEDS* THIS MASK ...?
HOW COULD THIS HAPPEN IN MAYFIELD HOUSE...?
AND MY DEAR EARL HARGREAVES IS INJURED... HOW CAN I EVER MAKE IT UP TO YOU...?!

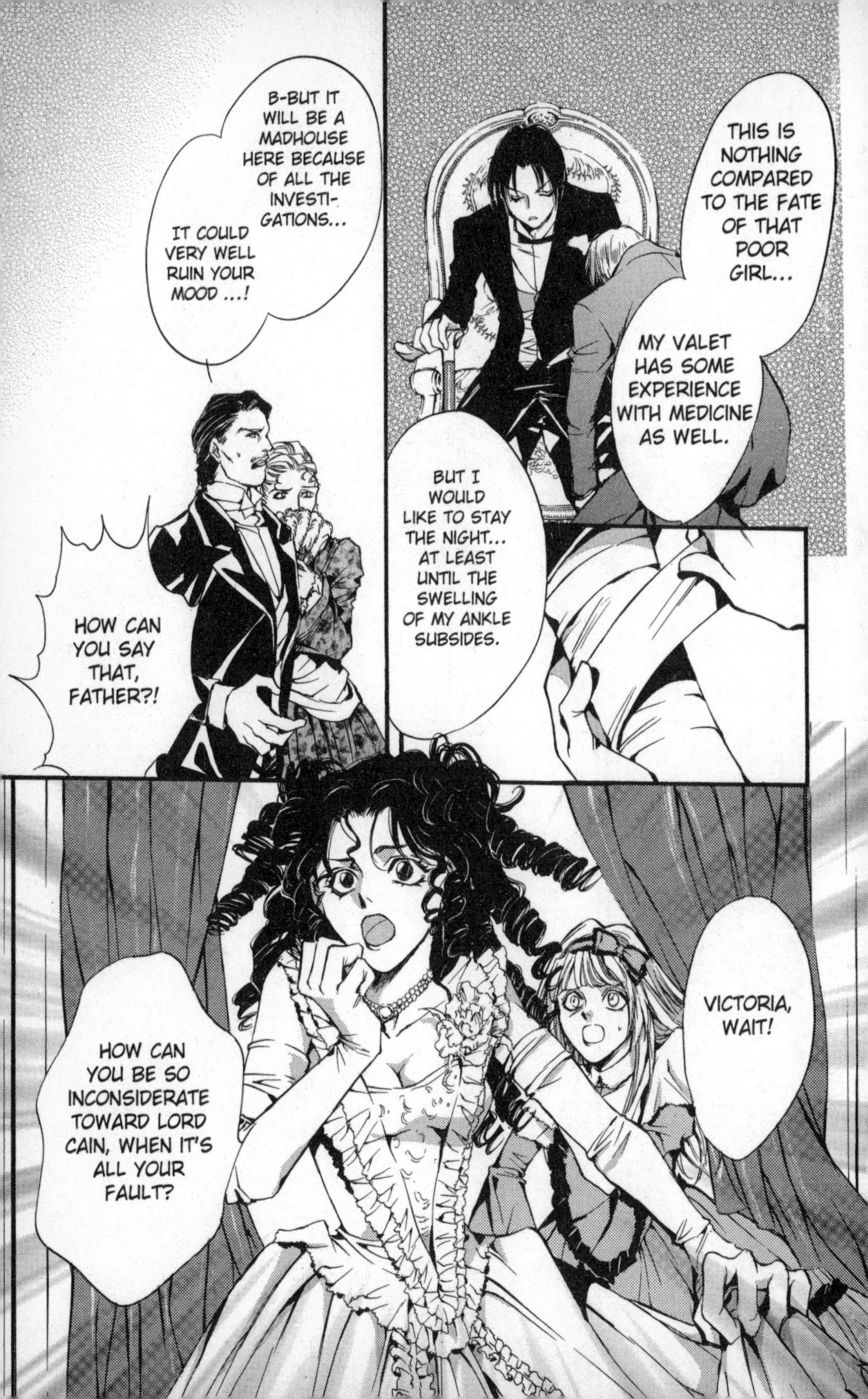
THIS IS NOTHING COMPARED TO THE FATE OF THAT POOR GIRL...
MY VALET HAS SOME EXPERIENCE WITH MEDICINE AS WELL.
BUT I WOULD LIKE TO STAY THE NIGHT... AT LEAST UNTIL THE SWELLING OF MY ANKLE SUBSIDES.
B-BUT IT WILL BE A MADHOUSE HERE BECAUSE OF ALL THE INVESTI-GATIONS...
IT COULD VERY WELL RUIN YOUR MOOD ...!
HOW CAN YOU SAY THAT, FATHER?!
VICTORIA, WAIT!
HOW CAN YOU BE SO INCONSIDERATE TOWARD LORD CAIN, WHEN IT'S ALL YOUR FAULT?

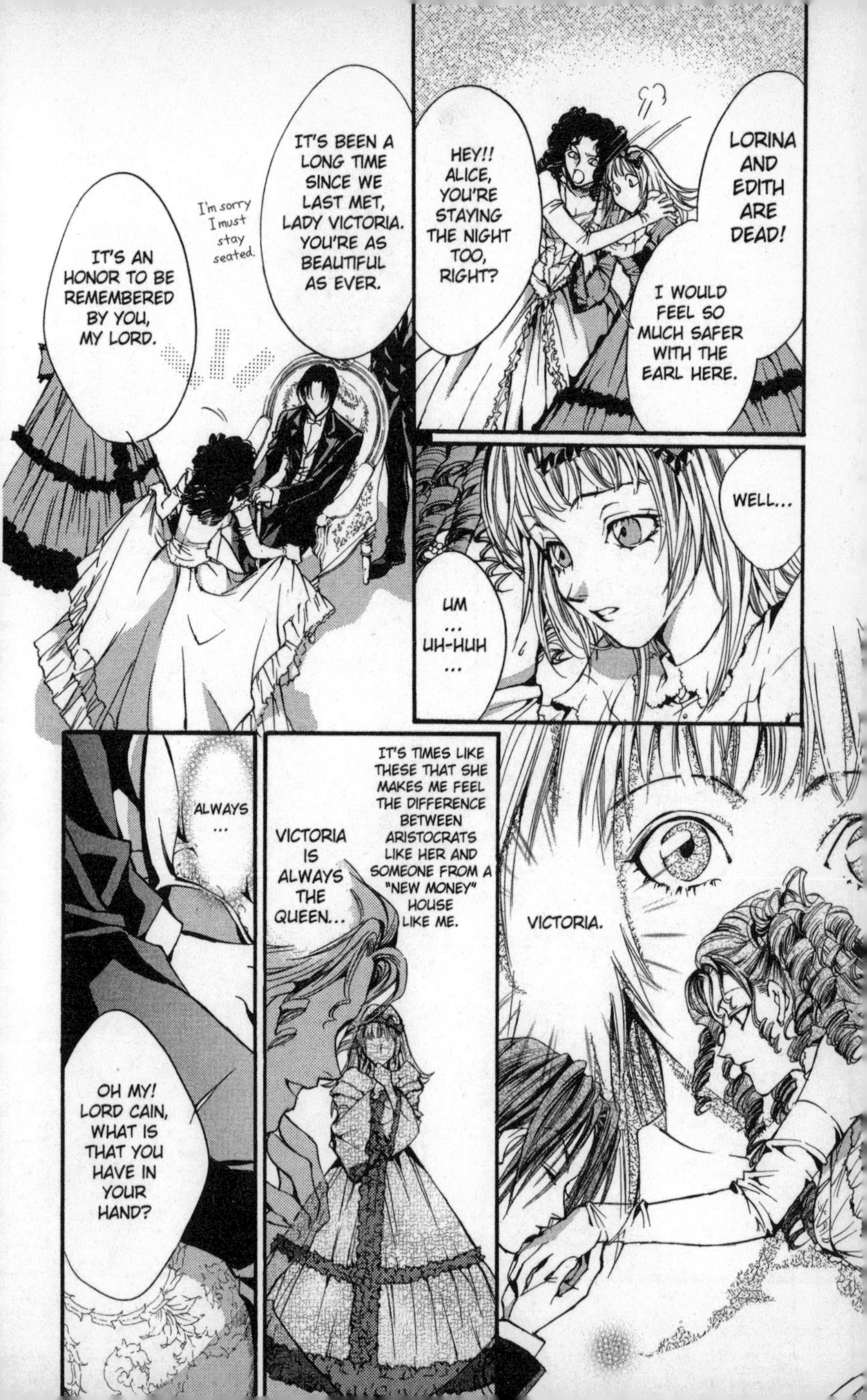
LORINA AND EDITH ARE DEAD!
I WOULD FEEL SO MUCH SAFER WITH THE EARL HERE.
HEY!! ALICE, YOU'RE STAYING THE NIGHT TOO, RIGHT?
WELL...
UM ... UH-HUH ...
IT'S BEEN A LONG TIME SINCE WE LAST MET, LADY VICTORIA. YOU'RE AS BEAUTIFUL AS EVER.
I'm sorry I must stay seated.
IT'S AN HONOR TO BE REMEMBERED BY YOU, MY LORD.
VICTORIA.
IT'S TIMES LIKE THESE THAT SHE MAKES ME FEEL THE DIFFERENCE BETWEEN ARISTOCRATS LIKE HER AND SOMEONE FROM A "NEW MONEY" HOUSE LIKE ME.
VICTORIA IS ALWAYS THE QUEEN...
ALWAYS ...
OH MY! LORD CAIN, WHAT IS THAT YOU HAVE IN YOUR HAND?

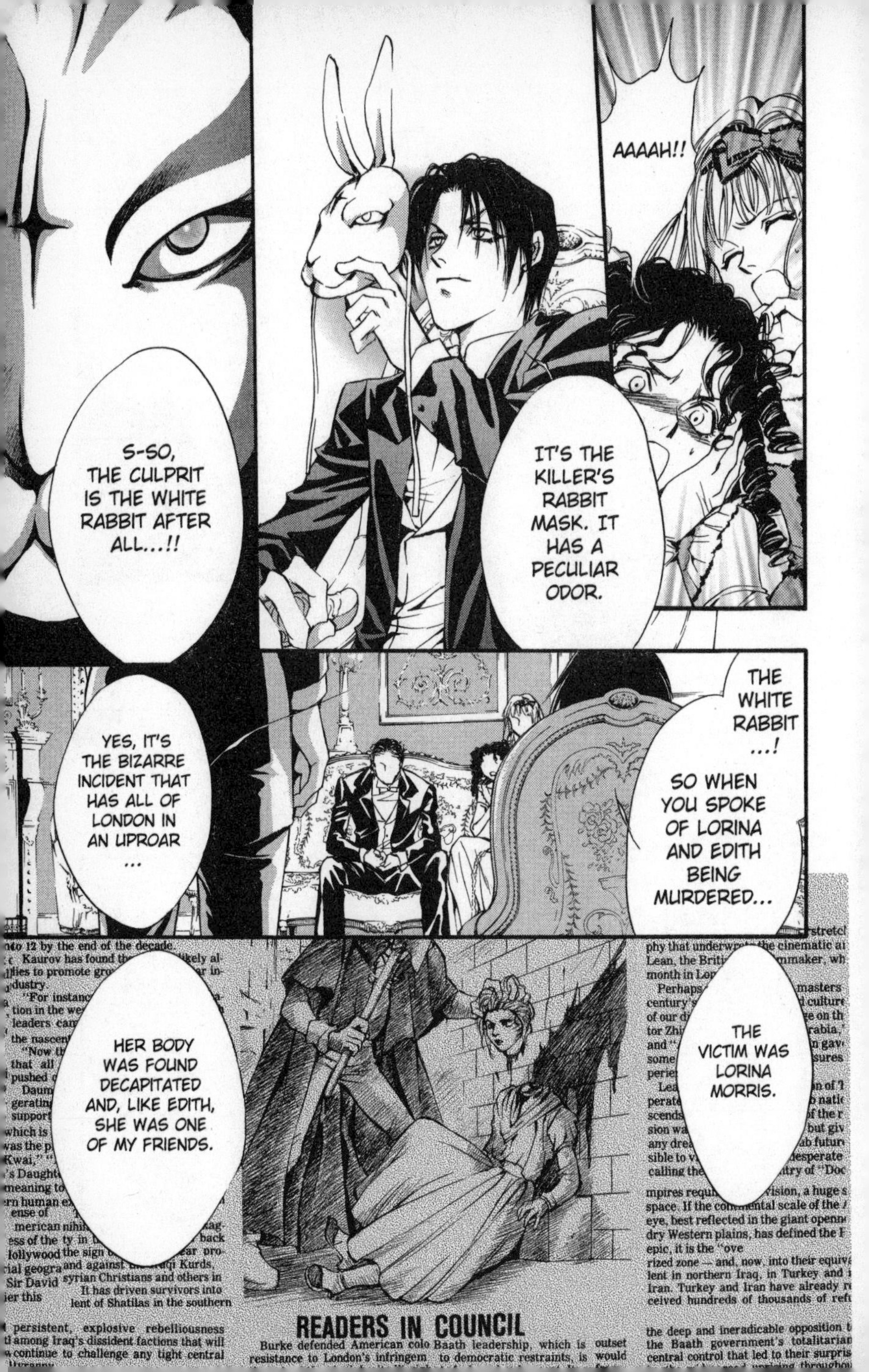
AAAAH!!
IT'S THE KILLER'S RABBIT MASK. IT HAS A PECULIAR ODOR.
S-SO, THE CULPRIT IS THE WHITE RABBIT AFTER ALL...!!
THE WHITE RABBIT ...!
SO WHEN YOU SPOKE OF LORINA AND EDITH BEING MURDERED...
YES, IT'S THE BIZARRE INCIDENT THAT HAS ALL OF LONDON IN AN UPROAR ...
THE VICTIM WAS LORINA MORRIS.
HER BODY WAS FOUND DECAPITATED AND, LIKE EDITH, SHE WAS ONE OF MY FRIENDS.
READERS IN COUNCIL

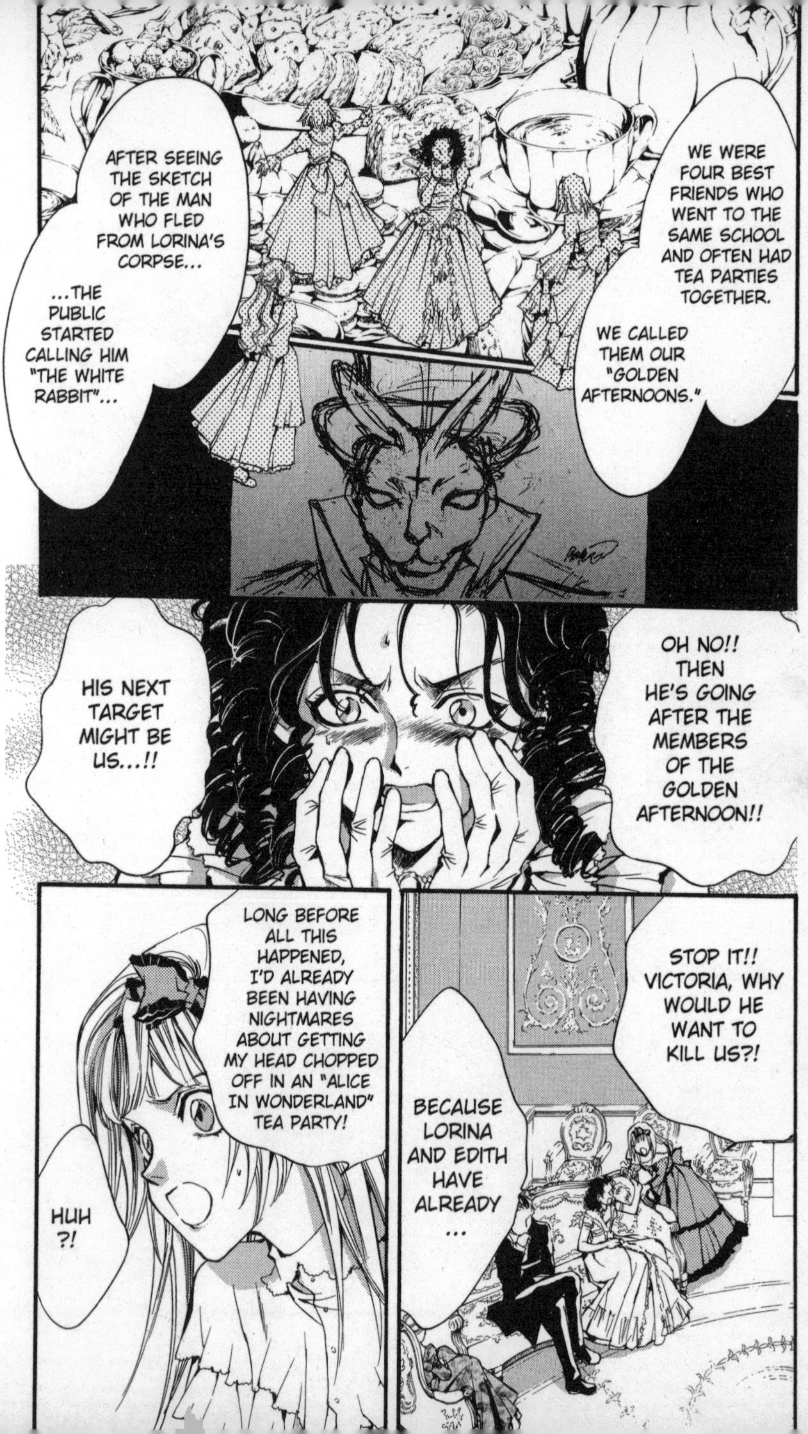
WE WERE FOUR BEST FRIENDS WHO WENT TO THE SAME SCHOOL AND OFTEN HAD TEA PARTIES TOGETHER.
WE CALLED THEM OUR "GOLDEN AFTERNOONS."
AFTER SEEING THE SKETCH OF THE MAN WHO FLED FROM LORINA'S CORPSE...
...THE PUBLIC STARTED CALLING HIM "THE WHITE RABBIT"...
OH NO!! THEN HE'S GOING AFTER THE MEMBERS OF THE GOLDEN AFTERNOON!!
HIS NEXT TARGET MIGHT BE US...!!
STOP IT!! VICTORIA, WHY WOULD HE WANT TO KILL US?!
BECAUSE LORINA AND EDITH HAVE ALREADY ...
LONG BEFORE ALL THIS HAPPENED, I'D ALREADY BEEN HAVING NIGHTMARES ABOUT GETTING MY HEAD CHOPPED OFF IN AN "ALICE IN WONDERLAND" TEA PARTY!
HUH ?!

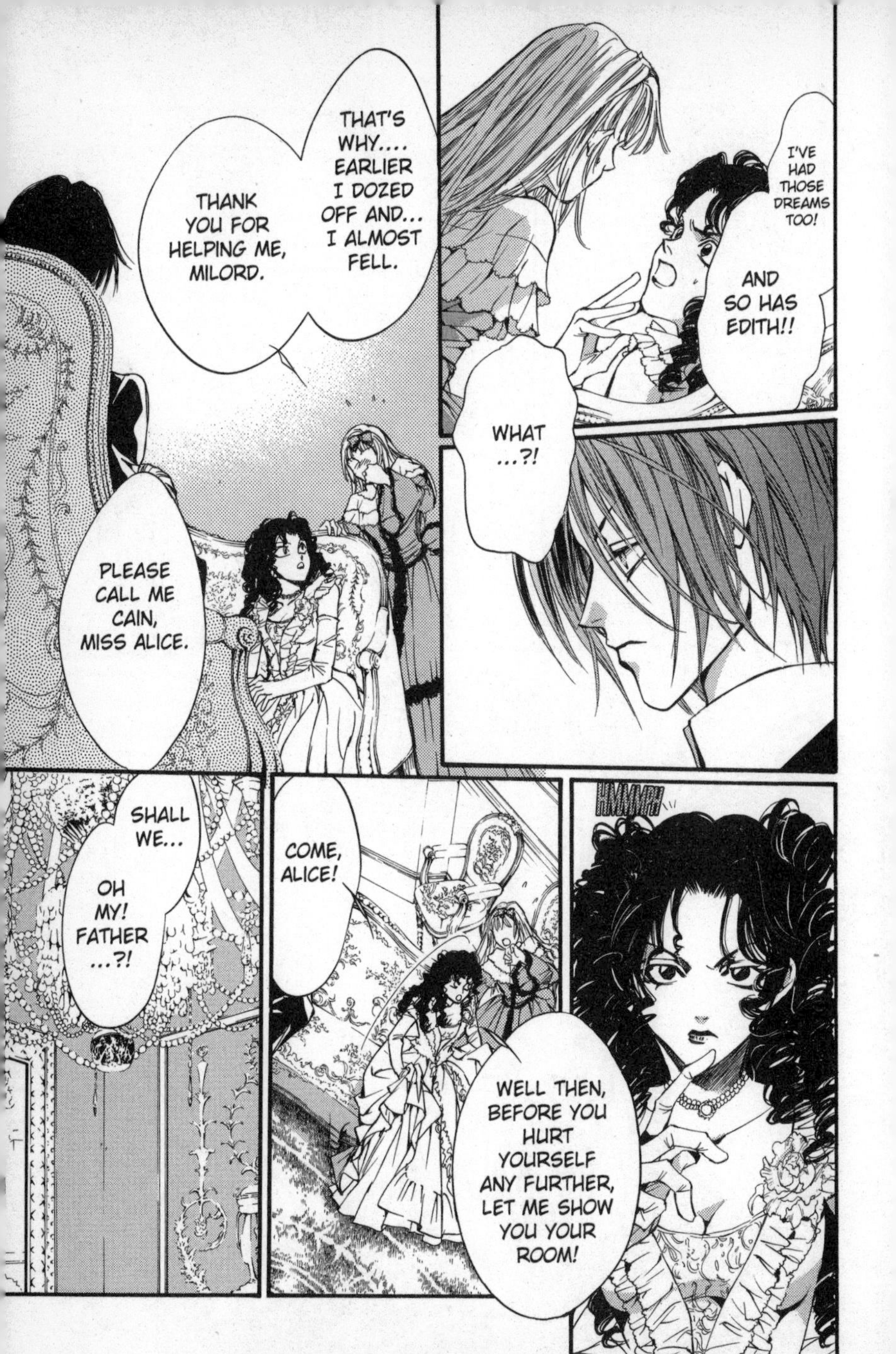
I'VE HAD THOSE DREAMS TOO!
AND SO HAS EDITH!!
WHAT ...?!
THAT'S WHY.... EARLIER I DOZED OFF AND... I ALMOST FELL.
THANK YOU FOR HELPING ME, MILORD.
PLEASE CALL ME CAIN, MISS ALICE.
HMMMPH
WELL THEN, BEFORE YOU HURT YOURSELF ANY FURTHER, LET ME SHOW YOU YOUR ROOM!
COME, ALICE!
SHALL WE...
OH MY! FATHER ...?!

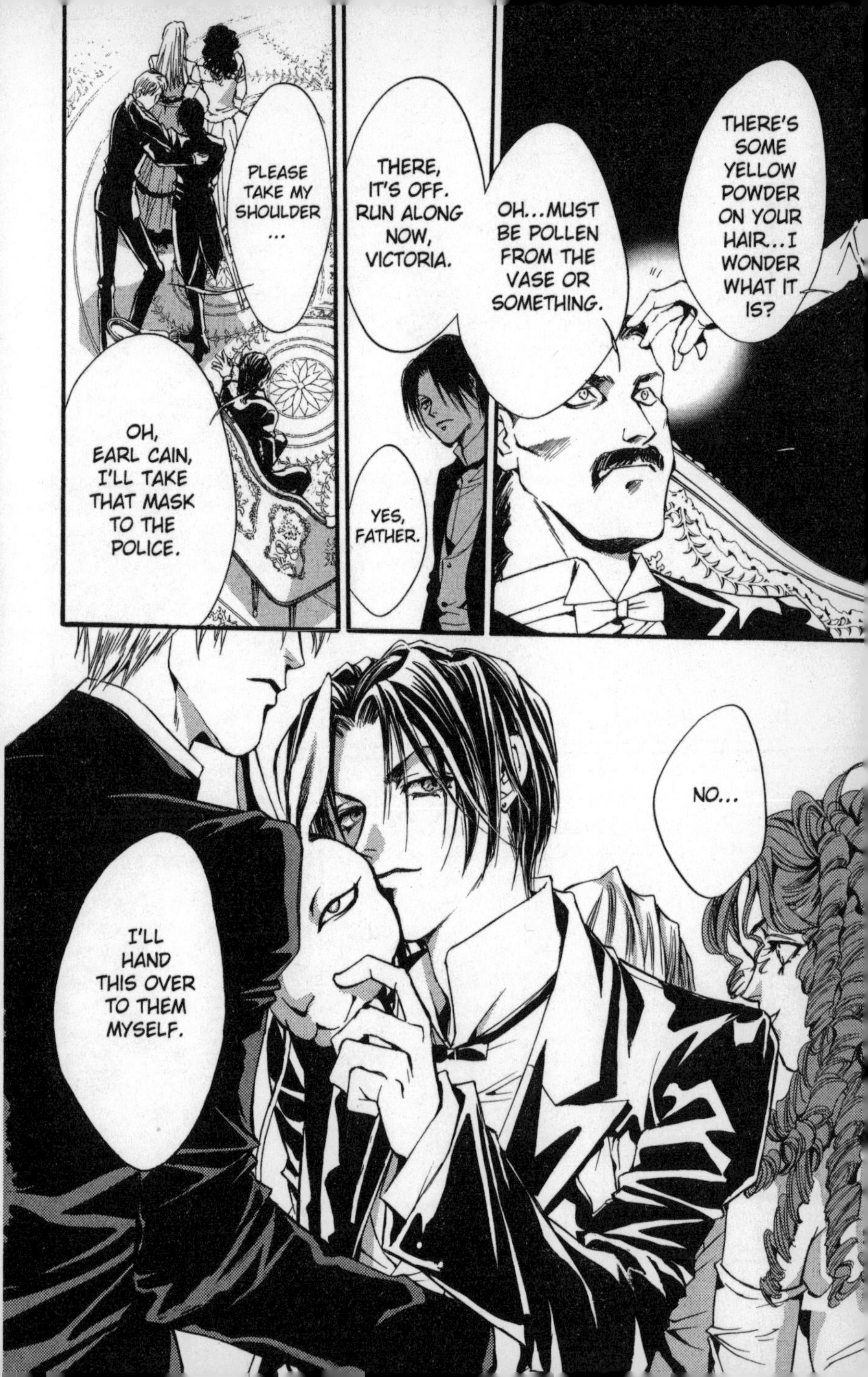
THERE'S SOME YELLOW POWDER ON YOUR HAIR...I WONDER WHAT IT IS?
OH...MUST BE POLLEN FROM THE VASE OR SOMETHING.
THERE, IT'S OFF. RUN ALONG NOW, VICTORIA.
YES, FATHER.
PLEASE TAKE MY SHOULDER...
OH, EARL CAIN, I'LL TAKE THAT MASK TO THE POLICE.
NO...
I'LL HAND THIS OVER TO THEM MYSELF.

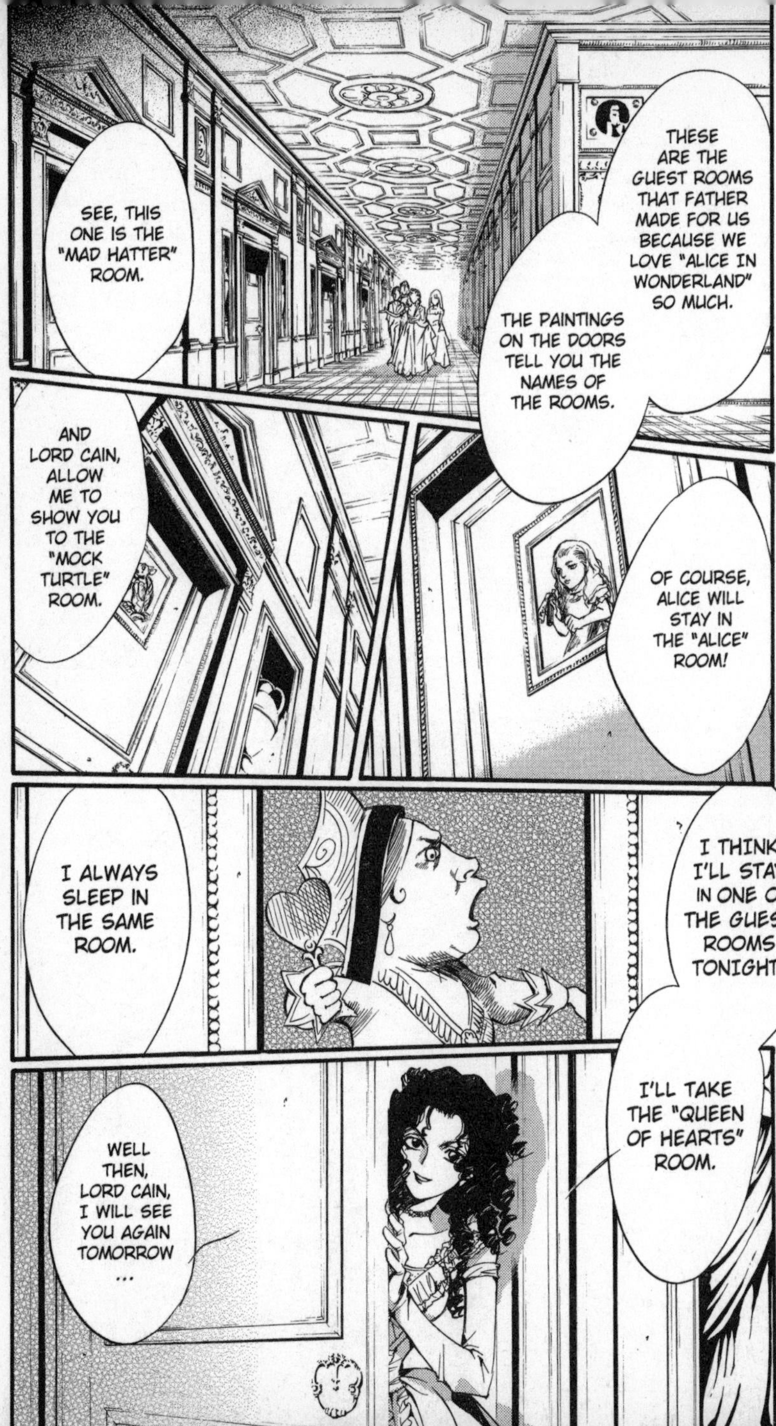
THESE ARE THE GUEST ROOMS THAT FATHER MADE FOR US BECAUSE WE LOVE "ALICE IN WONDERLAND" SO MUCH.
THE PAINTINGS ON THE DOORS TELL YOU THE NAMES OF THE ROOMS.
SEE, THIS ONE IS THE "MAD HATTER" ROOM.
OF COURSE, ALICE WILL STAY IN THE "ALICE" ROOM!
AND LORD CAIN, ALLOW ME TO SHOW YOU TO THE "MOCK TURTLE" ROOM.
I THINK I'LL STAY IN ONE OF THE GUEST ROOMS TONIGHT.
I ALWAYS SLEEP IN THE SAME ROOM.
I'LL TAKE THE "QUEEN OF HEARTS" ROOM.
WELL THEN, LORD CAIN, I WILL SEE YOU AGAIN TOMORROW ...

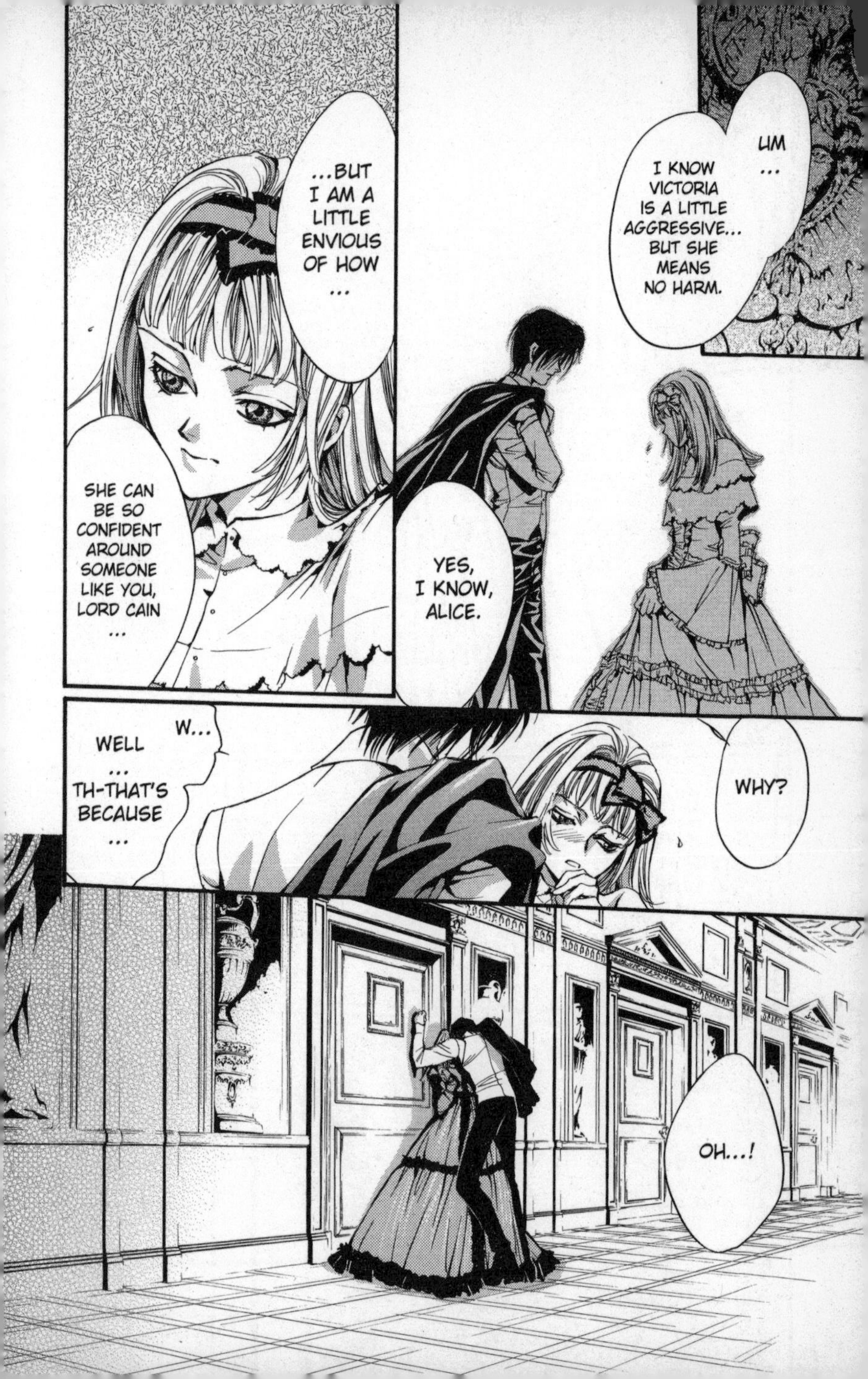
UM ...
I KNOW VICTORIA IS A LITTLE AGGRESSIVE... BUT SHE MEANS NO HARM.
YES, I KNOW, ALICE.
...BUT I AM A LITTLE ENVIOUS OF HOW ...
SHE CAN BE SO CONFIDENT AROUND SOMEONE LIKE YOU, LORD CAIN ...
WHY?
W...
WELL ... TH-THAT'S BECAUSE ...
OH...!

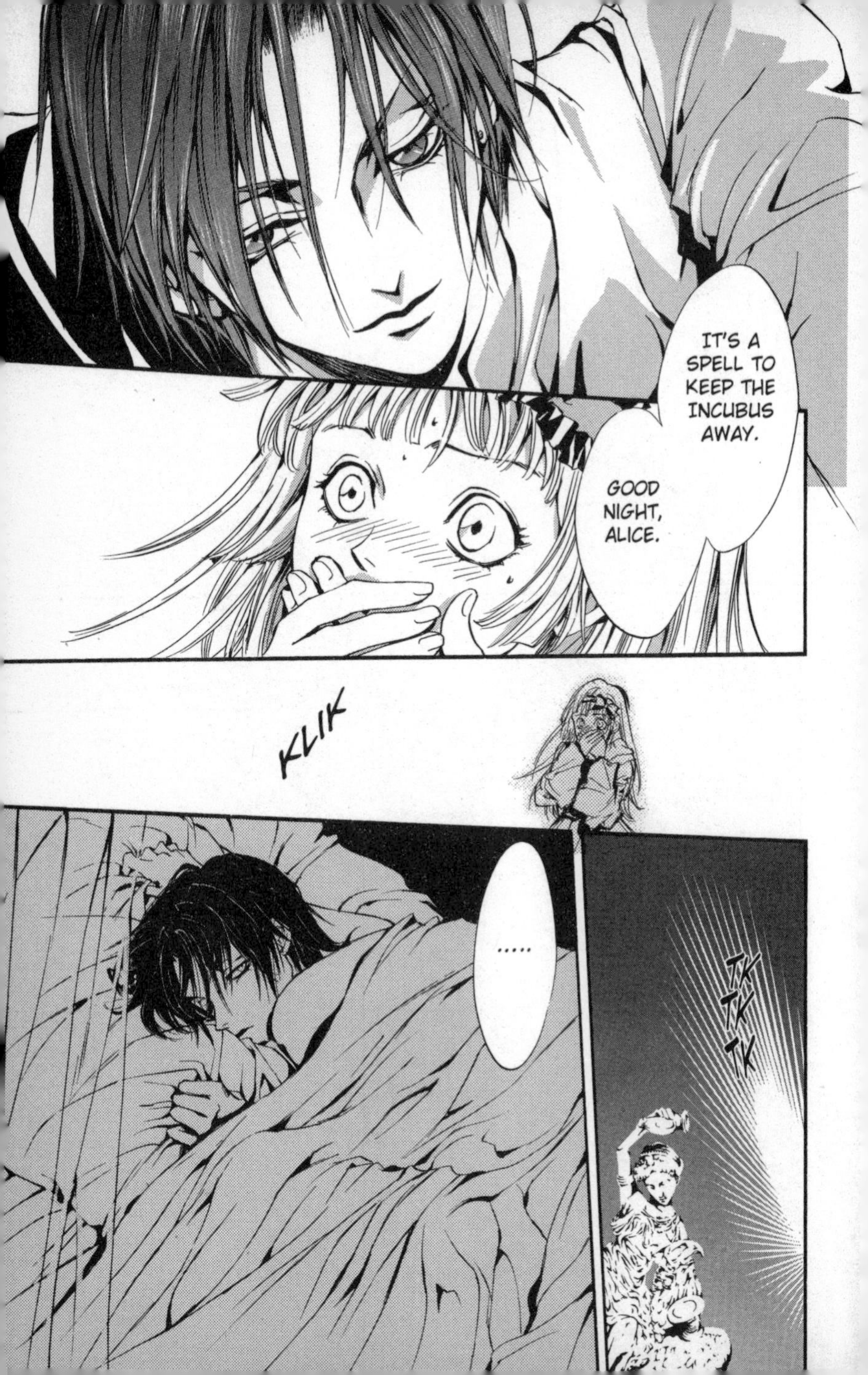
IT'S A SPELL TO KEEP THE INCUBUS AWAY.
GOOD NIGHT, ALICE.
KLIK
TK TK TK
.....

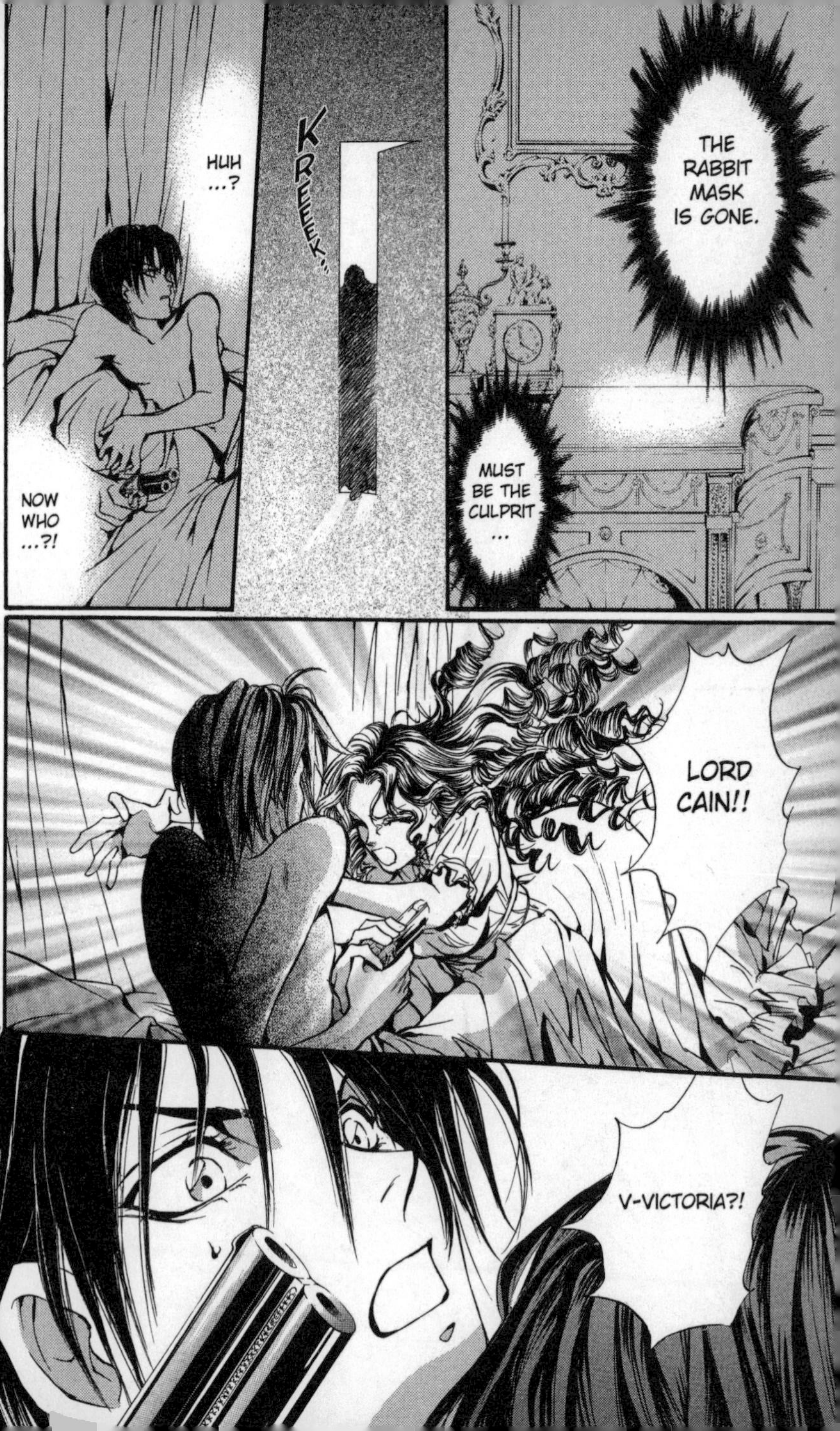
THE RABBIT MASK IS GONE.
MUST BE THE CULPRIT...
KREEEK...
HUH ...?
NOW WHO ...?!
LORD CAIN!!
V-VICTORIA?!

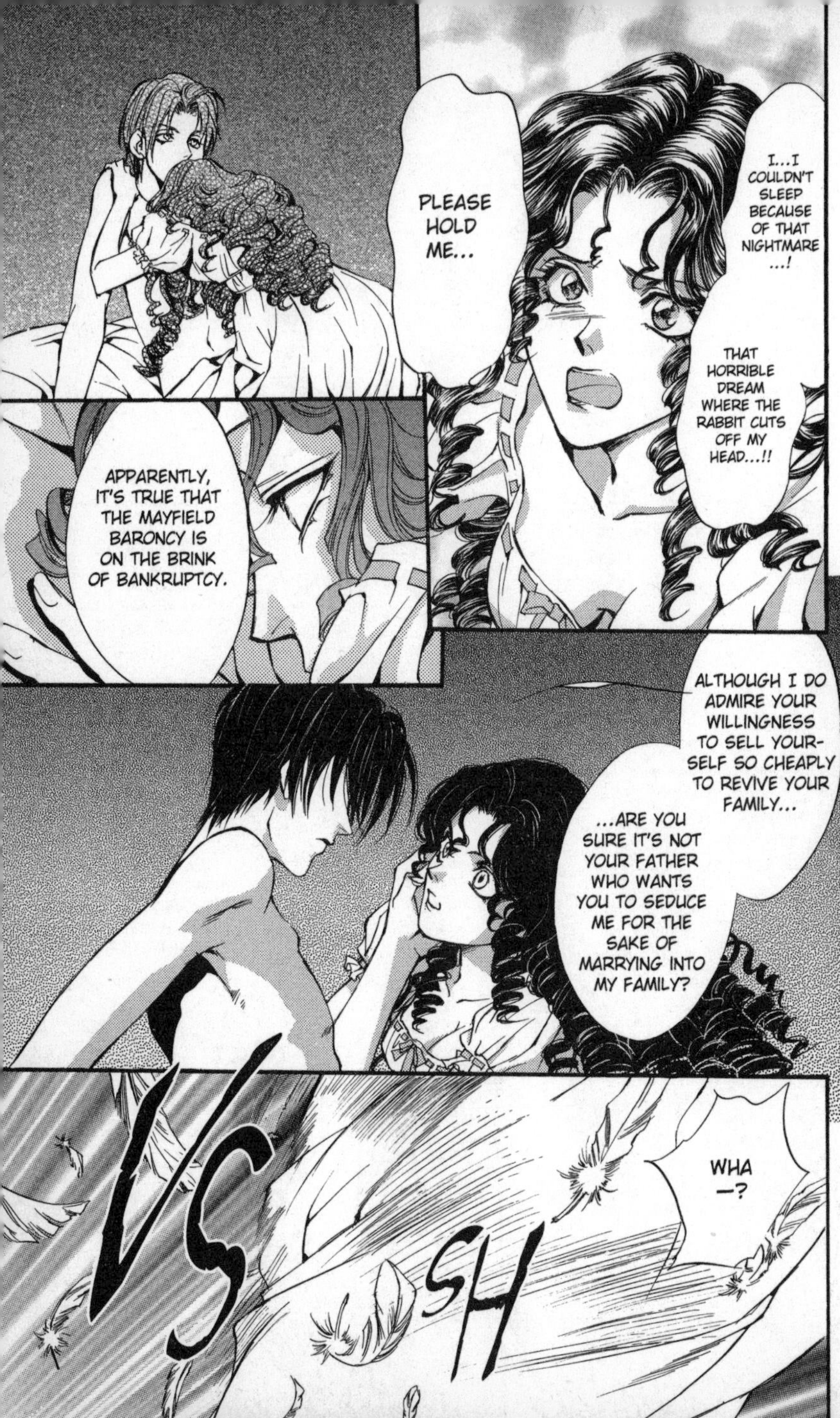
I...I COULDN'T SLEEP BECAUSE OF THAT NIGHTMARE ...!
THAT HORRIBLE DREAM WHERE THE RABBIT CUTS OFF MY HEAD...!!
PLEASE HOLD ME...
APPARENTLY, IT'S TRUE THAT THE MAYFIELD BARONCY IS ON THE BRINK OF BANKRUPTCY.
ALTHOUGH I DO ADMIRE YOUR WILLINGNESS TO SELL YOUR-SELF SO CHEAPLY TO REVIVE YOUR FAMILY...
...ARE YOU SURE IT'S NOT YOUR FATHER WHO WANTS YOU TO SEDUCE ME FOR THE SAKE OF MARRYING INTO MY FAMILY?
WHA —?
VS
SH

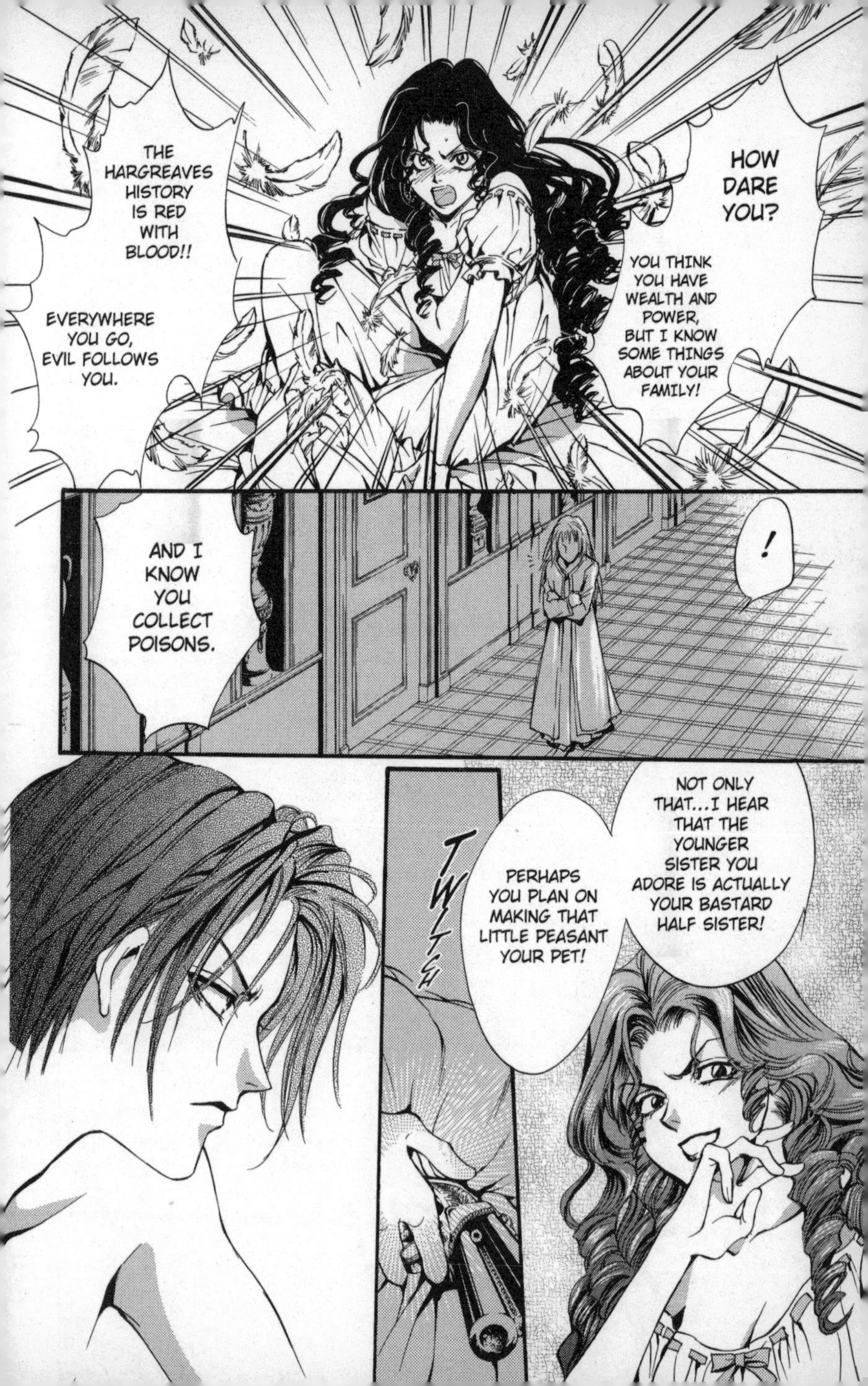
HOW DARE YOU?
YOU THINK YOU HAVE WEALTH AND POWER, BUT I KNOW SOME THINGS ABOUT YOUR FAMILY!
THE HARGREAVES HISTORY IS RED WITH BLOOD!!
EVERYWHERE YOU GO, EVIL FOLLOWS YOU.
!
AND I KNOW YOU COLLECT POISONS.
NOT ONLY THAT...I HEAR THAT THE YOUNGER SISTER YOU ADORE IS ACTUALLY YOUR BASTARD HALF SISTER!
PERHAPS YOU PLAN ON MAKING THAT LITTLE PEASANT YOUR PET!
TWITCH

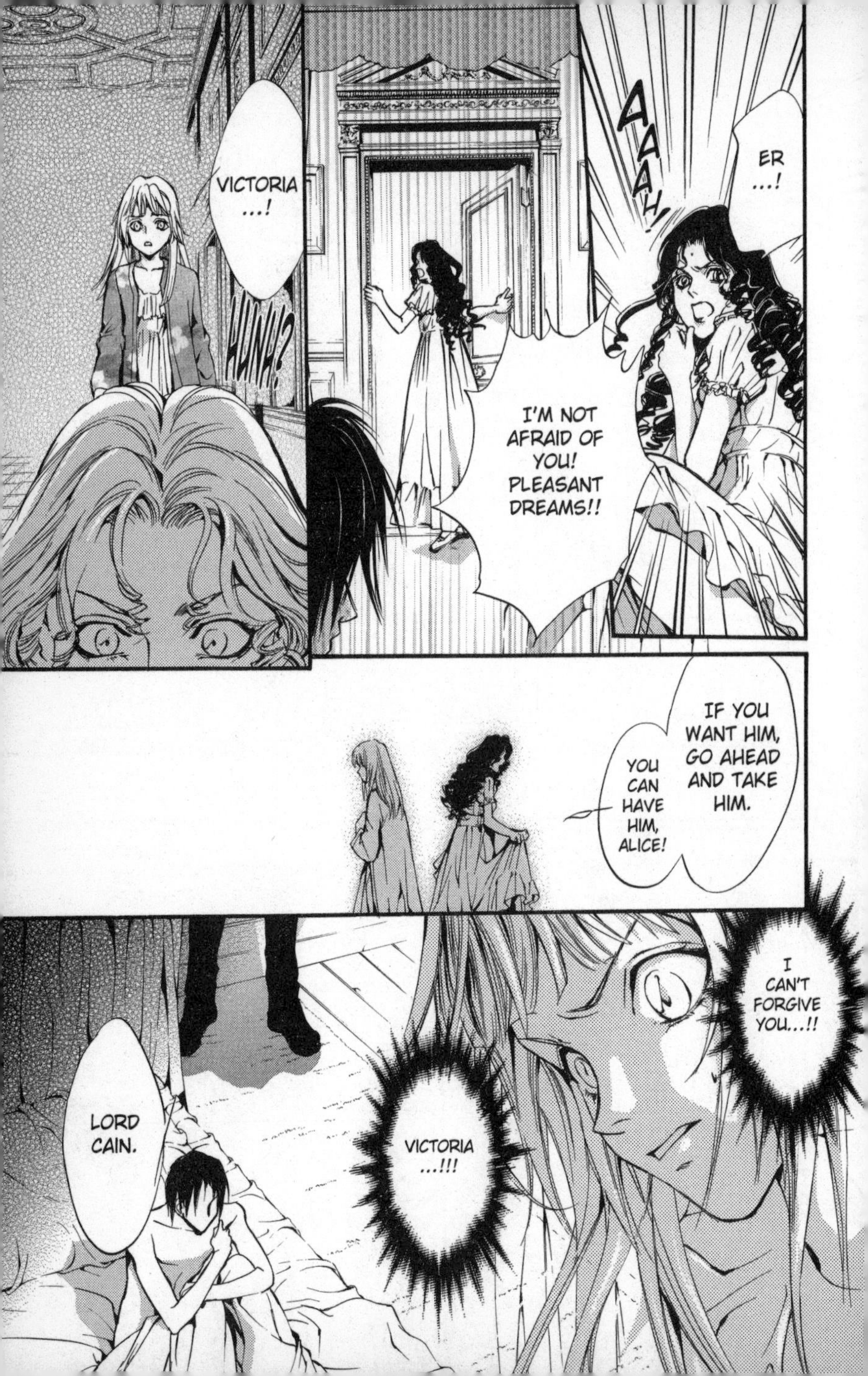
ER ...!
AAAH!
I'M NOT AFRAID OF YOU! PLEASANT DREAMS!!
VICTORIA ...!
HUNH?
IF YOU WANT HIM, GO AHEAD AND TAKE HIM.
YOU CAN HAVE HIM, ALICE!
I CAN'T FORGIVE YOU...!!
VICTORIA ...!!!
LORD CAIN.

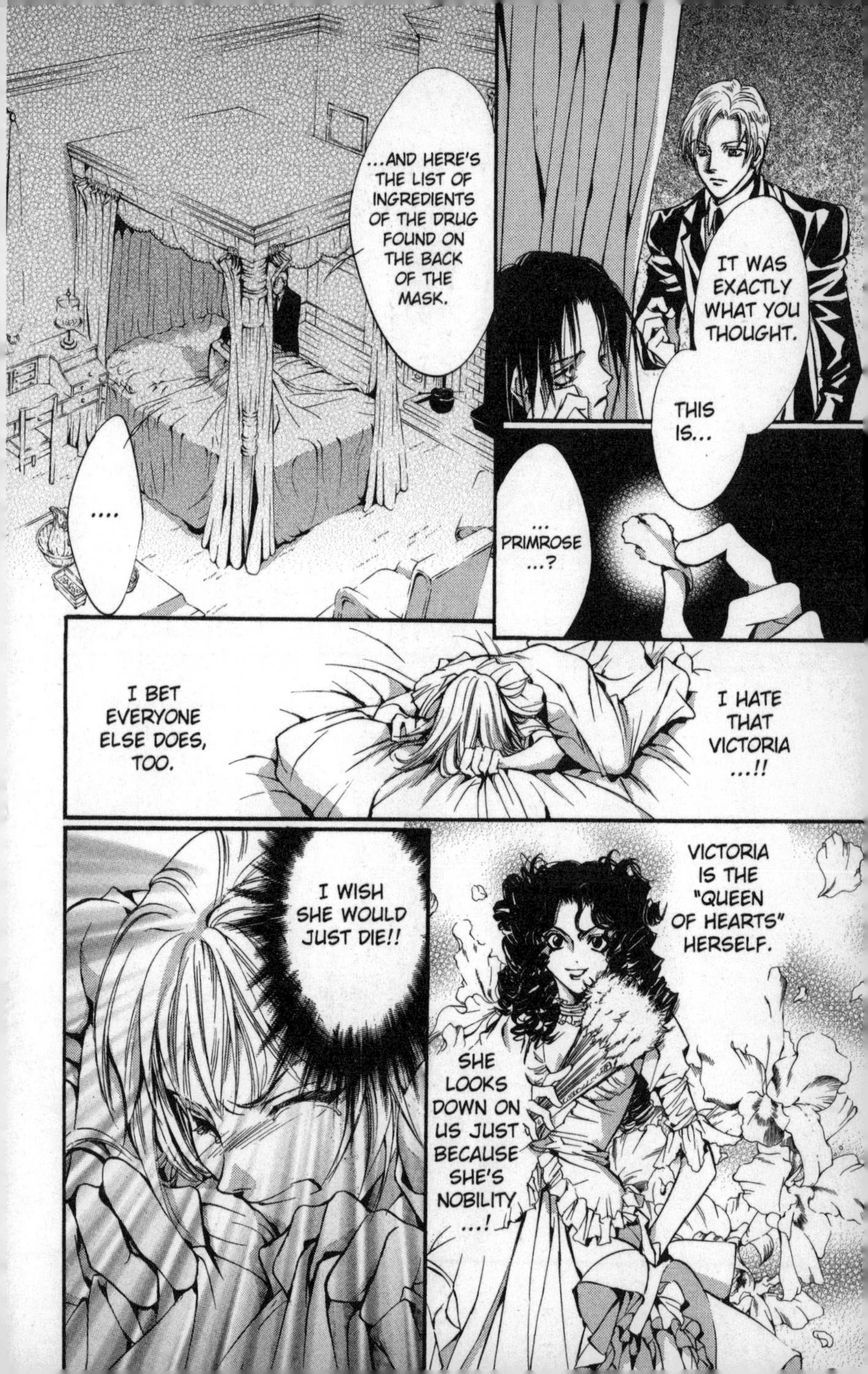
IT WAS EXACTLY WHAT YOU THOUGHT.
THIS IS...
...PRIMROSE...?
...AND HERE'S THE LIST OF INGREDIENTS OF THE DRUG FOUND ON THE BACK OF THE MASK.
....
I HATE THAT VICTORIA ...!!
I BET EVERYONE ELSE DOES, TOO.
VICTORIA IS THE "QUEEN OF HEARTS" HERSELF.
SHE LOOKS DOWN ON US JUST BECAUSE SHE'S NOBILITY ...!
I WISH SHE WOULD JUST DIE!!

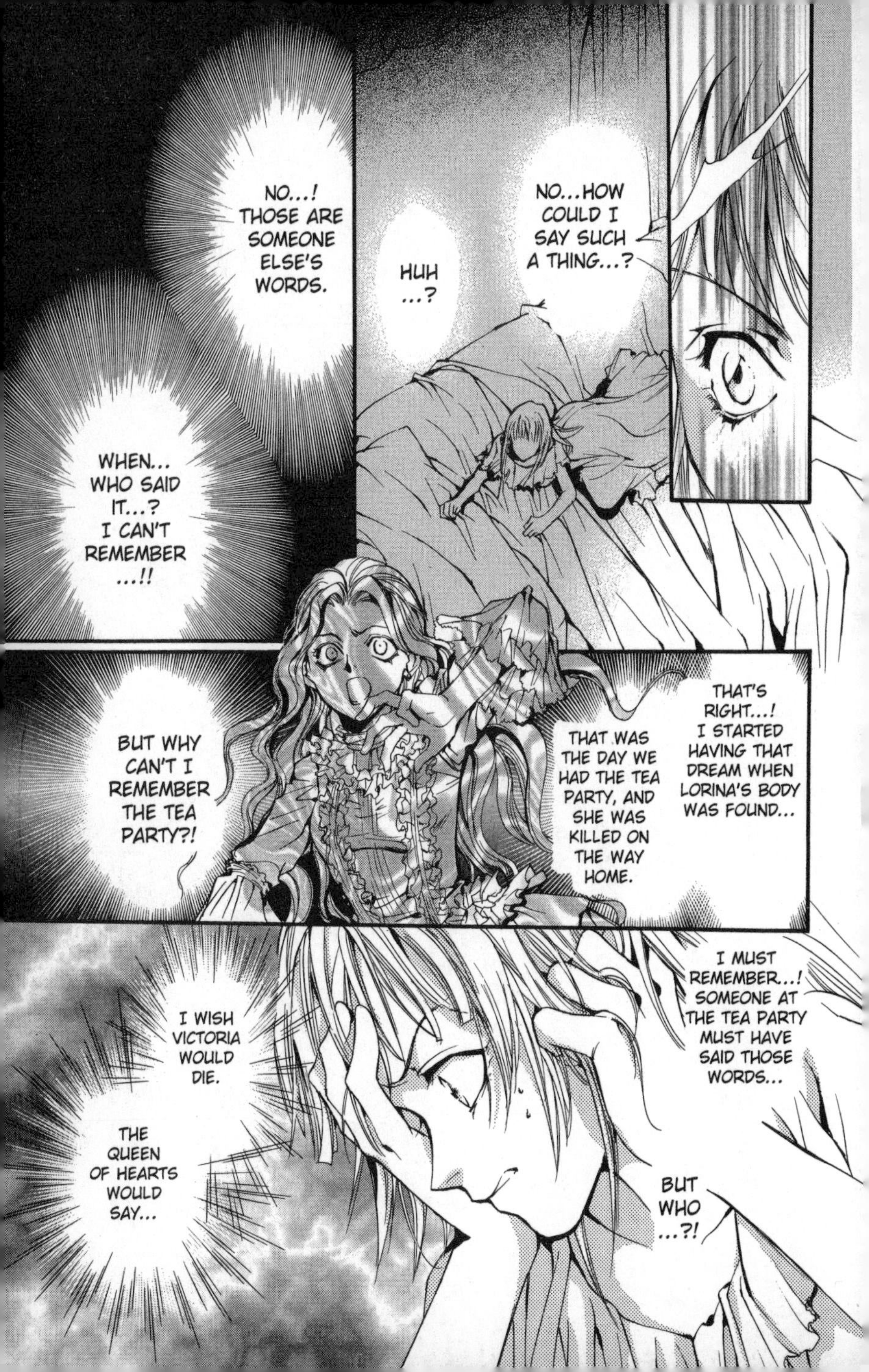

NO...HOW COULD I SAY SUCH A THING...?
HUH ...?
NO...! THOSE ARE SOMEONE ELSE'S WORDS.
WHEN... WHO SAID IT...? I CAN'T REMEMBER ...!!
THAT'S RIGHT...! I STARTED HAVING THAT DREAM WHEN LORINA'S BODY WAS FOUND...
THAT WAS THE DAY WE HAD THE TEA PARTY, AND SHE WAS KILLED ON THE WAY HOME.
BUT WHY CAN'T I REMEMBER THE TEA PARTY?!
I MUST REMEMBER...! SOMEONE AT THE TEA PARTY MUST HAVE SAID THOSE WORDS...
BUT WHO ...?!
I WISH VICTORIA WOULD DIE.
THE QUEEN OF HEARTS WOULD SAY...

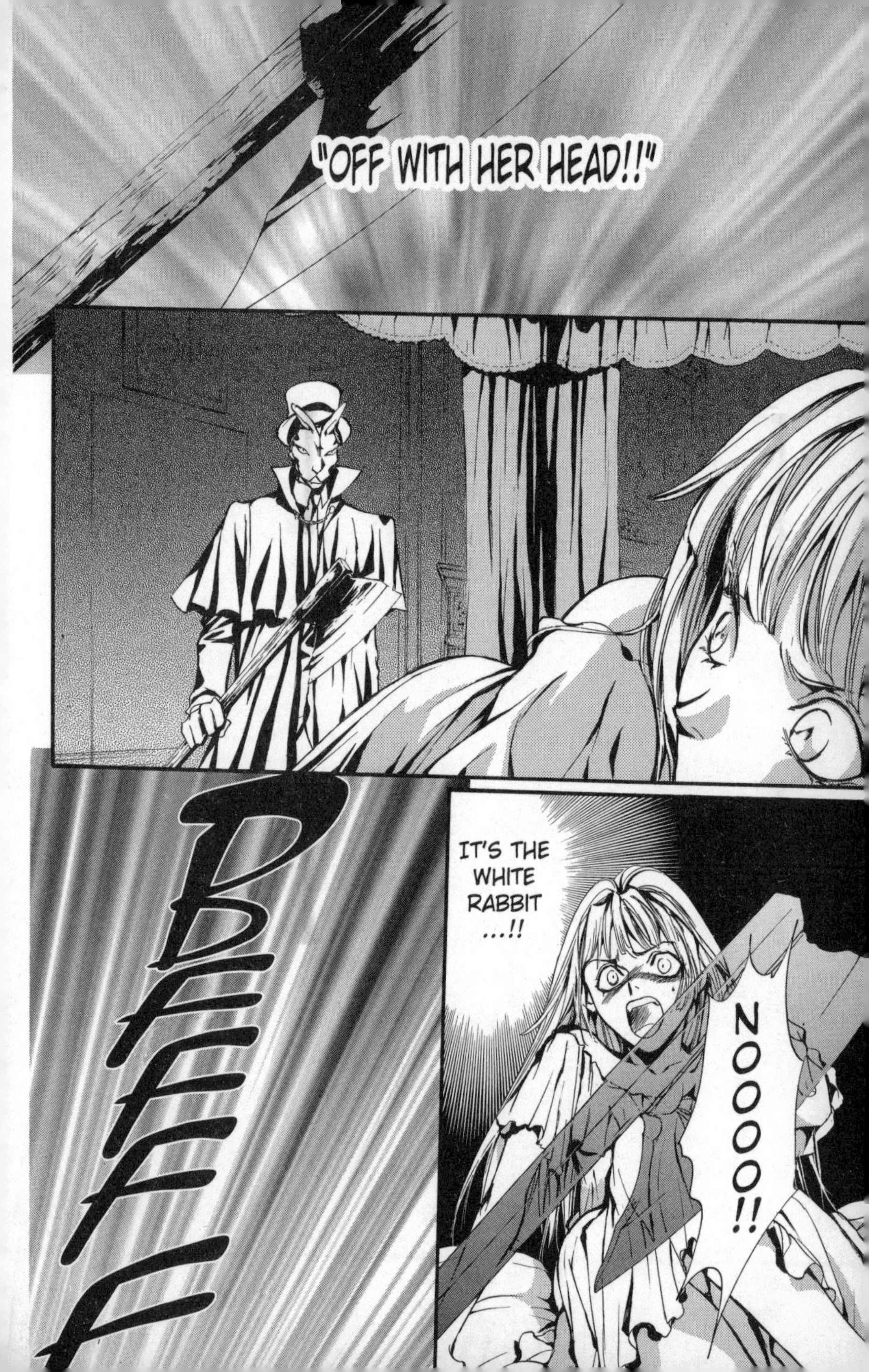
"OFF WITH HER HEAD!!"
IT'S THE WHITE RABBIT ...!!
NOOOOO!!

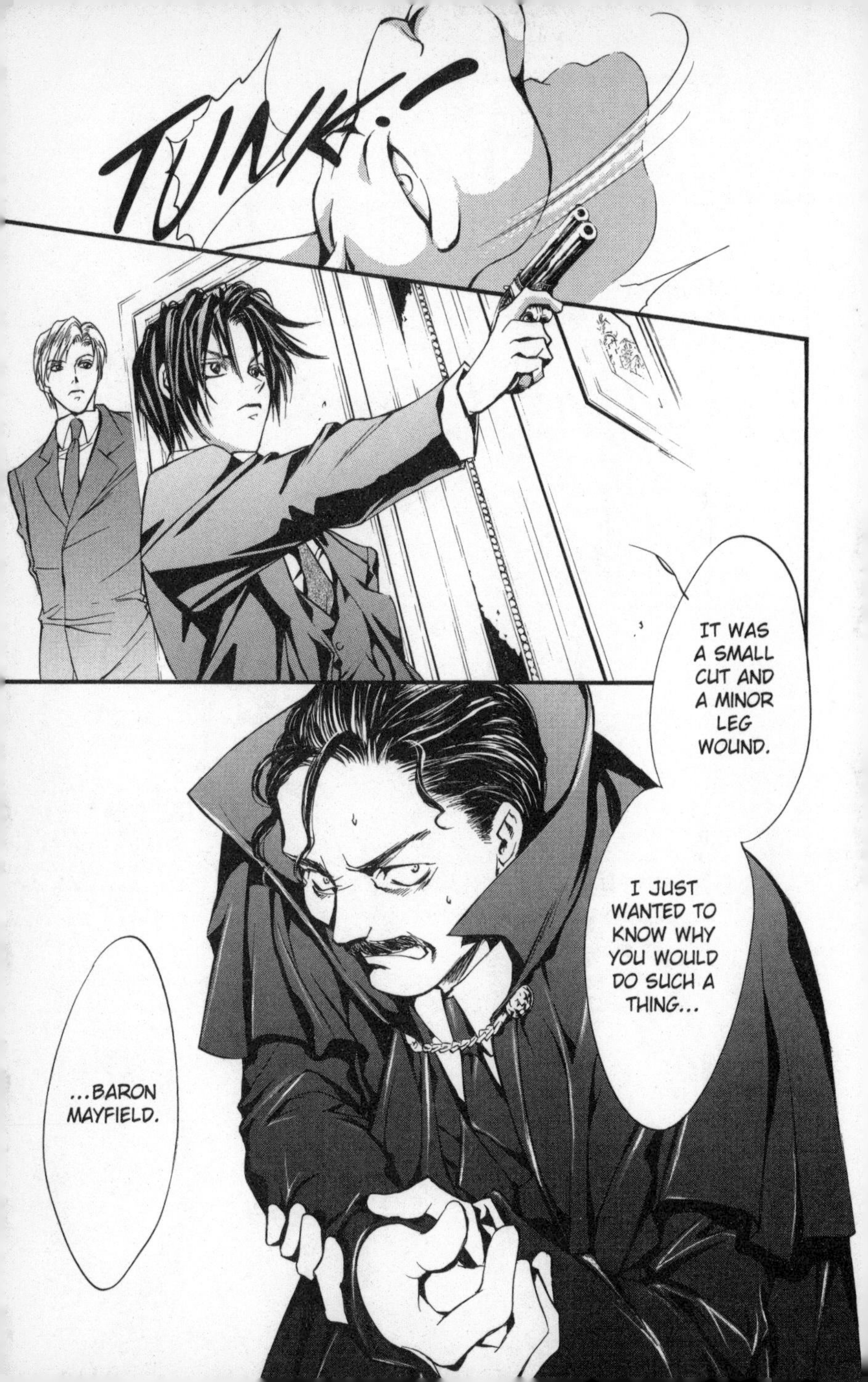
TUNK!
IT WAS A SMALL CUT AND A MINOR LEG WOUND.
I JUST WANTED TO KNOW WHY YOU WOULD DO SUCH A THING...
...BARON MAYFIELD.

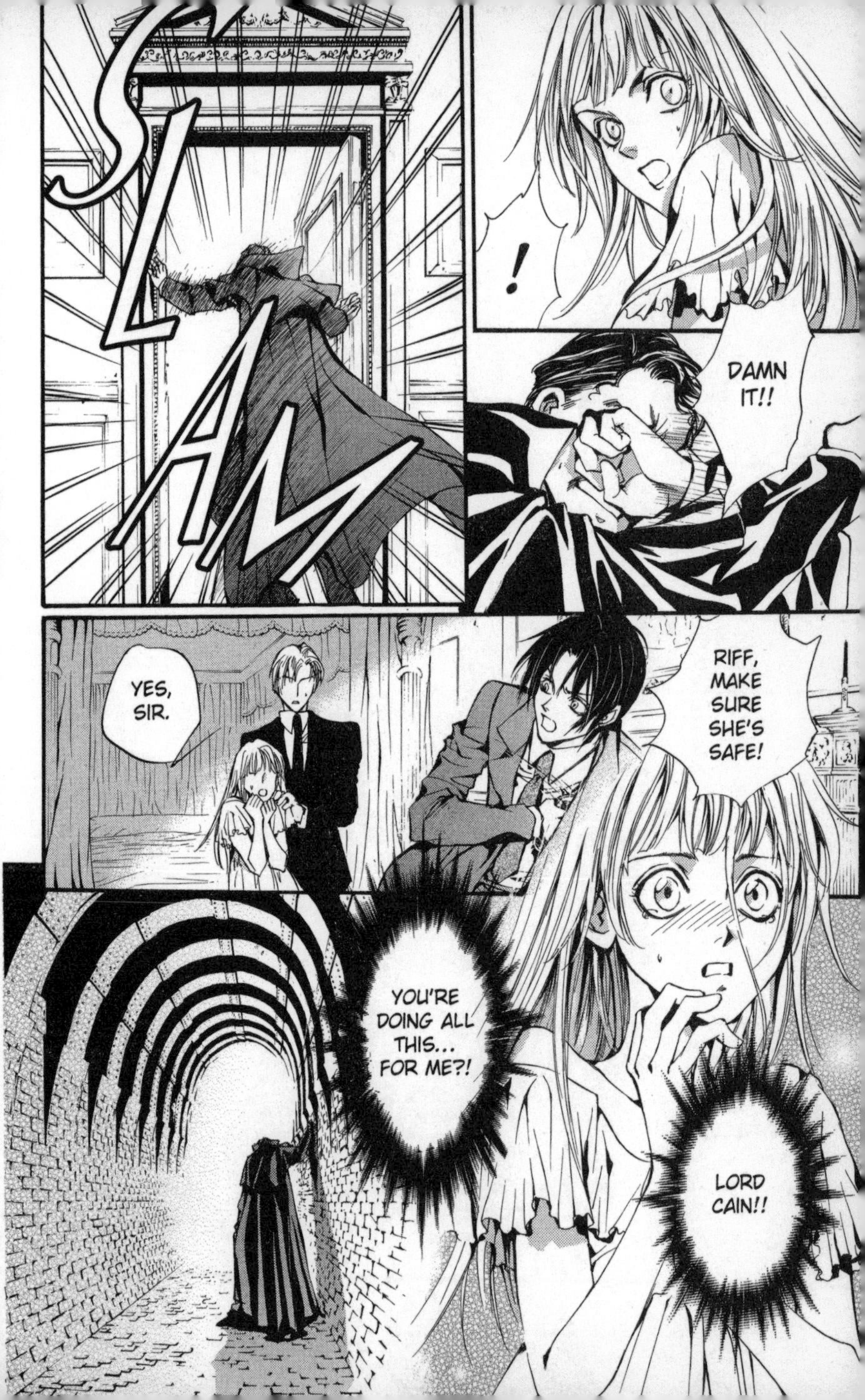
!
DAMN IT!!
SLAM
RIFF, MAKE SURE SHE'S SAFE!
YES, SIR.
YOU'RE DOING ALL THIS... FOR ME?!
LORD CAIN!!

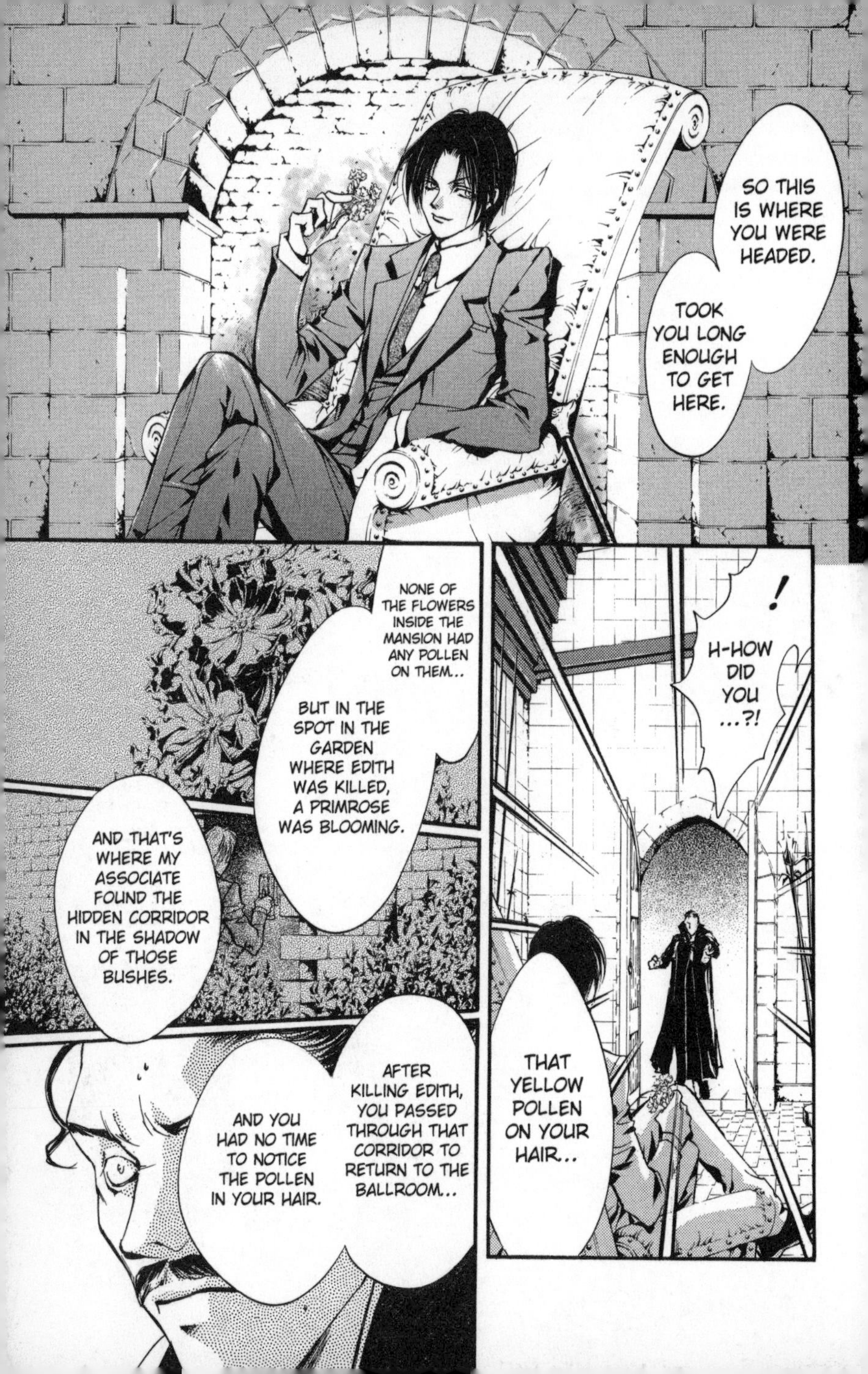
SO THIS IS WHERE YOU WERE HEADED.
TOOK YOU LONG ENOUGH TO GET HERE.
!
H-HOW DID YOU ...?!
THAT YELLOW POLLEN ON YOUR HAIR...
NONE OF THE FLOWERS INSIDE THE MANSION HAD ANY POLLEN ON THEM...
BUT IN THE SPOT IN THE GARDEN WHERE EDITH WAS KILLED, A PRIMROSE WAS BLOOMING.
AND THAT'S WHERE MY ASSOCIATE FOUND THE HIDDEN CORRIDOR IN THE SHADOW OF THOSE BUSHES.
AFTER KILLING EDITH, YOU PASSED THROUGH THAT CORRIDOR TO RETURN TO THE BALLROOM...
AND YOU HAD NO TIME TO NOTICE THE POLLEN IN YOUR HAIR.

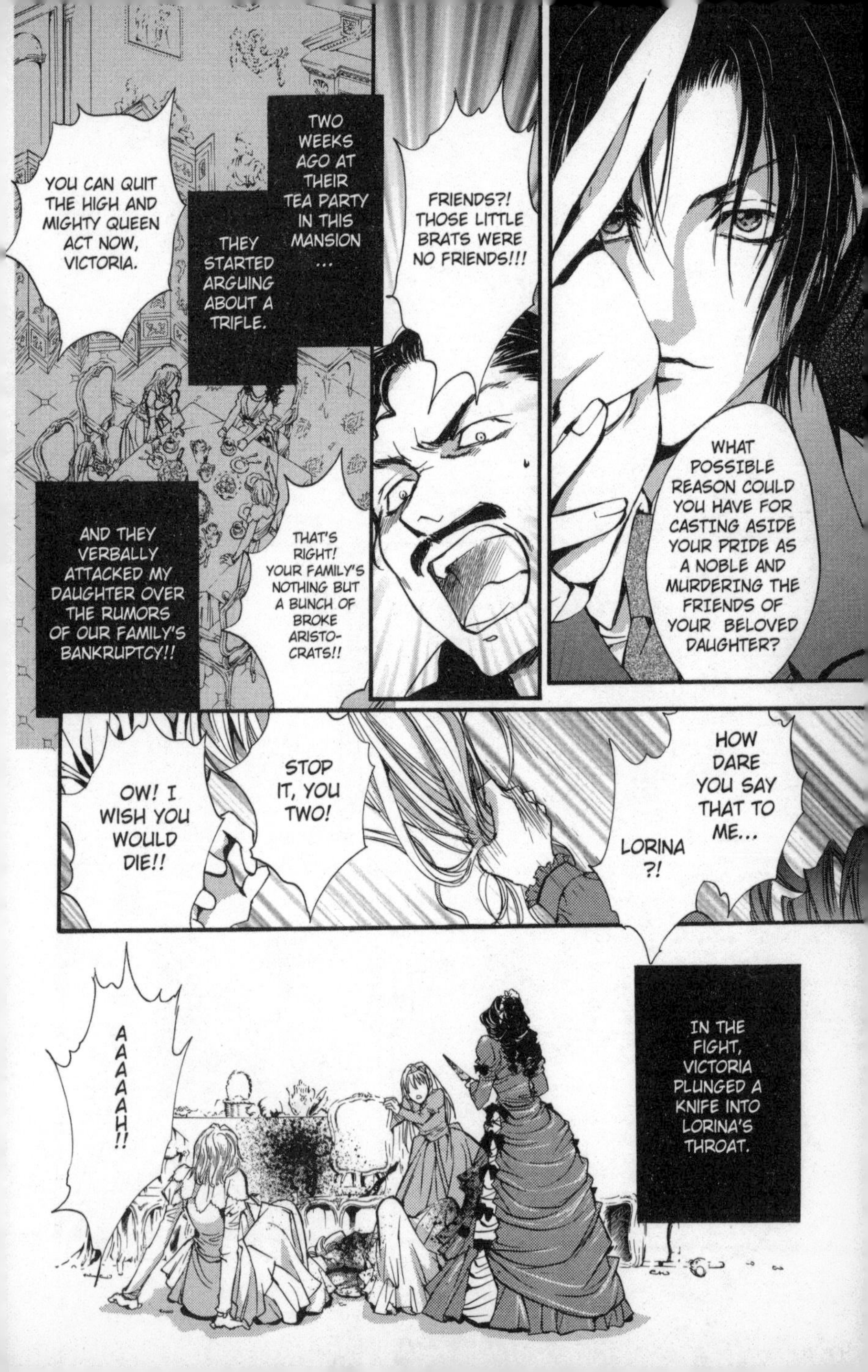
WHAT POSSIBLE REASON COULD YOU HAVE FOR CASTING ASIDE YOUR PRIDE AS A NOBLE AND MURDERING THE FRIENDS OF YOUR BELOVED DAUGHTER?
FRIENDS?! THOSE LITTLE BRATS WERE NO FRIENDS!!!
TWO WEEKS AGO AT THEIR TEA PARTY IN THIS MANSION ...
THEY STARTED ARGUING ABOUT A TRIFLE.
YOU CAN QUIT THE HIGH AND MIGHTY QUEEN ACT NOW, VICTORIA.
THAT'S RIGHT! YOUR FAMILY'S NOTHING BUT A BUNCH OF BROKE ARISTO-CRATS!!
AND THEY VERBALLY ATTACKED MY DAUGHTER OVER THE RUMORS OF OUR FAMILY'S BANKRUPTCY!!
HOW DARE YOU SAY THAT TO ME...
LORINA ?!
STOP IT, YOU TWO!
OW! I WISH YOU WOULD DIE!!
IN THE FIGHT, VICTORIA PLUNGED A KNIFE INTO LORINA'S THROAT.
AAAAAH!!

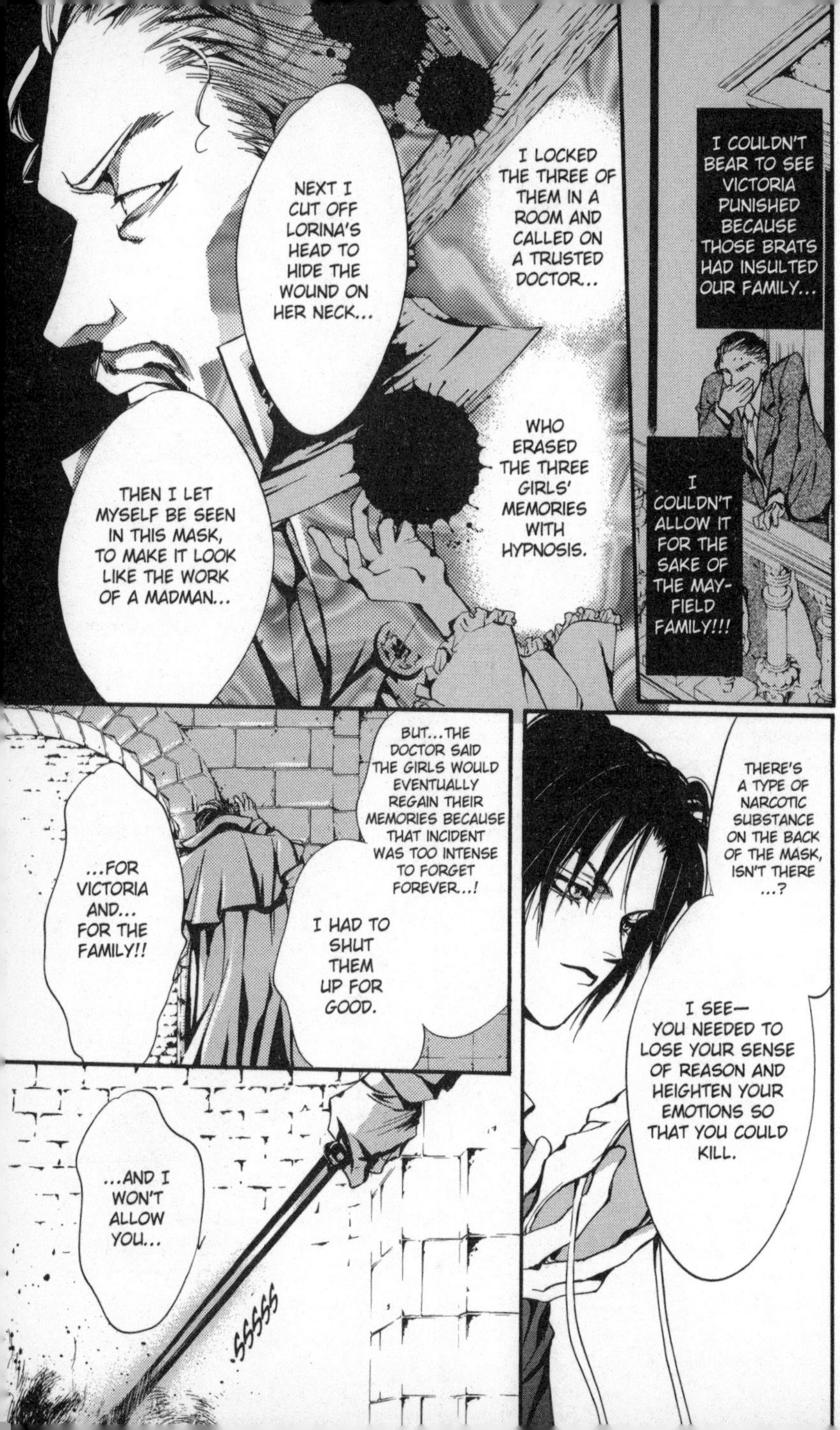
I COULDN'T BEAR TO SEE VICTORIA PUNISHED BECAUSE THOSE BRATS HAD INSULTED OUR FAMILY...
I COULDN'T ALLOW IT FOR THE SAKE OF THE MAY-FIELD FAMILY!!!
I LOCKED THE THREE OF THEM IN A ROOM AND CALLED ON A TRUSTED DOCTOR...
WHO ERASED THE THREE GIRLS' MEMORIES WITH HYPNOSIS.
NEXT I CUT OFF LORINA'S HEAD TO HIDE THE WOUND ON HER NECK...
THEN I LET MYSELF BE SEEN IN THIS MASK, TO MAKE IT LOOK LIKE THE WORK OF A MADMAN...
THERE'S A TYPE OF NARCOTIC SUBSTANCE ON THE BACK OF THE MASK, ISN'T THERE ...?
I SEE—YOU NEEDED TO LOSE YOUR SENSE OF REASON AND HEIGHTEN YOUR EMOTIONS SO THAT YOU COULD KILL.
BUT...THE DOCTOR SAID THE GIRLS WOULD EVENTUALLY REGAIN THEIR MEMORIES BECAUSE THAT INCIDENT WAS TOO INTENSE TO FORGET FOREVER...!
I HAD TO SHUT THEM UP FOR GOOD.
...FOR VICTORIA AND... FOR THE FAMILY!!
...AND I WON'T ALLOW YOU...
SSSSS

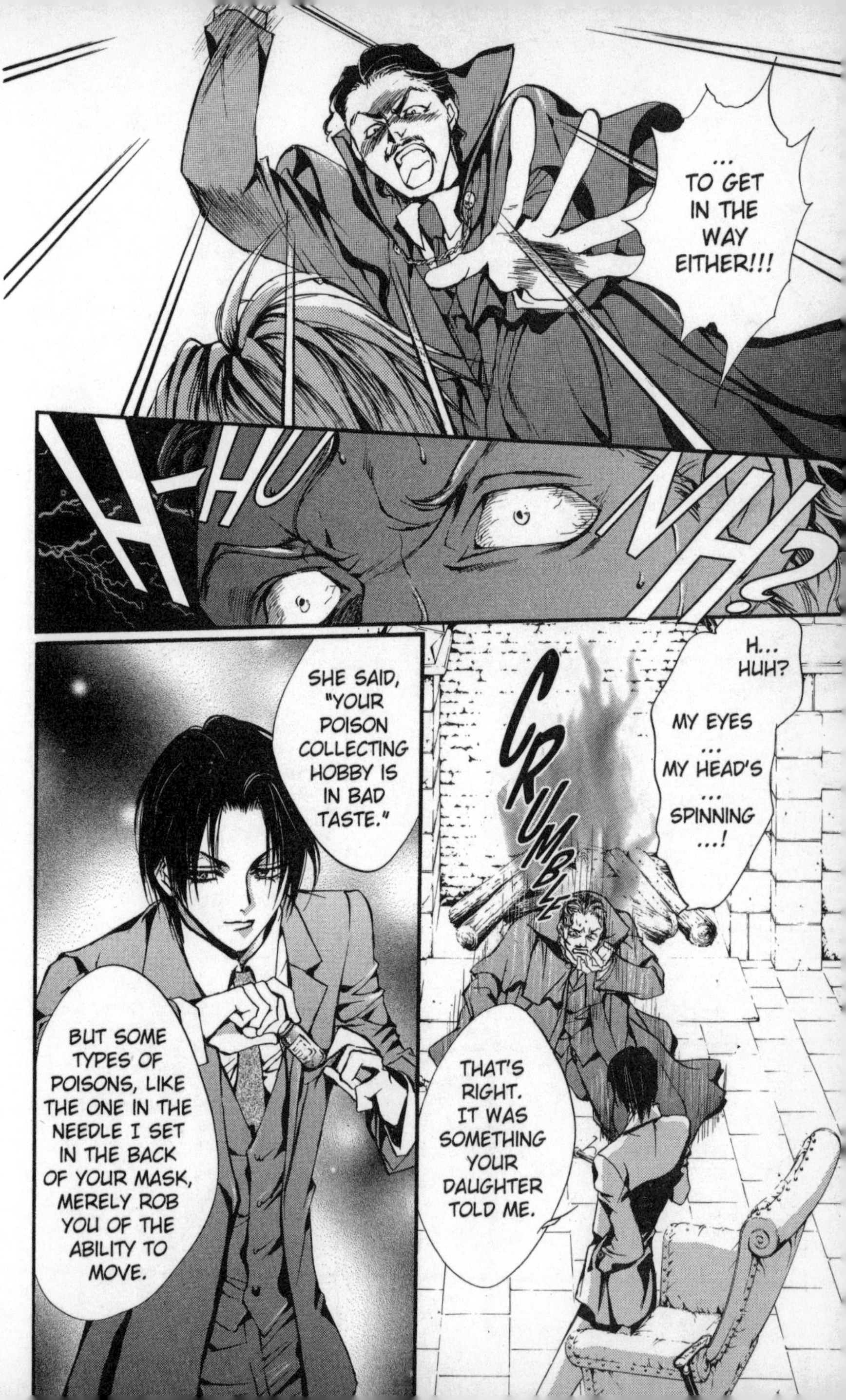
... TO GET IN THE WAY EITHER!!!
H-HUNH!?
H... HUH?
MY EYES ... MY HEAD'S ... SPINNING ...!
CRUMBLE
THAT'S RIGHT. IT WAS SOMETHING YOUR DAUGHTER TOLD ME.
SHE SAID, "YOUR POISON COLLECTING HOBBY IS IN BAD TASTE."
BUT SOME TYPES OF POISONS, LIKE THE ONE IN THE NEEDLE I SET IN THE BACK OF YOUR MASK, MERELY ROB YOU OF THE ABILITY TO MOVE.

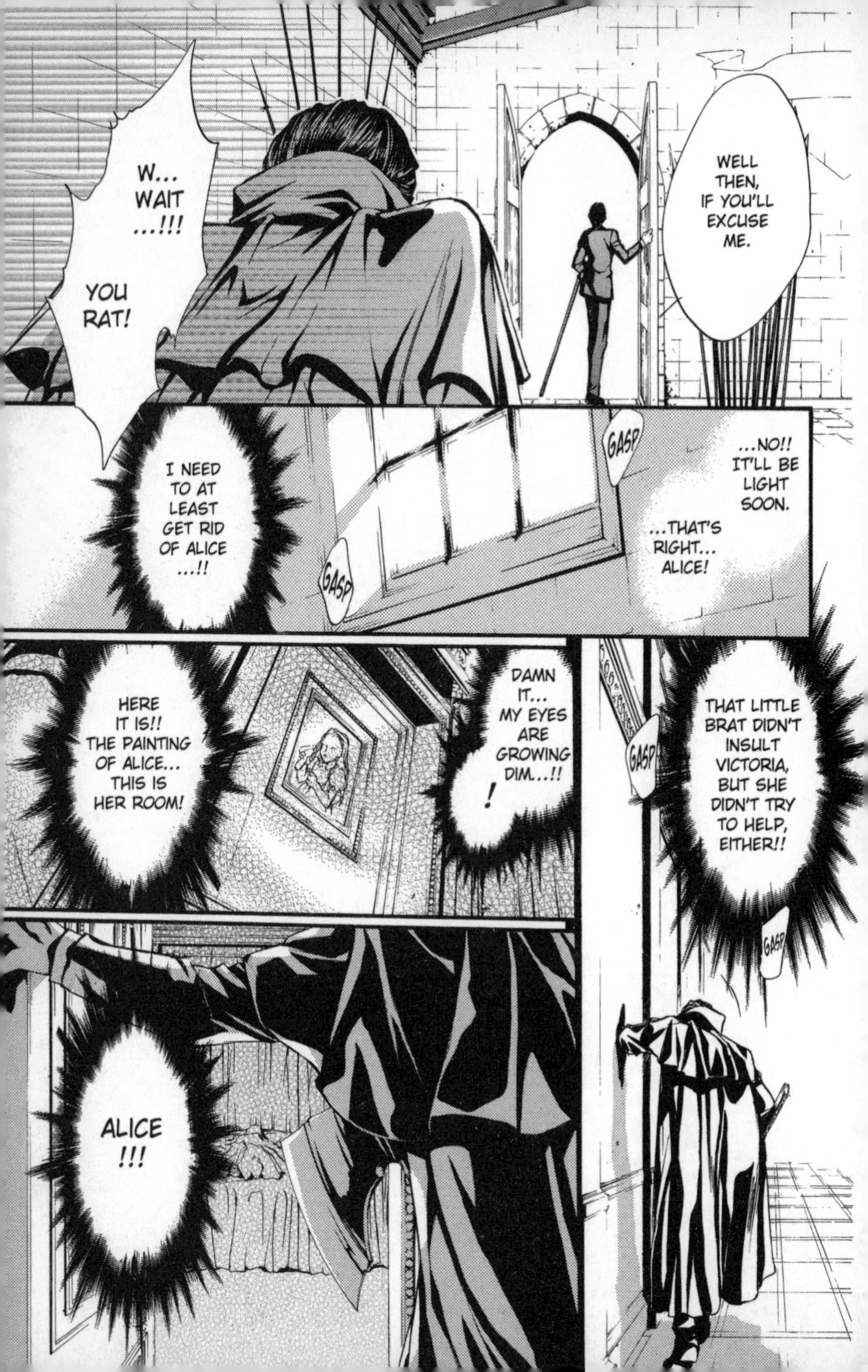
WELL THEN, IF YOU'LL EXCUSE ME.
W... WAIT ...!!!
YOU RAT!
GASP
...NO!! IT'LL BE LIGHT SOON.
...THAT'S RIGHT... ALICE!
GASP
I NEED TO AT LEAST GET RID OF ALICE ...!!
GASP
THAT LITTLE BRAT DIDN'T INSULT VICTORIA, BUT SHE DIDN'T TRY TO HELP, EITHER!!
GASP
DAMN IT... MY EYES ARE GROWING DIM...!!
!
HERE IT IS!! THE PAINTING OF ALICE... THIS IS HER ROOM!
ALICE !!!

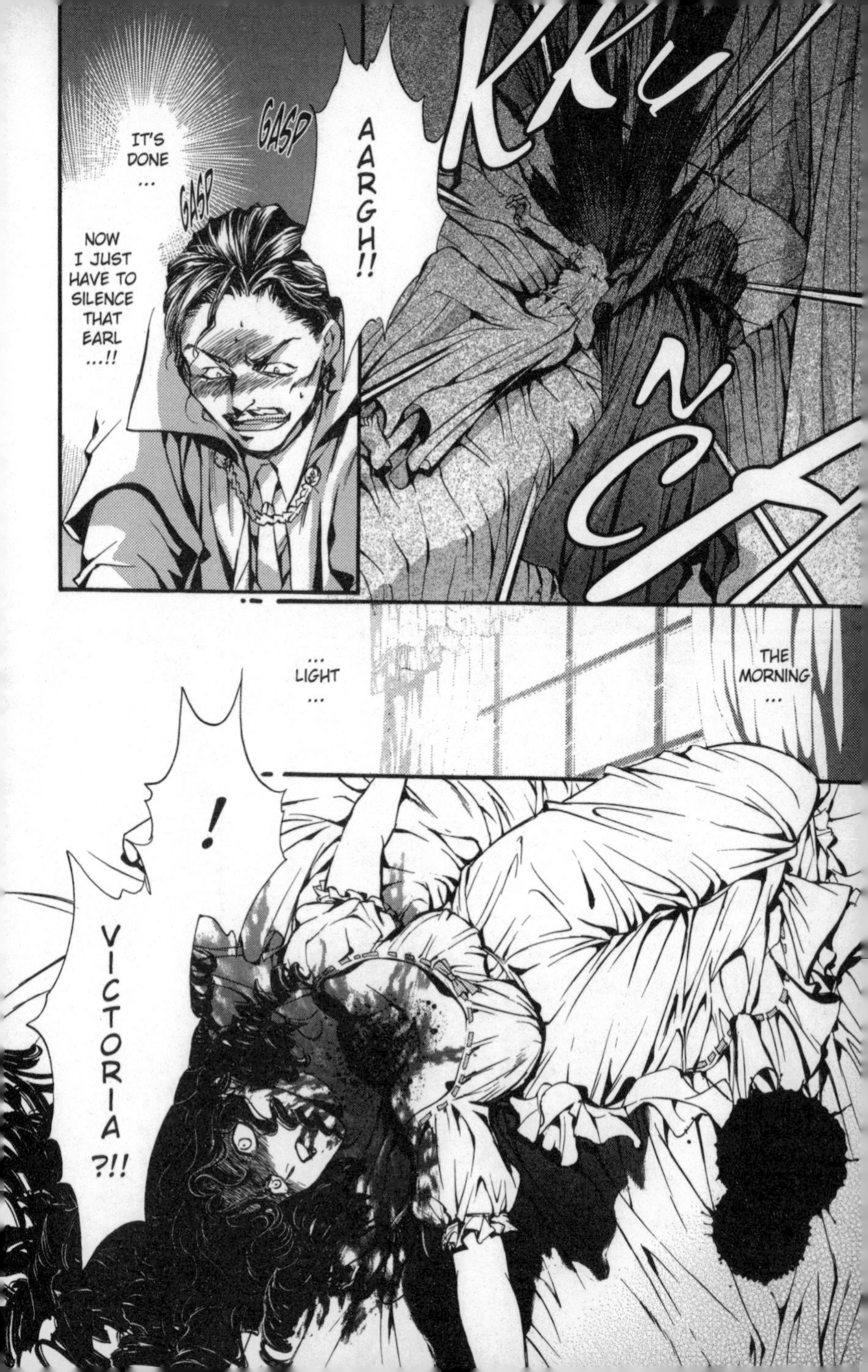
KKUNCH
AARGH!!
GASP
GASP
IT'S DONE ...
NOW I JUST HAVE TO SILENCE THAT EARL ...!!
THE MORNING ...
... LIGHT ...
!
VICTORIA ?!!

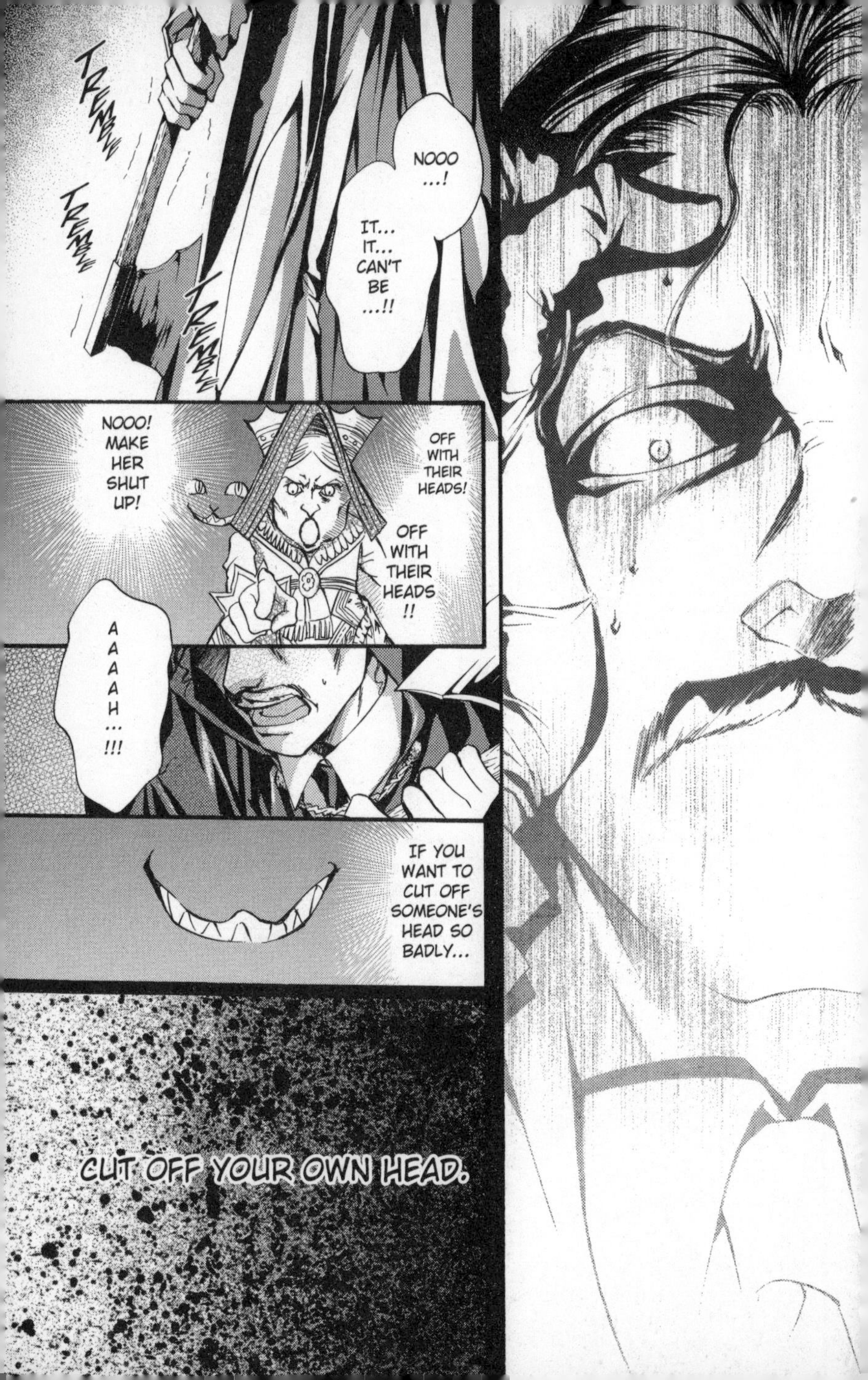
NOOO ...!
IT... IT... CAN'T BE ...!!
TREMBLE
TREMBLE
TREMBLE
OFF WITH THEIR HEADS!
OFF WITH THEIR HEADS !!
NOOO! MAKE HER SHUT UP!
AAAAH... !!!
IF YOU WANT TO CUT OFF SOMEONE'S HEAD SO BADLY...
CUT OFF YOUR OWN HEAD.

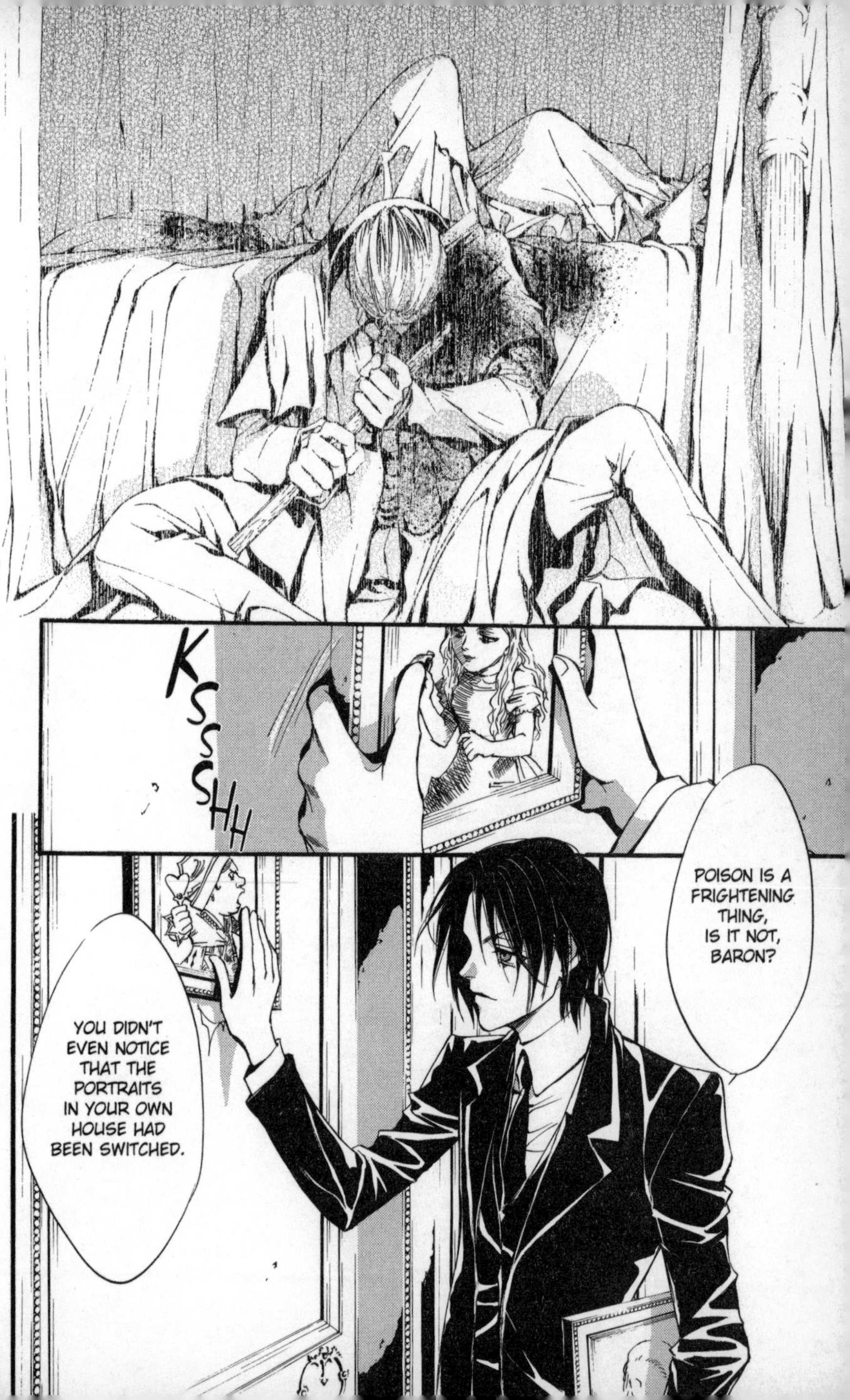
KSSSHH
POISON IS A FRIGHTENING THING, IS IT NOT, BARON?
YOU DIDN'T EVEN NOTICE THAT THE PORTRAITS IN YOUR OWN HOUSE HAD BEEN SWITCHED.

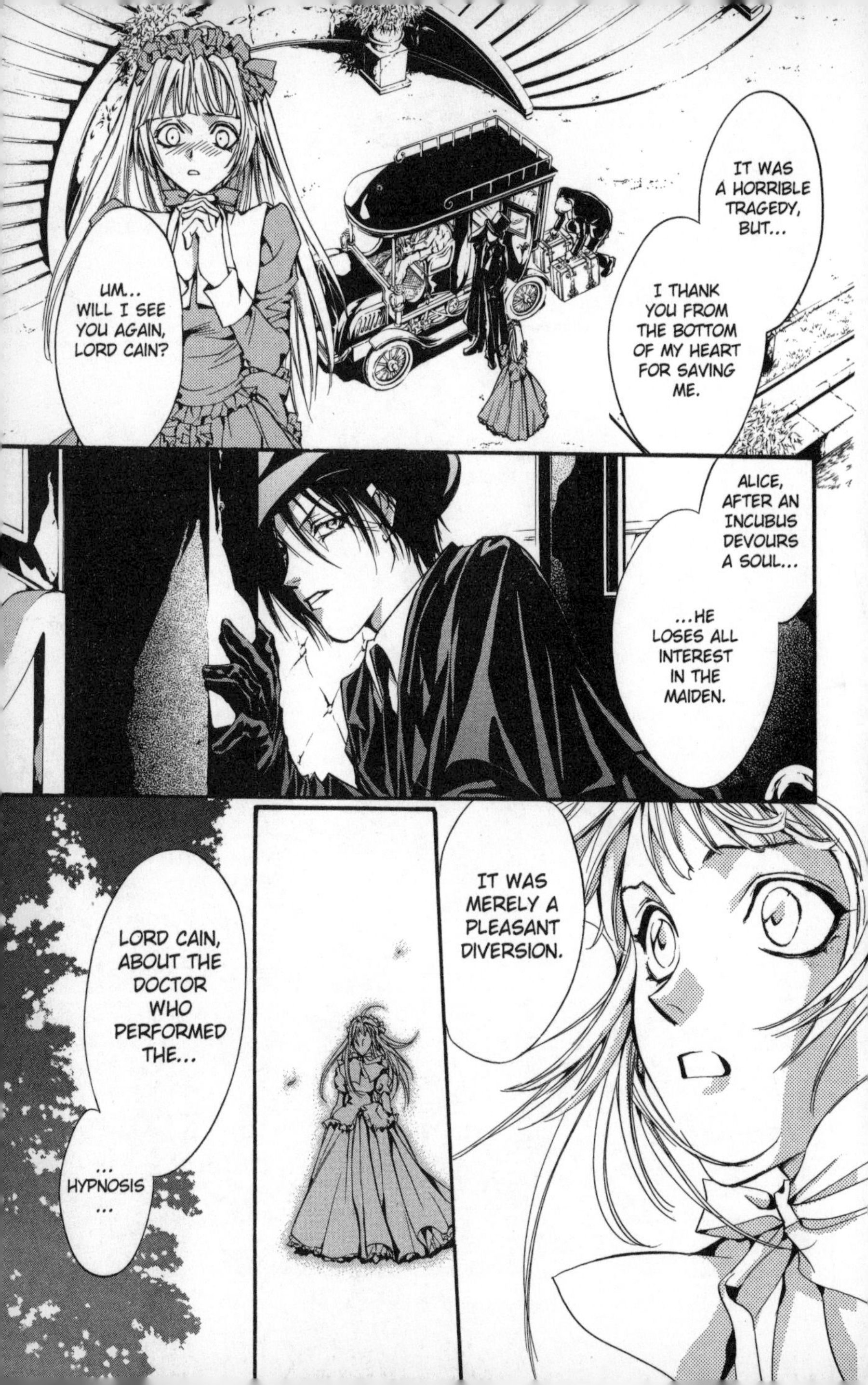
IT WAS A HORRIBLE TRAGEDY, BUT...
I THANK YOU FROM THE BOTTOM OF MY HEART FOR SAVING ME.
UM... WILL I SEE YOU AGAIN, LORD CAIN?
ALICE, AFTER AN INCUBUS DEVOURS A SOUL...
...HE LOSES ALL INTEREST IN THE MAIDEN.
IT WAS MERELY A PLEASANT DIVERSION.
LORD CAIN, ABOUT THE DOCTOR WHO PERFORMED THE...
...HYPNOSIS...

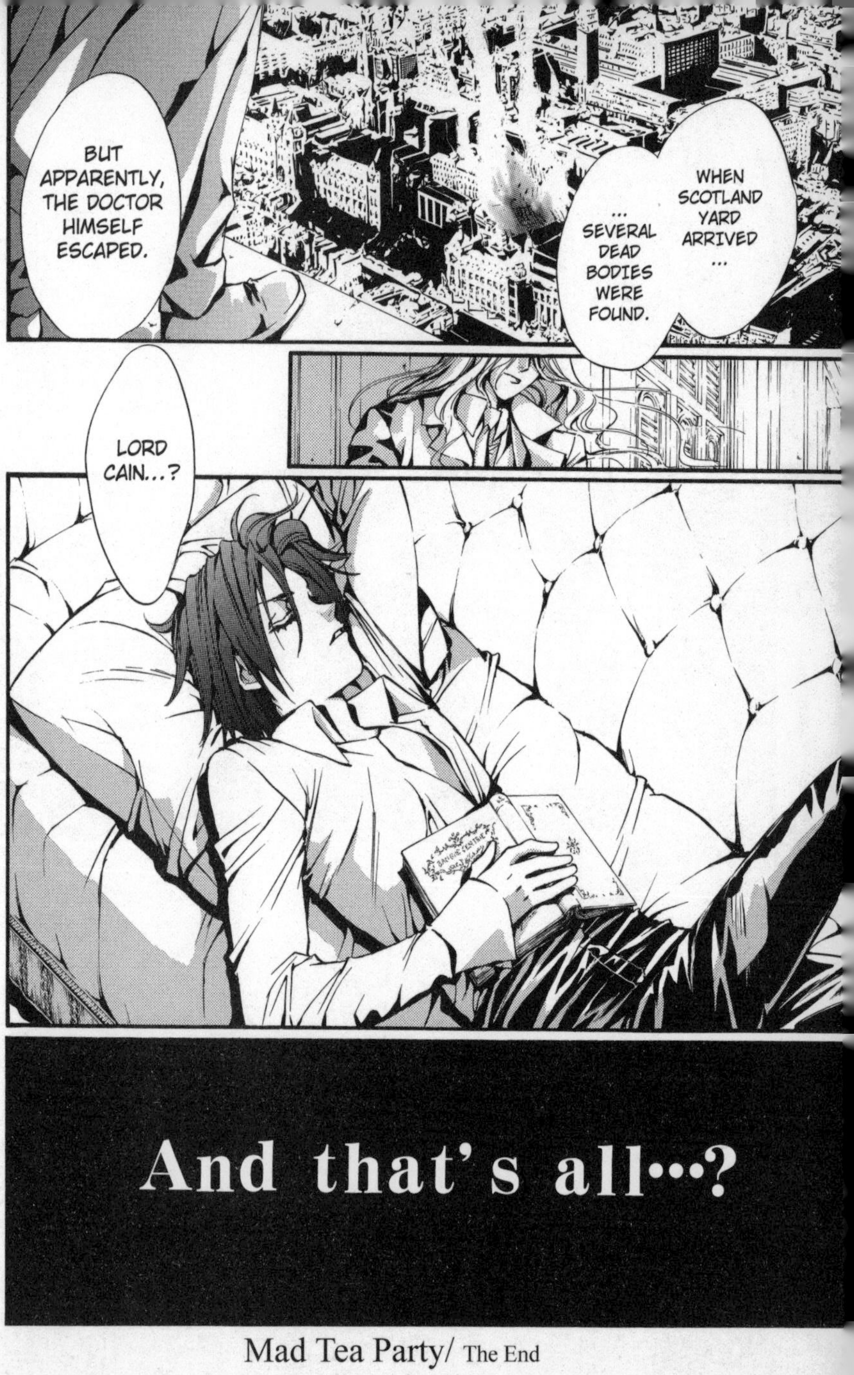

WHEN SCOTLAND YARD ARRIVED ...
... SEVERAL DEAD BODIES WERE FOUND.
BUT APPARENTLY, THE DOCTOR HIMSELF ESCAPED.
LORD CAIN...?

And that's all···?

Mad Tea Party/ The End

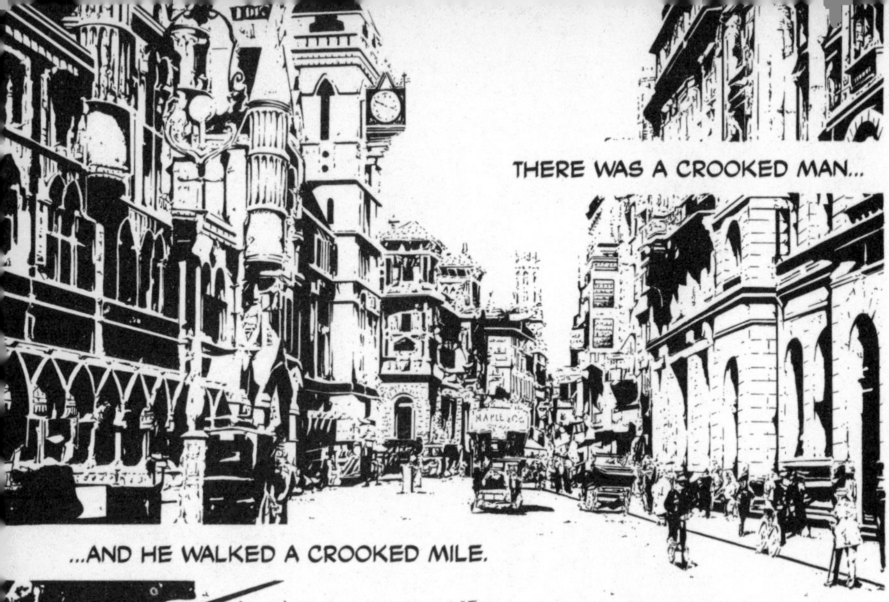
THERE WAS A CROOKED MAN...
...AND HE WALKED A CROOKED MILE.

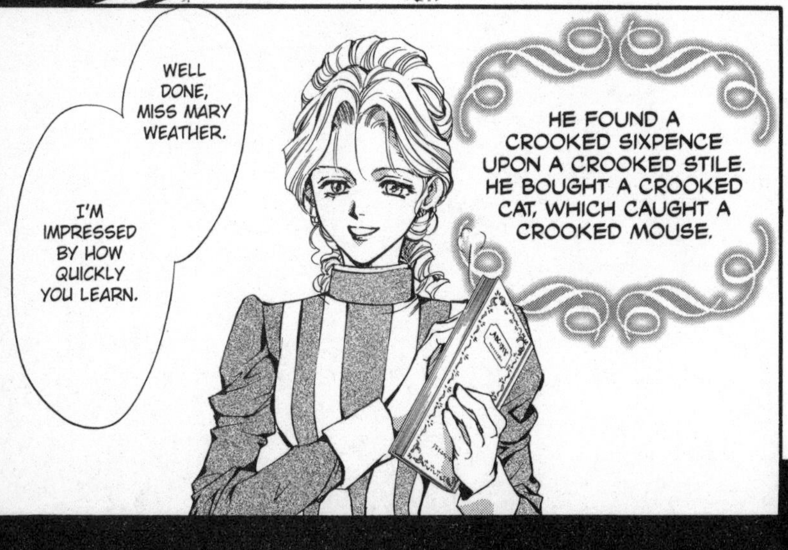
HE FOUND A CROOKED SIXPENCE UPON A CROOKED STILE. HE BOUGHT A CROOKED CAT, WHICH CAUGHT A CROOKED MOUSE.
WELL DONE, MISS MARY WEATHER.
I'M IMPRESSED BY HOW QUICKLY YOU LEARN.

The Little Crooked House

Part One

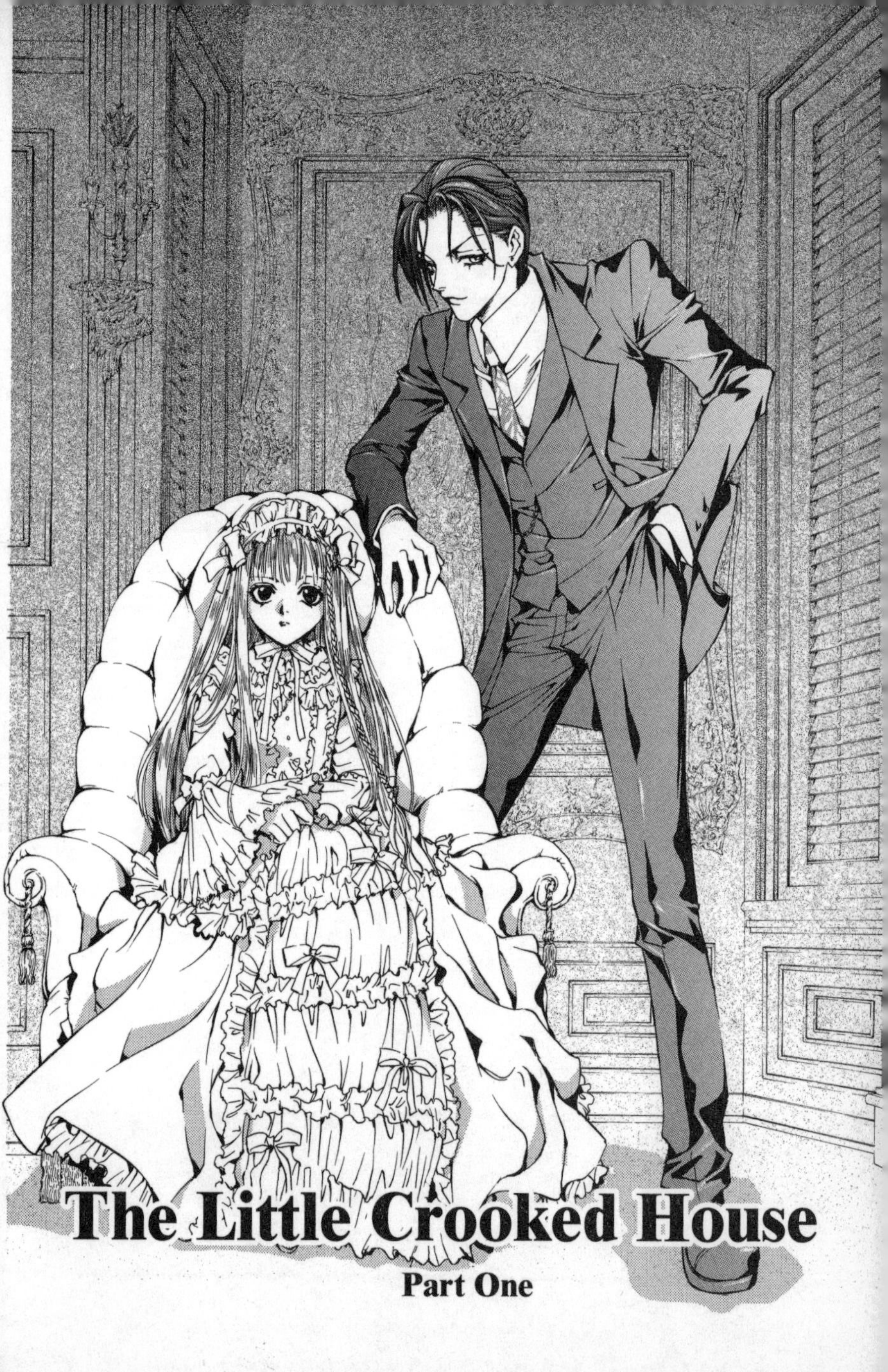

The Little Crooked House

Part One

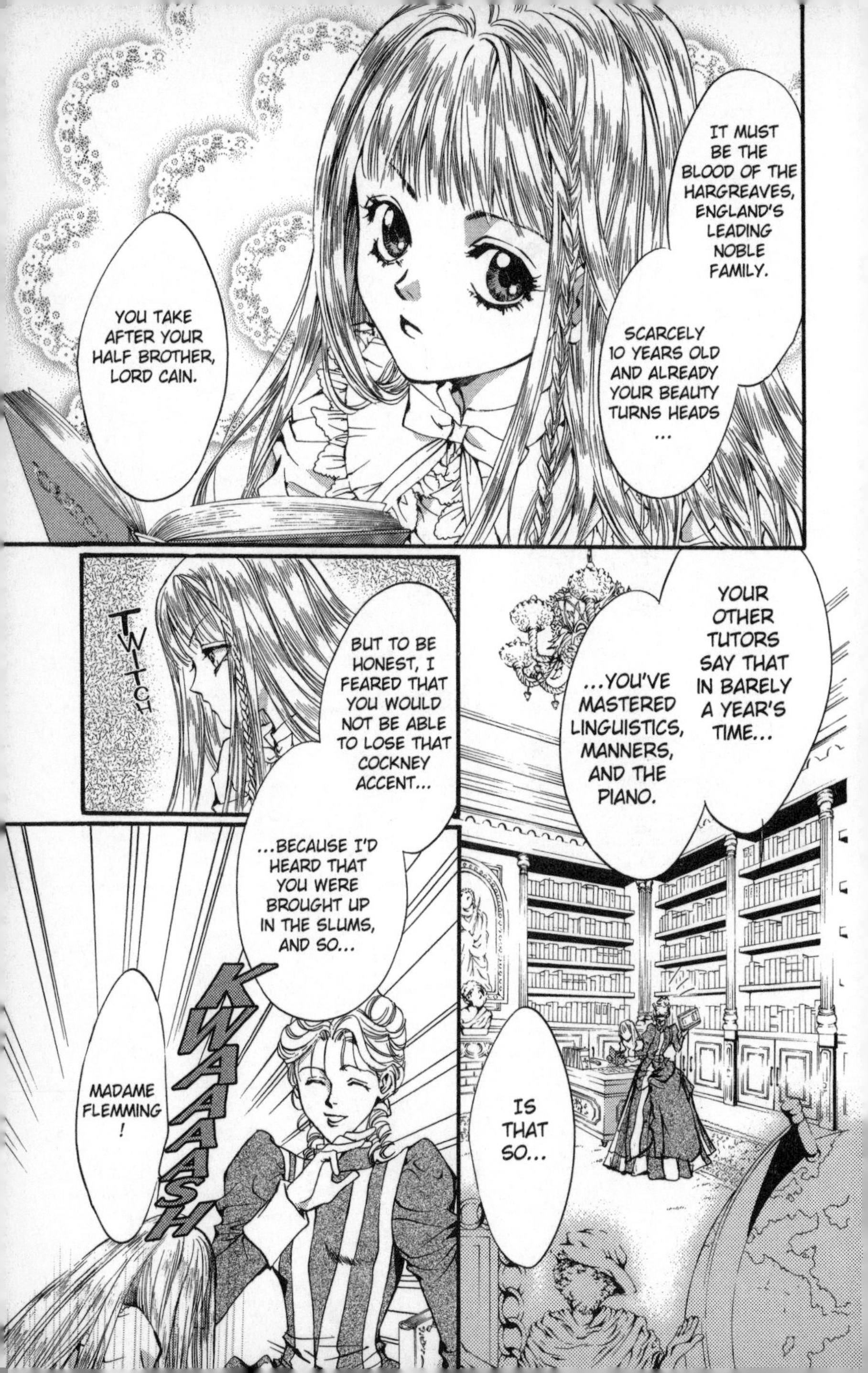
IT MUST BE THE BLOOD OF THE HARGREAVES, ENGLAND'S LEADING NOBLE FAMILY.
SCARCELY 10 YEARS OLD AND ALREADY YOUR BEAUTY TURNS HEADS ...
YOU TAKE AFTER YOUR HALF BROTHER, LORD CAIN.
YOUR OTHER TUTORS SAY THAT IN BARELY A YEAR'S TIME...
...YOU'VE MASTERED LINGUISTICS, MANNERS, AND THE PIANO.
IS THAT SO...
BUT TO BE HONEST, I FEARED THAT YOU WOULD NOT BE ABLE TO LOSE THAT COCKNEY ACCENT...
TWITCH
...BECAUSE I'D HEARD THAT YOU WERE BROUGHT UP IN THE SLUMS, AND SO...
KWAAAAASH
MADAME FLEMMING !

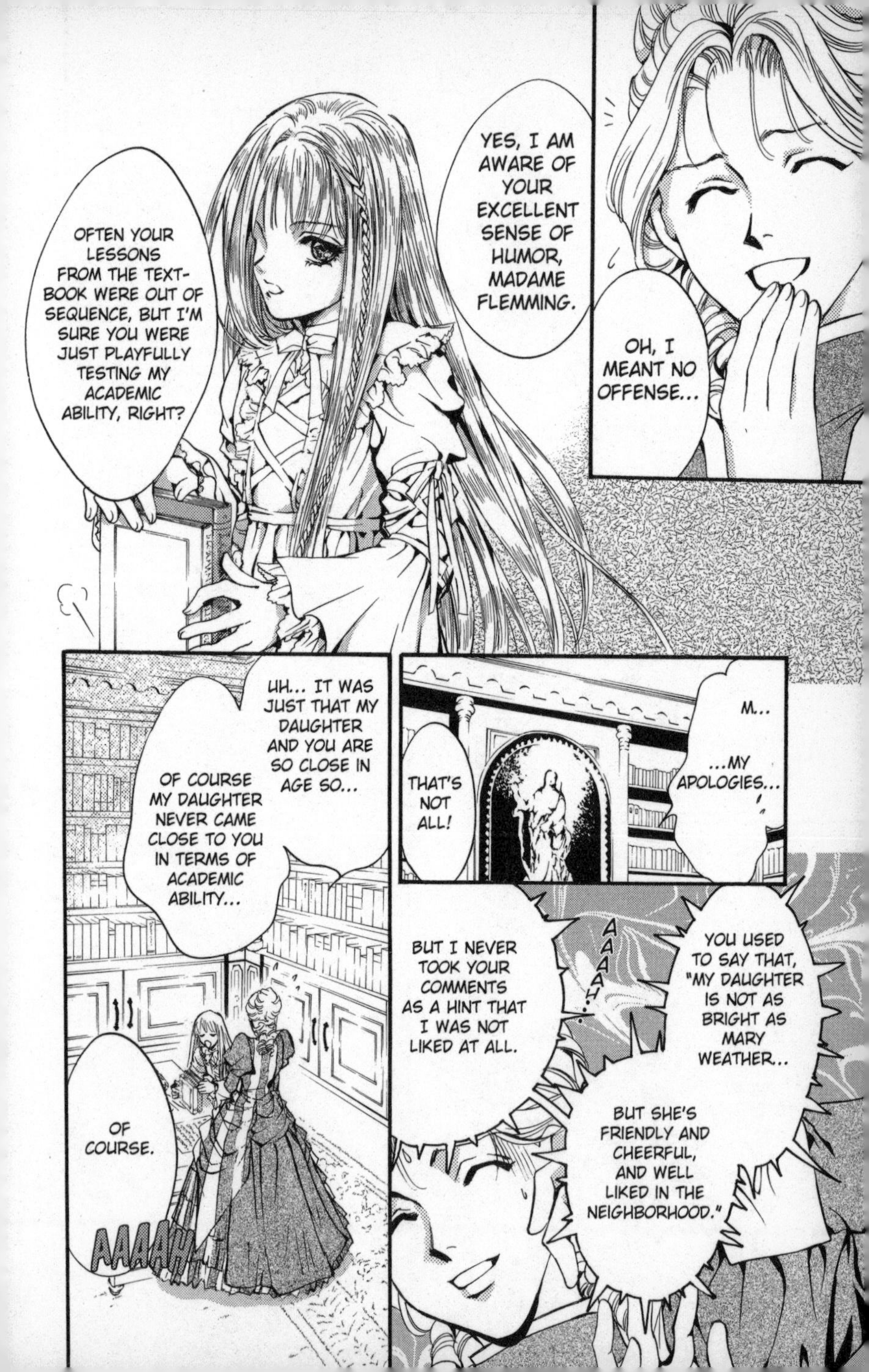
OH, I MEANT NO OFFENSE...
YES, I AM AWARE OF YOUR EXCELLENT SENSE OF HUMOR, MADAME FLEMMING.
OFTEN YOUR LESSONS FROM THE TEXT-BOOK WERE OUT OF SEQUENCE, BUT I'M SURE YOU WERE JUST PLAYFULLY TESTING MY ACADEMIC ABILITY, RIGHT?
M...
...MY APOLOGIES...
THAT'S NOT ALL!
YOU USED TO SAY THAT, "MY DAUGHTER IS NOT AS BRIGHT AS MARY WEATHER...
BUT SHE'S FRIENDLY AND CHEERFUL, AND WELL LIKED IN THE NEIGHBORHOOD."
BUT I NEVER TOOK YOUR COMMENTS AS A HINT THAT I WAS NOT LIKED AT ALL.
AAAAH!
UH... IT WAS JUST THAT MY DAUGHTER AND YOU ARE SO CLOSE IN AGE SO...
OF COURSE MY DAUGHTER NEVER CAME CLOSE TO YOU IN TERMS OF ACADEMIC ABILITY...
OF COURSE.
AAAAH

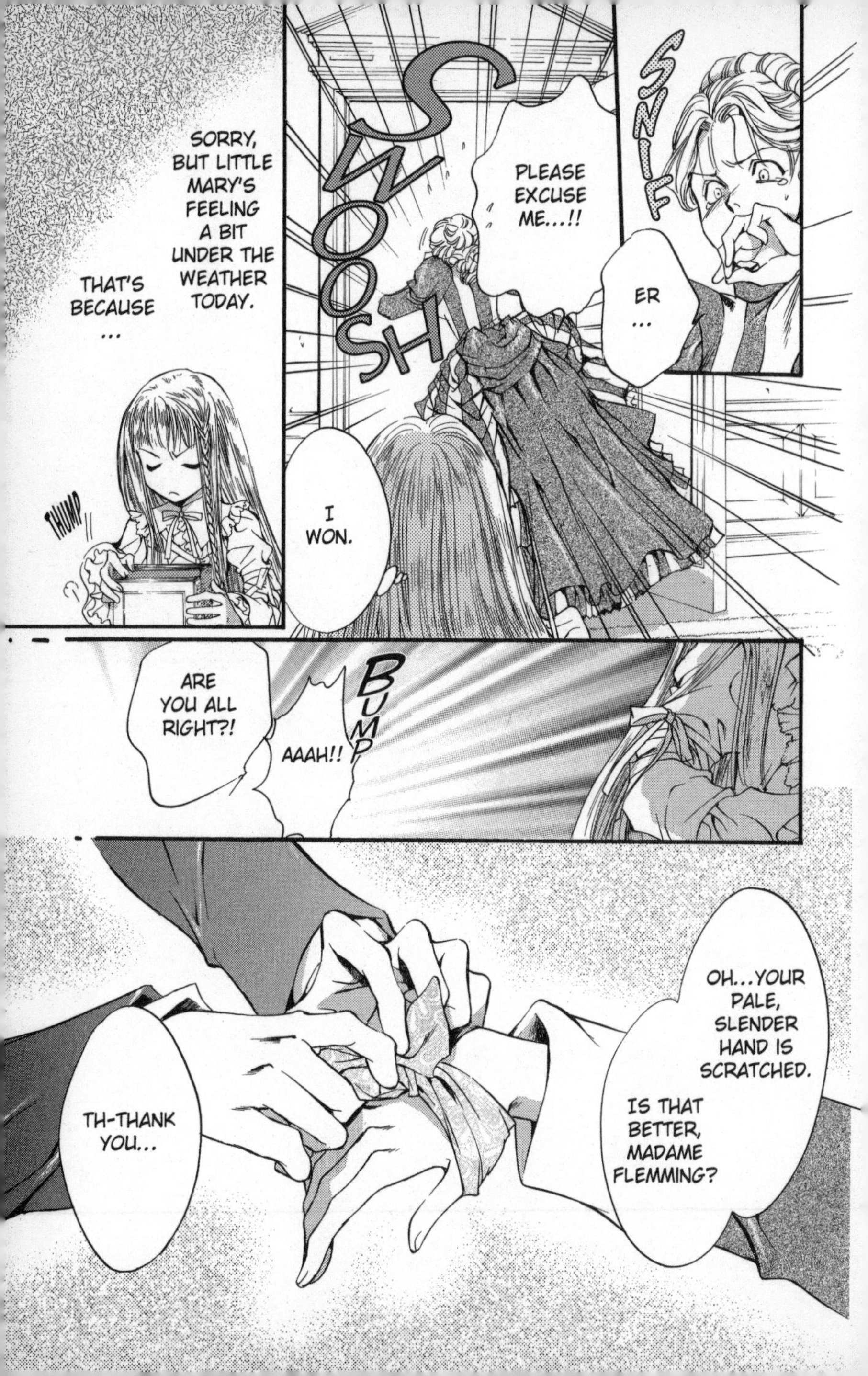
SNIF
ER ...
SWOOSH
PLEASE EXCUSE ME...!!
I WON.
SORRY, BUT LITTLE MARY'S FEELING A BIT UNDER THE WEATHER TODAY.
THAT'S BECAUSE ...
THUMP
BUMP
AAAH!!
ARE YOU ALL RIGHT?!
OH...YOUR PALE, SLENDER HAND IS SCRATCHED.
IS THAT BETTER, MADAME FLEMMING?
TH-THANK YOU...

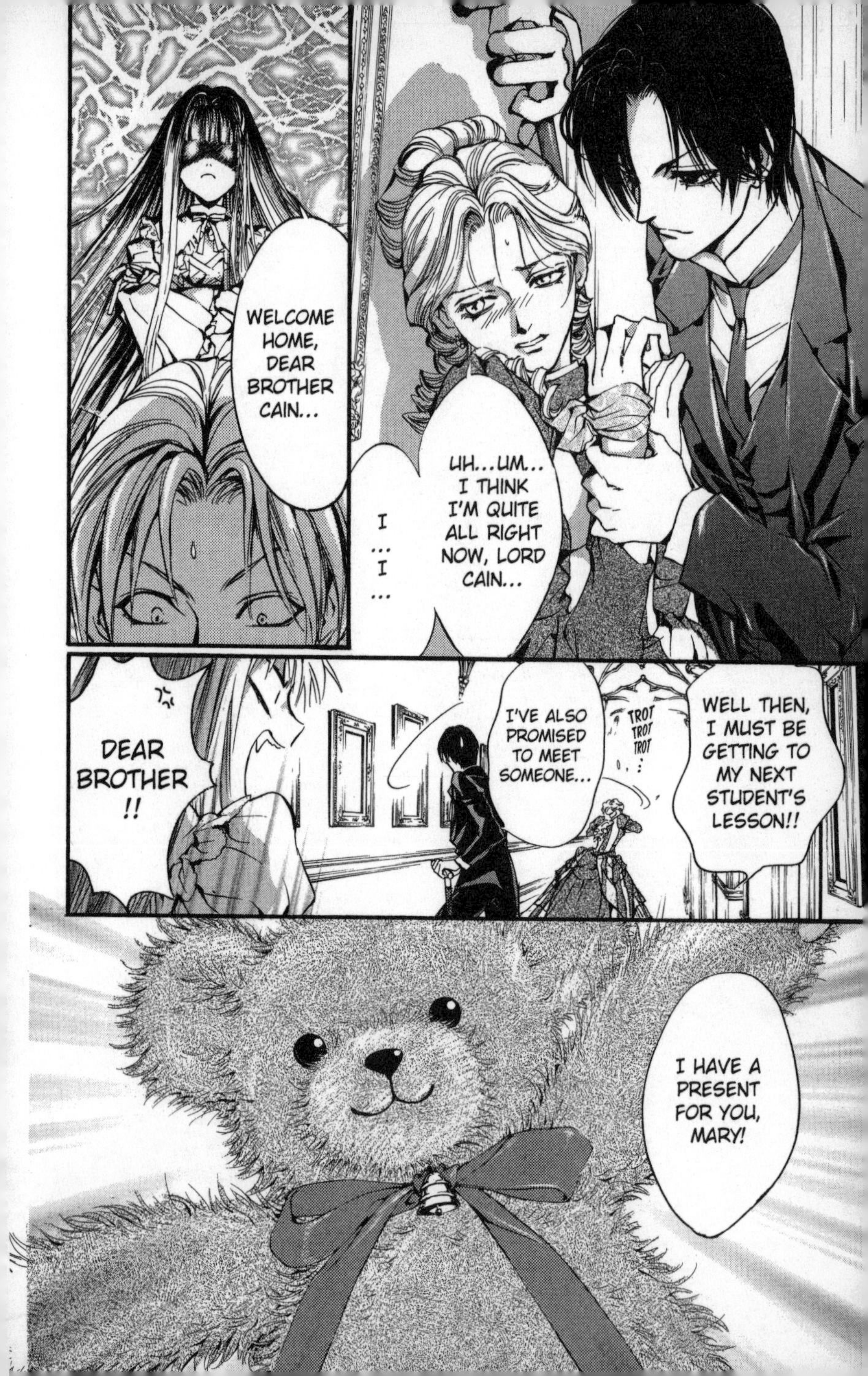
UH...UM... I THINK I'M QUITE ALL RIGHT NOW, LORD CAIN...
I ... I ...
WELCOME HOME, DEAR BROTHER CAIN...
WELL THEN, I MUST BE GETTING TO MY NEXT STUDENT'S LESSON!!
TROT TROT TROT
I'VE ALSO PROMISED TO MEET SOMEONE...
DEAR BROTHER !!
I HAVE A PRESENT FOR YOU, MARY!

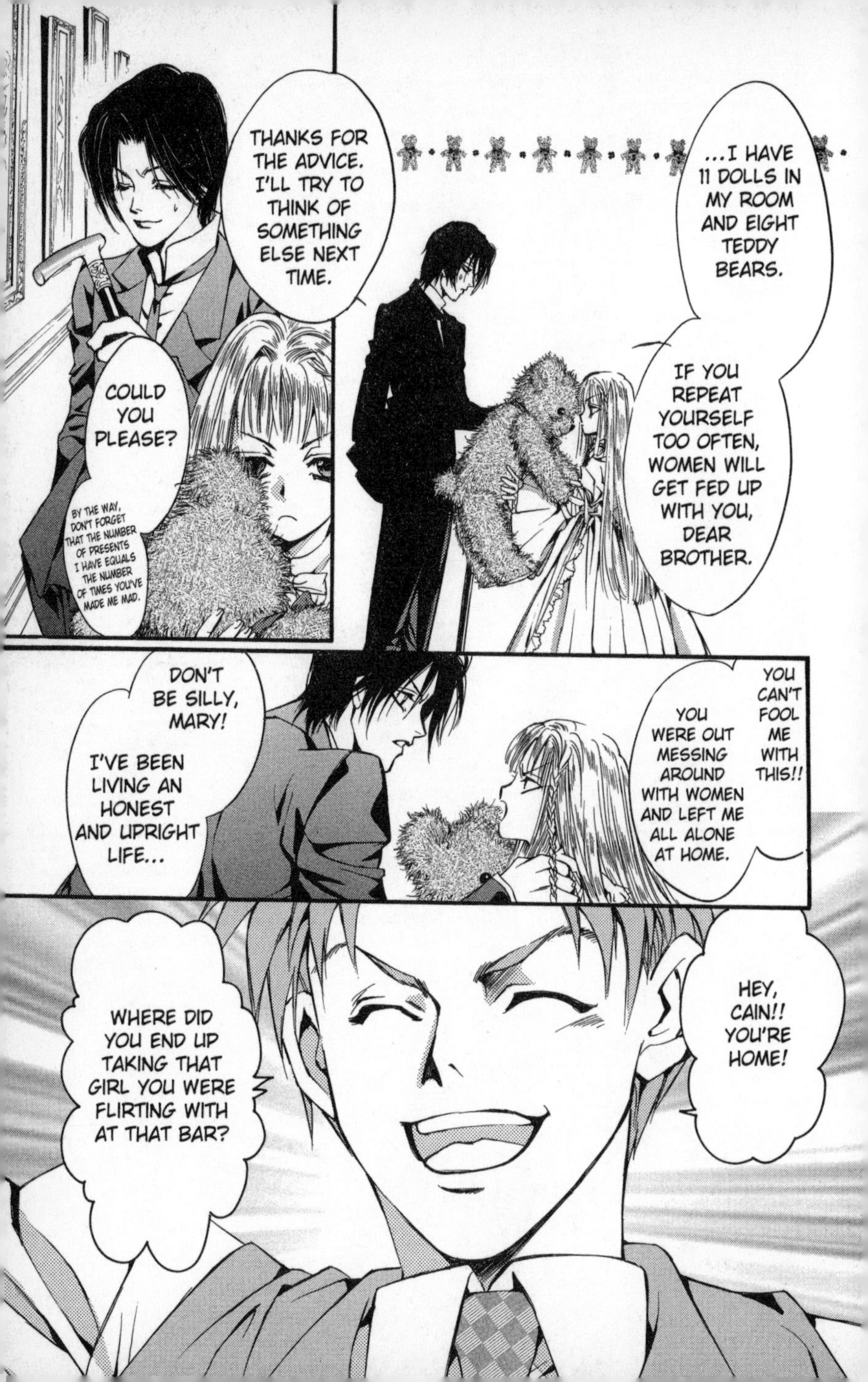
...I HAVE 11 DOLLS IN MY ROOM AND EIGHT TEDDY BEARS.
IF YOU REPEAT YOURSELF TOO OFTEN, WOMEN WILL GET FED UP WITH YOU, DEAR BROTHER.
THANKS FOR THE ADVICE. I'LL TRY TO THINK OF SOMETHING ELSE NEXT TIME.
COULD YOU PLEASE?
BY THE WAY, DON'T FORGET THAT THE NUMBER OF PRESENTS I HAVE EQUALS THE NUMBER OF TIMES YOU'VE MADE ME MAD.
YOU CAN'T FOOL ME WITH THIS!!
YOU WERE OUT MESSING AROUND WITH WOMEN AND LEFT ME ALL ALONE AT HOME.
DON'T BE SILLY, MARY!
I'VE BEEN LIVING AN HONEST AND UPRIGHT LIFE...
HEY, CAIN!! YOU'RE HOME!
WHERE DID YOU END UP TAKING THAT GIRL YOU WERE FLIRTING WITH AT THAT BAR?

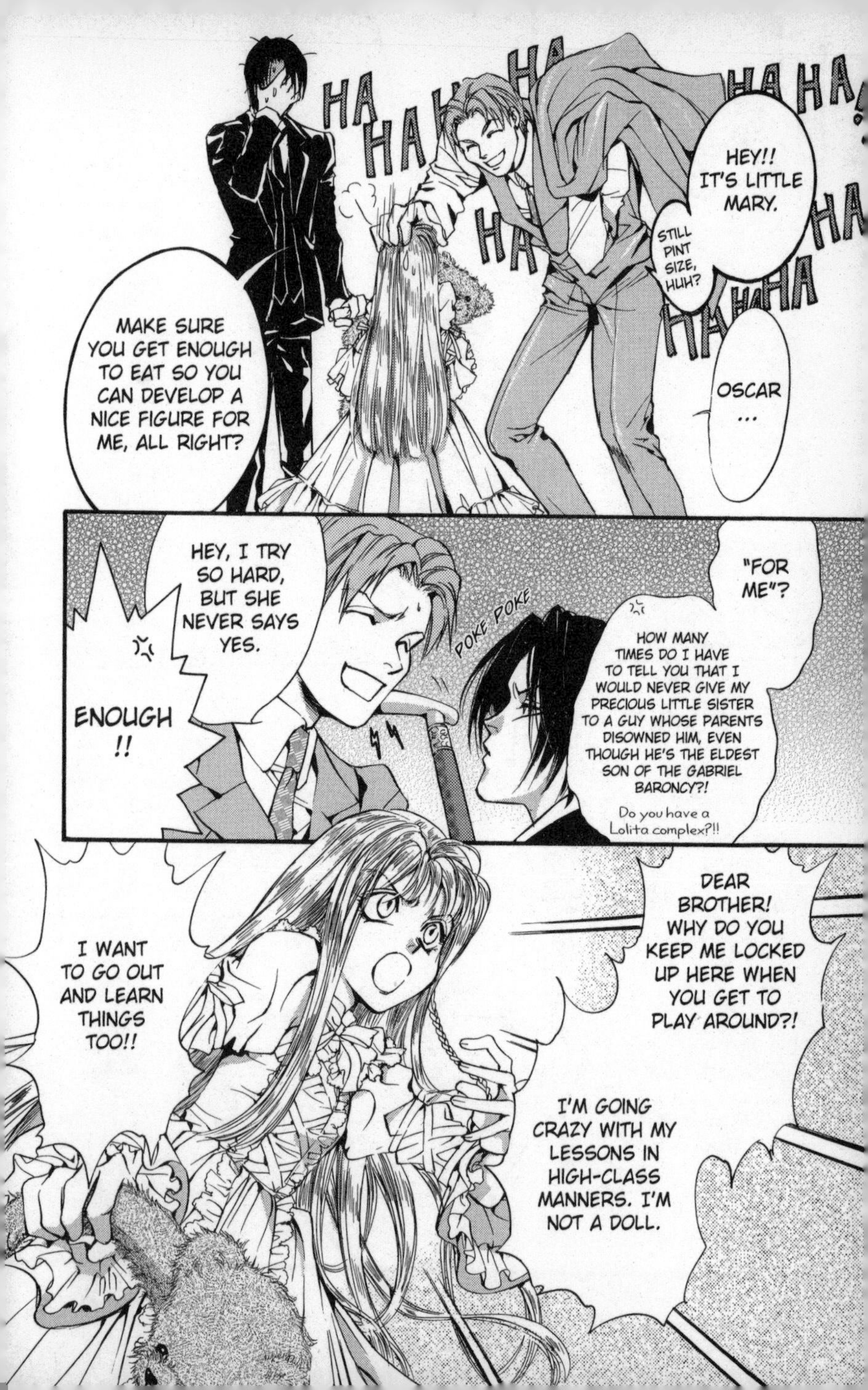
HA HA HAHAHA! HA HA HA HA HAHAHA
HEY!! IT'S LITTLE MARY.
STILL PINT SIZE, HUH?
OSCAR ...
MAKE SURE YOU GET ENOUGH TO EAT SO YOU CAN DEVELOP A NICE FIGURE FOR ME, ALL RIGHT?
"FOR ME"?
HOW MANY TIMES DO I HAVE TO TELL YOU THAT I WOULD NEVER GIVE MY PRECIOUS LITTLE SISTER TO A GUY WHOSE PARENTS DISOWNED HIM, EVEN THOUGH HE'S THE ELDEST SON OF THE GABRIEL BARONCY?!
Do you have a Lolita complex?!!
POKE POKE
HEY, I TRY SO HARD, BUT SHE NEVER SAYS YES.
ENOUGH !!
DEAR BROTHER! WHY DO YOU KEEP ME LOCKED UP HERE WHEN YOU GET TO PLAY AROUND?!
I'M GOING CRAZY WITH MY LESSONS IN HIGH-CLASS MANNERS. I'M NOT A DOLL.
I WANT TO GO OUT AND LEARN THINGS TOO!!

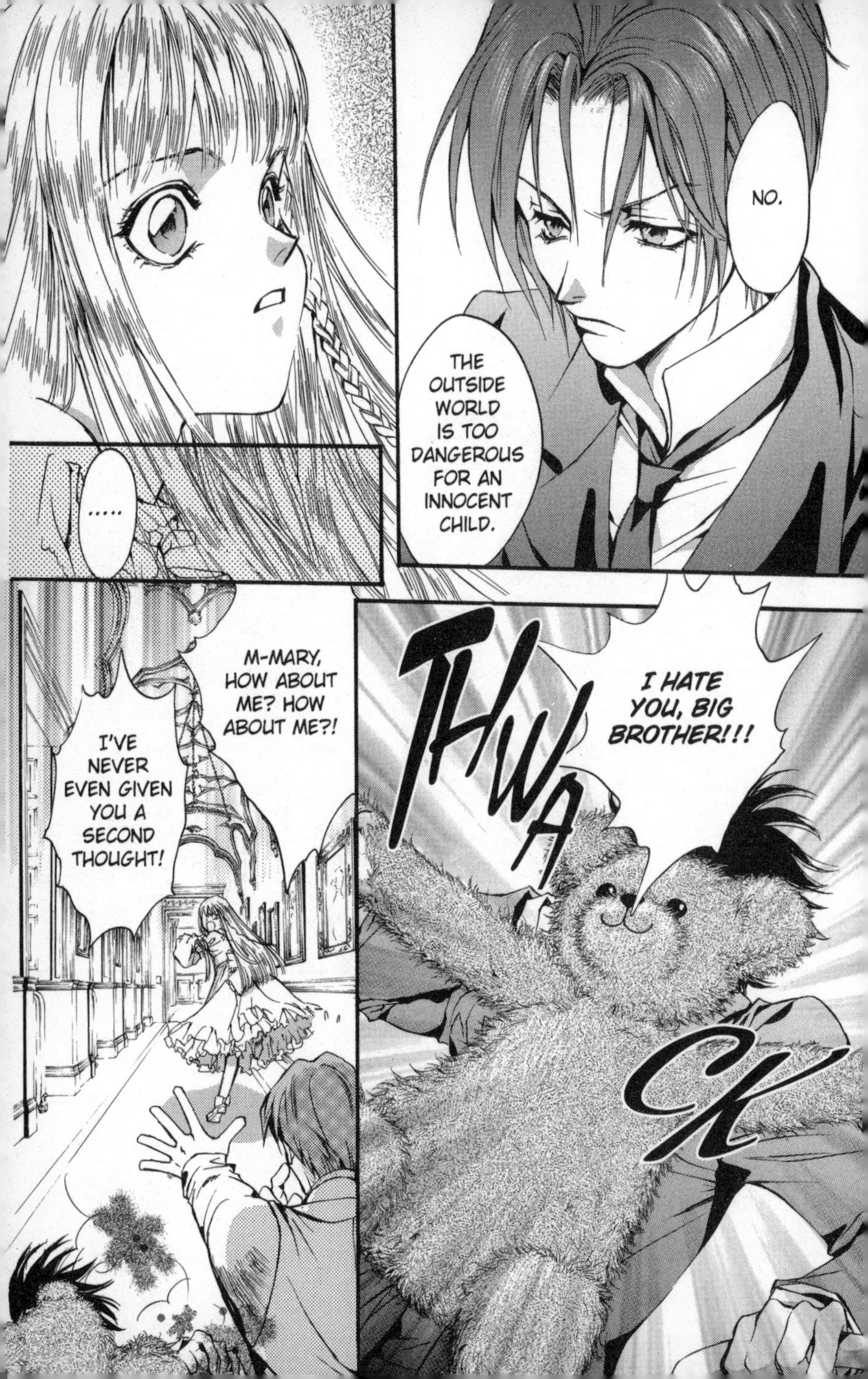
NO.
THE OUTSIDE WORLD IS TOO DANGEROUS FOR AN INNOCENT CHILD.
......
I HATE YOU, BIG BROTHER!!!
THWACK
M-MARY, HOW ABOUT ME? HOW ABOUT ME?!
I'VE NEVER EVEN GIVEN YOU A SECOND THOUGHT!

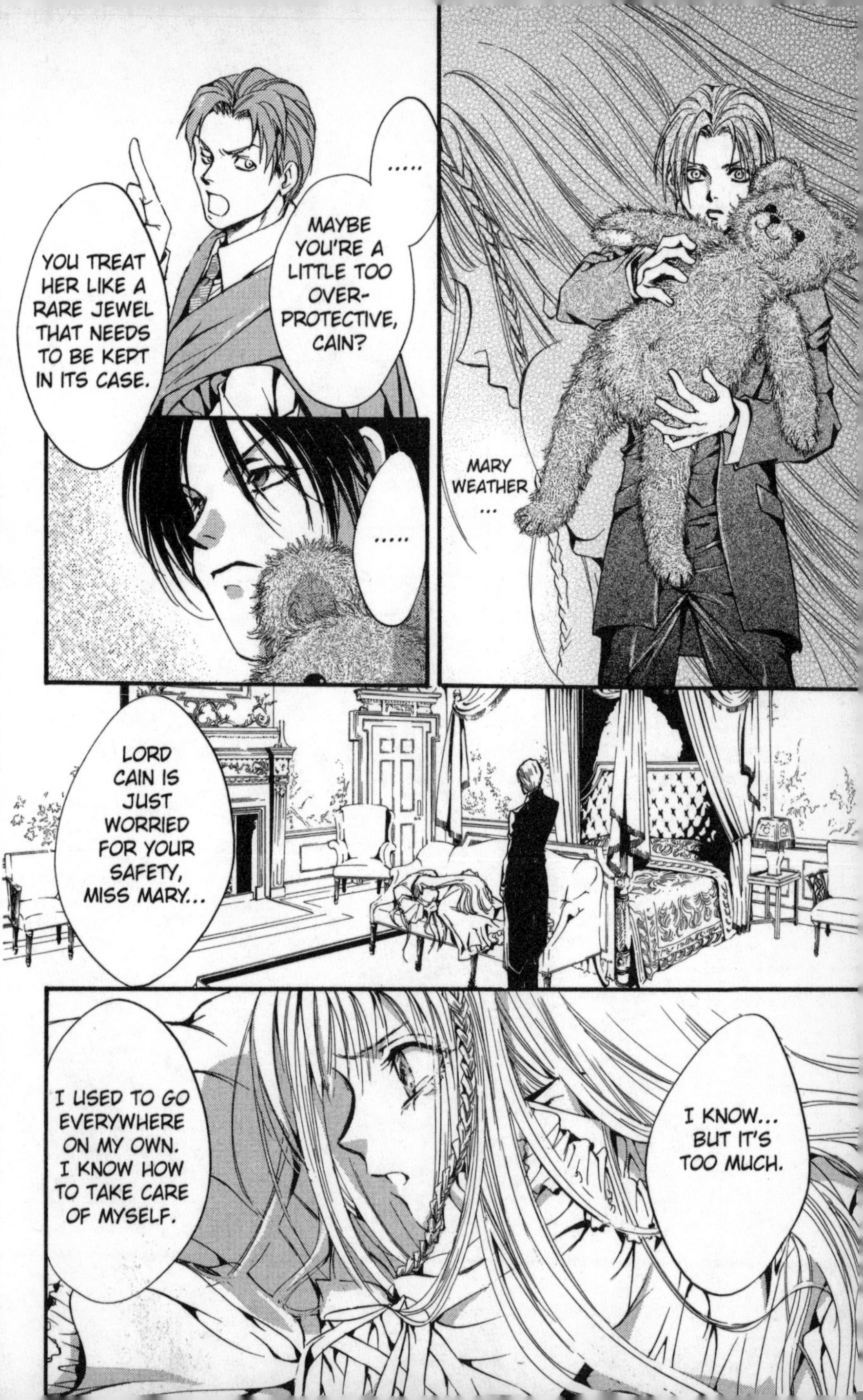
MARY WEATHER ...
.....
MAYBE YOU'RE A LITTLE TOO OVER-PROTECTIVE, CAIN?
YOU TREAT HER LIKE A RARE JEWEL THAT NEEDS TO BE KEPT IN ITS CASE.
.....
LORD CAIN IS JUST WORRIED FOR YOUR SAFETY, MISS MARY...
I KNOW... BUT IT'S TOO MUCH.
I USED TO GO EVERYWHERE ON MY OWN. I KNOW HOW TO TAKE CARE OF MYSELF.

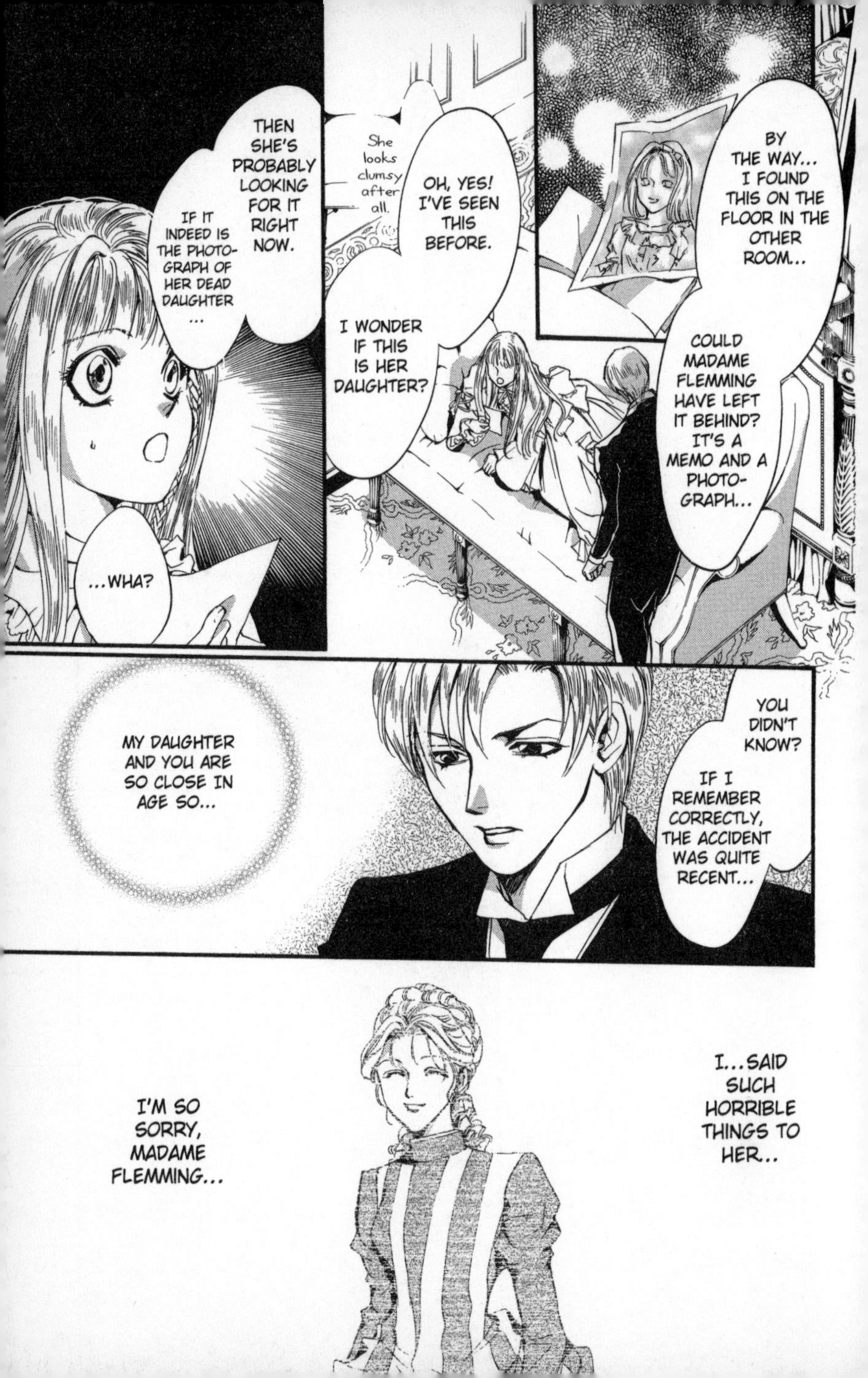
BY THE WAY... I FOUND THIS ON THE FLOOR IN THE OTHER ROOM...
COULD MADAME FLEMMING HAVE LEFT IT BEHIND? IT'S A MEMO AND A PHOTOGRAPH...
OH, YES! I'VE SEEN THIS BEFORE.
She looks clumsy after all.
I WONDER IF THIS IS HER DAUGHTER?
THEN SHE'S PROBABLY LOOKING FOR IT RIGHT NOW.
IF IT INDEED IS THE PHOTOGRAPH OF HER DEAD DAUGHTER...
...WHA?
YOU DIDN'T KNOW?
IF I REMEMBER CORRECTLY, THE ACCIDENT WAS QUITE RECENT...
MY DAUGHTER AND YOU ARE SO CLOSE IN AGE SO...
I...SAID SUCH HORRIBLE THINGS TO HER...
I'M SO SORRY, MADAME FLEMMING...

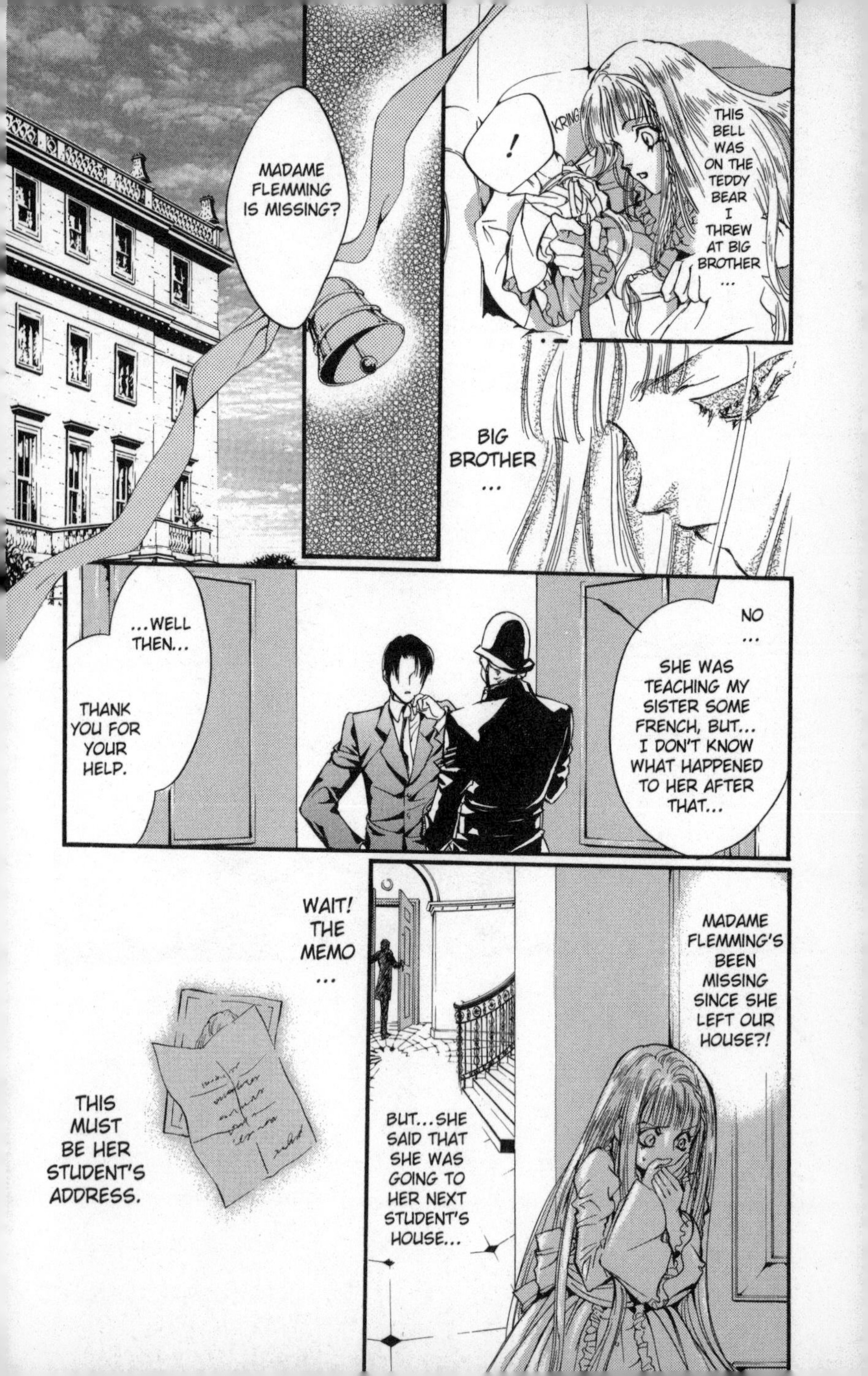
!
KRING
THIS BELL WAS ON THE TEDDY BEAR I THREW AT BIG BROTHER ...
BIG BROTHER ...
MADAME FLEMMING IS MISSING?
NO ...
SHE WAS TEACHING MY SISTER SOME FRENCH, BUT... I DON'T KNOW WHAT HAPPENED TO HER AFTER THAT...
...WELL THEN...
THANK YOU FOR YOUR HELP.
MADAME FLEMMING'S BEEN MISSING SINCE SHE LEFT OUR HOUSE?!
BUT...SHE SAID THAT SHE WAS GOING TO HER NEXT STUDENT'S HOUSE...
WAIT! THE MEMO ...
THIS MUST BE HER STUDENT'S ADDRESS.

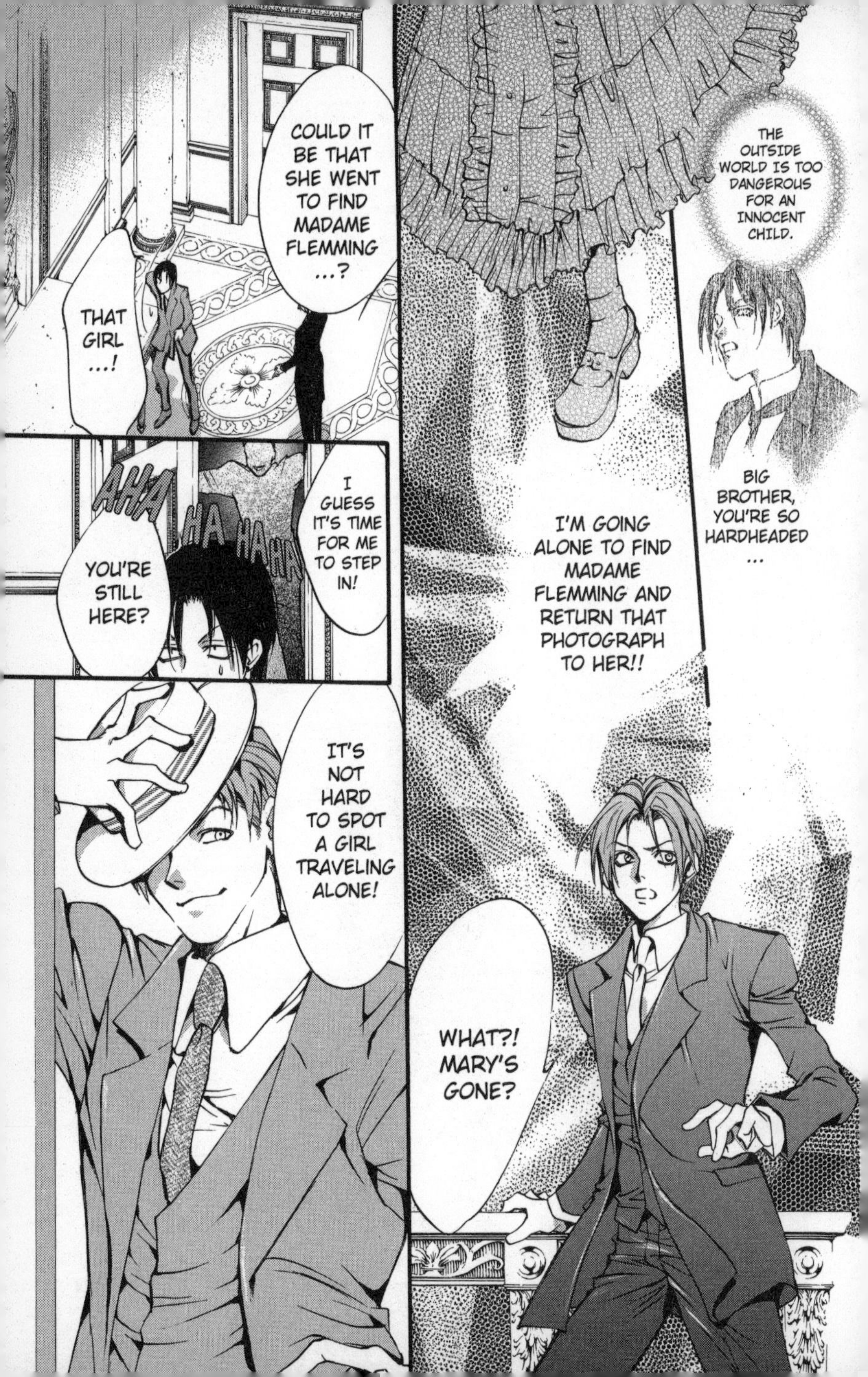
THE OUTSIDE WORLD IS TOO DANGEROUS FOR AN INNOCENT CHILD.
BIG BROTHER, YOU'RE SO HARDHEADED ...
I'M GOING ALONE TO FIND MADAME FLEMMING AND RETURN THAT PHOTOGRAPH TO HER!!
WHAT?! MARY'S GONE?
COULD IT BE THAT SHE WENT TO FIND MADAME FLEMMING ...?
THAT GIRL ...!
I GUESS IT'S TIME FOR ME TO STEP IN!
AHA HA HAHA
YOU'RE STILL HERE?
IT'S NOT HARD TO SPOT A GIRL TRAVELING ALONE!

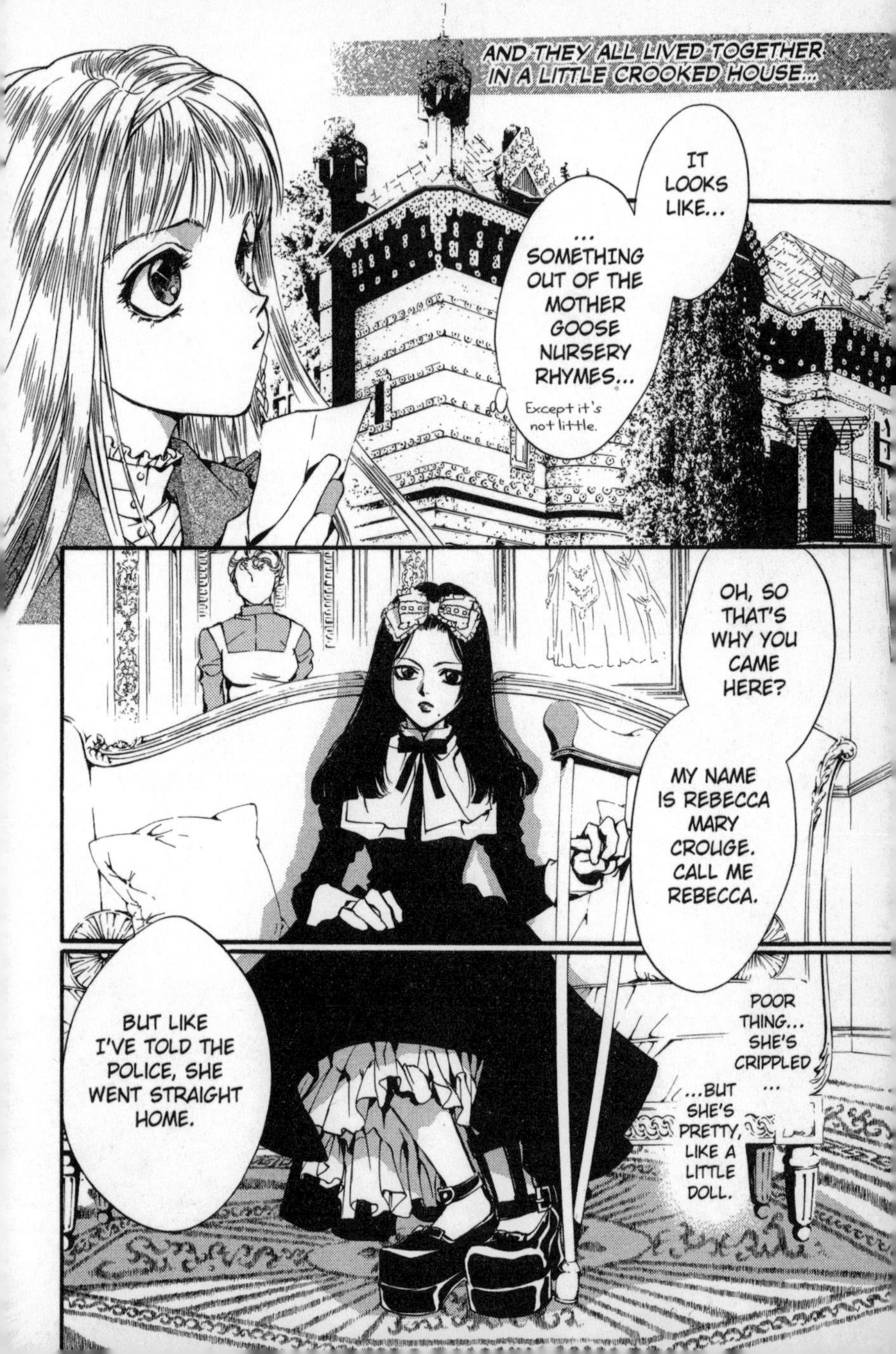
AND THEY ALL LIVED TOGETHER IN A LITTLE CROOKED HOUSE...
IT LOOKS LIKE...
... SOMETHING OUT OF THE MOTHER GOOSE NURSERY RHYMES...
Except it's not little.
OH, SO THAT'S WHY YOU CAME HERE?
MY NAME IS REBECCA MARY CROUGE. CALL ME REBECCA.
POOR THING... SHE'S CRIPPLED ...
...BUT SHE'S PRETTY, LIKE A LITTLE DOLL.
BUT LIKE I'VE TOLD THE POLICE, SHE WENT STRAIGHT HOME.

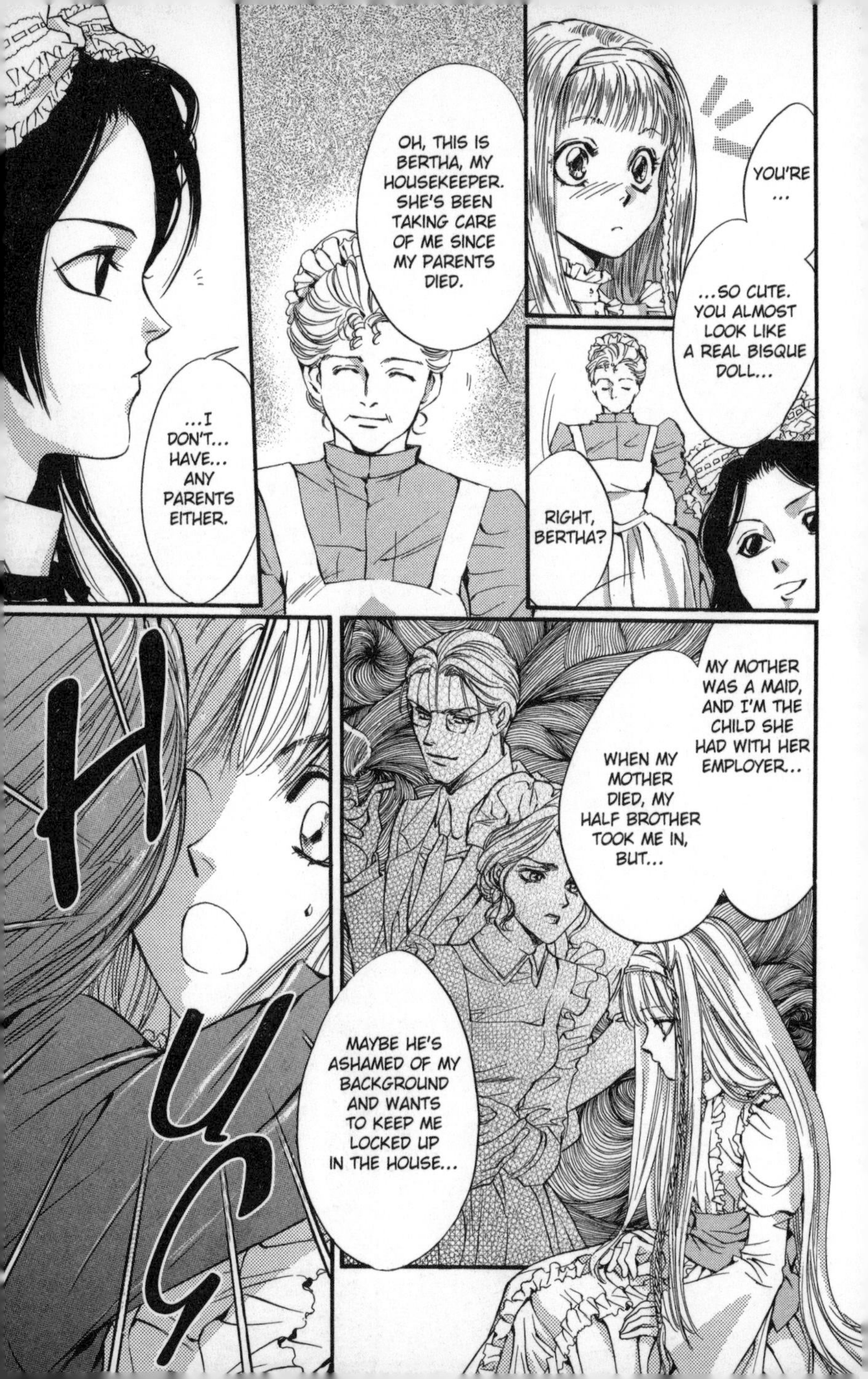
YOU'RE ...
...SO CUTE. YOU ALMOST LOOK LIKE A REAL BISQUE DOLL...
RIGHT, BERTHA?
OH, THIS IS BERTHA, MY HOUSEKEEPER. SHE'S BEEN TAKING CARE OF ME SINCE MY PARENTS DIED.
...I DON'T... HAVE... ANY PARENTS EITHER.
MY MOTHER WAS A MAID, AND I'M THE CHILD SHE HAD WITH HER EMPLOYER...
WHEN MY MOTHER DIED, MY HALF BROTHER TOOK ME IN, BUT...
MAYBE HE'S ASHAMED OF MY BACKGROUND AND WANTS TO KEEP ME LOCKED UP IN THE HOUSE...

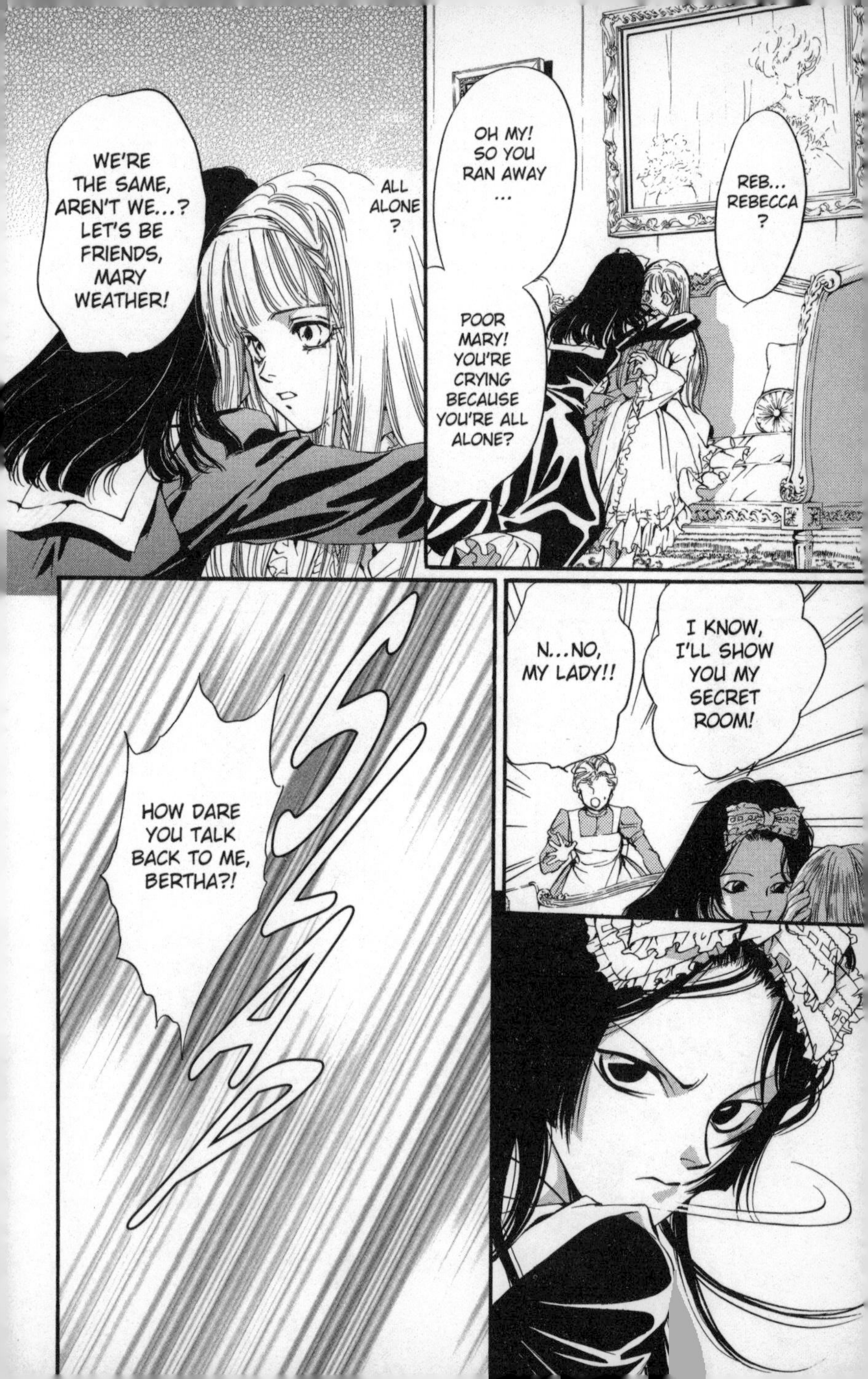
REB... REBECCA?
OH MY! SO YOU RAN AWAY...
POOR MARY! YOU'RE CRYING BECAUSE YOU'RE ALL ALONE?
ALL ALONE?
WE'RE THE SAME, AREN'T WE...? LET'S BE FRIENDS, MARY WEATHER!
I KNOW, I'LL SHOW YOU MY SECRET ROOM!
N...NO, MY LADY!!
HOW DARE YOU TALK BACK TO ME, BERTHA?!

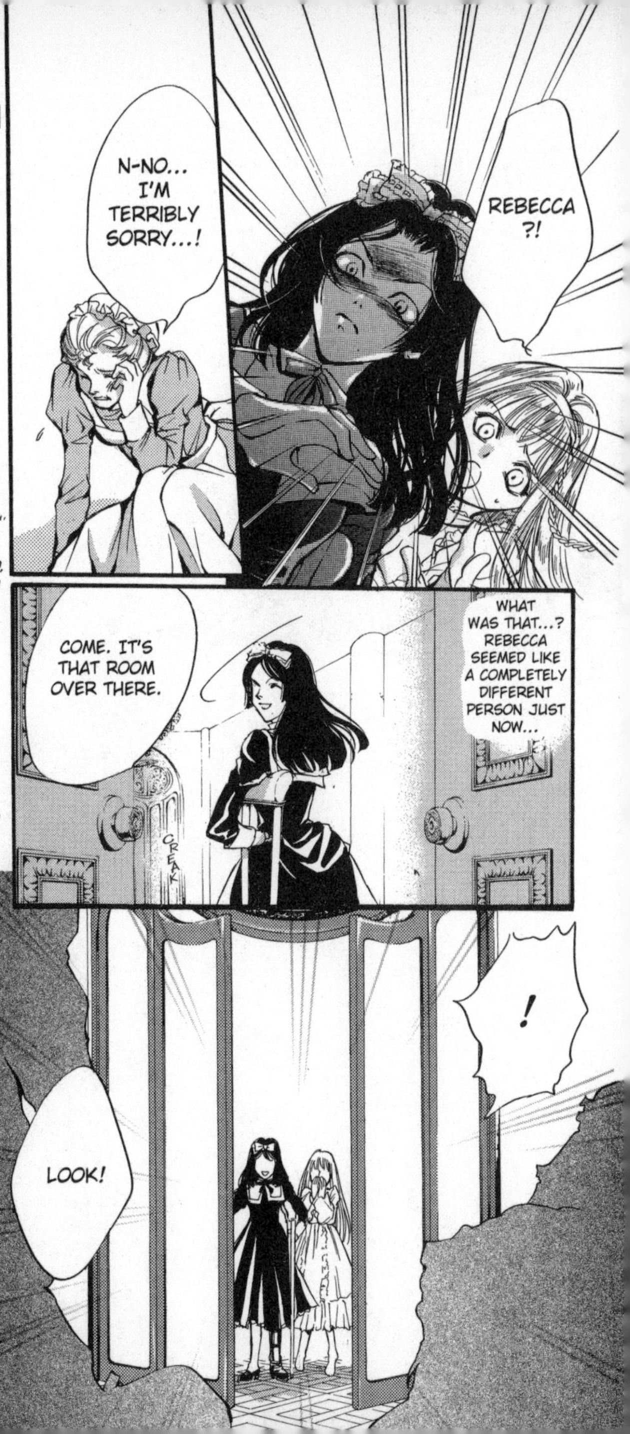
REBECCA ?!
N-NO... I'M TERRIBLY SORRY...!
WHAT WAS THAT...? REBECCA SEEMED LIKE A COMPLETELY DIFFERENT PERSON JUST NOW...
COME. IT'S THAT ROOM OVER THERE.
CREAK
!
LOOK!

Crooked House

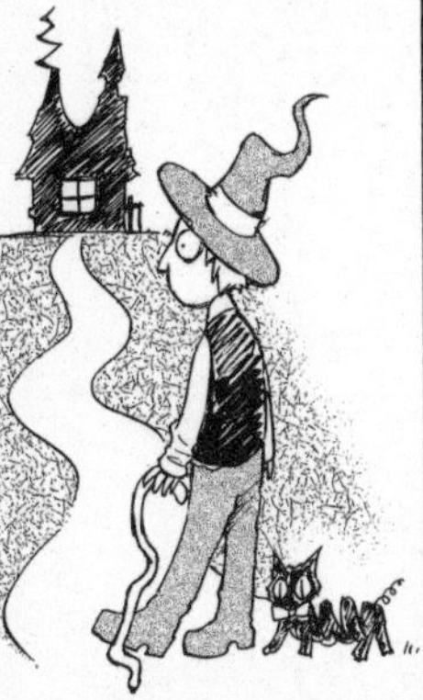

There was a crooked man, and he walked a crooked mile. He found a crooked sixpence against a crooked mouse, ~

This is a line from a Mother Goose poem. Nursery rhymes like this are often used in movies. Some famous novels with nursery rhyme themes are "And Then There Were None" and "To Kill a Mocking-bird." It was once believed that an actual person named Mother Goose sang these poems, but this turned out to be a myth.

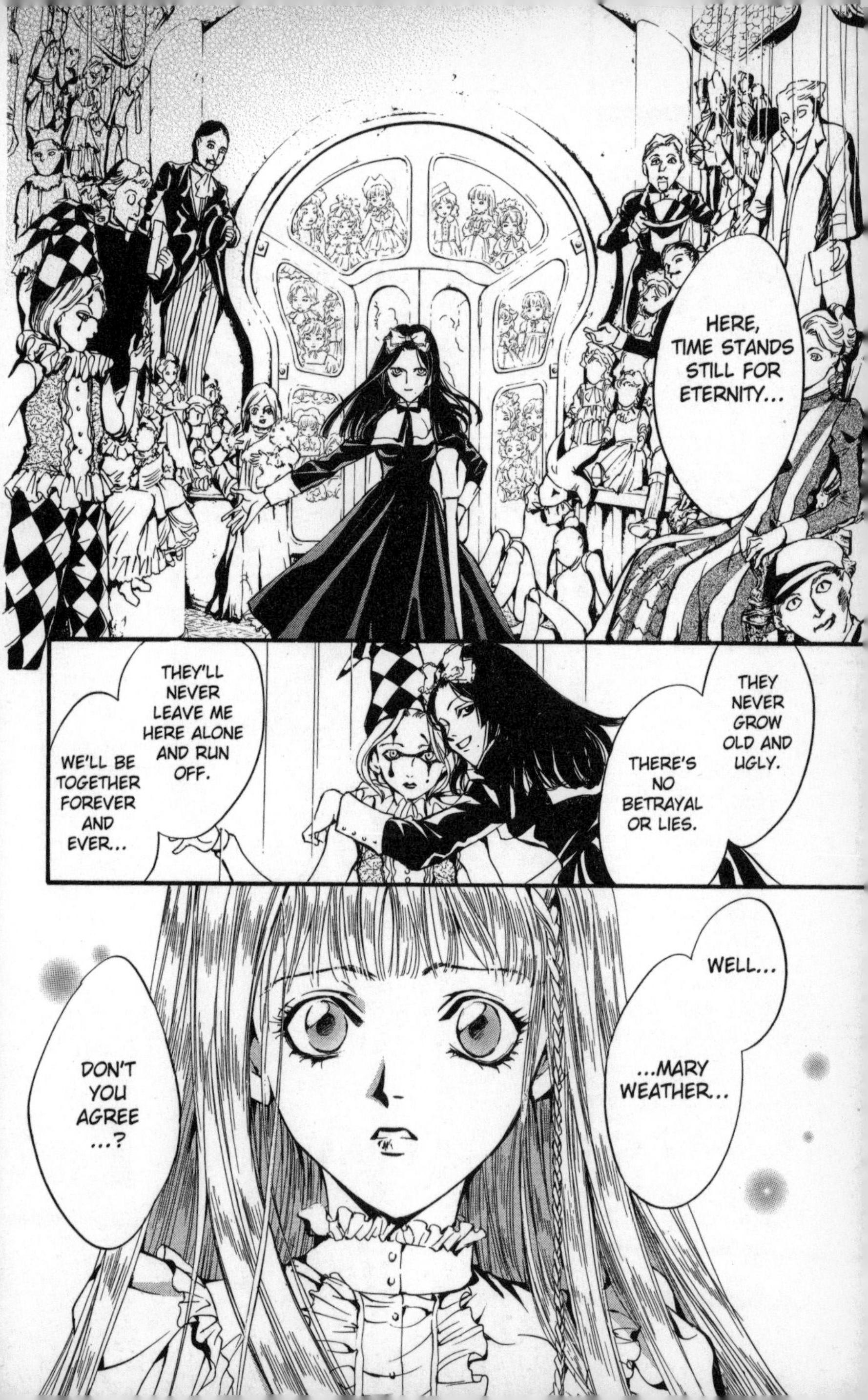
HERE, TIME STANDS STILL FOR ETERNITY...
THEY NEVER GROW OLD AND UGLY.
THERE'S NO BETRAYAL OR LIES.
THEY'LL NEVER LEAVE ME HERE ALONE AND RUN OFF.
WE'LL BE TOGETHER FOREVER AND EVER...
WELL...
...MARY WEATHER...
DON'T YOU AGREE ...?

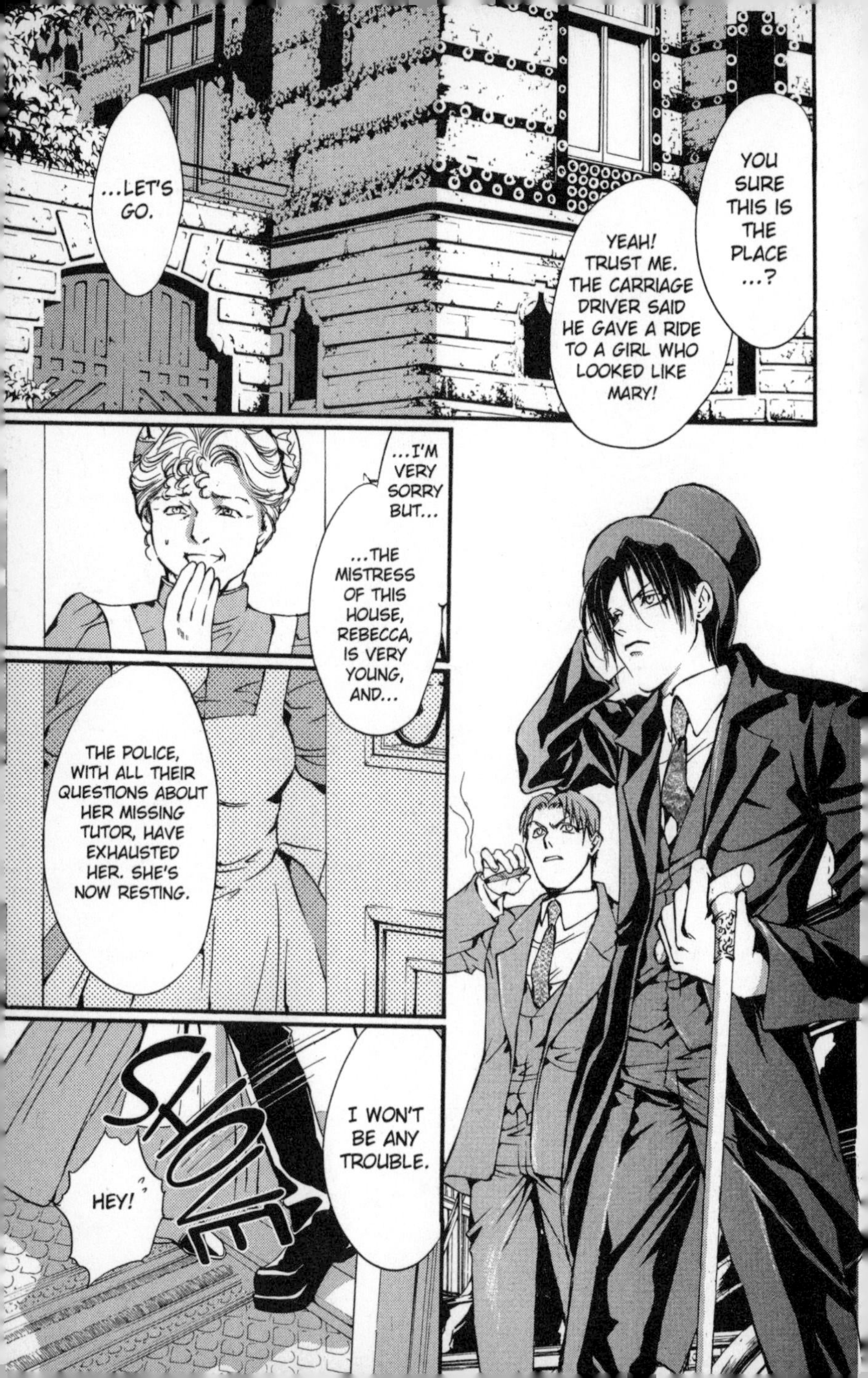
YOU SURE THIS IS THE PLACE ...?
YEAH! TRUST ME. THE CARRIAGE DRIVER SAID HE GAVE A RIDE TO A GIRL WHO LOOKED LIKE MARY!
...LET'S GO.
...I'M VERY SORRY BUT...
...THE MISTRESS OF THIS HOUSE, REBECCA, IS VERY YOUNG, AND...
THE POLICE, WITH ALL THEIR QUESTIONS ABOUT HER MISSING TUTOR, HAVE EXHAUSTED HER. SHE'S NOW RESTING.
I WON'T BE ANY TROUBLE.
SHOVE
HEY!

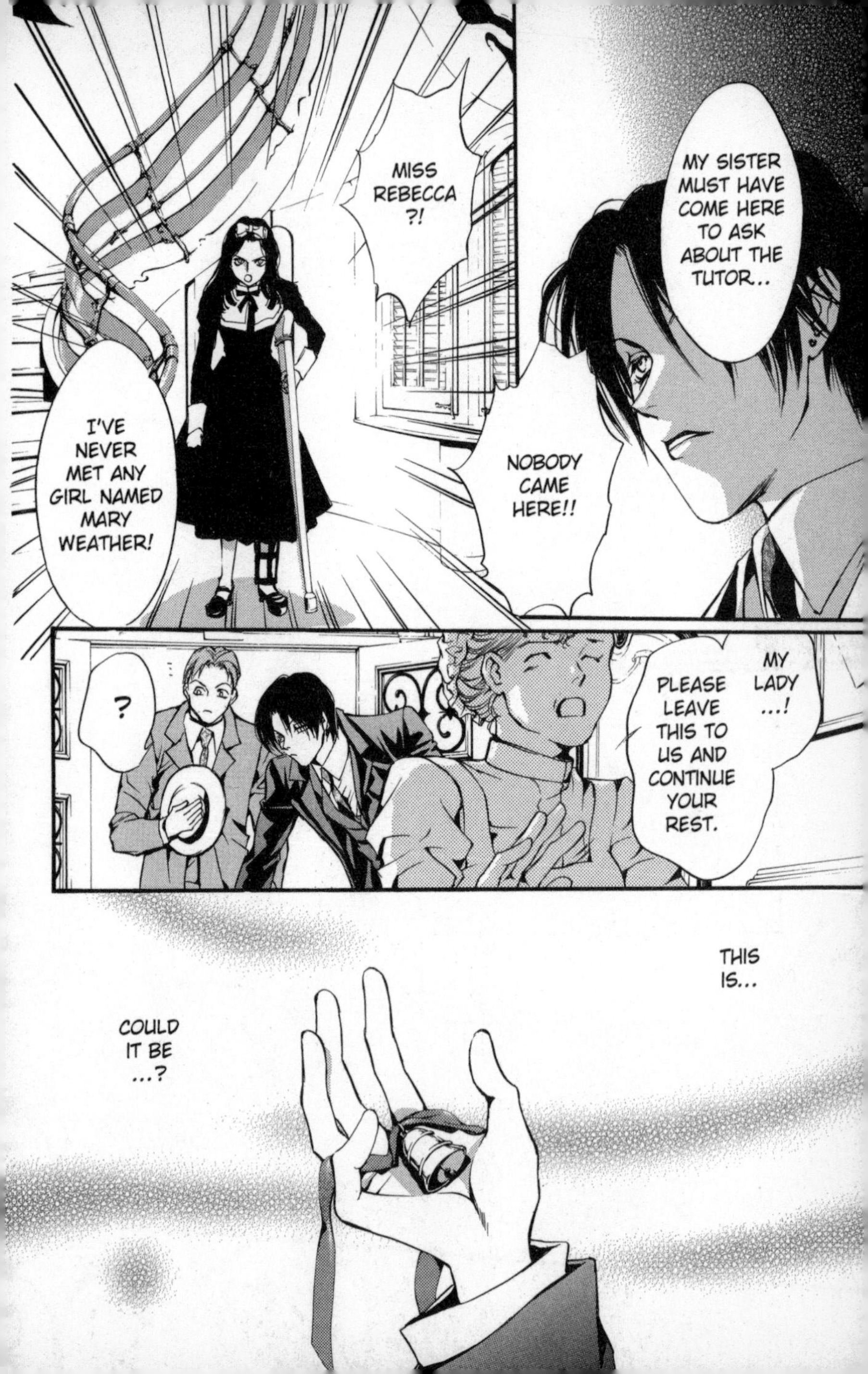
MY SISTER MUST HAVE COME HERE TO ASK ABOUT THE TUTOR...
MISS REBECCA ?!
NOBODY CAME HERE!!
I'VE NEVER MET ANY GIRL NAMED MARY WEATHER!
MY LADY ...!
PLEASE LEAVE THIS TO US AND CONTINUE YOUR REST.
?
THIS IS...
COULD IT BE ...?

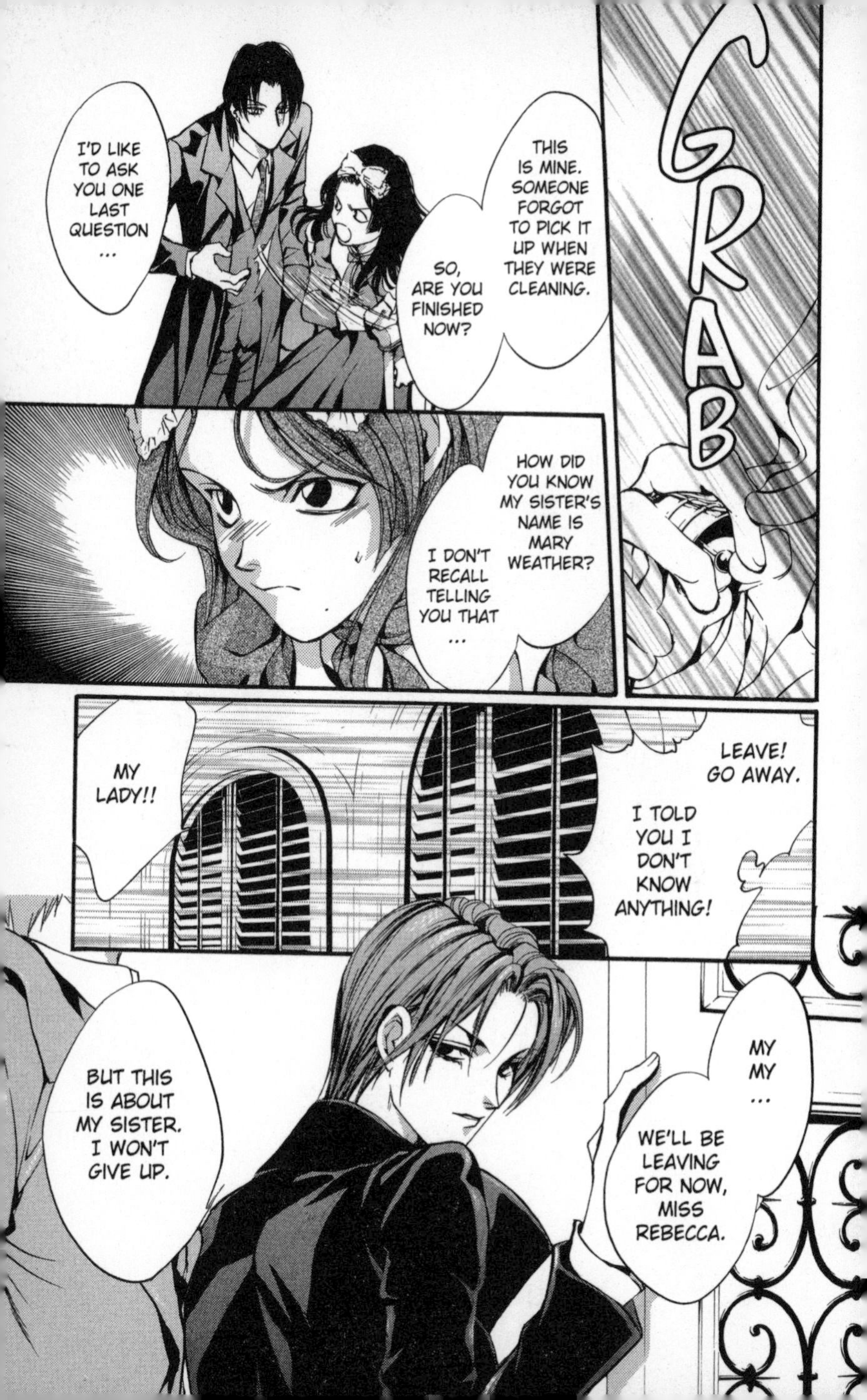
GRAB
THIS IS MINE. SOMEONE FORGOT TO PICK IT UP WHEN THEY WERE CLEANING.
SO, ARE YOU FINISHED NOW?
I'D LIKE TO ASK YOU ONE LAST QUESTION ...
HOW DID YOU KNOW MY SISTER'S NAME IS MARY WEATHER?
I DON'T RECALL TELLING YOU THAT ...
LEAVE! GO AWAY.
I TOLD YOU I DON'T KNOW ANYTHING!
MY LADY!!
MY MY ...
WE'LL BE LEAVING FOR NOW, MISS REBECCA.
BUT THIS IS ABOUT MY SISTER. I WON'T GIVE UP.

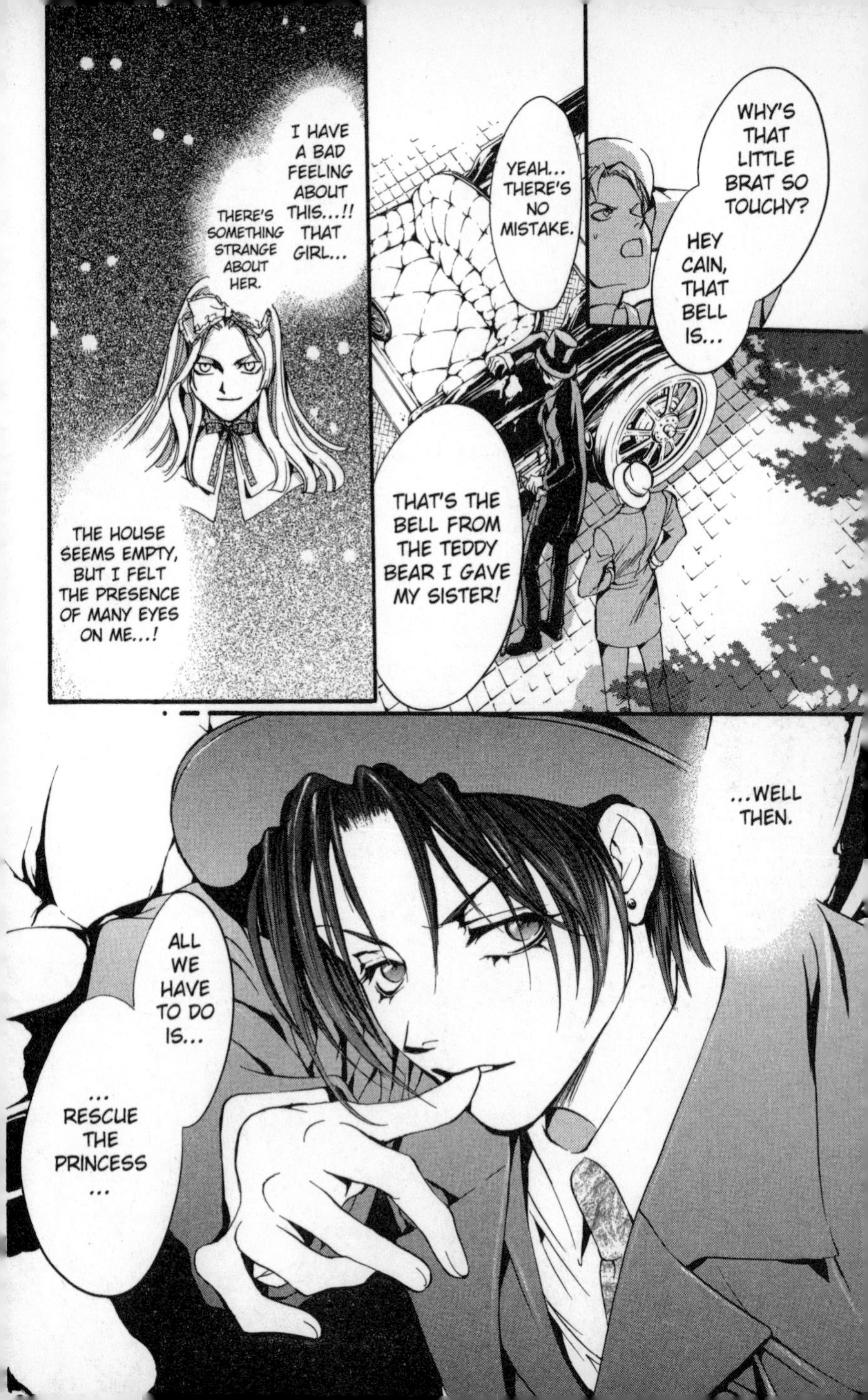
WHY'S THAT LITTLE BRAT SO TOUCHY?
HEY CAIN, THAT BELL IS...
YEAH... THERE'S NO MISTAKE.
THAT'S THE BELL FROM THE TEDDY BEAR I GAVE MY SISTER!
I HAVE A BAD FEELING ABOUT THIS...!! THAT GIRL...
THERE'S SOMETHING STRANGE ABOUT HER.
THE HOUSE SEEMS EMPTY, BUT I FELT THE PRESENCE OF MANY EYES ON ME...!
...WELL THEN.
ALL WE HAVE TO DO IS...
...RESCUE THE PRINCESS...

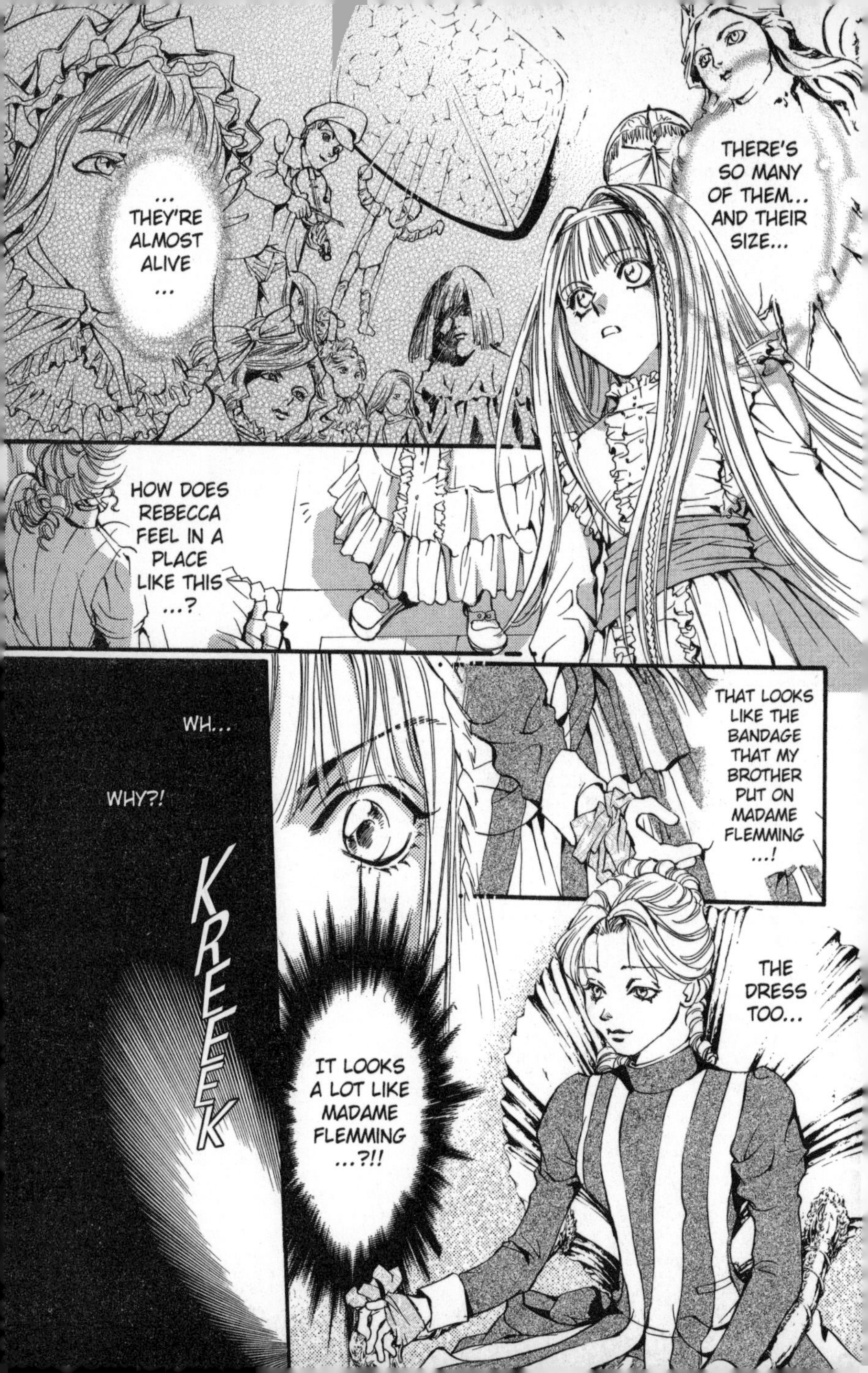
THERE'S SO MANY OF THEM... AND THEIR SIZE...
...THEY'RE ALMOST ALIVE...
HOW DOES REBECCA FEEL IN A PLACE LIKE THIS...?
THAT LOOKS LIKE THE BANDAGE THAT MY BROTHER PUT ON MADAME FLEMMING...!
THE DRESS TOO...
IT LOOKS A LOT LIKE MADAME FLEMMING...?!!
WH...
WHY?!
KREEEK

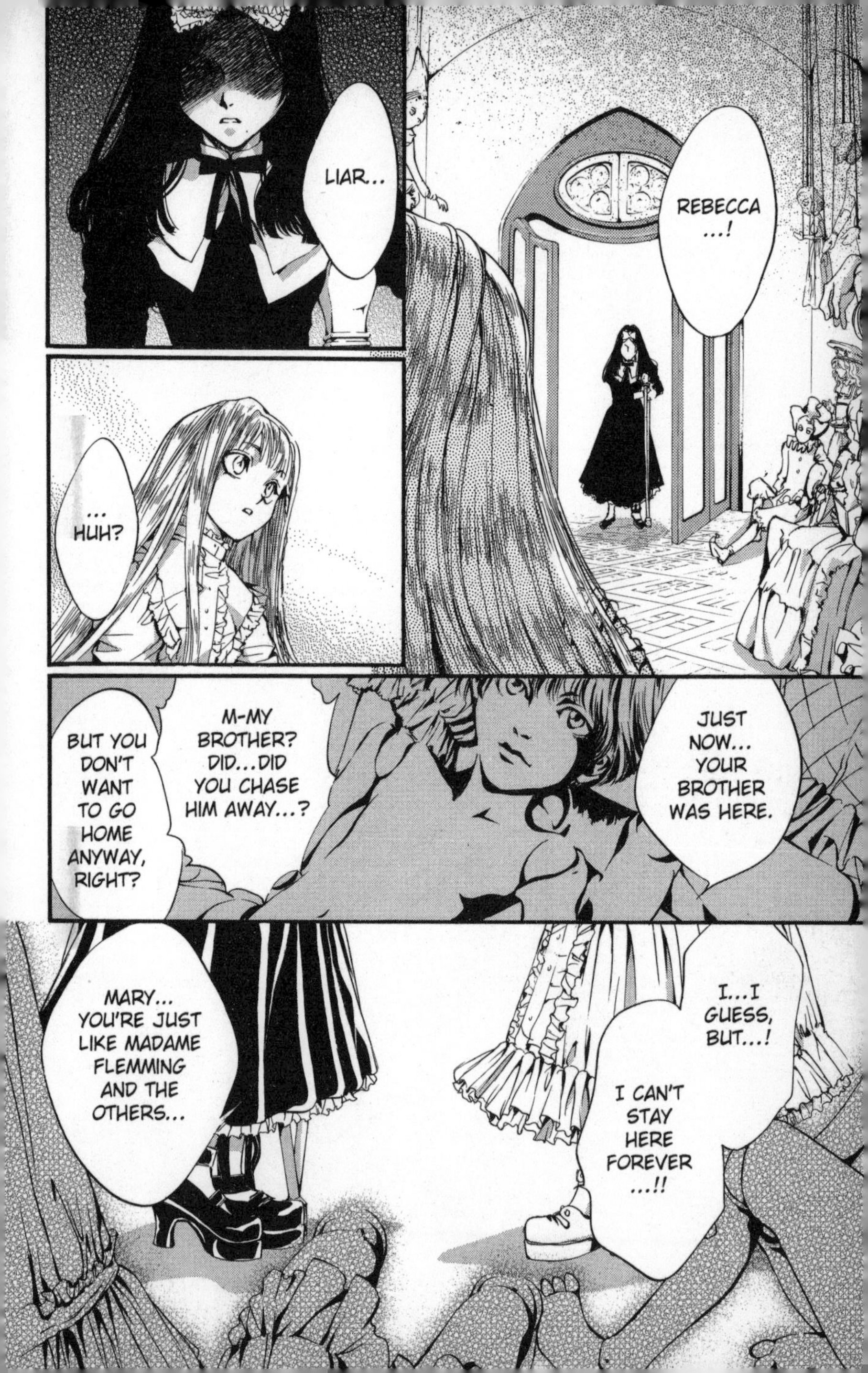
REBECCA...!
LIAR...
...HUH?
JUST NOW... YOUR BROTHER WAS HERE.
M-MY BROTHER? DID...DID YOU CHASE HIM AWAY...?
BUT YOU DON'T WANT TO GO HOME ANYWAY, RIGHT?
I...I GUESS, BUT...!
I CAN'T STAY HERE FOREVER...!!
MARY... YOU'RE JUST LIKE MADAME FLEMMING AND THE OTHERS...

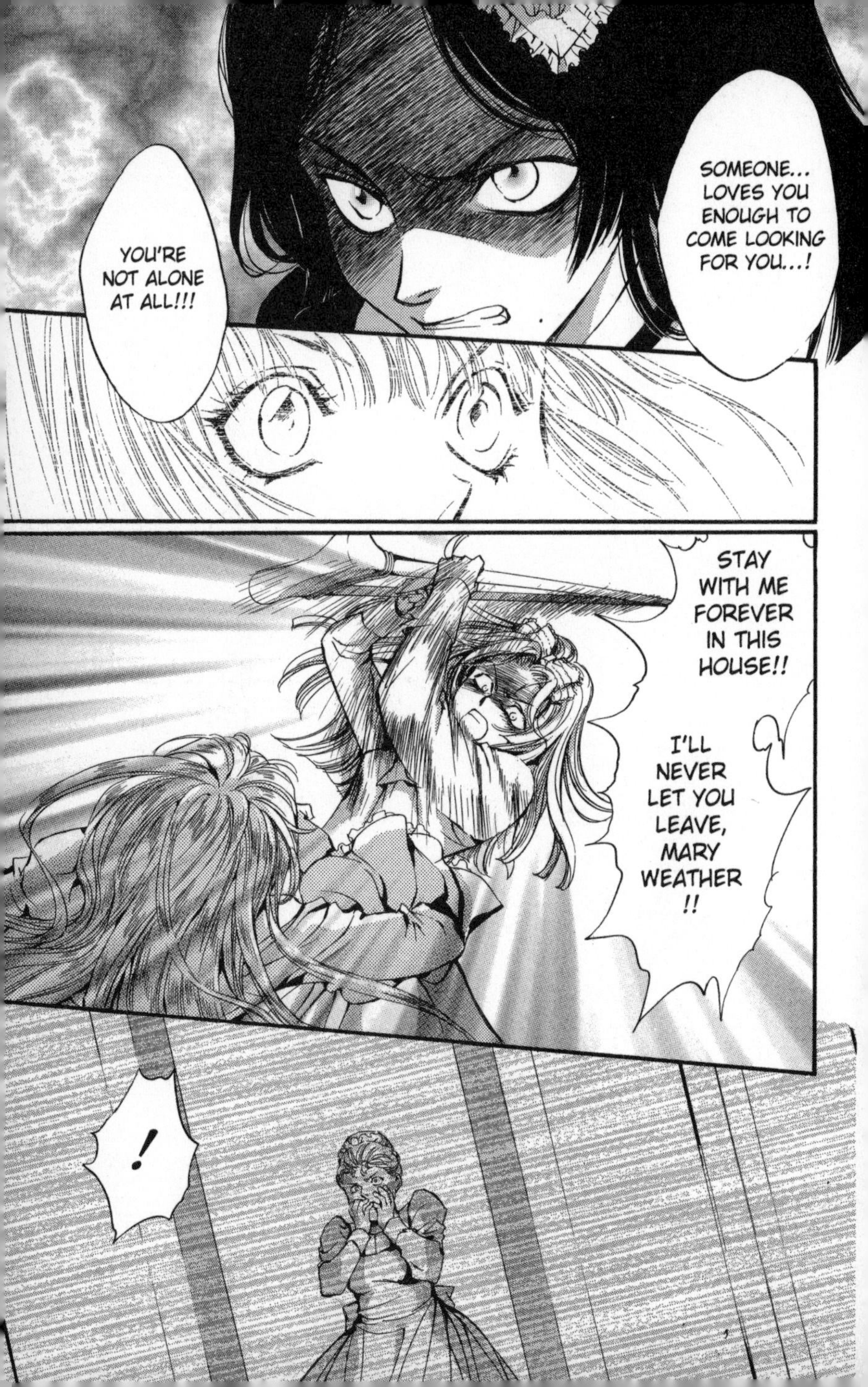
SOMEONE... LOVES YOU ENOUGH TO COME LOOKING FOR YOU...!
YOU'RE NOT ALONE AT ALL!!!
STAY WITH ME FOREVER IN THIS HOUSE!!
I'LL NEVER LET YOU LEAVE, MARY WEATHER !!
!

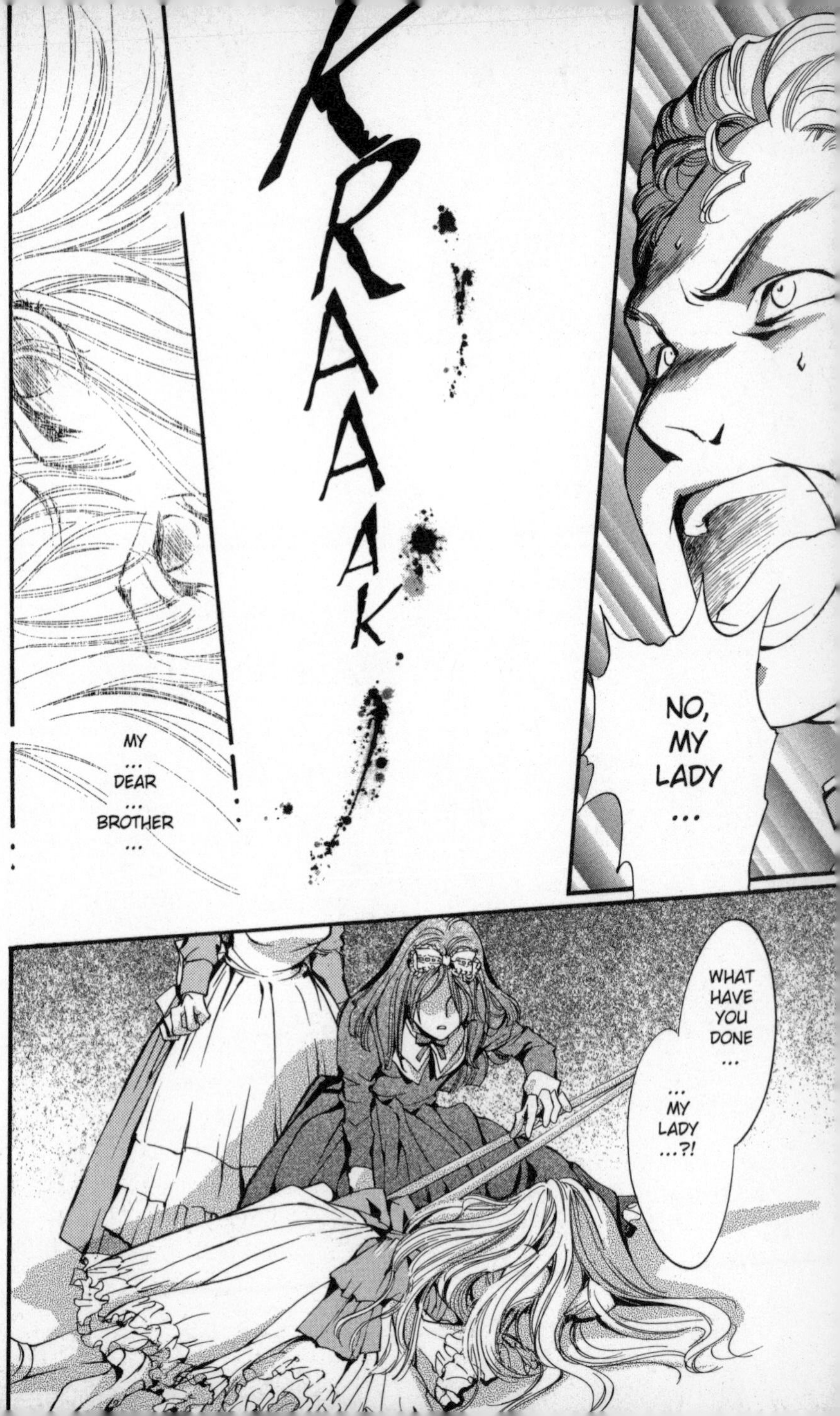
NO, MY LADY ...
KRAAAAK
MY ... DEAR ... BROTHER ...
WHAT HAVE YOU DONE ...
... MY LADY ...?!

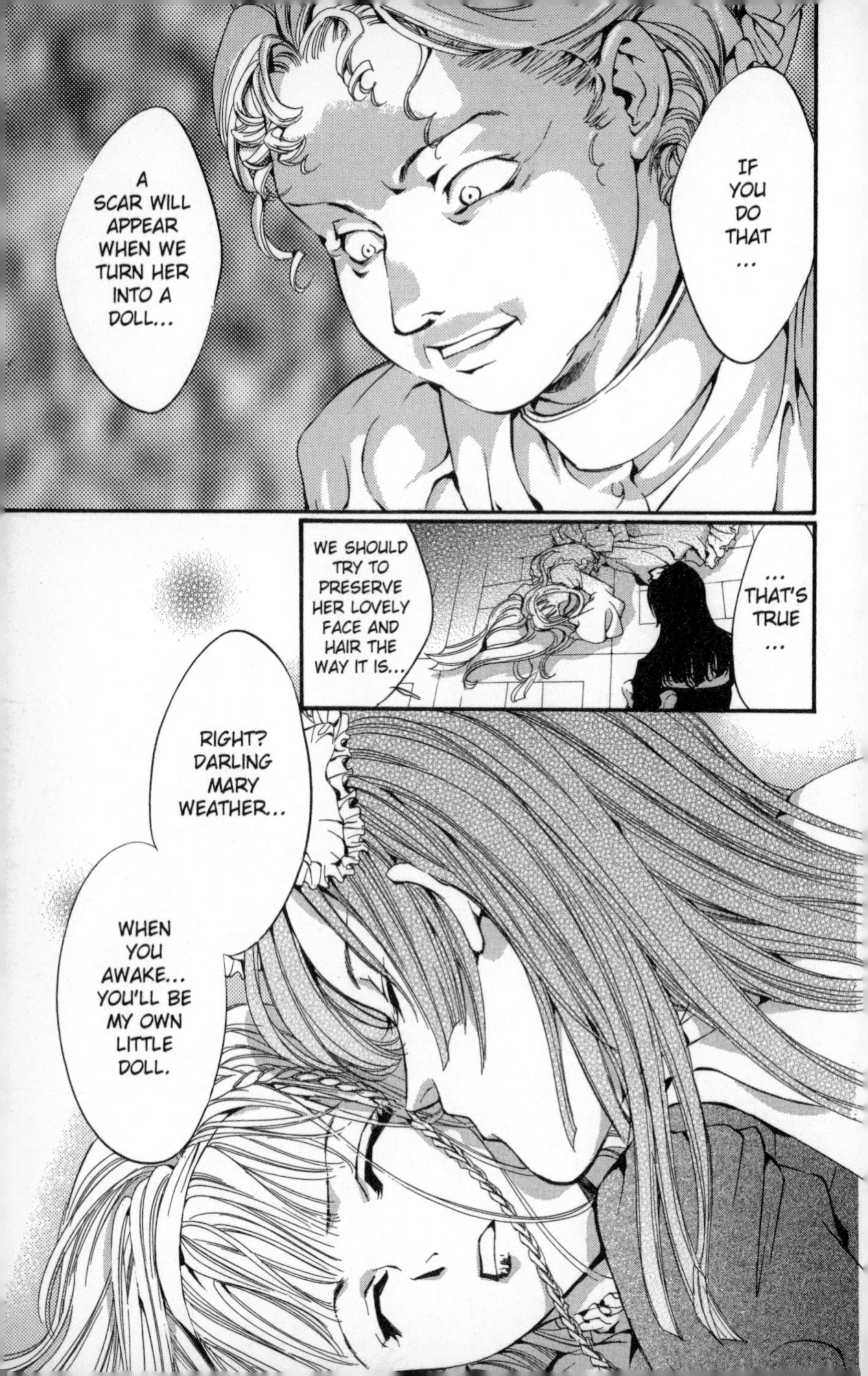
IF YOU DO THAT ...
A SCAR WILL APPEAR WHEN WE TURN HER INTO A DOLL...
... THAT'S TRUE ...
WE SHOULD TRY TO PRESERVE HER LOVELY FACE AND HAIR THE WAY IT IS...
RIGHT? DARLING MARY WEATHER...
WHEN YOU AWAKE... YOU'LL BE MY OWN LITTLE DOLL.

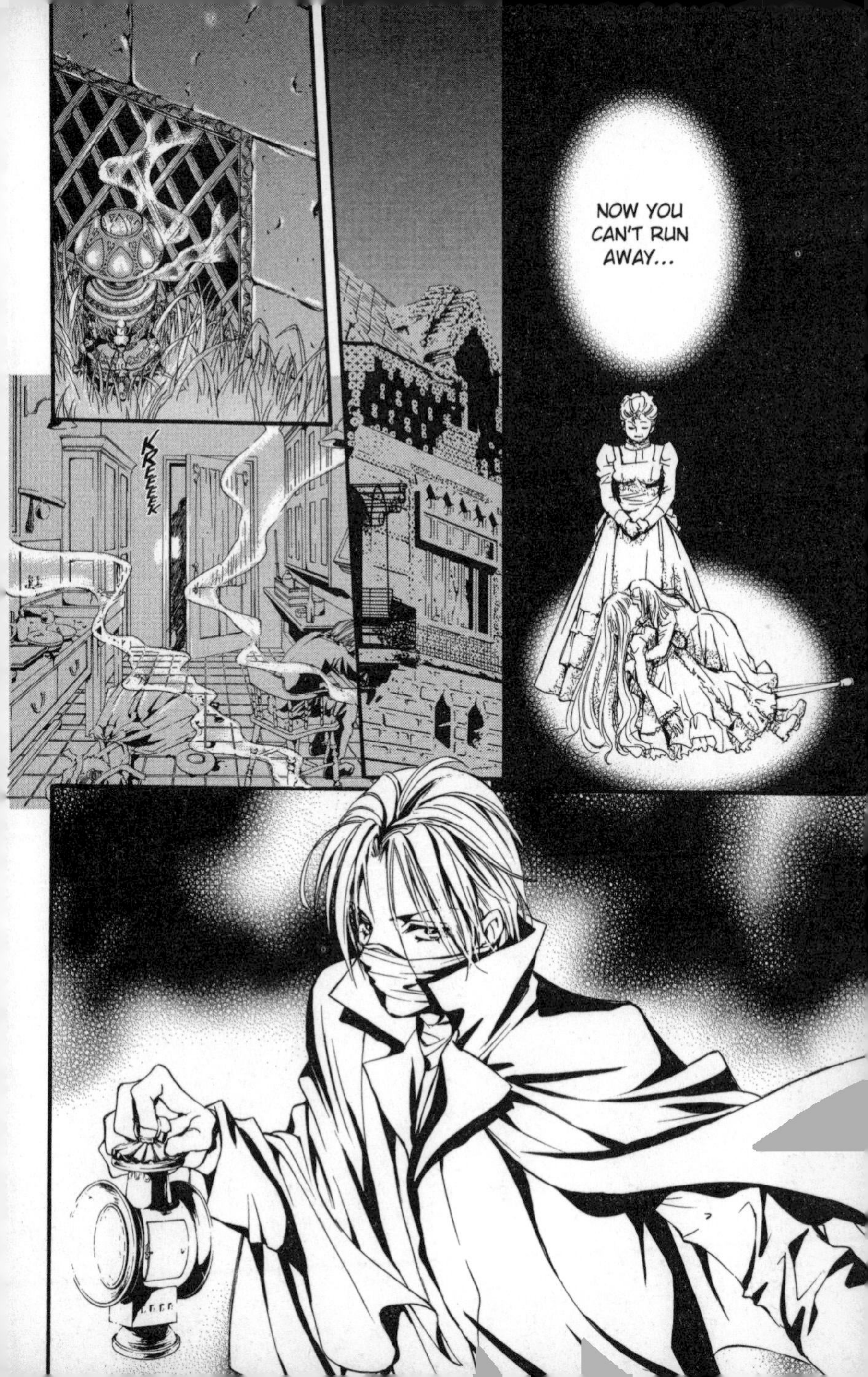
NOW YOU CAN'T RUN AWAY...
KREEEK

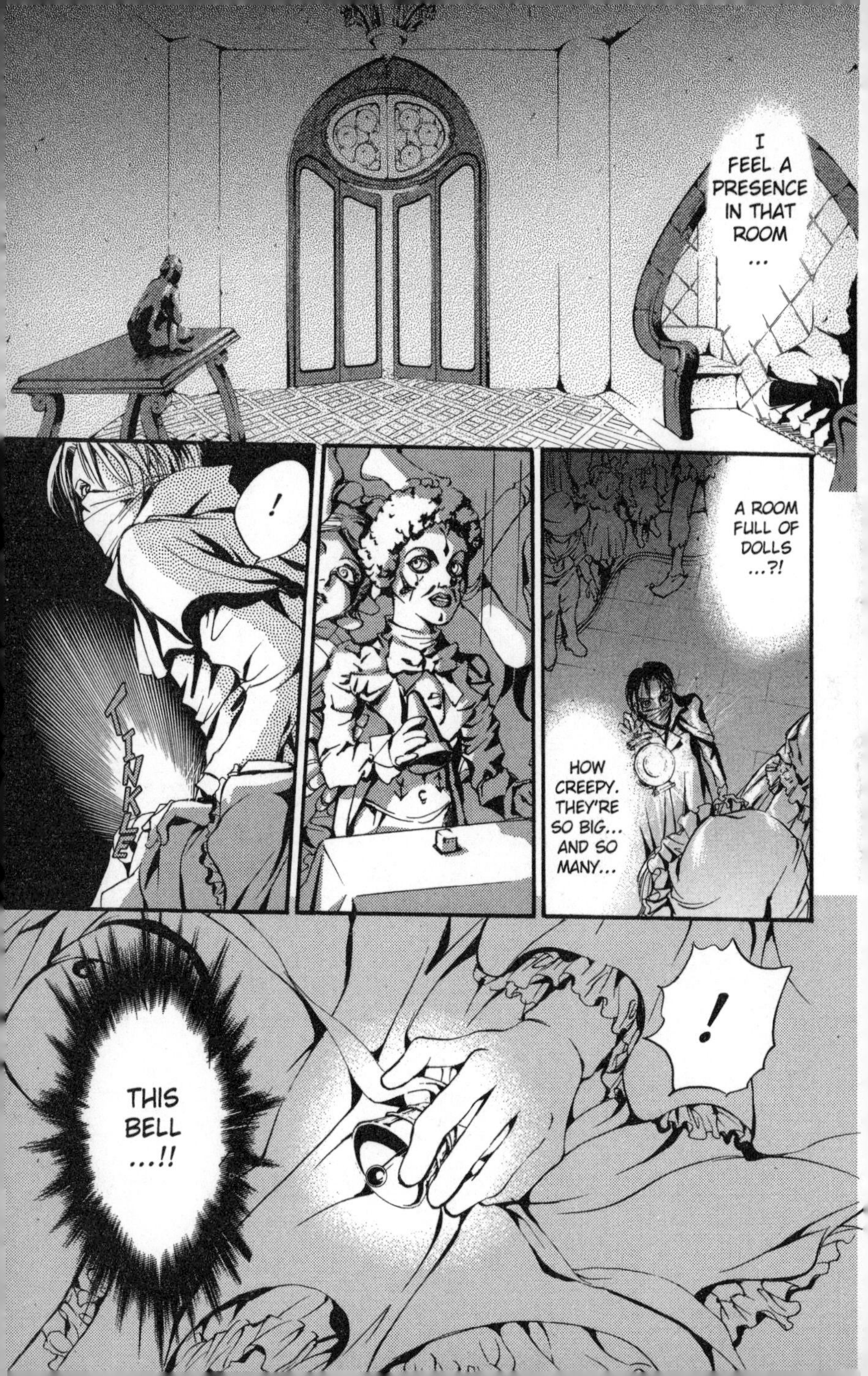

I FEEL A PRESENCE IN THAT ROOM ...
A ROOM FULL OF DOLLS ...?!
HOW CREEPY. THEY'RE SO BIG... AND SO MANY...
!
TINKLE
!
THIS BELL ...!!

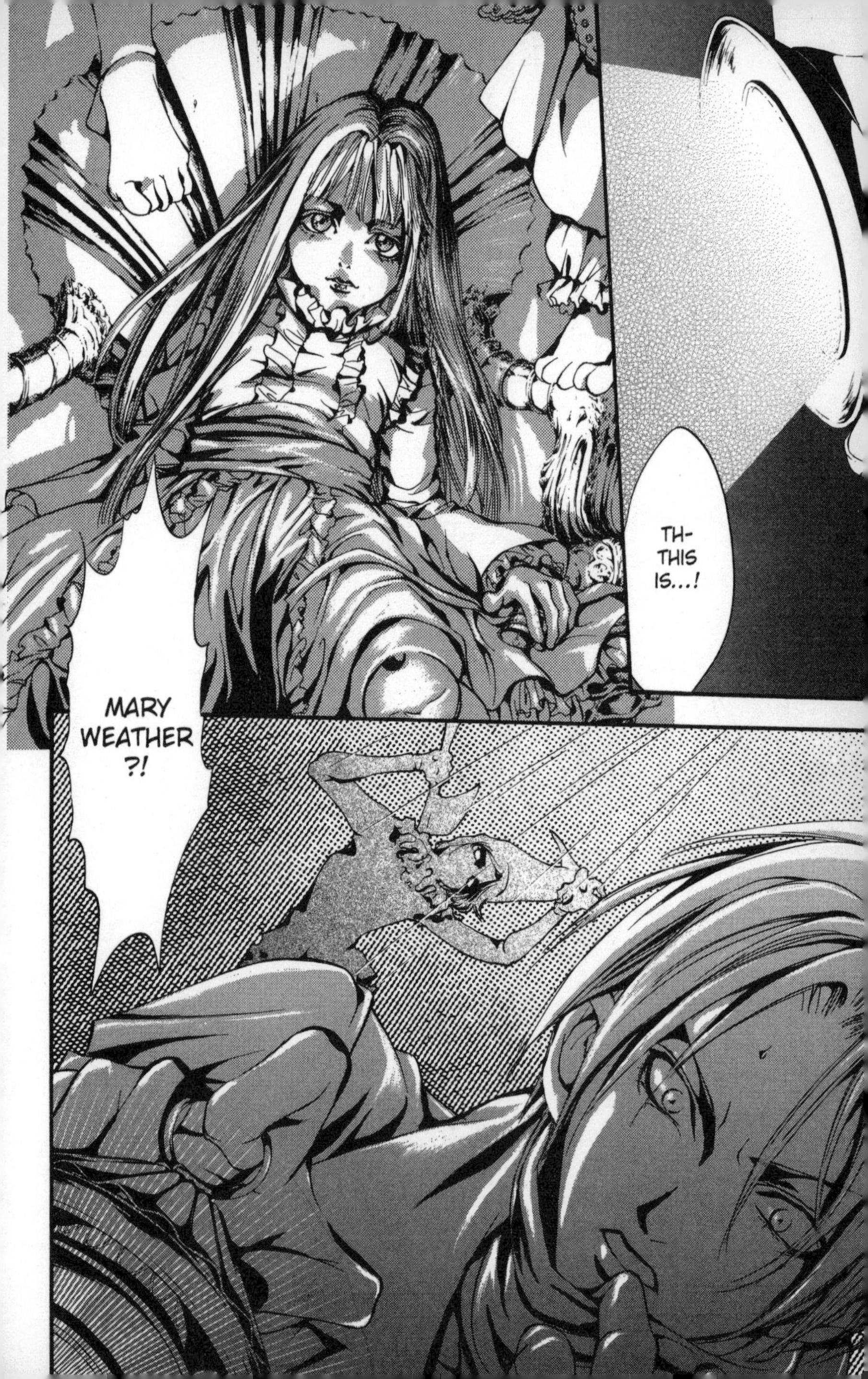
TH- THIS IS...!
MARY WEATHER ?!

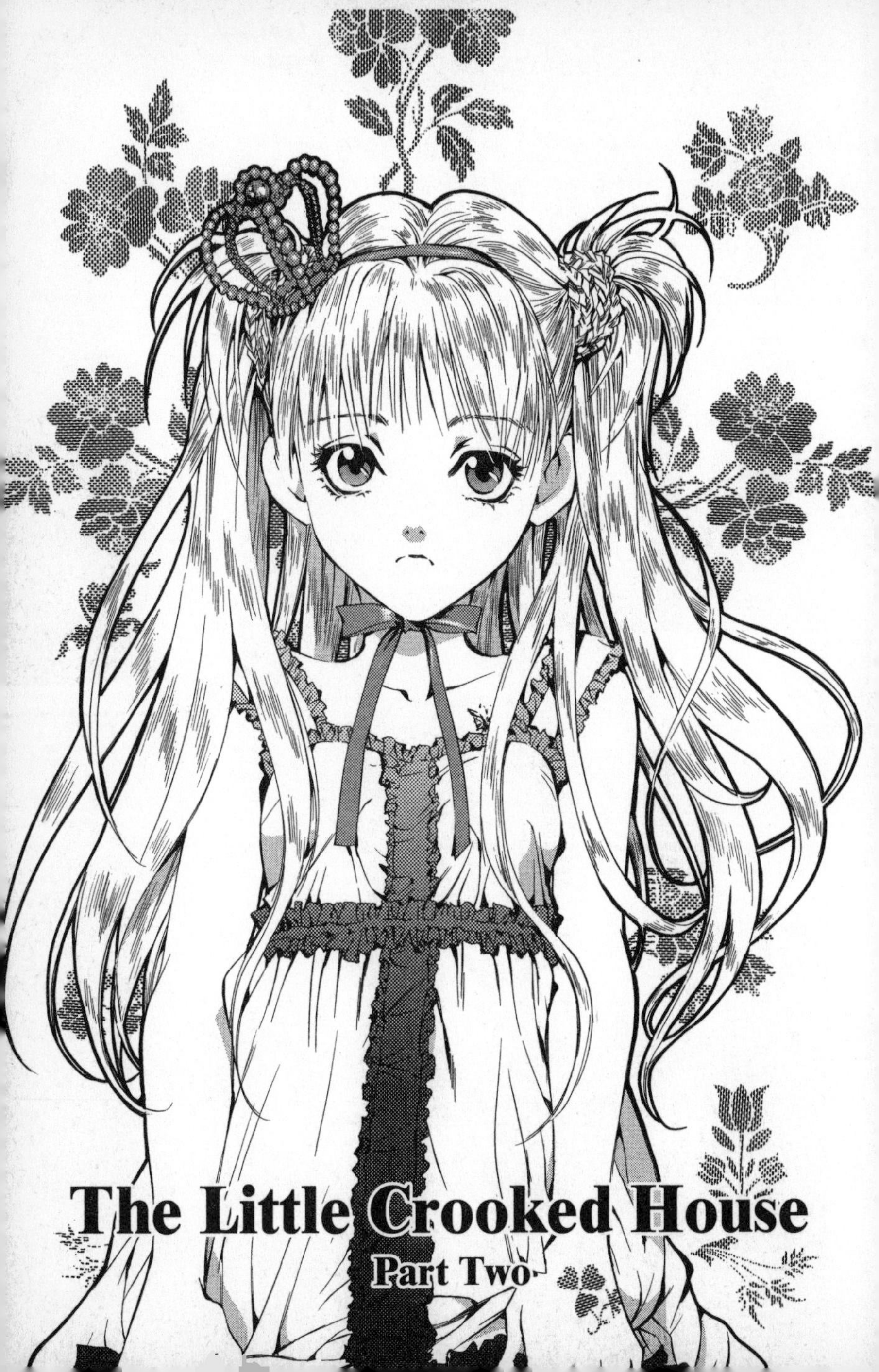
The Little Crooked House
Part Two

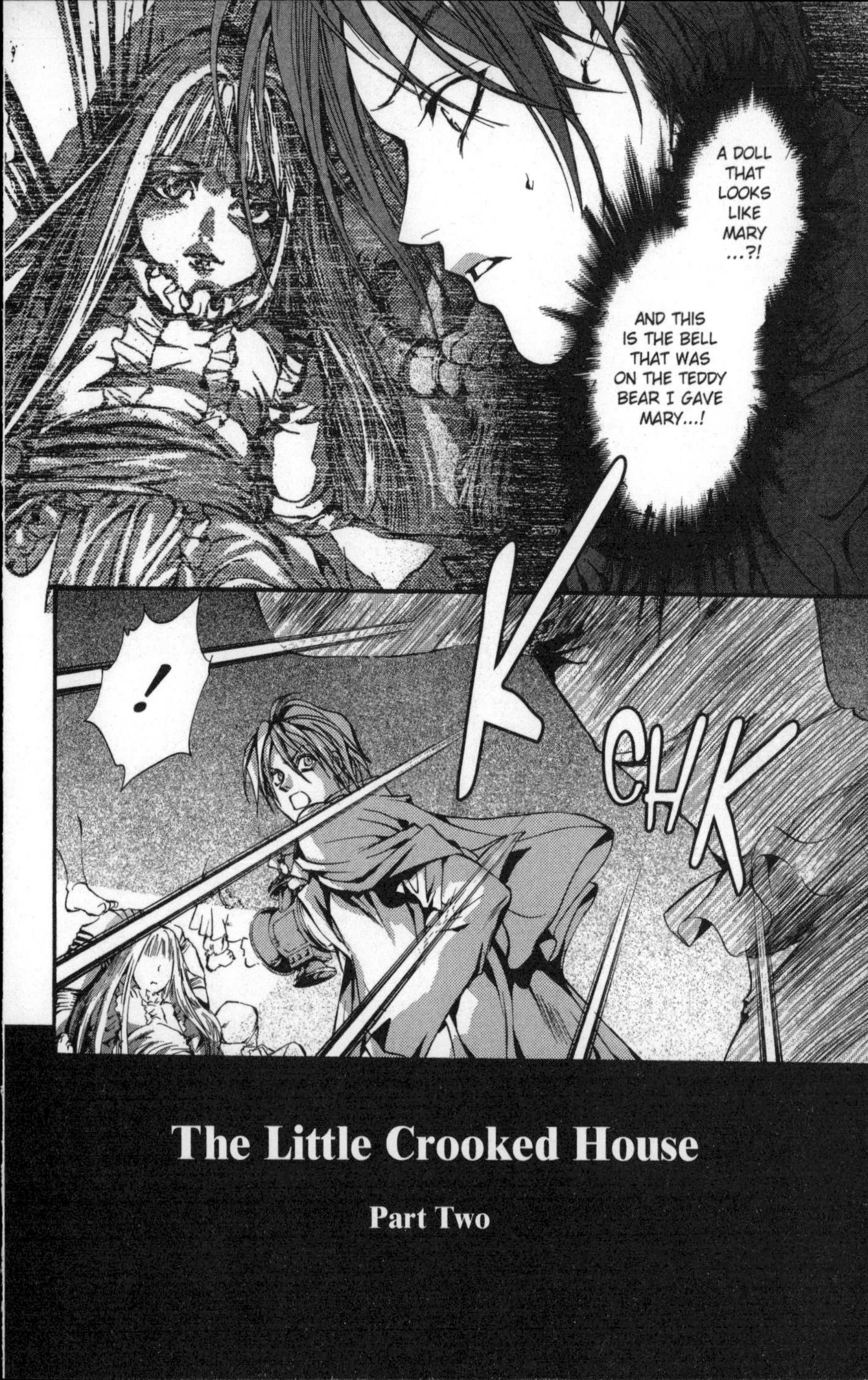
A DOLL THAT LOOKS LIKE MARY ...?!
AND THIS IS THE BELL THAT WAS ON THE TEDDY BEAR I GAVE MARY...!
K
CHK
!

The Little Crooked House

Part Two

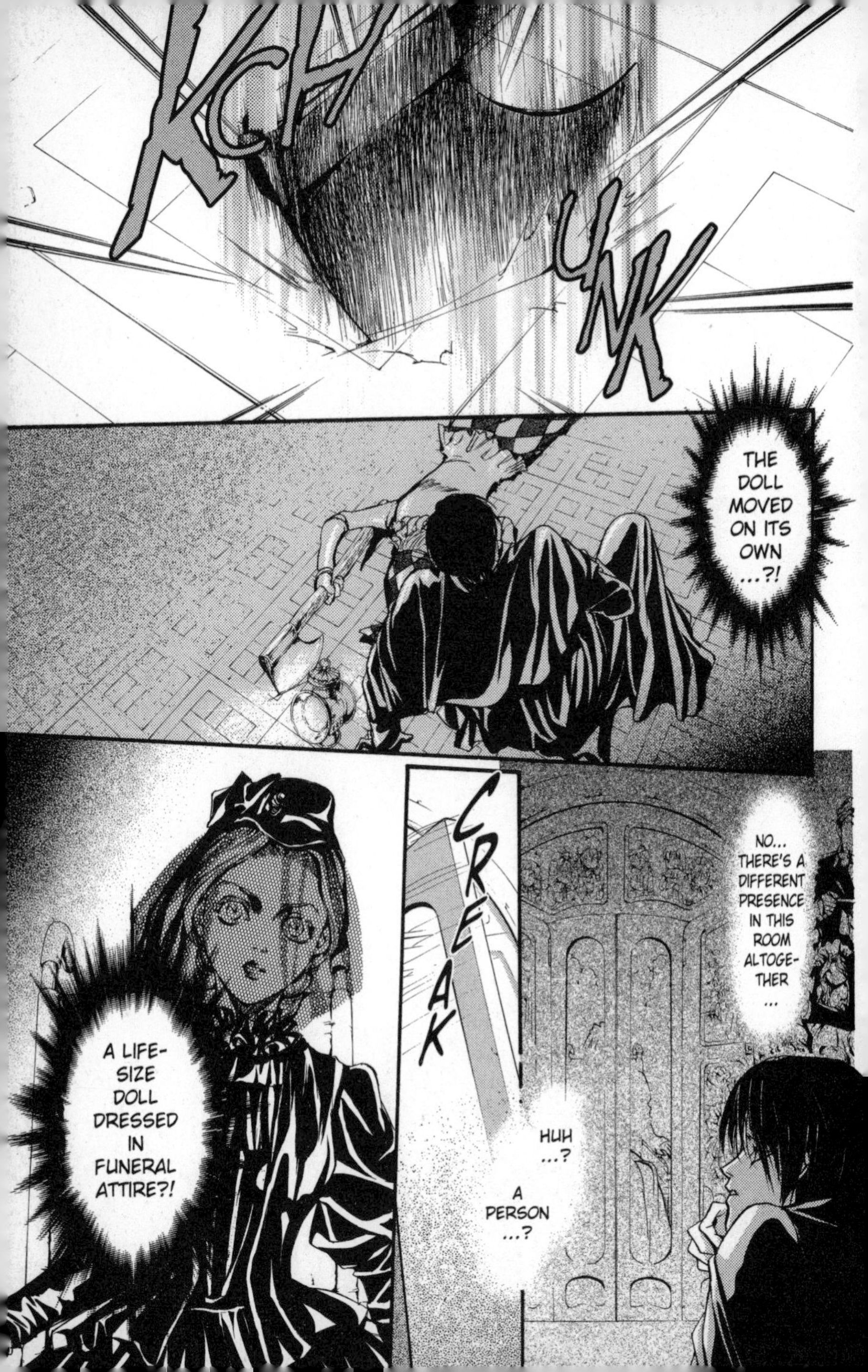
KCHUNK
THE DOLL MOVED ON ITS OWN ...?!
NO... THERE'S A DIFFERENT PRESENCE IN THIS ROOM ALTOGETHER ...
HUH ...?
A PERSON ...?
CREAK
A LIFE-SIZE DOLL DRESSED IN FUNERAL ATTIRE?!

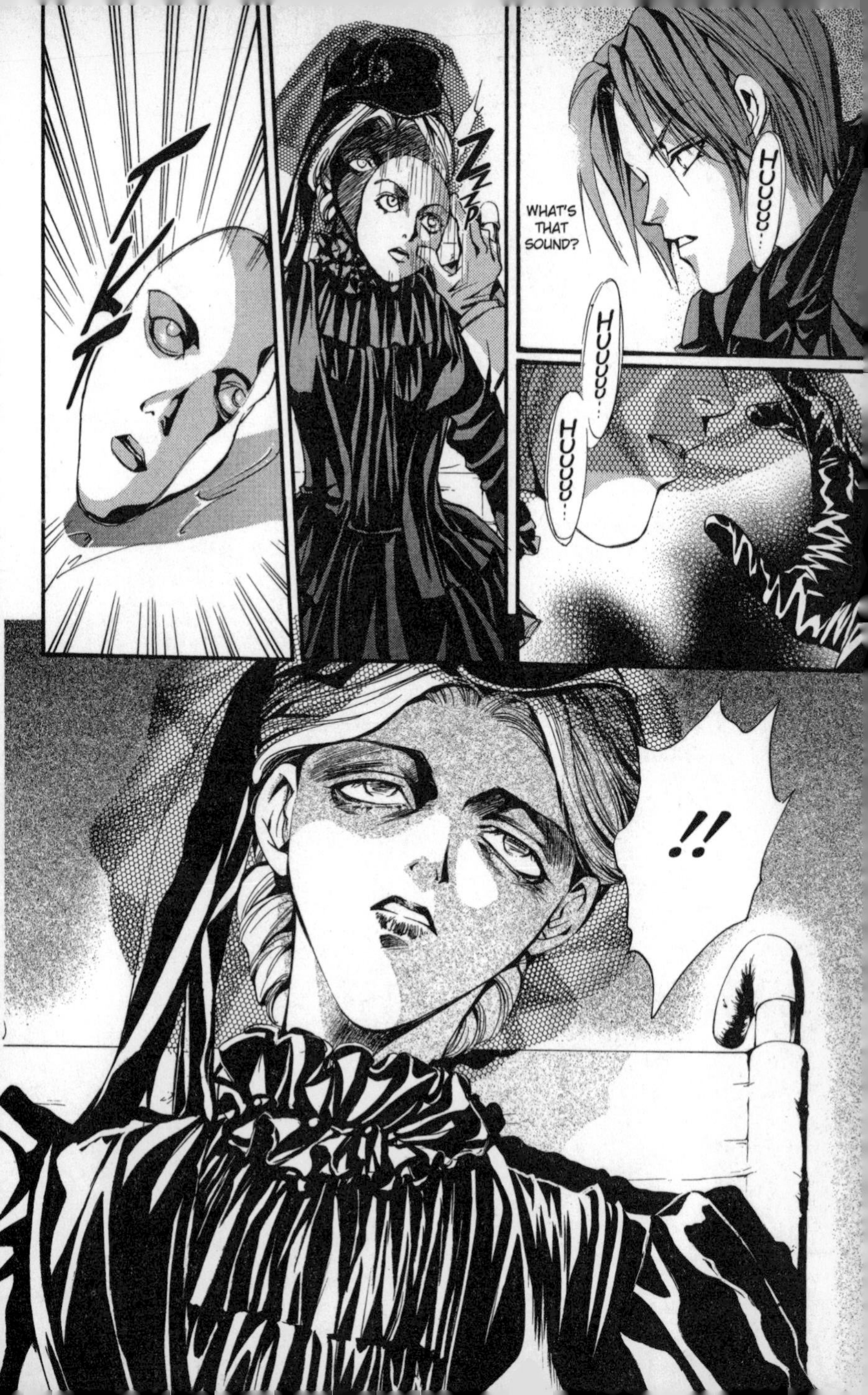
HUUUUU...
WHAT'S THAT SOUND?
HUUUUU...
HUUUUU...
ZZZP
!!

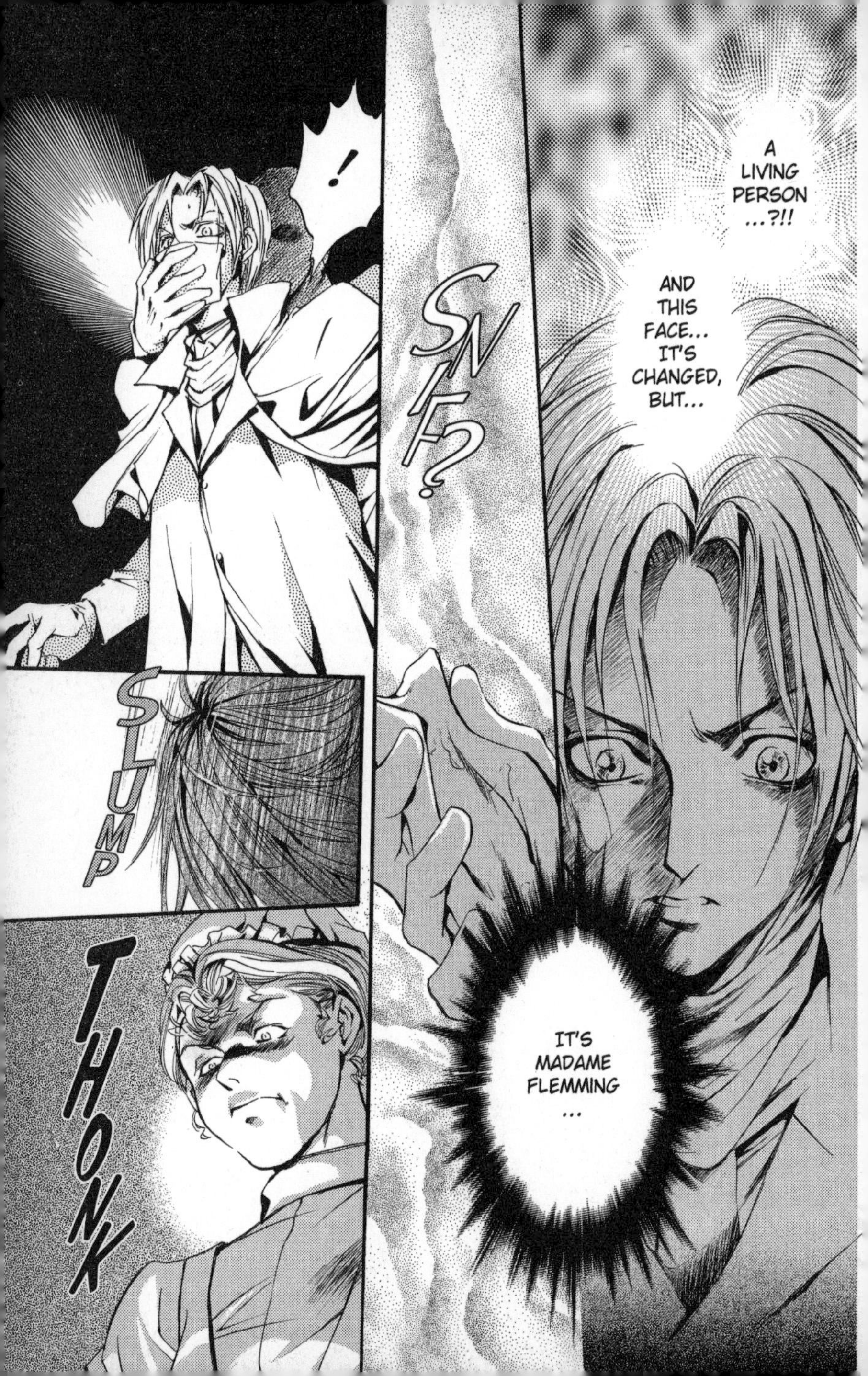
A LIVING PERSON ...?!!
AND THIS FACE... IT'S CHANGED, BUT...
IT'S MADAME FLEMMING ...
SNIFF?
!
SLUMP
THONK

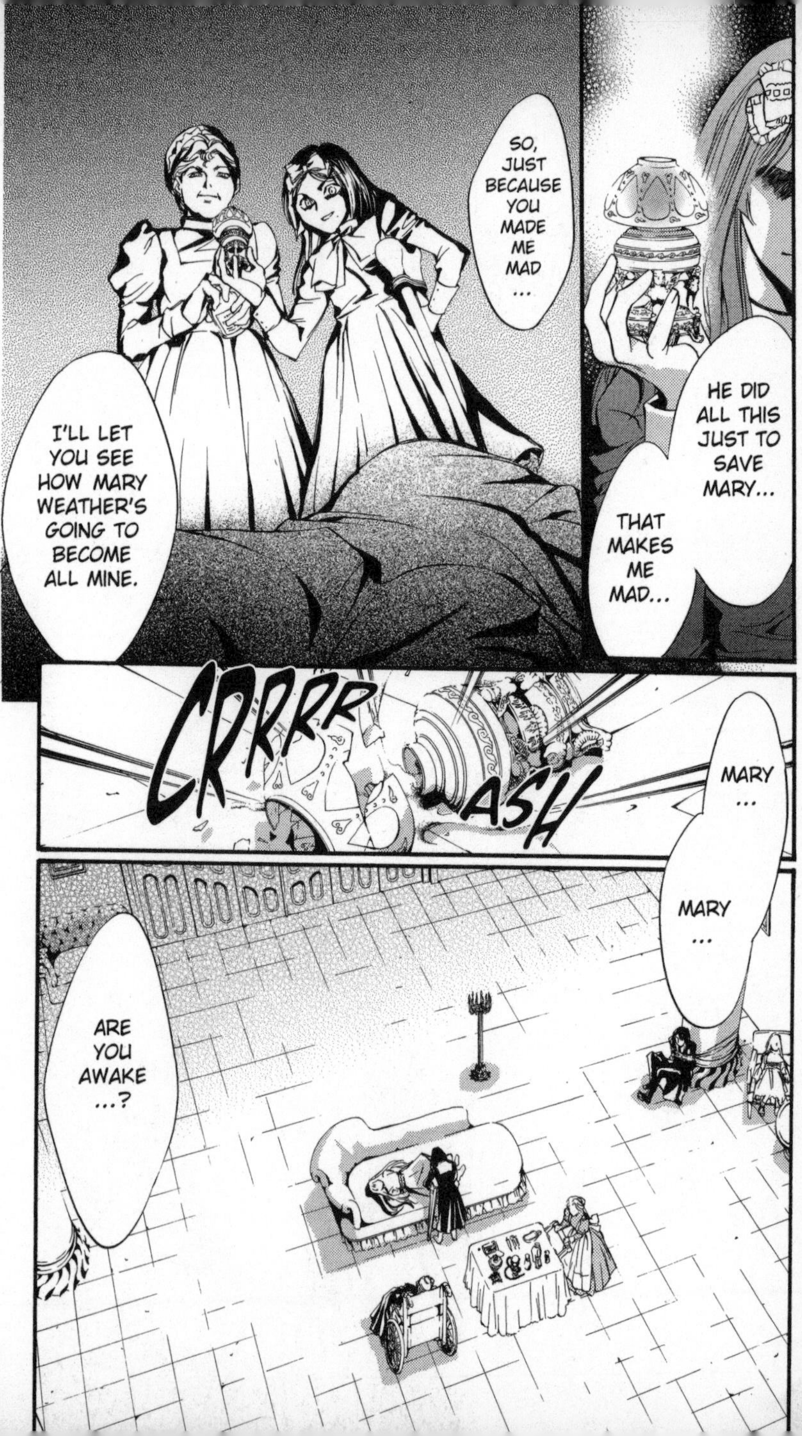
HE DID ALL THIS JUST TO SAVE MARY...
THAT MAKES ME MAD...
SO, JUST BECAUSE YOU MADE ME MAD ...
I'LL LET YOU SEE HOW MARY WEATHER'S GOING TO BECOME ALL MINE.
CRRRRASH
MARY ...
MARY ...
ARE YOU AWAKE ...?

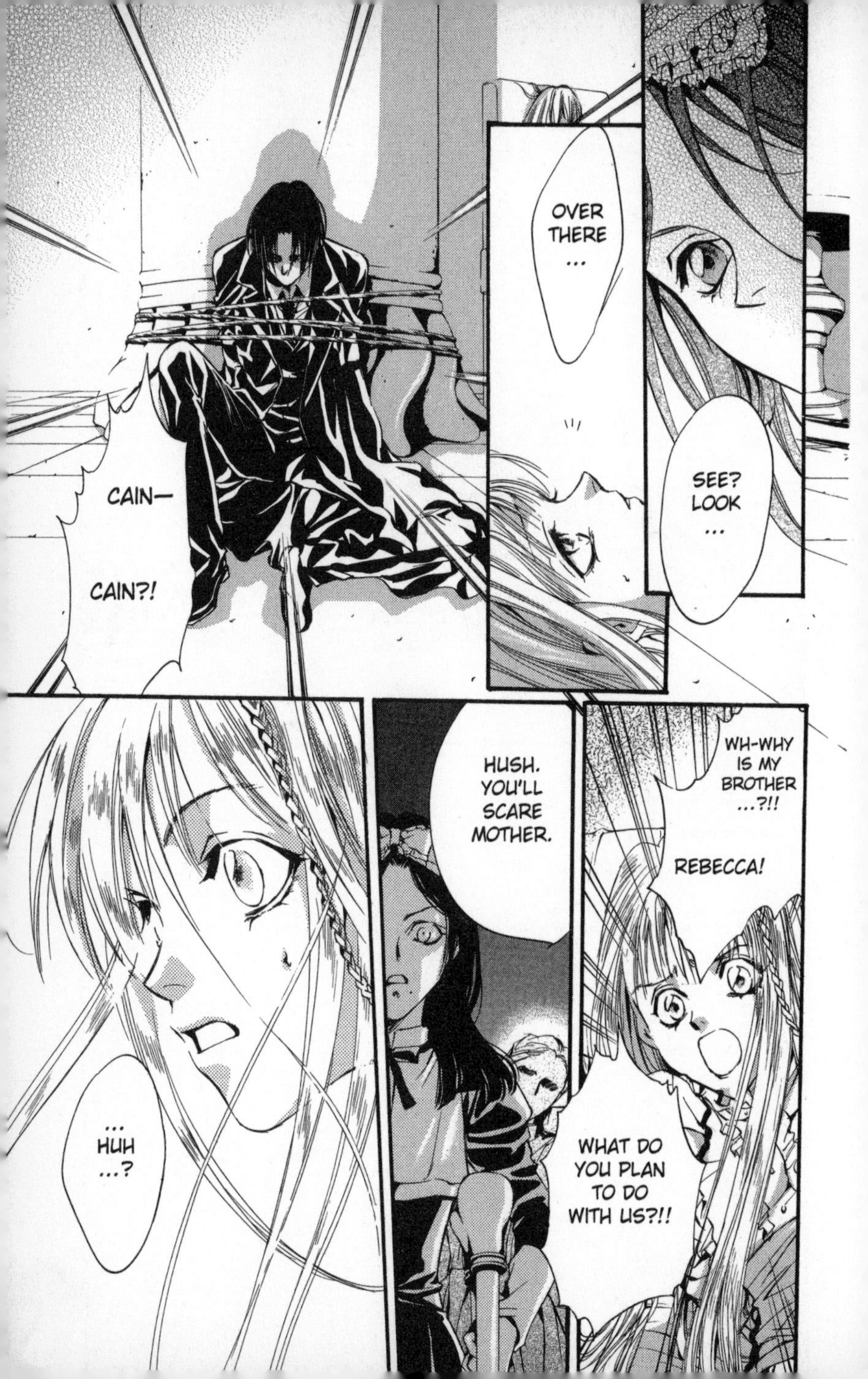
OVER THERE …
SEE? LOOK …
CAIN—
CAIN?!
WH-WHY IS MY BROTHER …?!!
REBECCA!
WHAT DO YOU PLAN TO DO WITH US?!!
HUSH. YOU'LL SCARE MOTHER.
… HUH …?

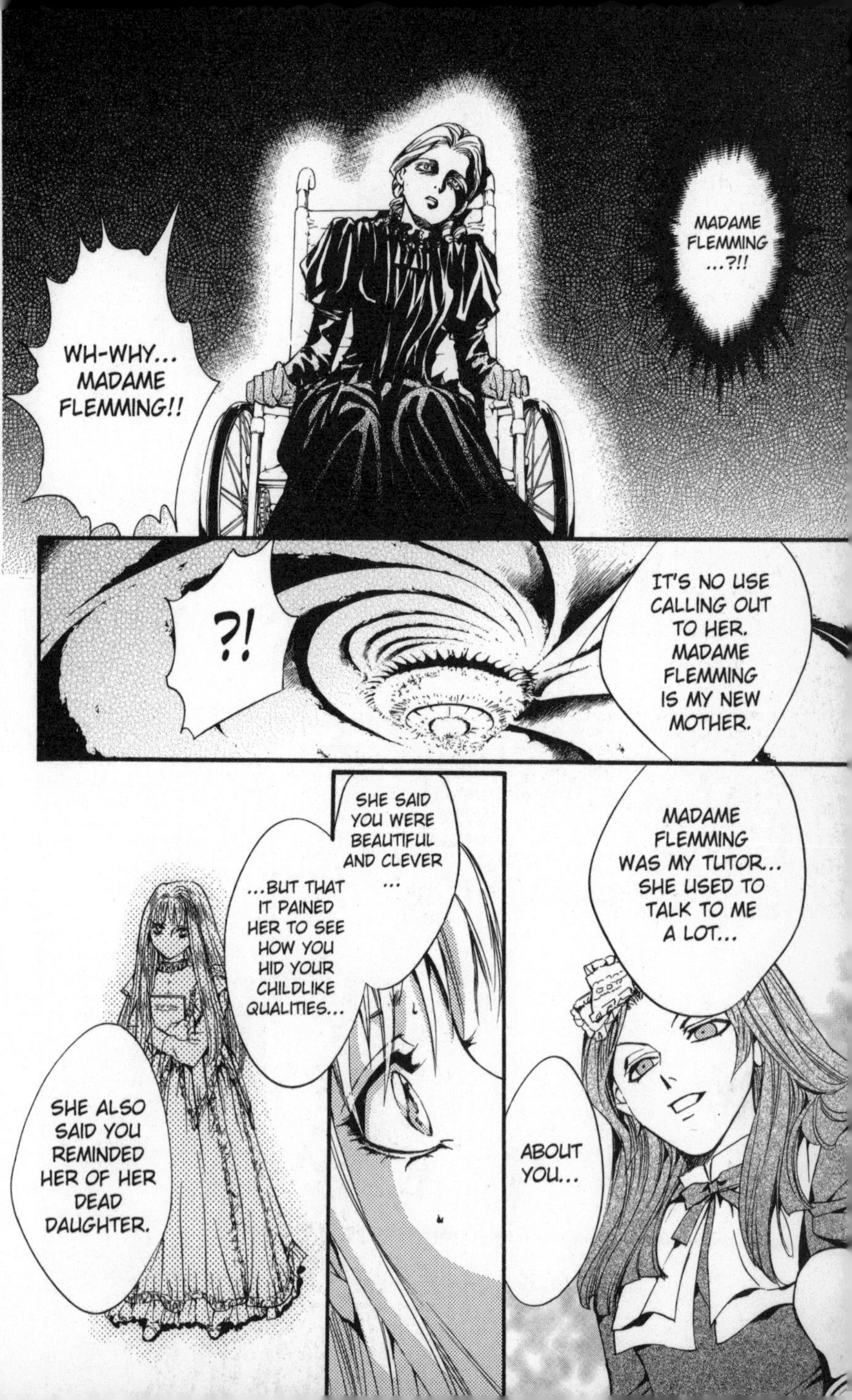
MADAME FLEMMING ...?!!
WH-WHY... MADAME FLEMMING!!
IT'S NO USE CALLING OUT TO HER. MADAME FLEMMING IS MY NEW MOTHER.
?!
MADAME FLEMMING WAS MY TUTOR... SHE USED TO TALK TO ME A LOT...
ABOUT YOU...
SHE SAID YOU WERE BEAUTIFUL AND CLEVER ...
...BUT THAT IT PAINED HER TO SEE HOW YOU HID YOUR CHILDLIKE QUALITIES...
SHE ALSO SAID YOU REMINDED HER OF HER DEAD DAUGHTER.

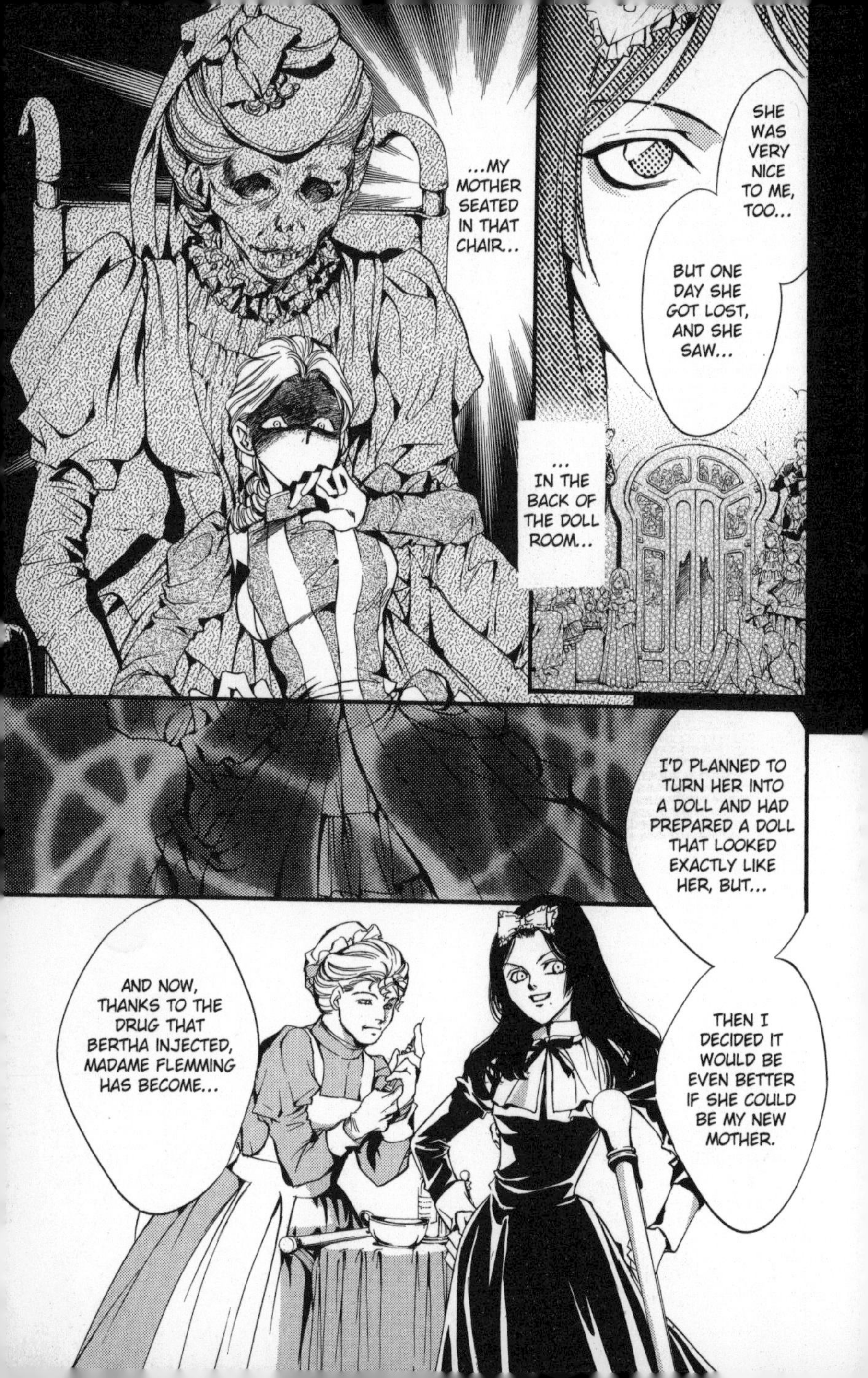
SHE WAS VERY NICE TO ME, TOO...
BUT ONE DAY SHE GOT LOST, AND SHE SAW...
... IN THE BACK OF THE DOLL ROOM...
...MY MOTHER SEATED IN THAT CHAIR...
I'D PLANNED TO TURN HER INTO A DOLL AND HAD PREPARED A DOLL THAT LOOKED EXACTLY LIKE HER, BUT...
THEN I DECIDED IT WOULD BE EVEN BETTER IF SHE COULD BE MY NEW MOTHER.
AND NOW, THANKS TO THE DRUG THAT BERTHA INJECTED, MADAME FLEMMING HAS BECOME...

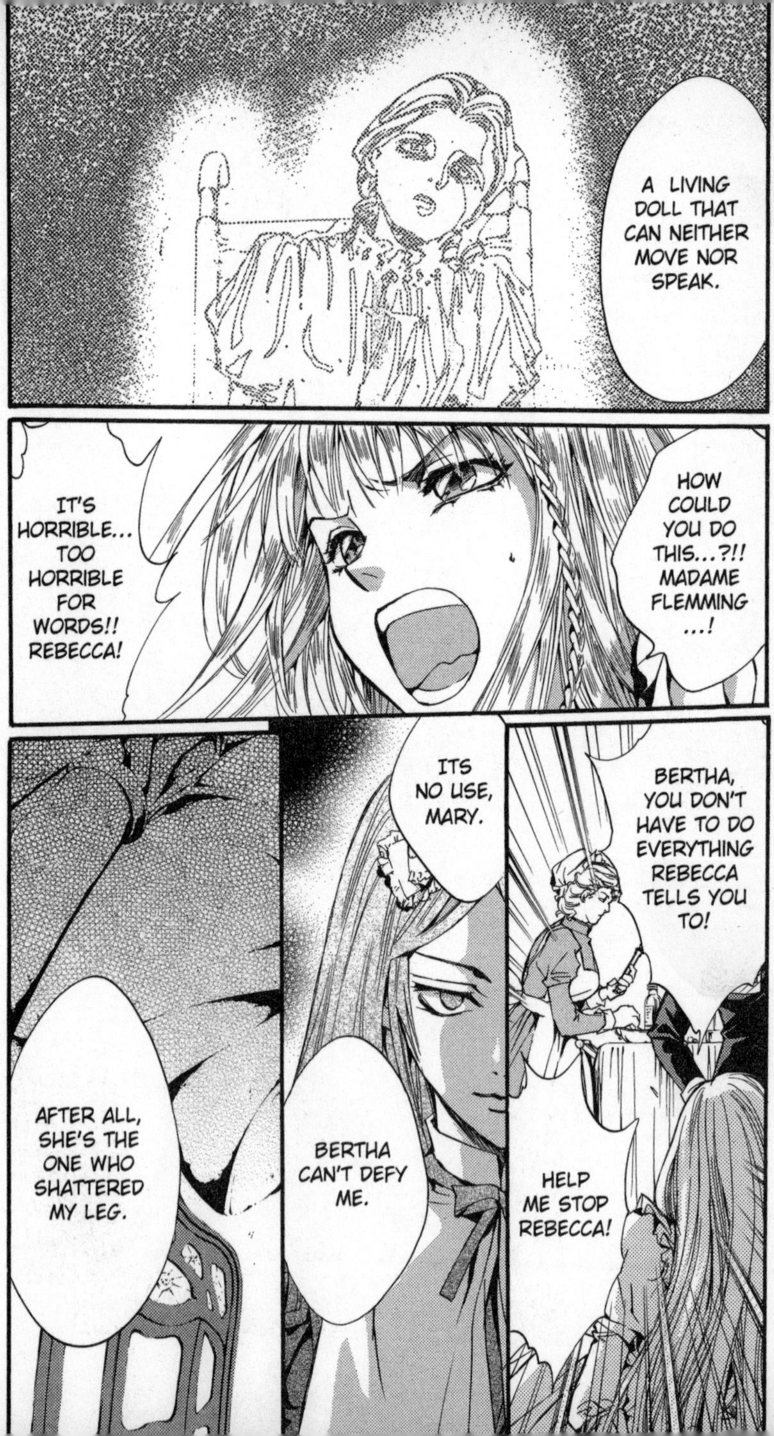
A LIVING DOLL THAT CAN NEITHER MOVE NOR SPEAK.
HOW COULD YOU DO THIS...?!! MADAME FLEMMING ...!
IT'S HORRIBLE... TOO HORRIBLE FOR WORDS!! REBECCA!
BERTHA, YOU DON'T HAVE TO DO EVERYTHING REBECCA TELLS YOU TO!
HELP ME STOP REBECCA!
ITS NO USE, MARY.
BERTHA CAN'T DEFY ME.
AFTER ALL, SHE'S THE ONE WHO SHATTERED MY LEG.

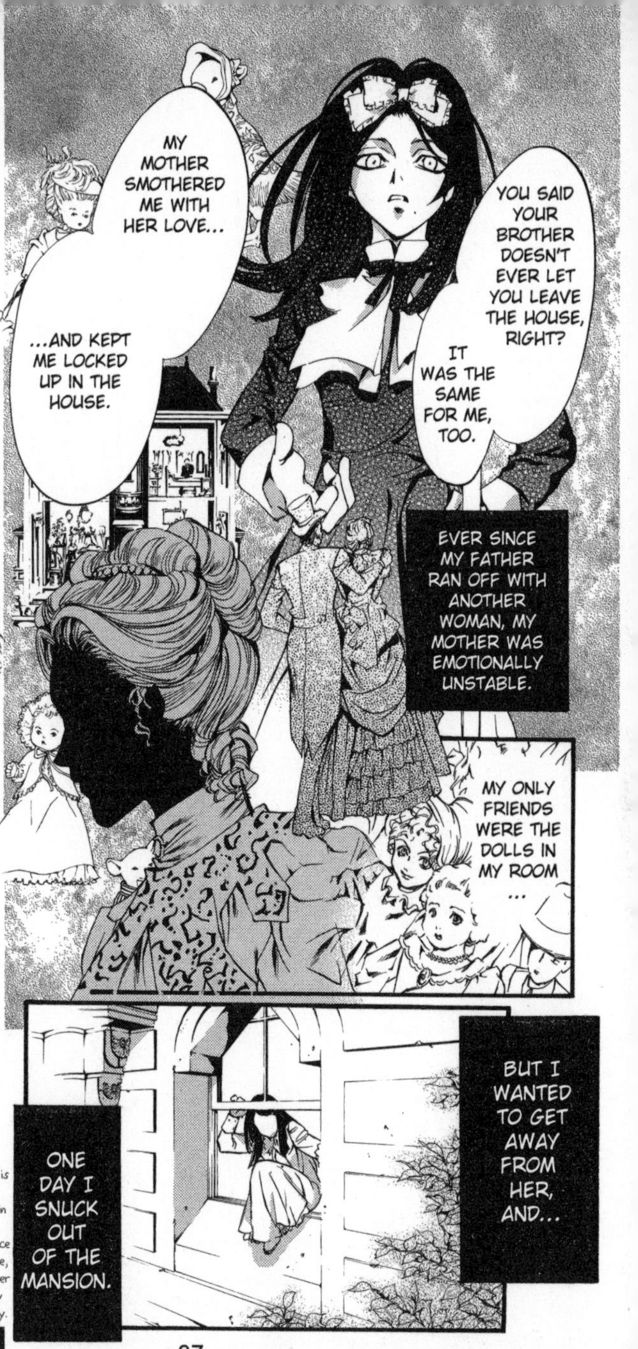
YOU SAID YOUR BROTHER DOESN'T EVER LET YOU LEAVE THE HOUSE, RIGHT?
IT WAS THE SAME FOR ME, TOO.
MY MOTHER SMOTHERED ME WITH HER LOVE...
...AND KEPT ME LOCKED UP IN THE HOUSE.
EVER SINCE MY FATHER RAN OFF WITH ANOTHER WOMAN, MY MOTHER WAS EMOTIONALLY UNSTABLE.
MY ONLY FRIENDS WERE THE DOLLS IN MY ROOM ...
BUT I WANTED TO GET AWAY FROM HER, AND...
ONE DAY I SNUCK OUT OF THE MANSION.

About Mary Weather.

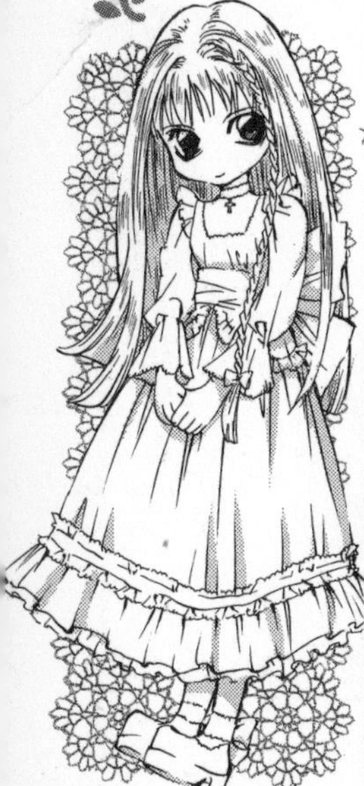

She first appeared in the comic "The Sound Hatched By the Boy" in "The Hung Man" episode. In the beginning, she had curly hair, but as time passed her hair became straight...! She did Tarot readings to earn a living on her way to London in search of her brother Cain. She's the child of Cain's dad and the maid, Alegra, and is Cain's half sister. Her last name has also been changed from Duke to Hargreaves now.

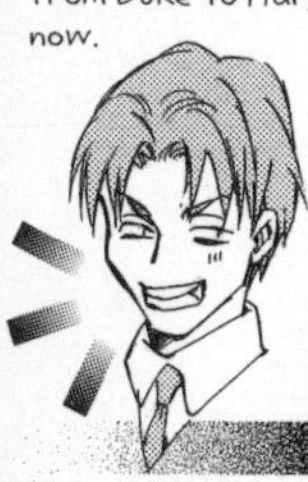

Oscar. His brain is made of muscle. He's interested in Cain because of Cain's resemblance to his dead fiance, but now he's after Mary. Either way he's kind of scary.

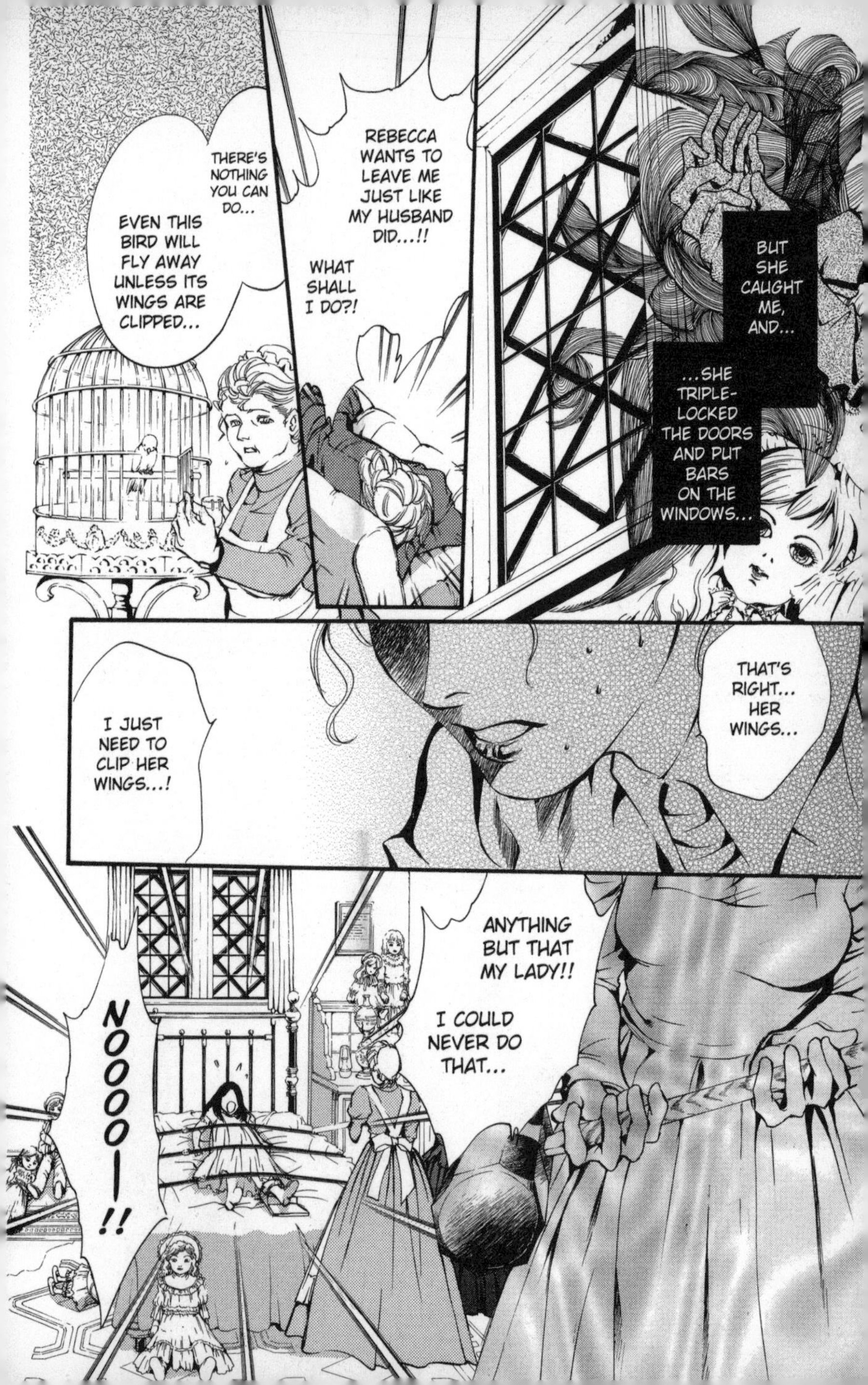

BUT SHE CAUGHT ME, AND...
...SHE TRIPLE-LOCKED THE DOORS AND PUT BARS ON THE WINDOWS...
REBECCA WANTS TO LEAVE ME JUST LIKE MY HUSBAND DID...!!
WHAT SHALL I DO?!
THERE'S NOTHING YOU CAN DO...
EVEN THIS BIRD WILL FLY AWAY UNLESS ITS WINGS ARE CLIPPED...
THAT'S RIGHT... HER WINGS...
I JUST NEED TO CLIP HER WINGS...!
ANYTHING BUT THAT MY LADY!!
I COULD NEVER DO THAT...
NOOOOO—!!

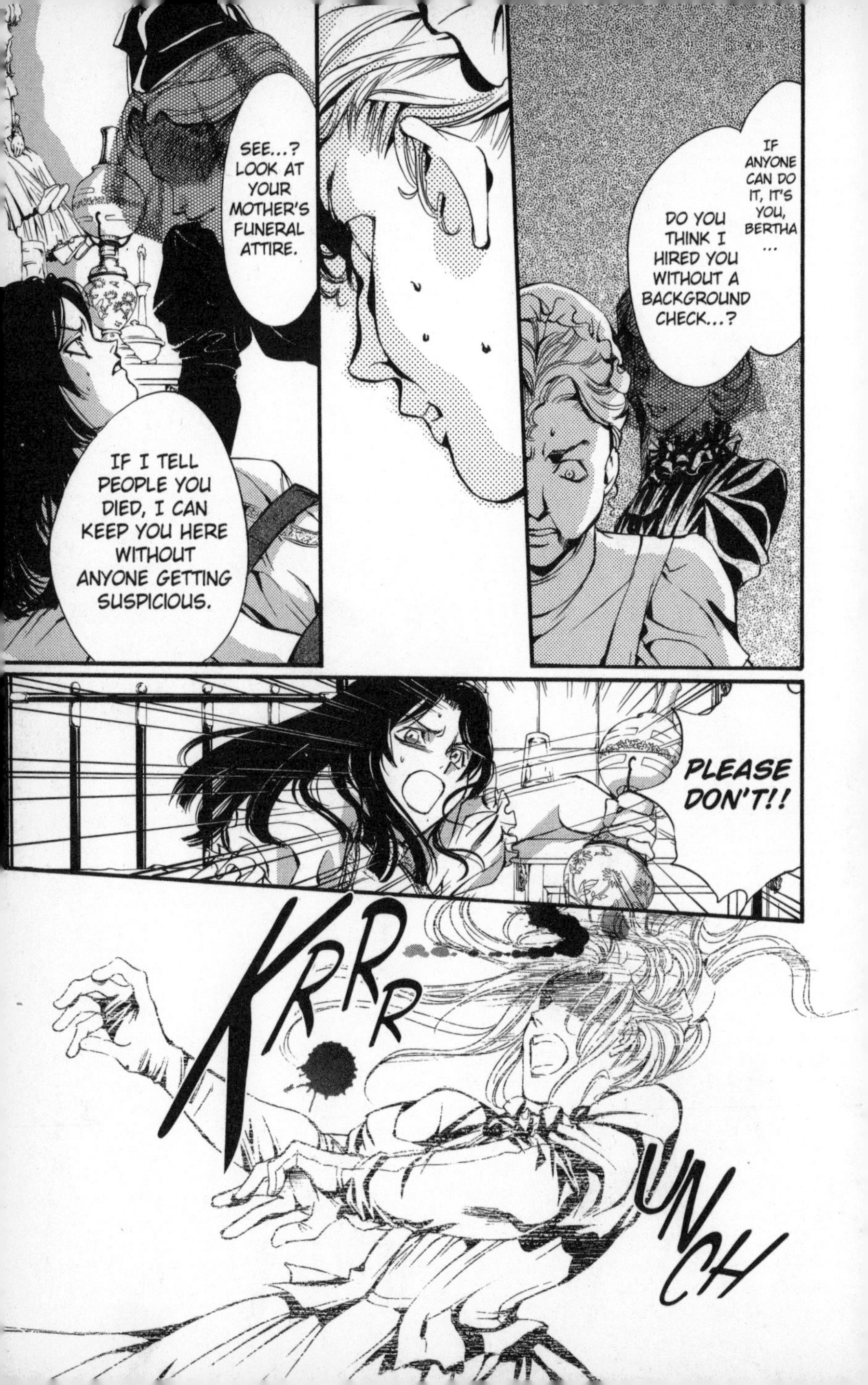
IF ANYONE CAN DO IT, IT'S YOU, BERTHA...
DO YOU THINK I HIRED YOU WITHOUT A BACKGROUND CHECK...?
SEE...? LOOK AT YOUR MOTHER'S FUNERAL ATTIRE.
IF I TELL PEOPLE YOU DIED, I CAN KEEP YOU HERE WITHOUT ANYONE GETTING SUSPICIOUS.
PLEASE DON'T!!
KRRRUNCH

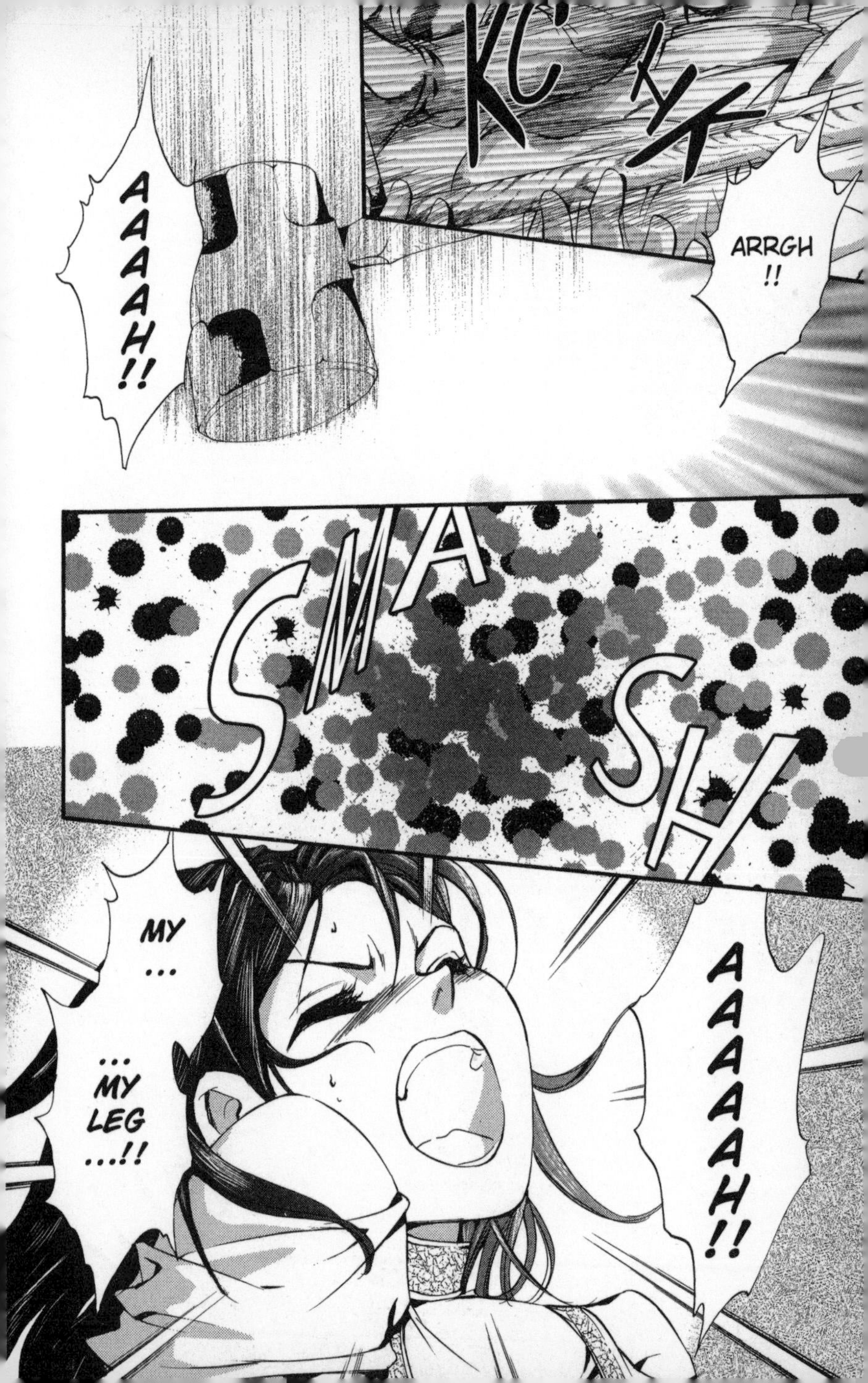
KC'KYK
ARRGH !!
AAAAAH!!
SMASH
AAAAAAH!!
MY ...
... MY LEG ...!!

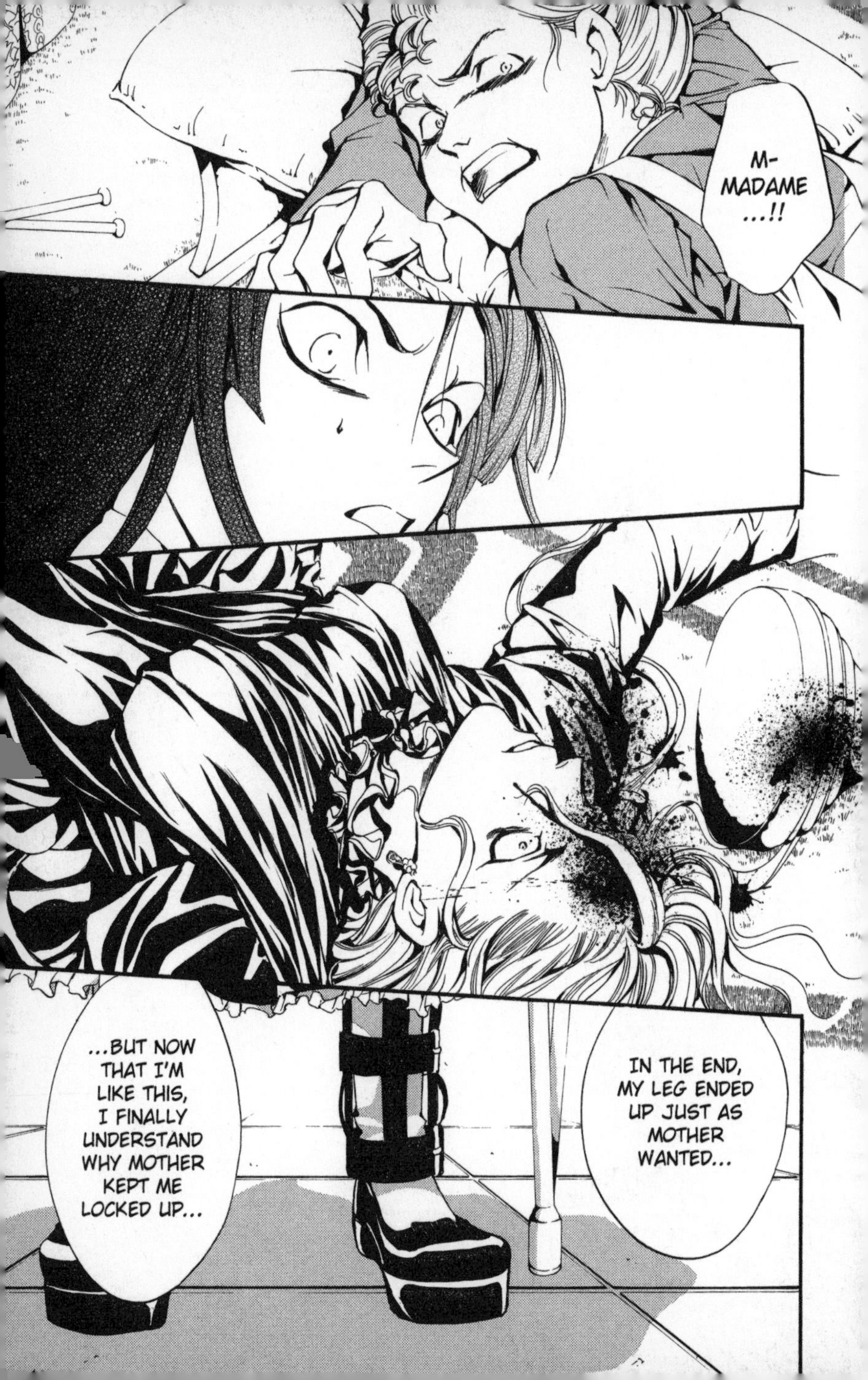
M-MADAME ...!!
IN THE END, MY LEG ENDED UP JUST AS MOTHER WANTED...
...BUT NOW THAT I'M LIKE THIS, I FINALLY UNDERSTAND WHY MOTHER KEPT ME LOCKED UP...

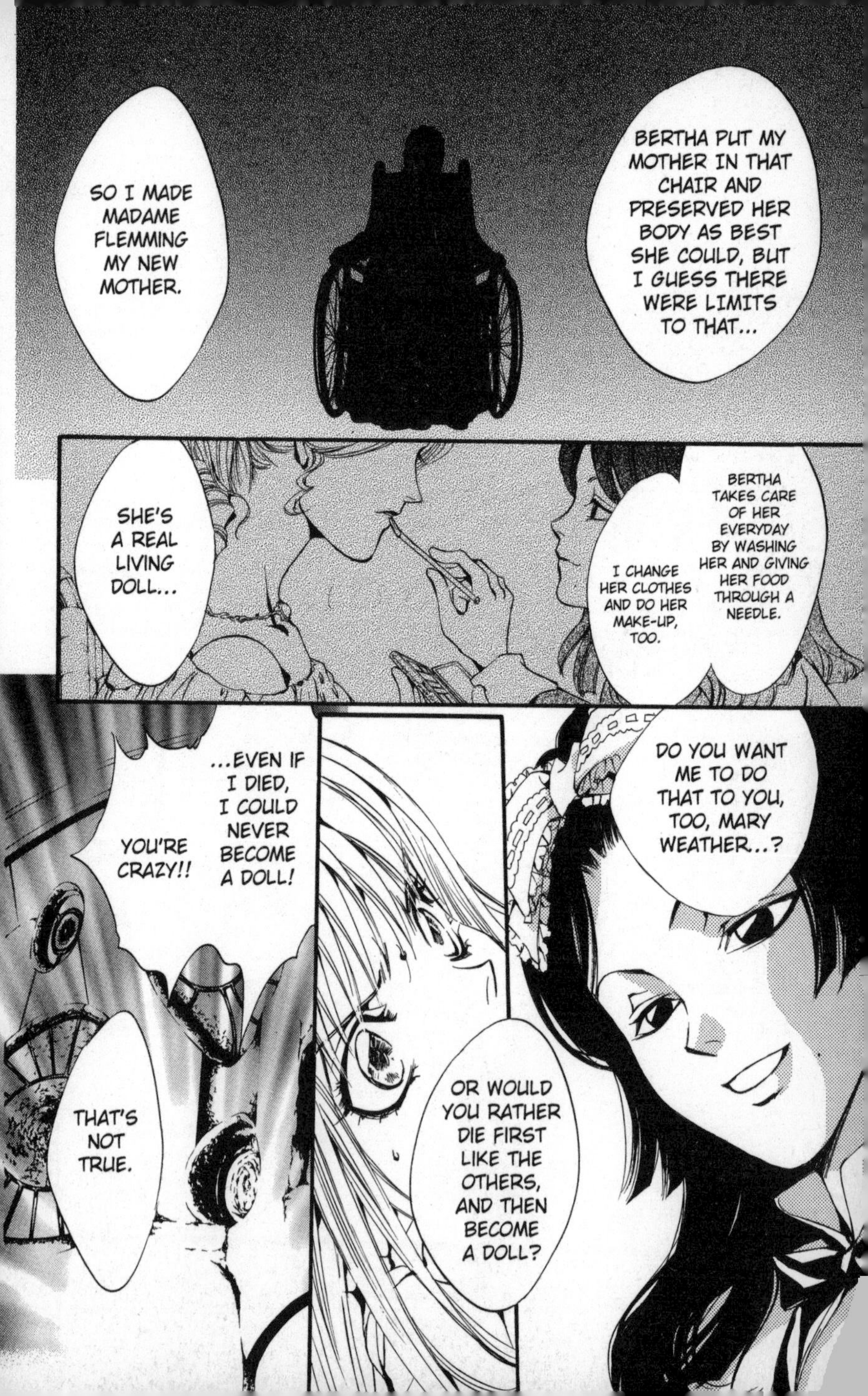
BERTHA PUT MY MOTHER IN THAT CHAIR AND PRESERVED HER BODY AS BEST SHE COULD, BUT I GUESS THERE WERE LIMITS TO THAT...
SO I MADE MADAME FLEMMING MY NEW MOTHER.
BERTHA TAKES CARE OF HER EVERYDAY BY WASHING HER AND GIVING HER FOOD THROUGH A NEEDLE.
I CHANGE HER CLOTHES AND DO HER MAKE-UP, TOO.
SHE'S A REAL LIVING DOLL...
DO YOU WANT ME TO DO THAT TO YOU, TOO, MARY WEATHER..?
OR WOULD YOU RATHER DIE FIRST LIKE THE OTHERS, AND THEN BECOME A DOLL?
...EVEN IF I DIED, I COULD NEVER BECOME A DOLL!
YOU'RE CRAZY!!
THAT'S NOT TRUE.

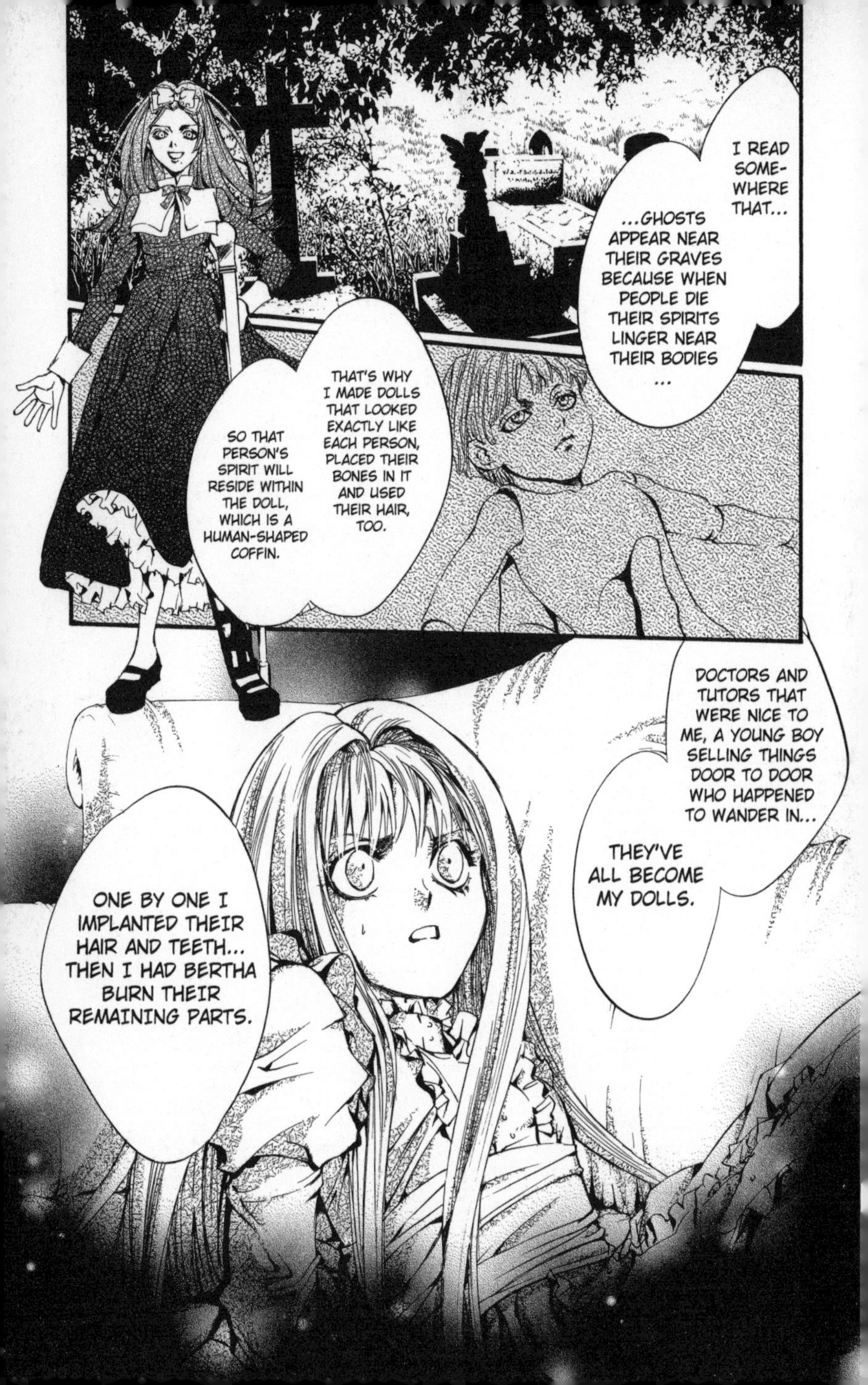
I READ SOME-WHERE THAT...
...GHOSTS APPEAR NEAR THEIR GRAVES BECAUSE WHEN PEOPLE DIE THEIR SPIRITS LINGER NEAR THEIR BODIES ...
THAT'S WHY I MADE DOLLS THAT LOOKED EXACTLY LIKE EACH PERSON, PLACED THEIR BONES IN IT AND USED THEIR HAIR, TOO.
SO THAT PERSON'S SPIRIT WILL RESIDE WITHIN THE DOLL, WHICH IS A HUMAN-SHAPED COFFIN.
DOCTORS AND TUTORS THAT WERE NICE TO ME, A YOUNG BOY SELLING THINGS DOOR TO DOOR WHO HAPPENED TO WANDER IN...
THEY'VE ALL BECOME MY DOLLS.
ONE BY ONE I IMPLANTED THEIR HAIR AND TEETH... THEN I HAD BERTHA BURN THEIR REMAINING PARTS.

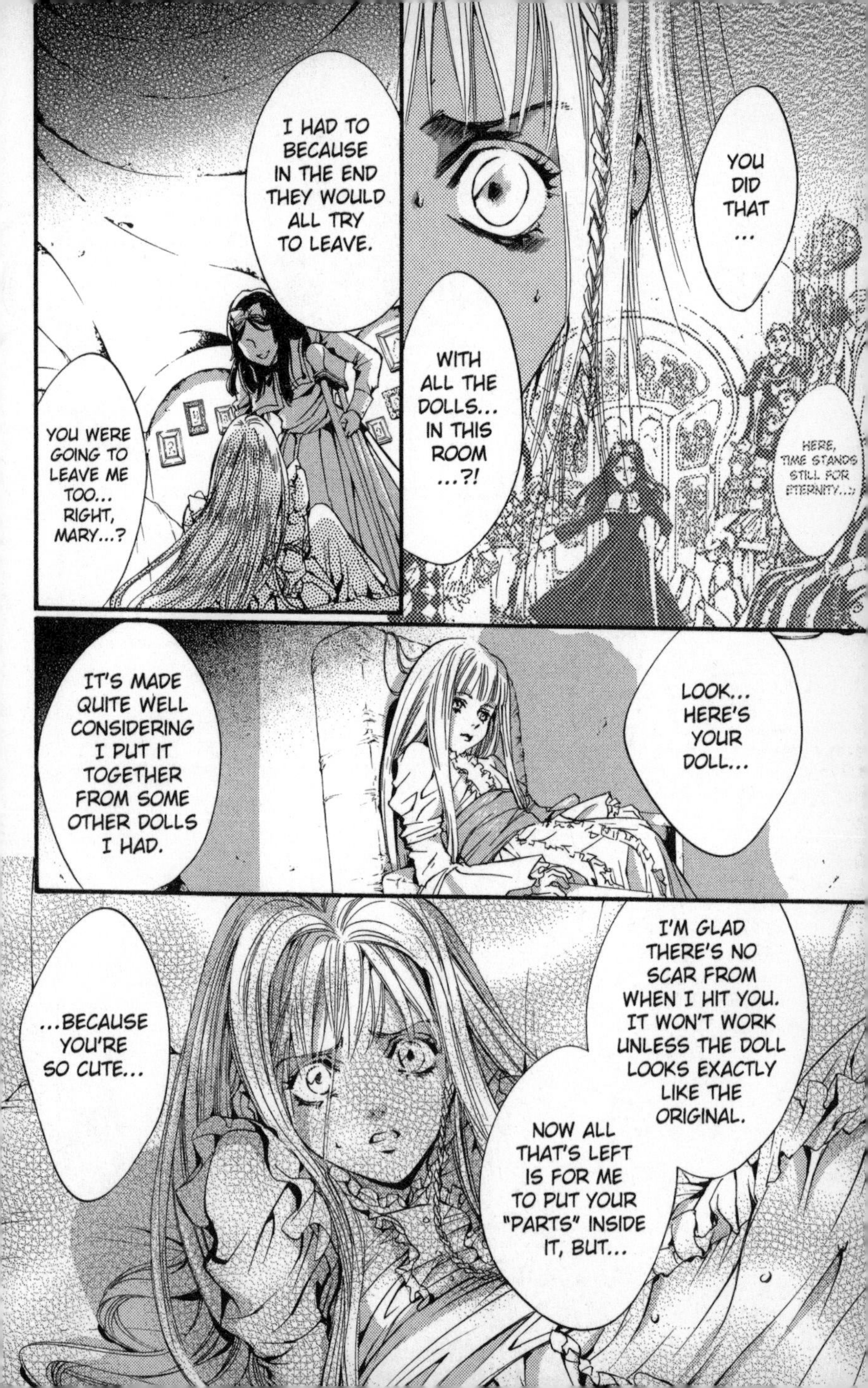
YOU DID THAT ...
WITH ALL THE DOLLS... IN THIS ROOM ...?!
HERE, TIME STANDS STILL FOR ETERNITY...
I HAD TO BECAUSE IN THE END THEY WOULD ALL TRY TO LEAVE.
YOU WERE GOING TO LEAVE ME TOO... RIGHT, MARY...?
LOOK... HERE'S YOUR DOLL...
IT'S MADE QUITE WELL CONSIDERING I PUT IT TOGETHER FROM SOME OTHER DOLLS I HAD.
I'M GLAD THERE'S NO SCAR FROM WHEN I HIT YOU. IT WON'T WORK UNLESS THE DOLL LOOKS EXACTLY LIKE THE ORIGINAL.
NOW ALL THAT'S LEFT IS FOR ME TO PUT YOUR "PARTS" INSIDE IT, BUT...
...BECAUSE YOU'RE SO CUTE...

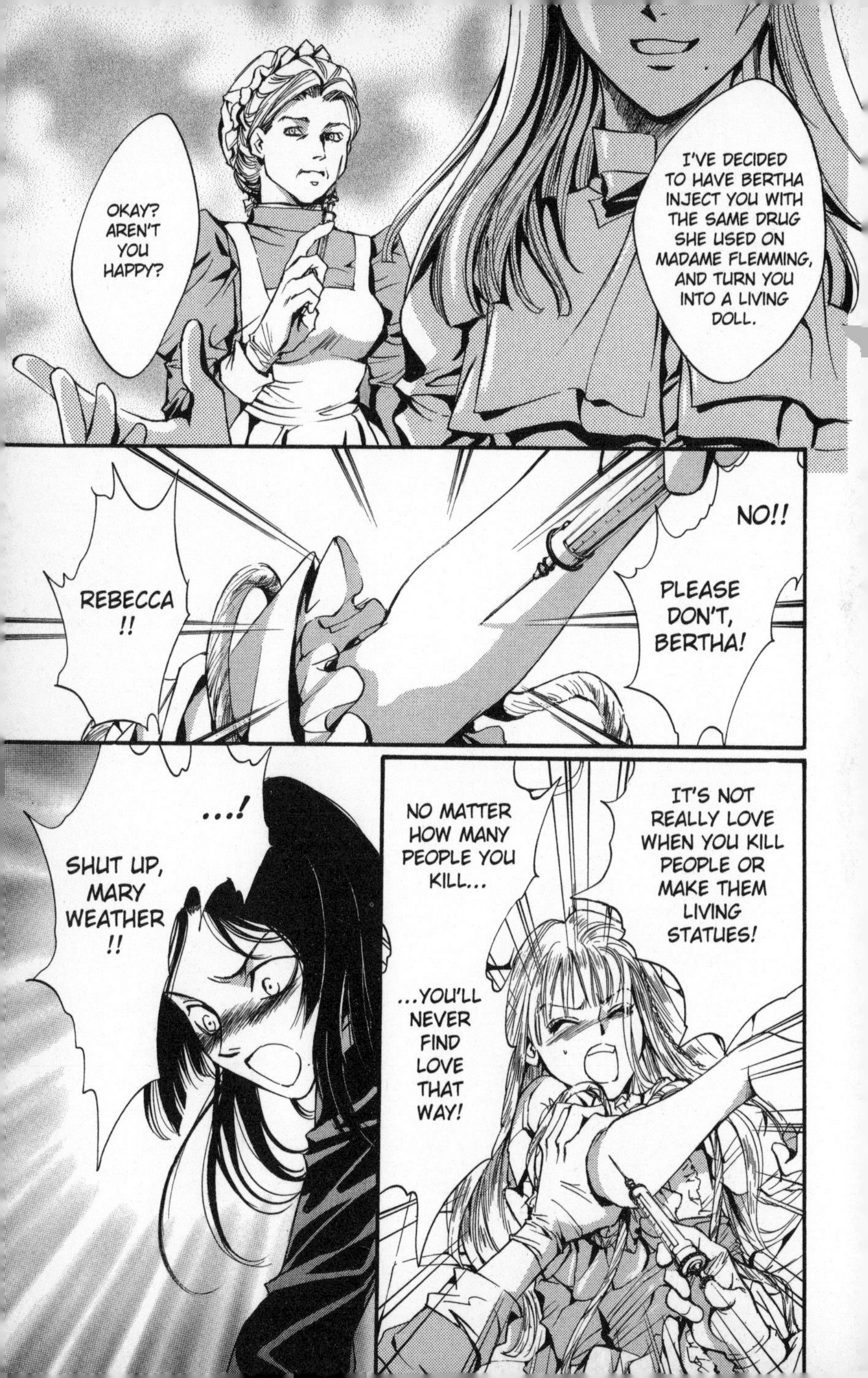

I'VE DECIDED TO HAVE BERTHA INJECT YOU WITH THE SAME DRUG SHE USED ON MADAME FLEMMING, AND TURN YOU INTO A LIVING DOLL.
OKAY? AREN'T YOU HAPPY?
NO!!
PLEASE DON'T, BERTHA!
REBECCA !!
IT'S NOT REALLY LOVE WHEN YOU KILL PEOPLE OR MAKE THEM LIVING STATUES!
NO MATTER HOW MANY PEOPLE YOU KILL...
...YOU'LL NEVER FIND LOVE THAT WAY!
...!
SHUT UP, MARY WEATHER !!

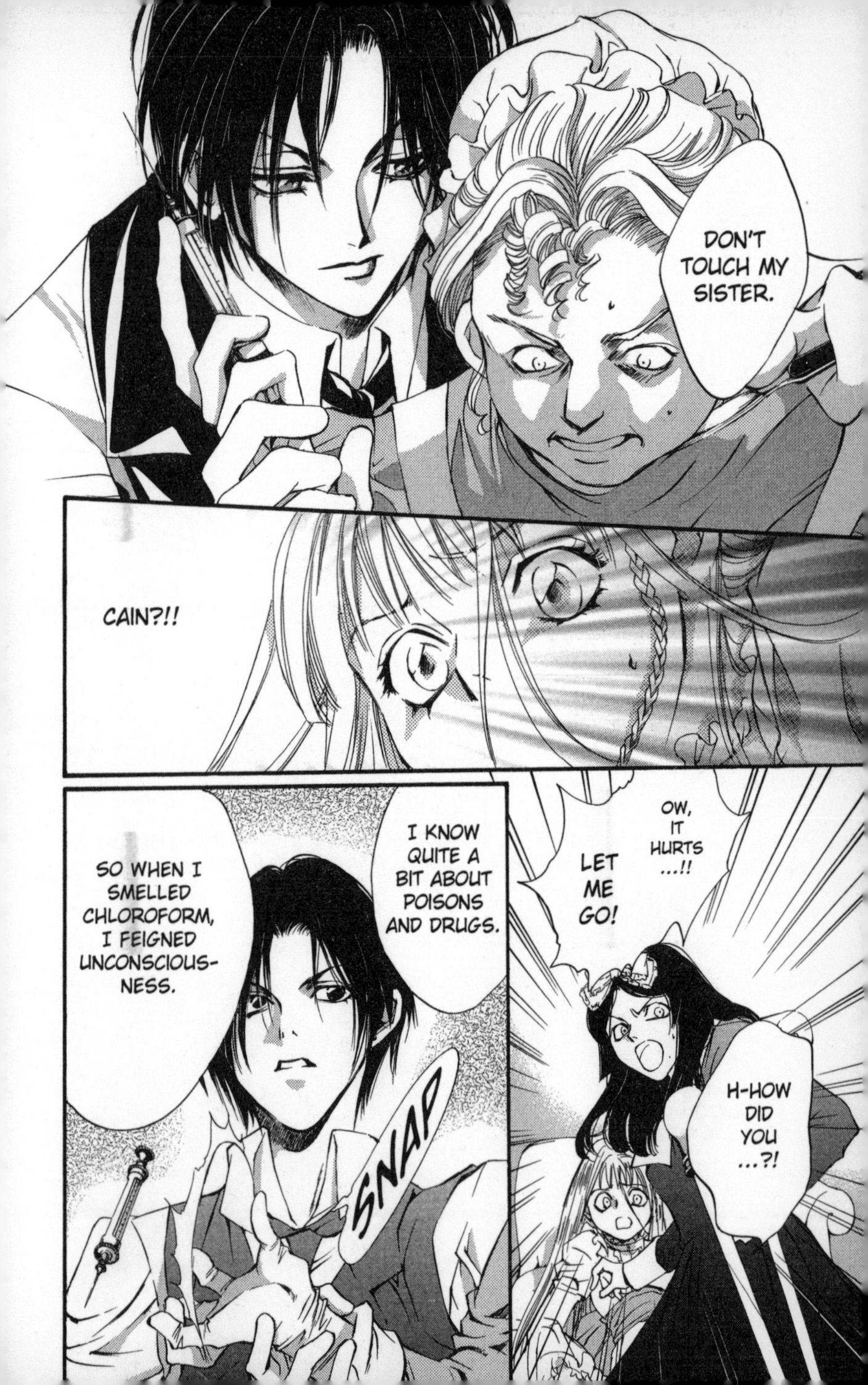
DON'T TOUCH MY SISTER.
CAIN?!!
OW, IT HURTS ...!!
LET ME GO!
H-HOW DID YOU ...?!
I KNOW QUITE A BIT ABOUT POISONS AND DRUGS.
SO WHEN I SMELLED CHLOROFORM, I FEIGNED UNCONSCIOUSNESS.
SNAP

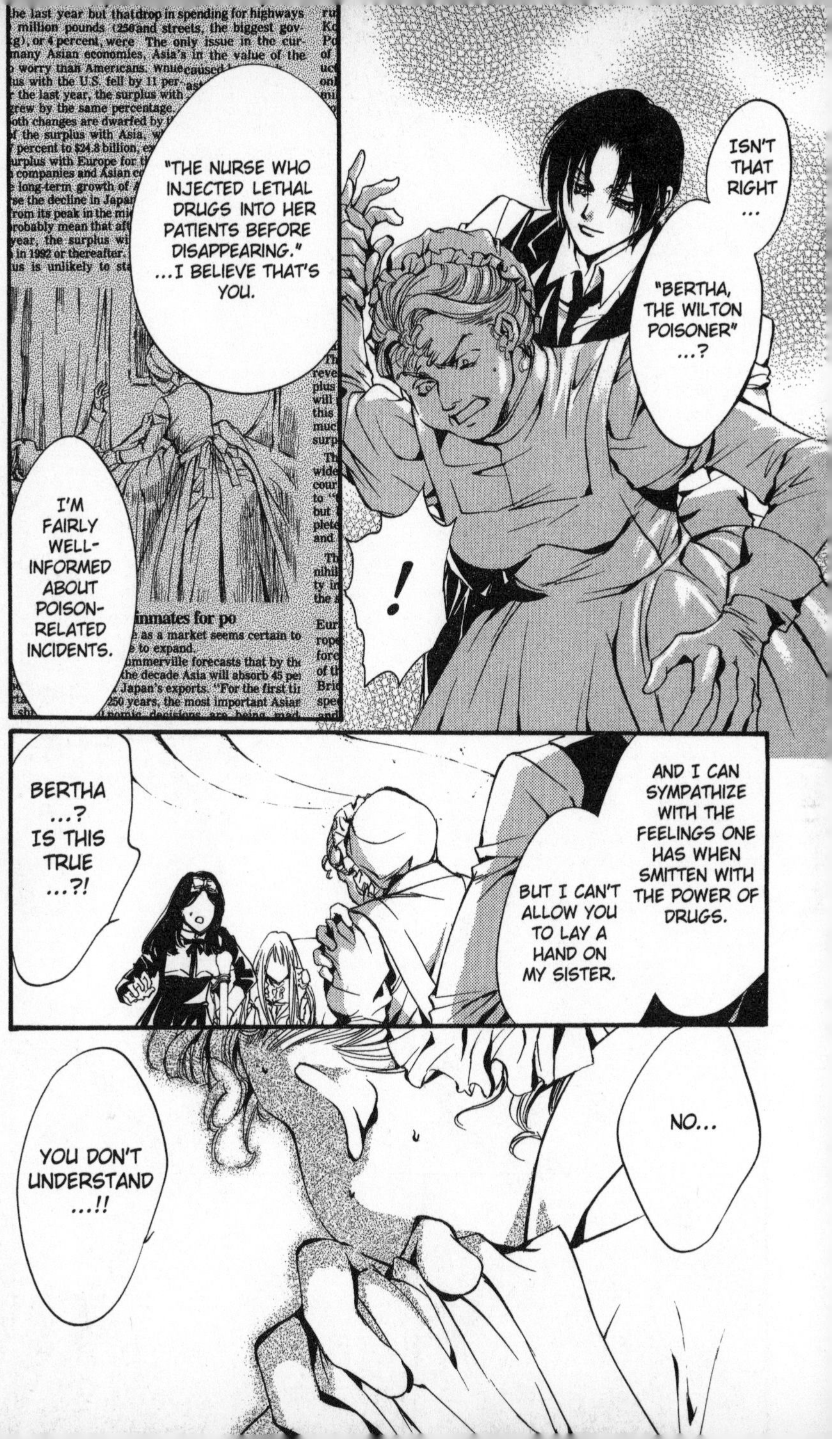
ISN'T THAT RIGHT ...
"BERTHA, THE WILTON POISONER" ...?
!
"THE NURSE WHO INJECTED LETHAL DRUGS INTO HER PATIENTS BEFORE DISAPPEARING." ...I BELIEVE THAT'S YOU.
I'M FAIRLY WELL-INFORMED ABOUT POISON-RELATED INCIDENTS.
AND I CAN SYMPATHIZE WITH THE FEELINGS ONE HAS WHEN SMITTEN WITH THE POWER OF DRUGS.
BUT I CAN'T ALLOW YOU TO LAY A HAND ON MY SISTER.
BERTHA ...? IS THIS TRUE ...?!
NO...
YOU DON'T UNDERSTAND ...!!

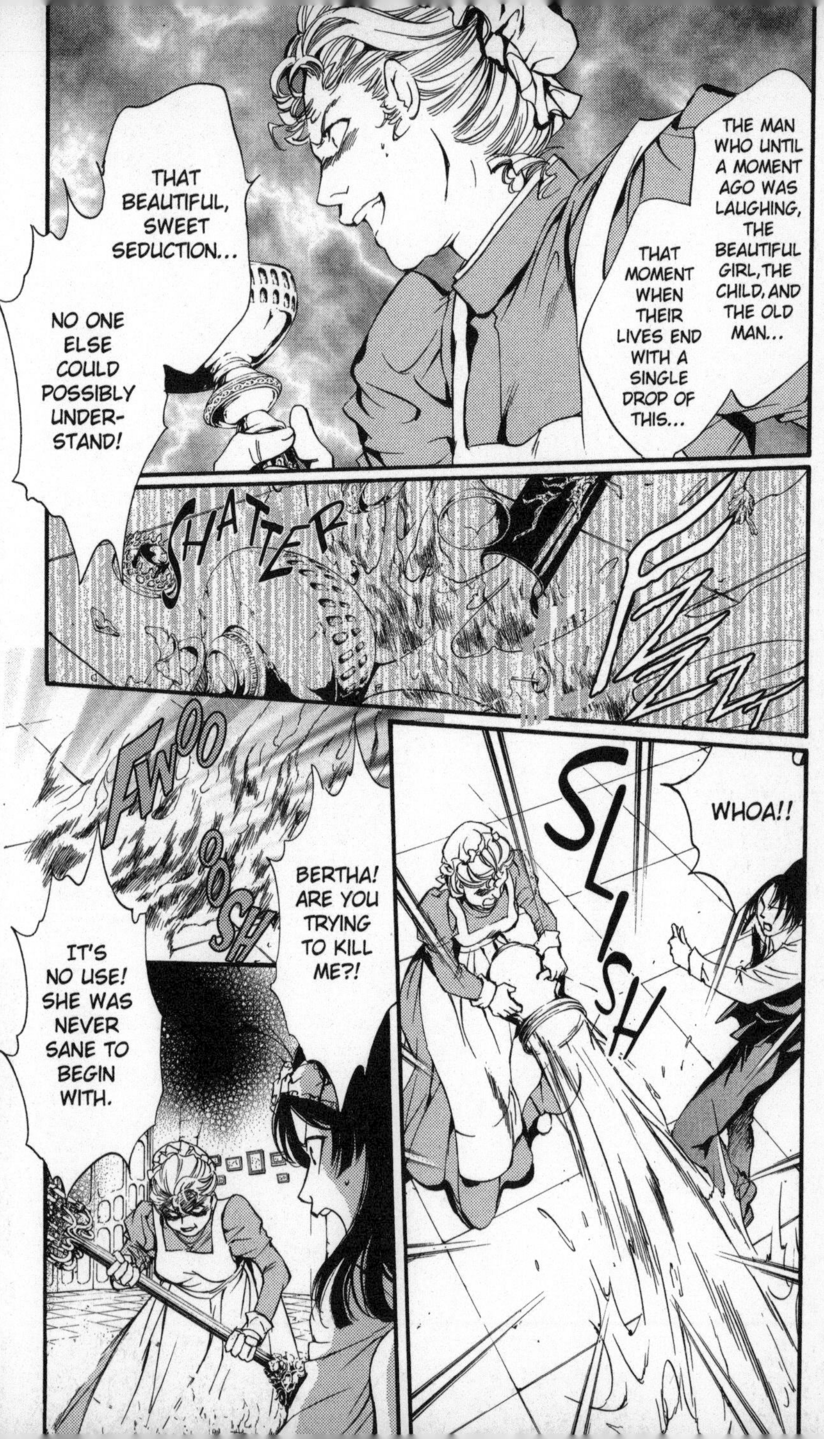
THE MAN WHO UNTIL A MOMENT AGO WAS LAUGHING, THE BEAUTIFUL GIRL, THE CHILD, AND THE OLD MAN...
THAT MOMENT WHEN THEIR LIVES END WITH A SINGLE DROP OF THIS...
THAT BEAUTIFUL, SWEET SEDUCTION...
NO ONE ELSE COULD POSSIBLY UNDER-STAND!
FZZZT
SHATTER
WHOA!!
SLISH
FWOOOOOSH
BERTHA! ARE YOU TRYING TO KILL ME?!
IT'S NO USE! SHE WAS NEVER SANE TO BEGIN WITH.

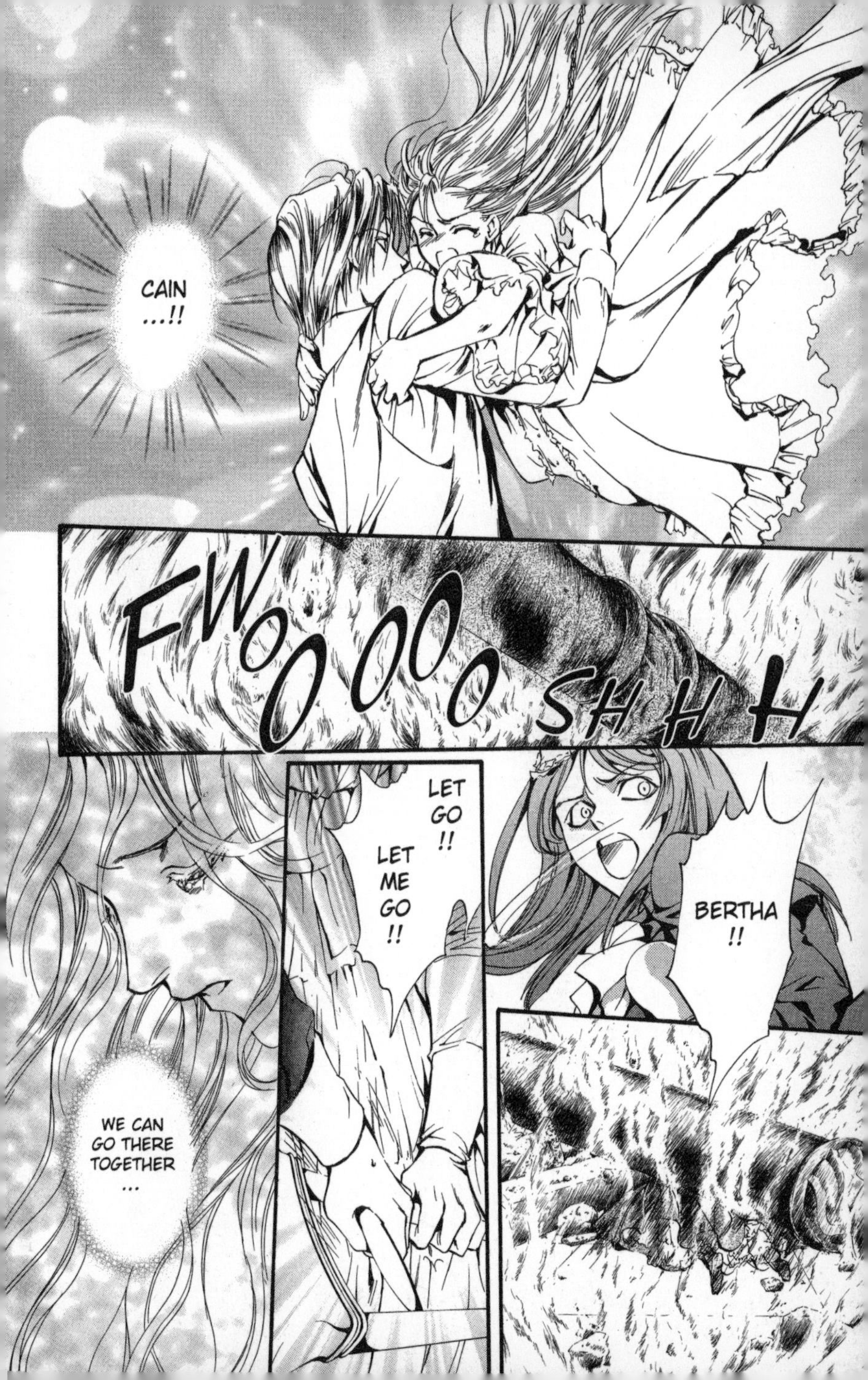
CAIN ...!!
FWOOOOOSHHH
BERTHA !!
LET GO !!
LET ME GO !!
WE CAN GO THERE TOGETHER ...

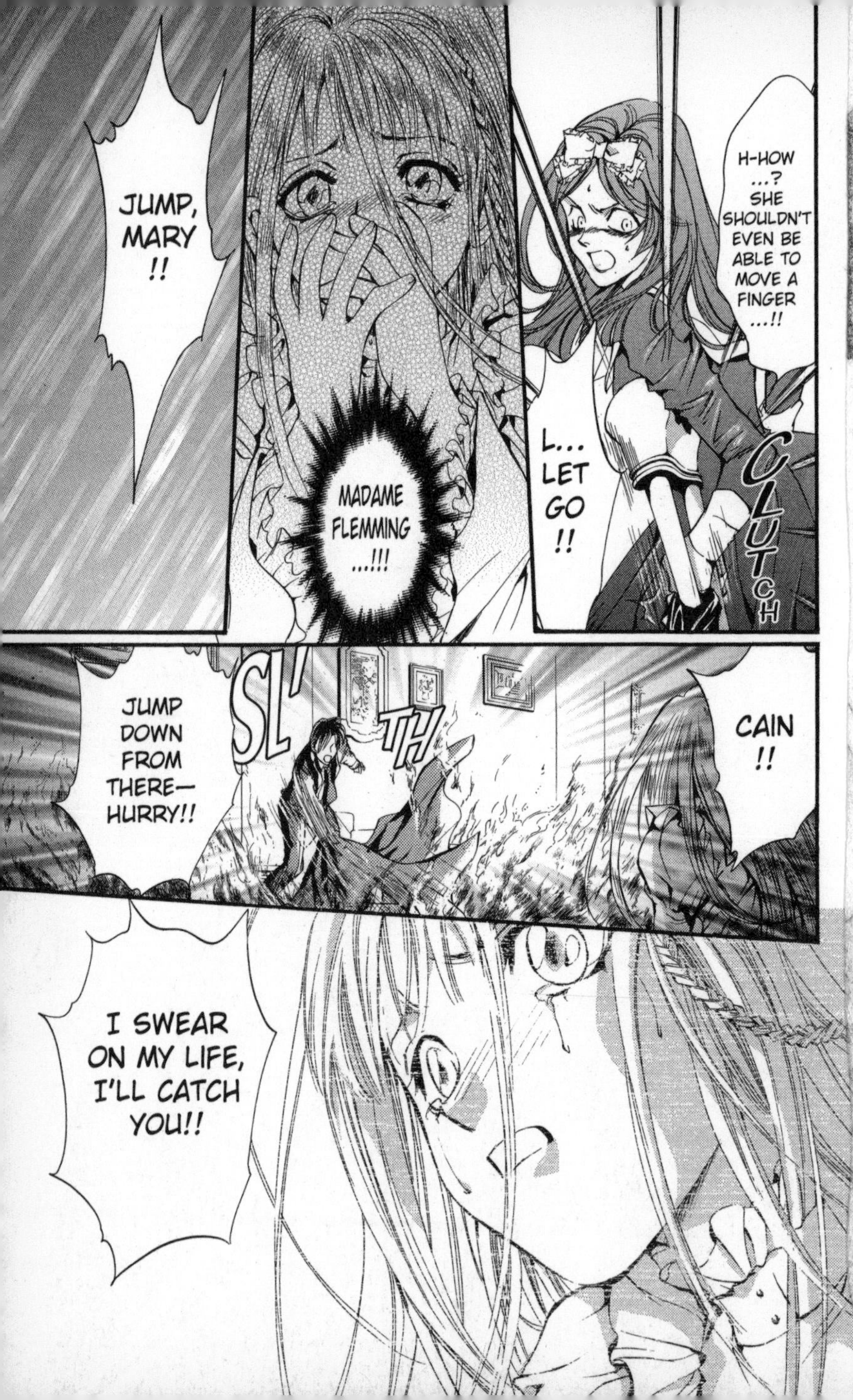
H-HOW ...? SHE SHOULDN'T EVEN BE ABLE TO MOVE A FINGER ...!!
L... LET GO !!
CLUTCH
MADAME FLEMMING ...!!!
JUMP, MARY !!
CAIN !!
SL'TH
JUMP DOWN FROM THERE— HURRY!!
I SWEAR ON MY LIFE, I'LL CATCH YOU!!

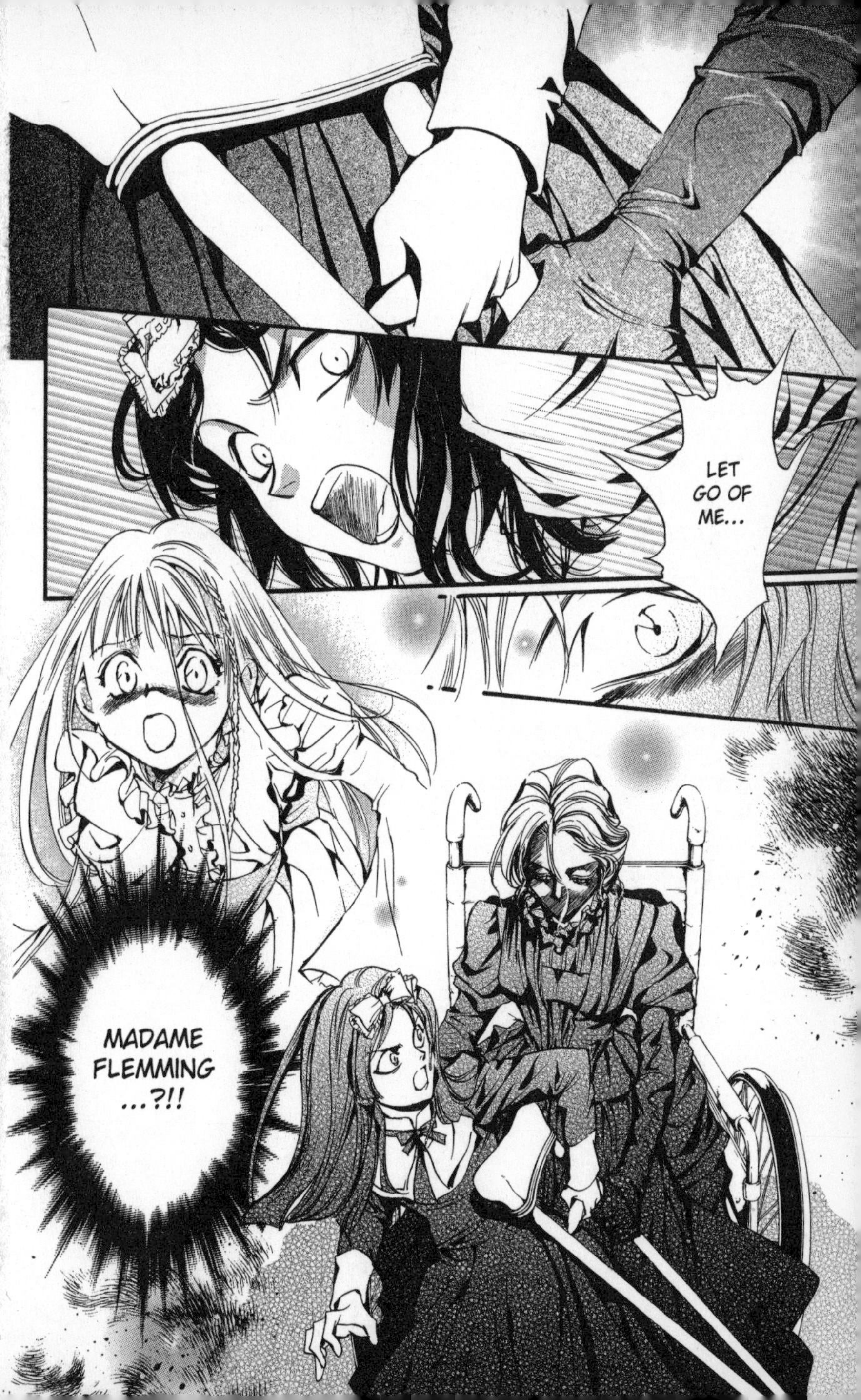
LET GO OF ME...
MADAME FLEMMING ...?!!

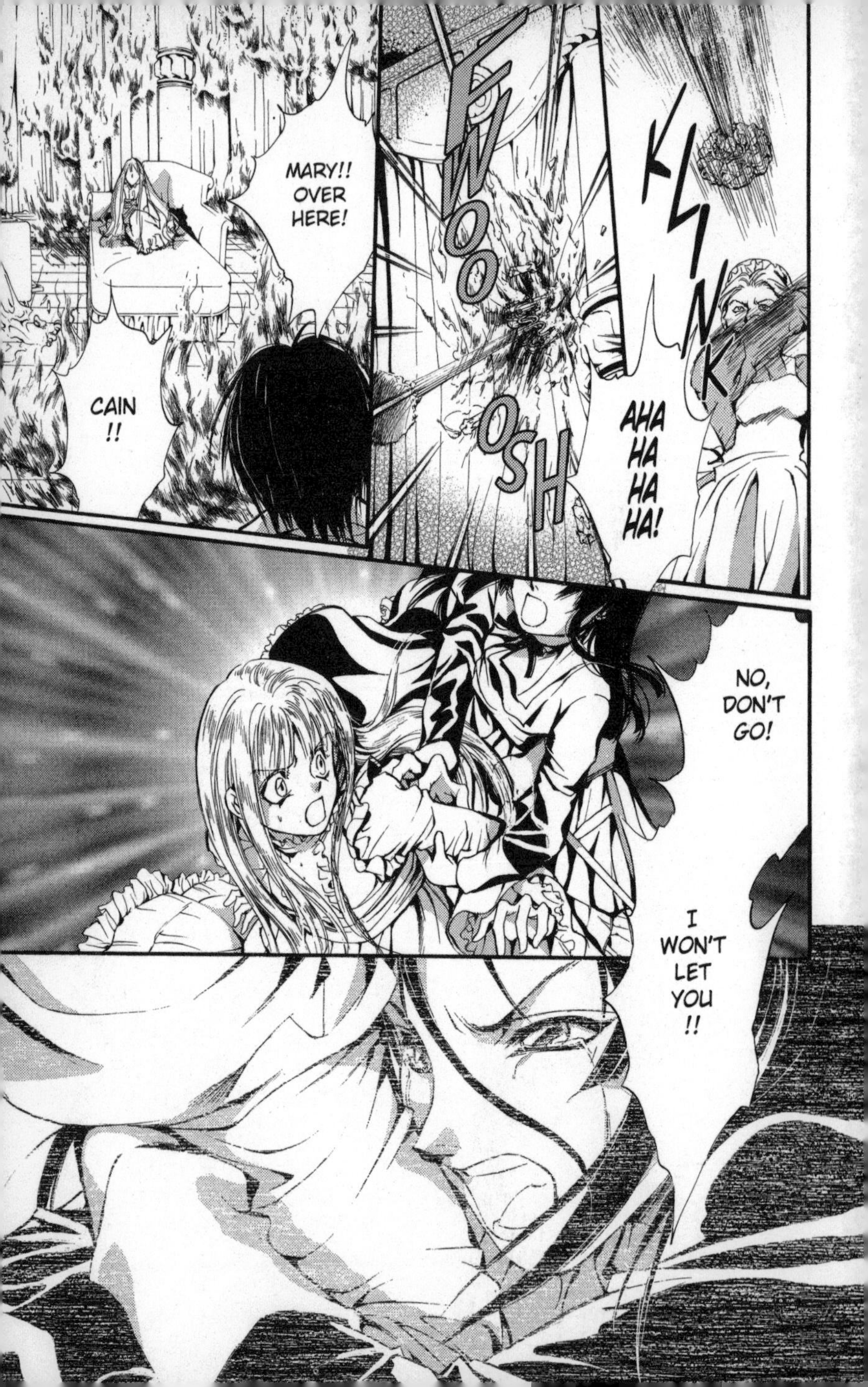
KLINK
FWOOOSH
AHA HA HA HA!
MARY!! OVER HERE!
CAIN !!
NO, DON'T GO!
I WON'T LET YOU !!

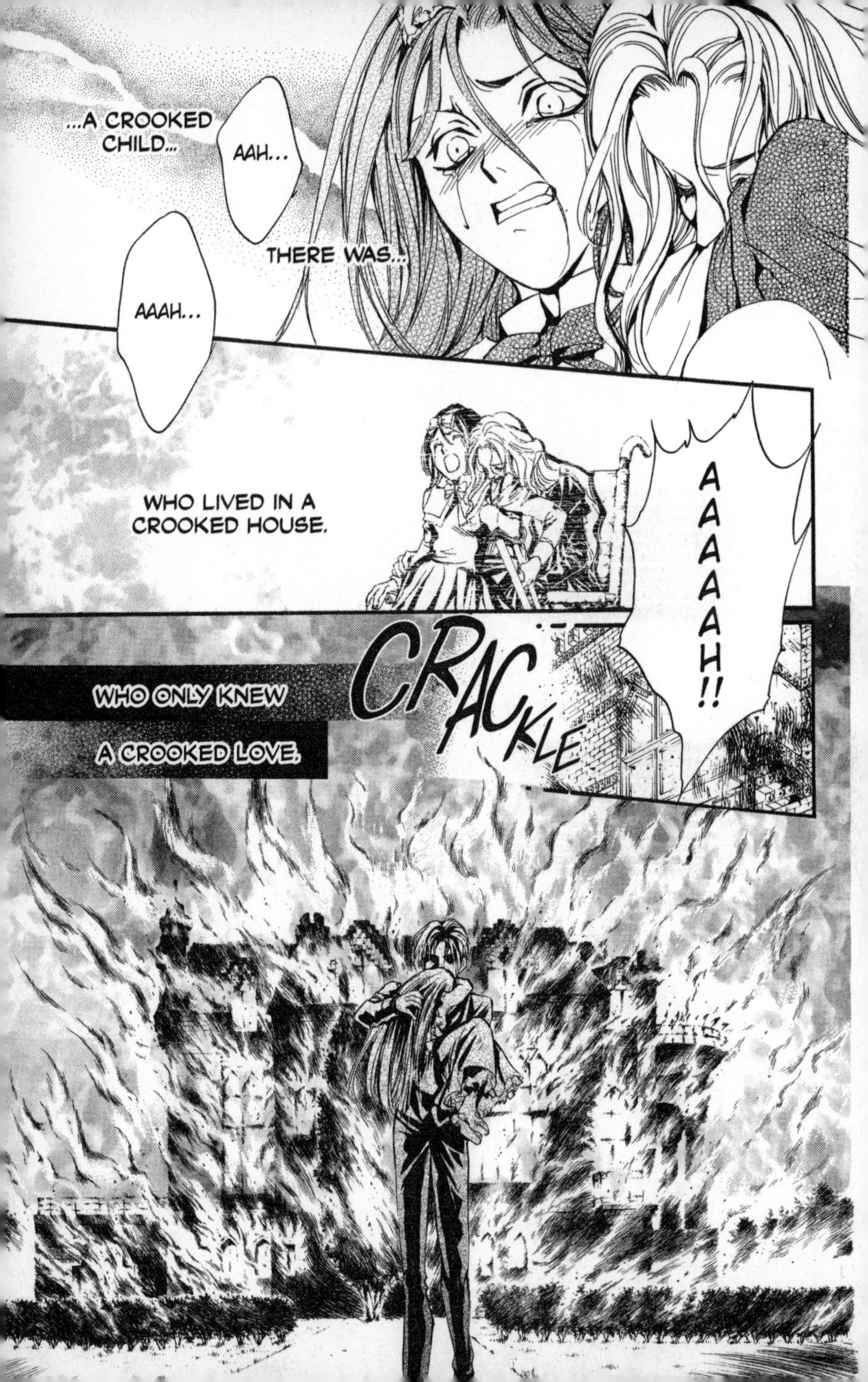
THERE WAS...
AAH...
...A CROOKED CHILD...
AAAH...
AAAAAAH!!
WHO LIVED IN A CROOKED HOUSE.
CRACKLE
WHO ONLY KNEW A CROOKED LOVE.

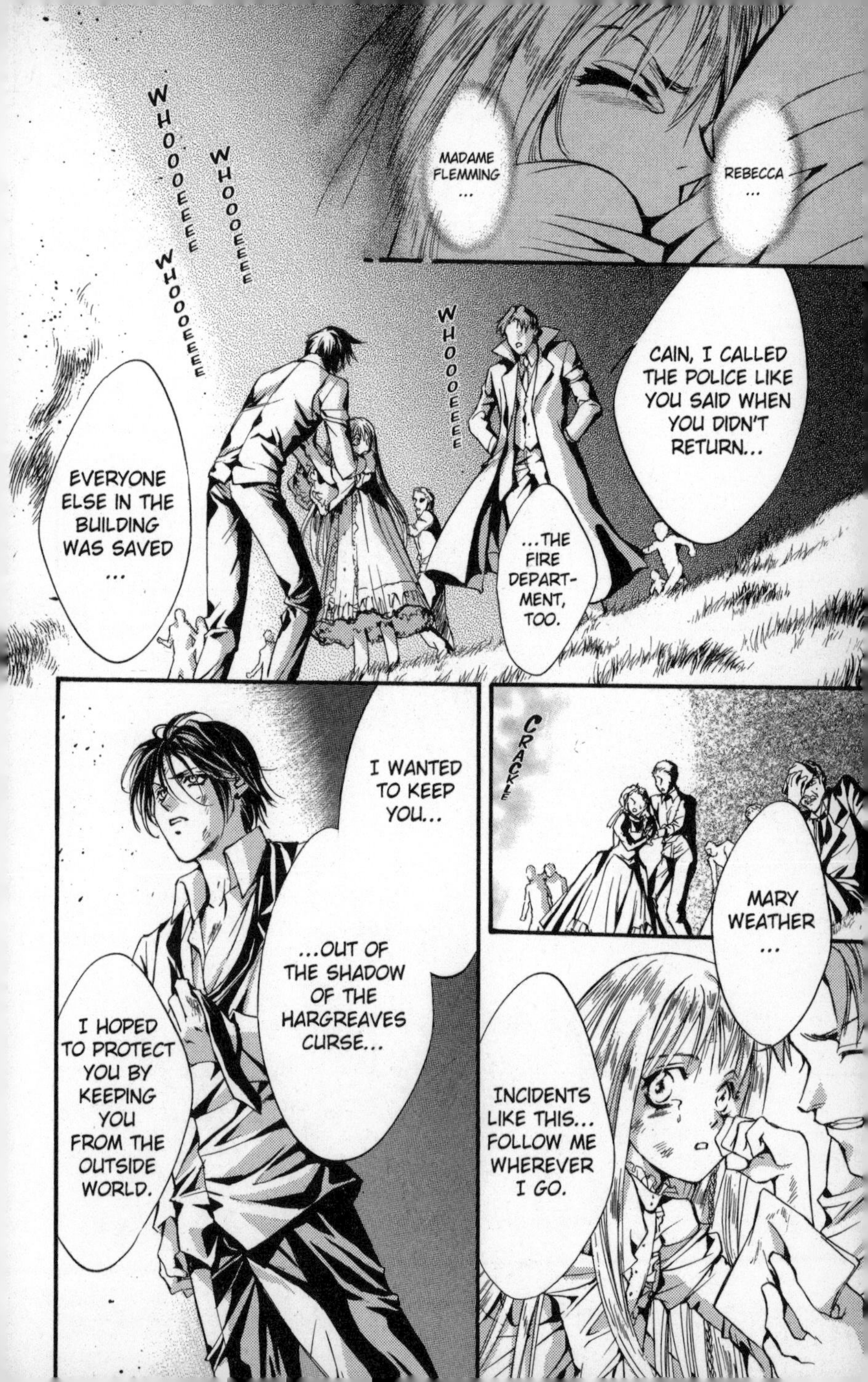
REBECCA...
MADAME FLEMMING...
WHOOOEEEE
WHOOOEEEE
WHOOOEEEE
CAIN, I CALLED THE POLICE LIKE YOU SAID WHEN YOU DIDN'T RETURN...
...THE FIRE DEPARTMENT, TOO.
WHOOOEEEE
EVERYONE ELSE IN THE BUILDING WAS SAVED...
CRACKLE
MARY WEATHER...
INCIDENTS LIKE THIS... FOLLOW ME WHEREVER I GO.
I WANTED TO KEEP YOU...
...OUT OF THE SHADOW OF THE HARGREAVES CURSE...
I HOPED TO PROTECT YOU BY KEEPING YOU FROM THE OUTSIDE WORLD.

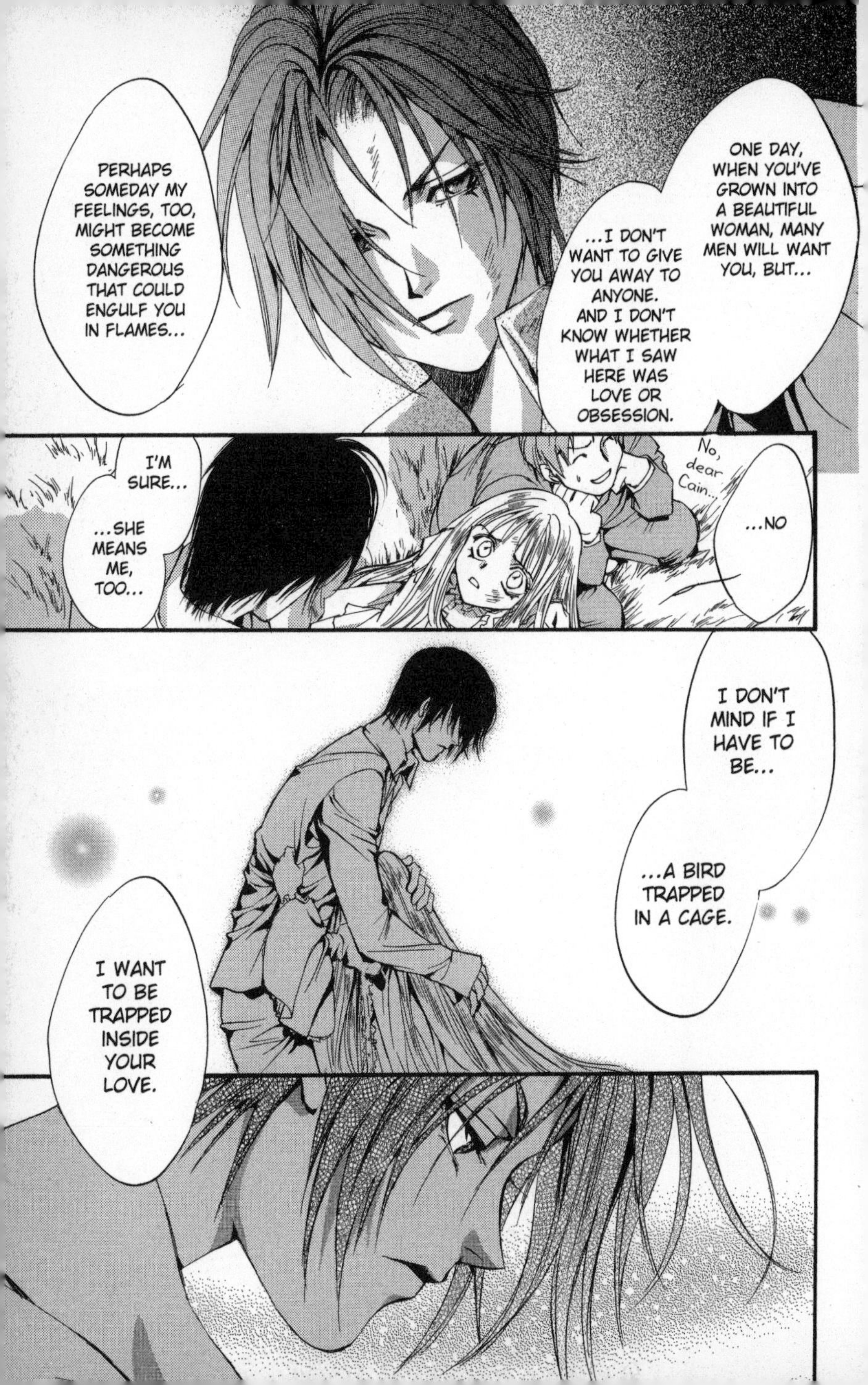
ONE DAY, WHEN YOU'VE GROWN INTO A BEAUTIFUL WOMAN, MANY MEN WILL WANT YOU, BUT...
...I DON'T WANT TO GIVE YOU AWAY TO ANYONE. AND I DON'T KNOW WHETHER WHAT I SAW HERE WAS LOVE OR OBSESSION.
PERHAPS SOMEDAY MY FEELINGS, TOO, MIGHT BECOME SOMETHING DANGEROUS THAT COULD ENGULF YOU IN FLAMES...
No, dear Cain...
...NO
I'M SURE...
...SHE MEANS ME, TOO...
I DON'T MIND IF I HAVE TO BE...
...A BIRD TRAPPED IN A CAGE.
I WANT TO BE TRAPPED INSIDE YOUR LOVE.

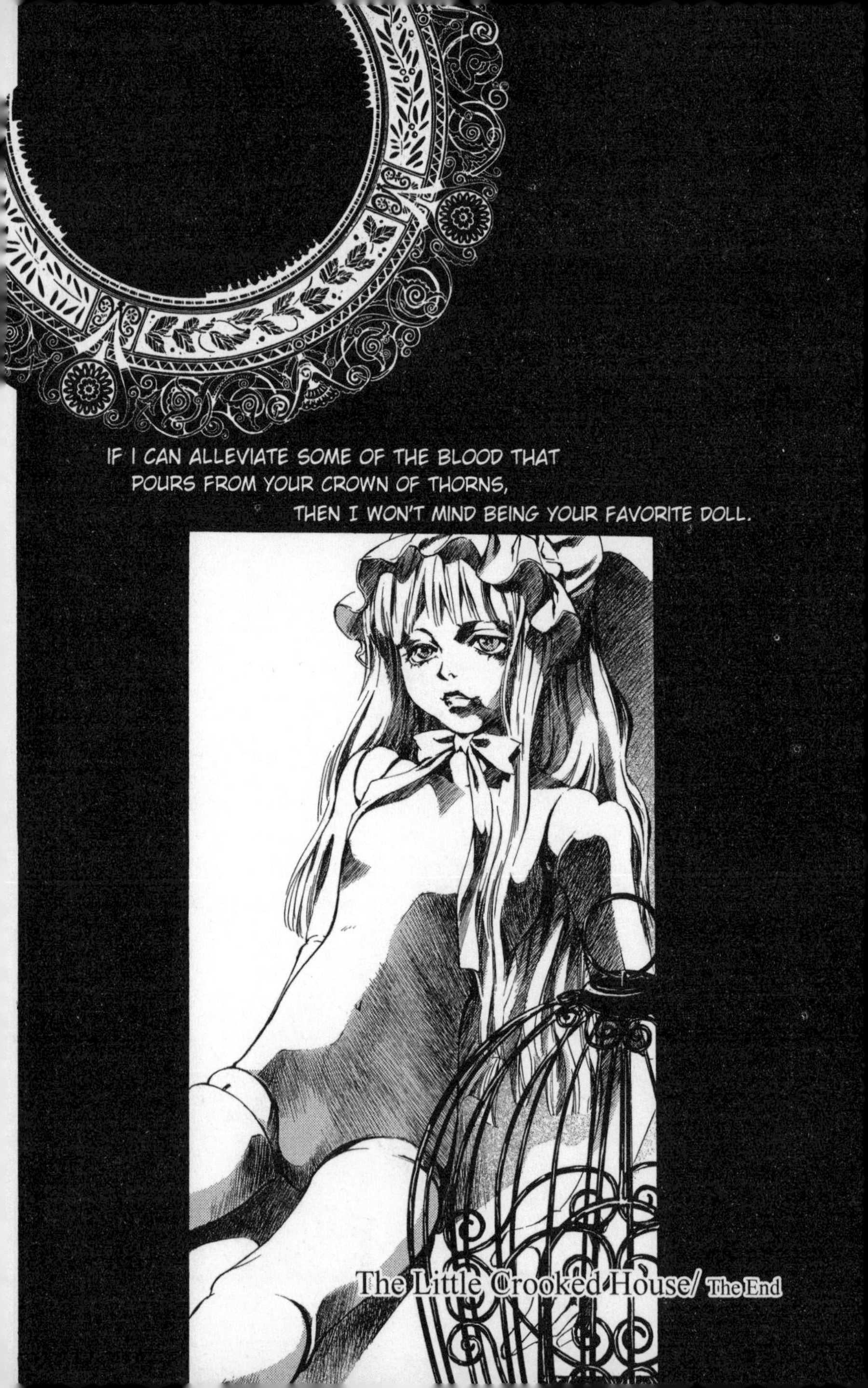
IF I CAN ALLEVIATE SOME OF THE BLOOD THAT POURS FROM YOUR CROWN OF THORNS, THEN I WON'T MIND BEING YOUR FAVORITE DOLL.
The Little Crooked House/ The End

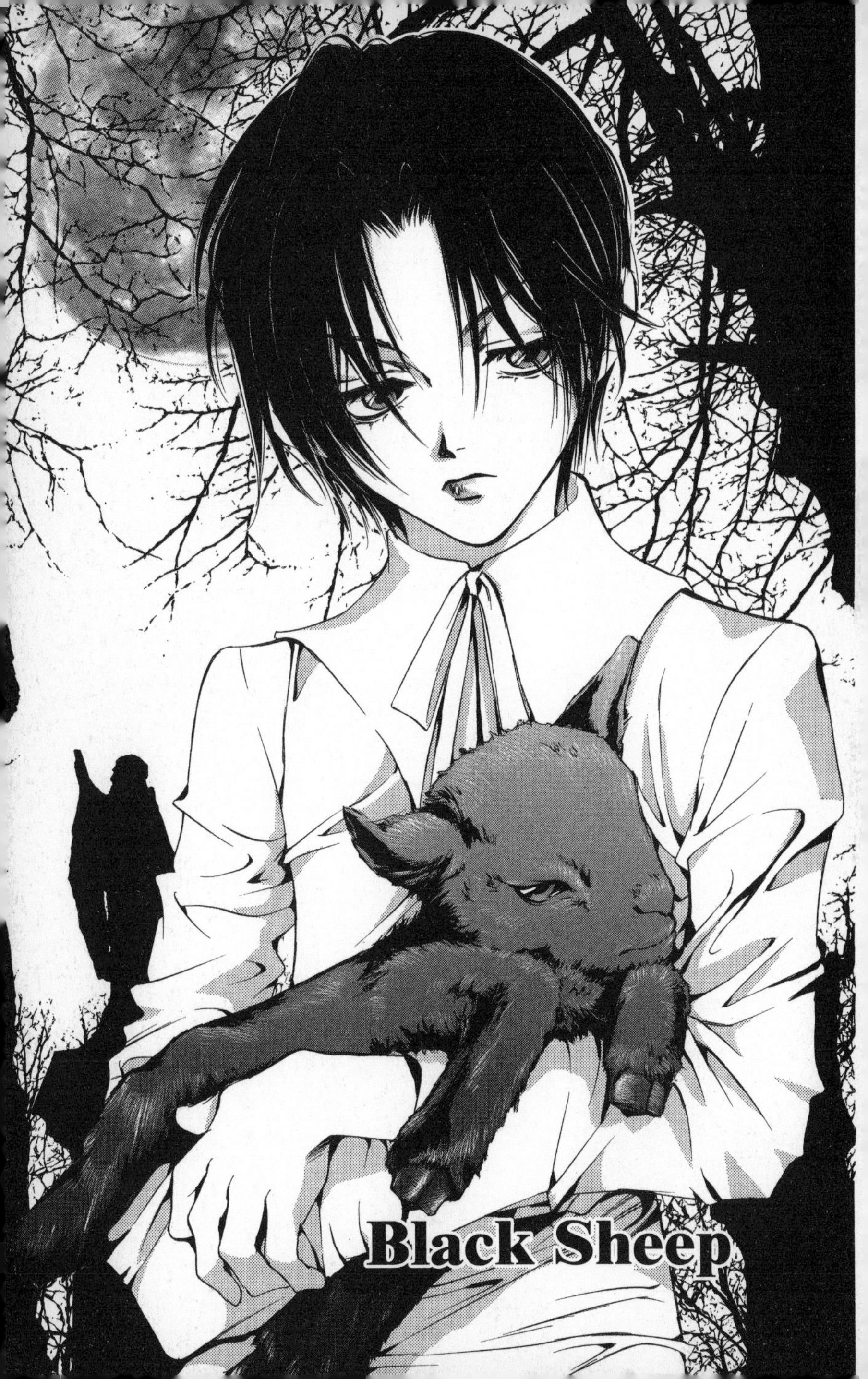
Black Sheep

Black Sheep

BAA, BAA,
BLACK SHEEP...
...HAVE YOU ANY WOOL?
YES SIR, YES SIR, THREE BAGS FULL.
ONE FOR THE MASTER, ONE FOR THE DAME...
...AND ONE FOR THE LITTLE BOY WHO LIVES DOWN THE LANE.
THE ONE BLACK SHEEP WITHIN THE ALL-WHITE FLOCK...
SOUNDS LIKE ME.

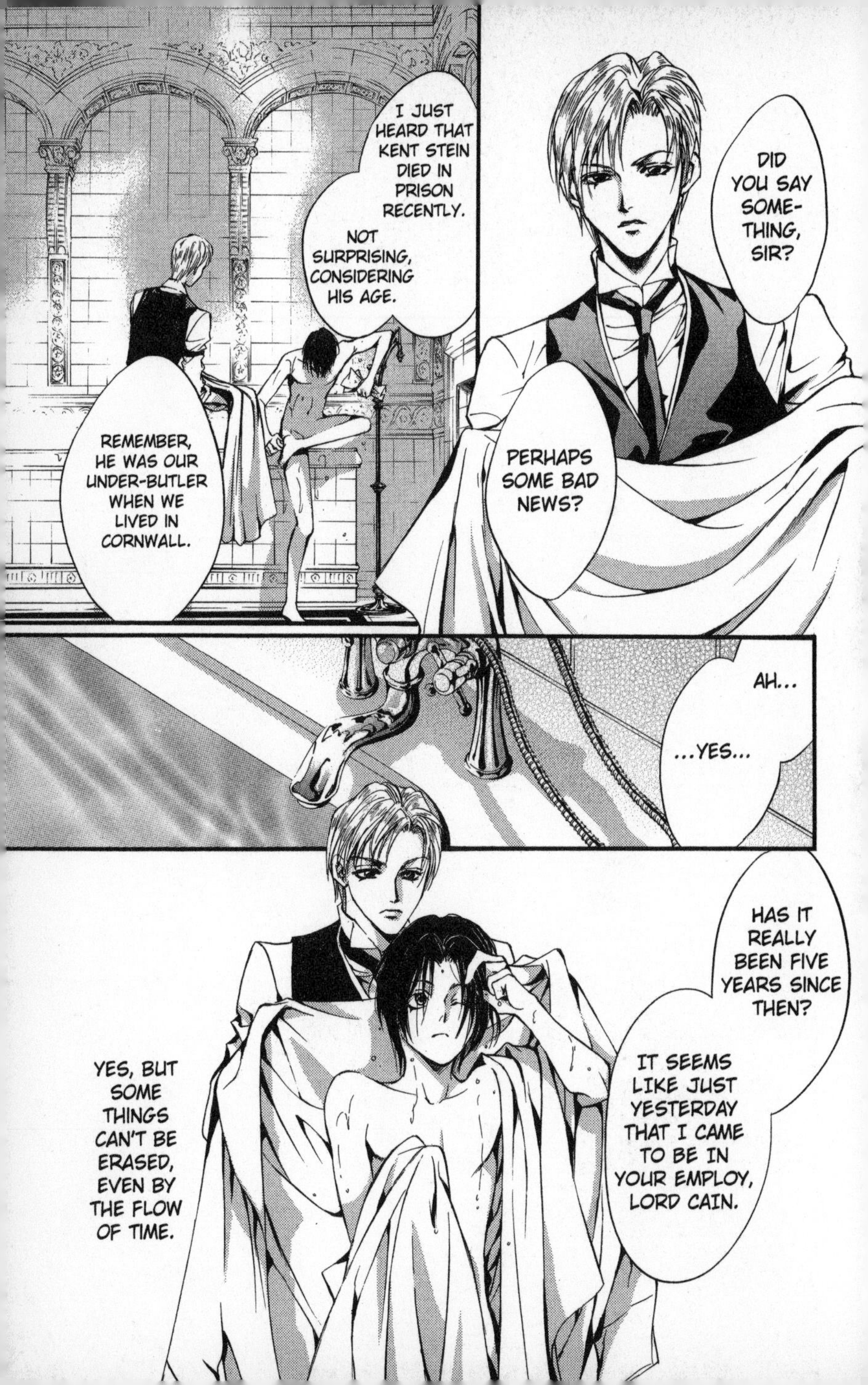
DID YOU SAY SOME-THING, SIR?
PERHAPS SOME BAD NEWS?
I JUST HEARD THAT KENT STEIN DIED IN PRISON RECENTLY.
NOT SURPRISING, CONSIDERING HIS AGE.
REMEMBER, HE WAS OUR UNDER-BUTLER WHEN WE LIVED IN CORNWALL.
AH...
...YES...
HAS IT REALLY BEEN FIVE YEARS SINCE THEN?
IT SEEMS LIKE JUST YESTERDAY THAT I CAME TO BE IN YOUR EMPLOY, LORD CAIN.
YES, BUT SOME THINGS CAN'T BE ERASED, EVEN BY THE FLOW OF TIME.

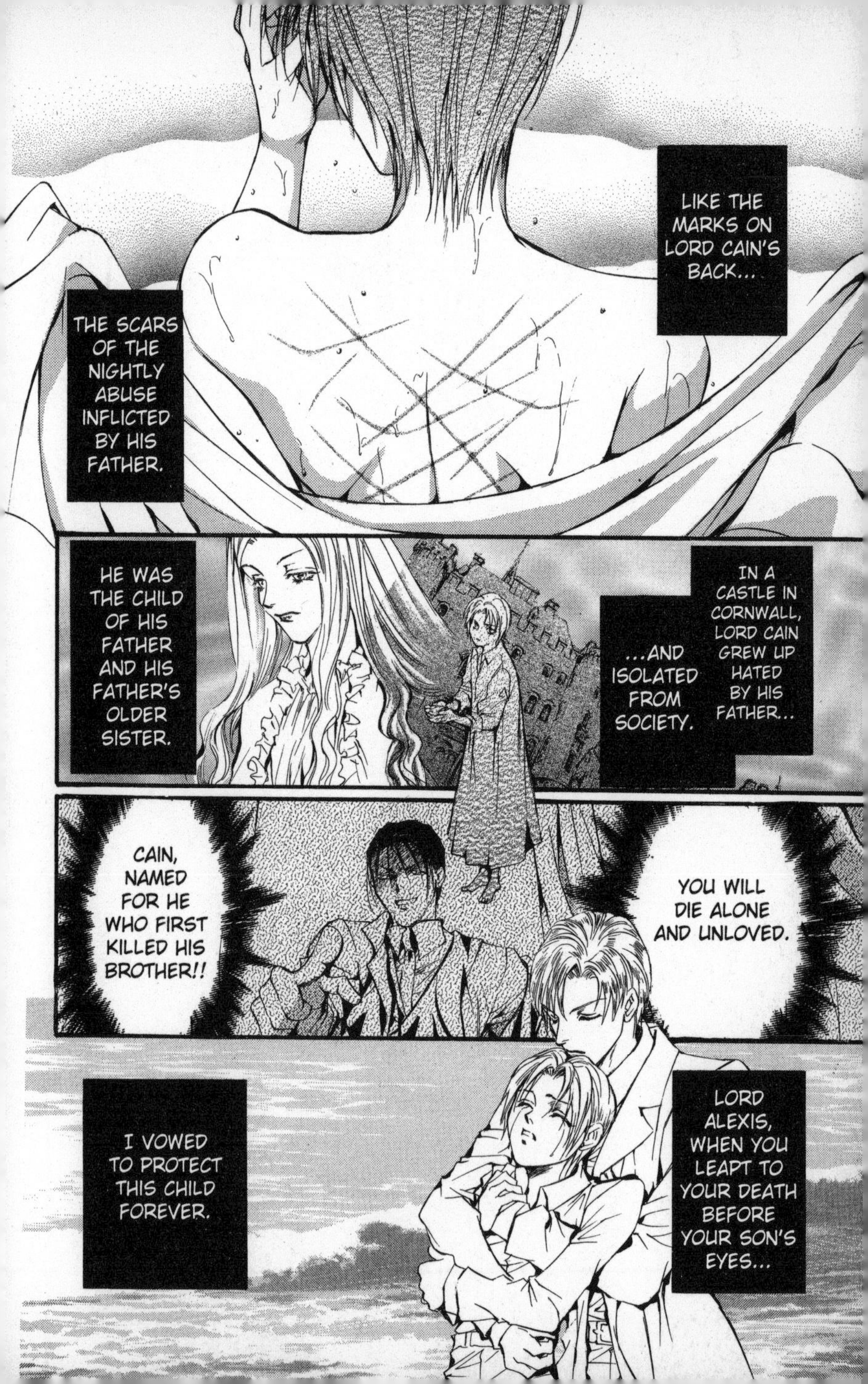
LIKE THE MARKS ON LORD CAIN'S BACK...
THE SCARS OF THE NIGHTLY ABUSE INFLICTED BY HIS FATHER.
IN A CASTLE IN CORNWALL, LORD CAIN GREW UP HATED BY HIS FATHER...
...AND ISOLATED FROM SOCIETY.
HE WAS THE CHILD OF HIS FATHER AND HIS FATHER'S OLDER SISTER.
YOU WILL DIE ALONE AND UNLOVED.
CAIN, NAMED FOR HE WHO FIRST KILLED HIS BROTHER!!
LORD ALEXIS, WHEN YOU LEAPT TO YOUR DEATH BEFORE YOUR SON'S EYES...
I VOWED TO PROTECT THIS CHILD FOREVER.

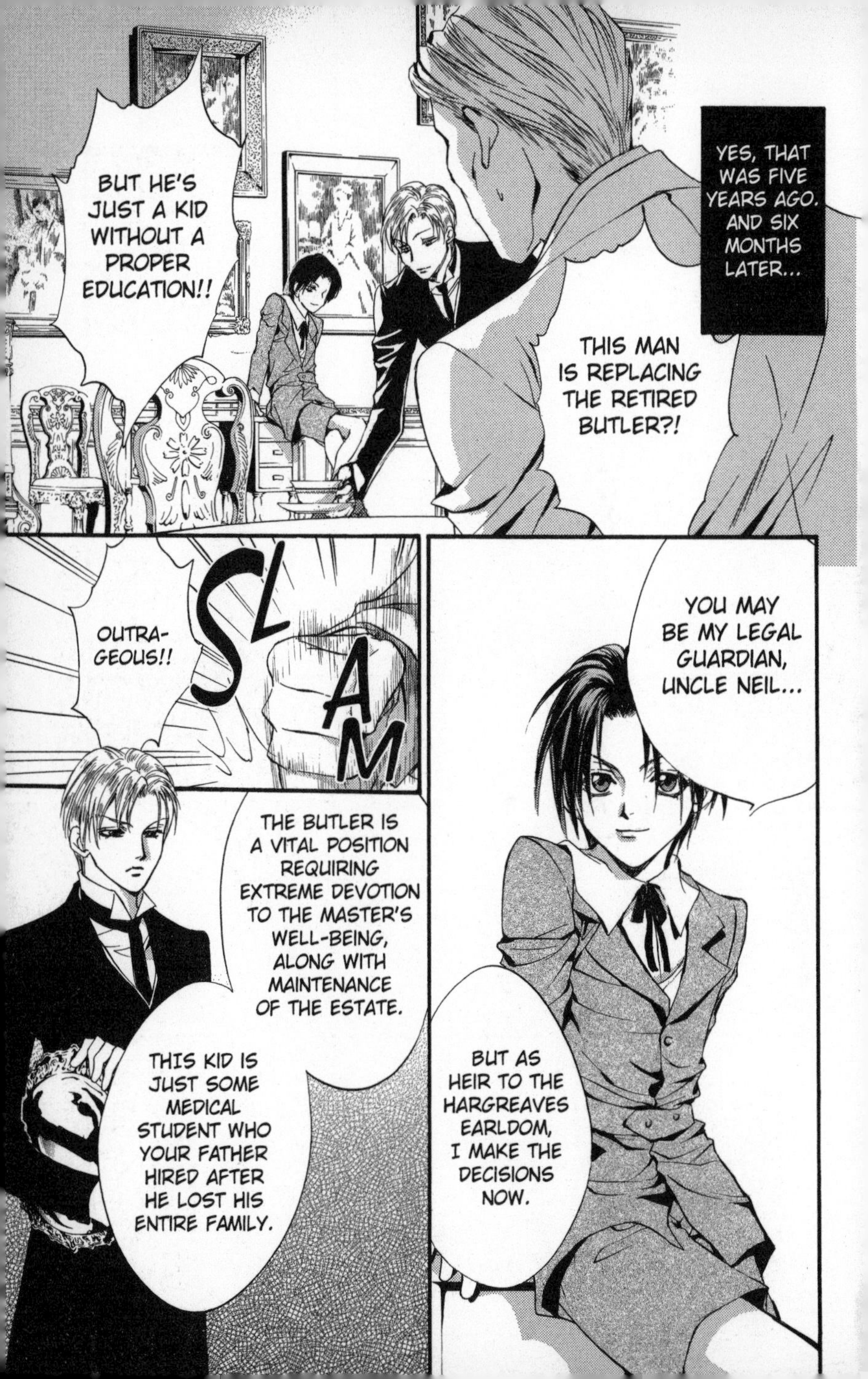
YES, THAT WAS FIVE YEARS AGO. AND SIX MONTHS LATER...
THIS MAN IS REPLACING THE RETIRED BUTLER?!
BUT HE'S JUST A KID WITHOUT A PROPER EDUCATION!!
YOU MAY BE MY LEGAL GUARDIAN, UNCLE NEIL...
BUT AS HEIR TO THE HARGREAVES EARLDOM, I MAKE THE DECISIONS NOW.
SLAM
OUTRA-GEOUS!!
THE BUTLER IS A VITAL POSITION REQUIRING EXTREME DEVOTION TO THE MASTER'S WELL-BEING, ALONG WITH MAINTENANCE OF THE ESTATE.
THIS KID IS JUST SOME MEDICAL STUDENT WHO YOUR FATHER HIRED AFTER HE LOST HIS ENTIRE FAMILY.

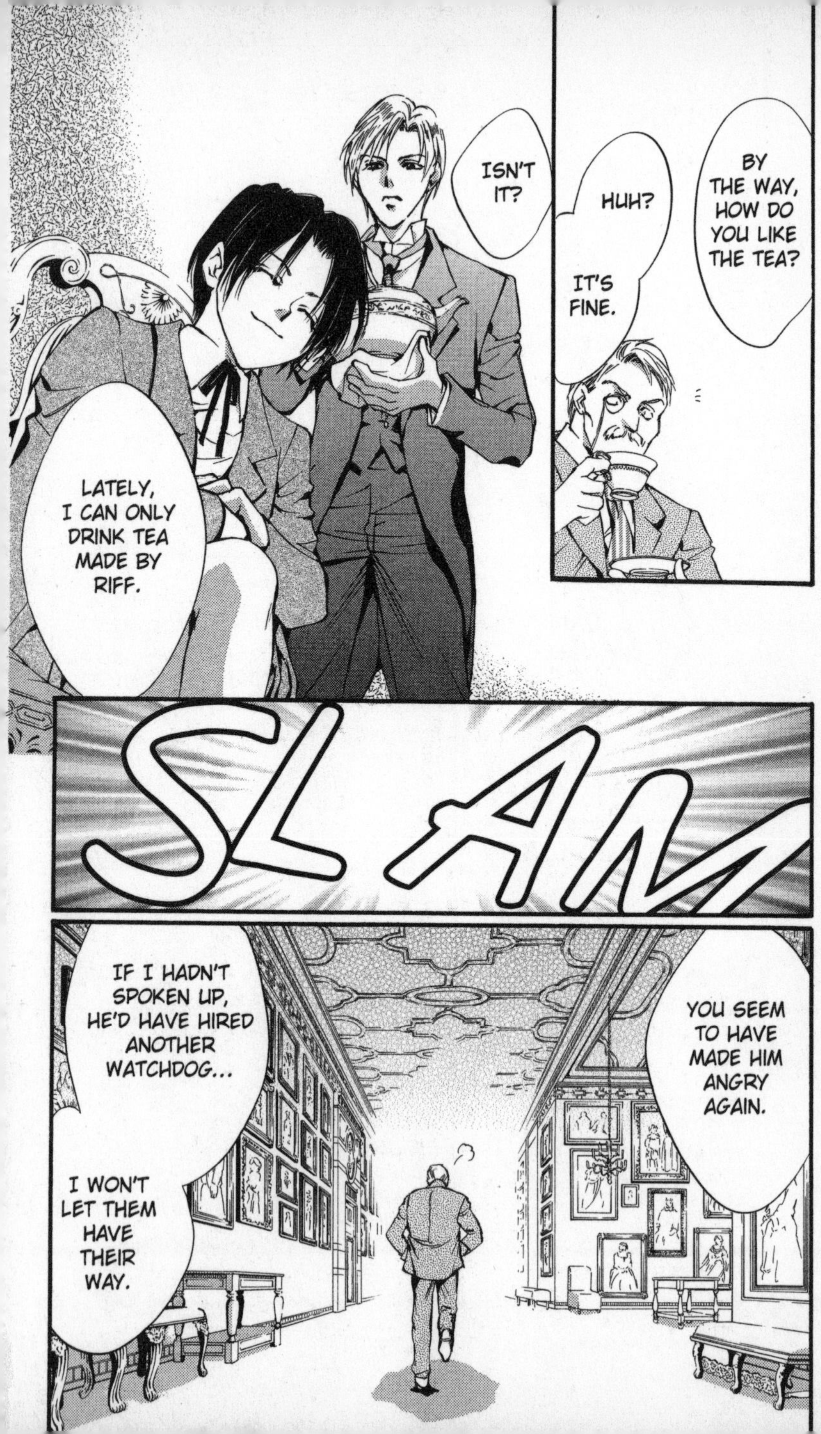
BY THE WAY, HOW DO YOU LIKE THE TEA?
HUH?
IT'S FINE.
ISN'T IT?
LATELY, I CAN ONLY DRINK TEA MADE BY RIFF.
SLAM
YOU SEEM TO HAVE MADE HIM ANGRY AGAIN.
IF I HADN'T SPOKEN UP, HE'D HAVE HIRED ANOTHER WATCHDOG...
I WON'T LET THEM HAVE THEIR WAY.

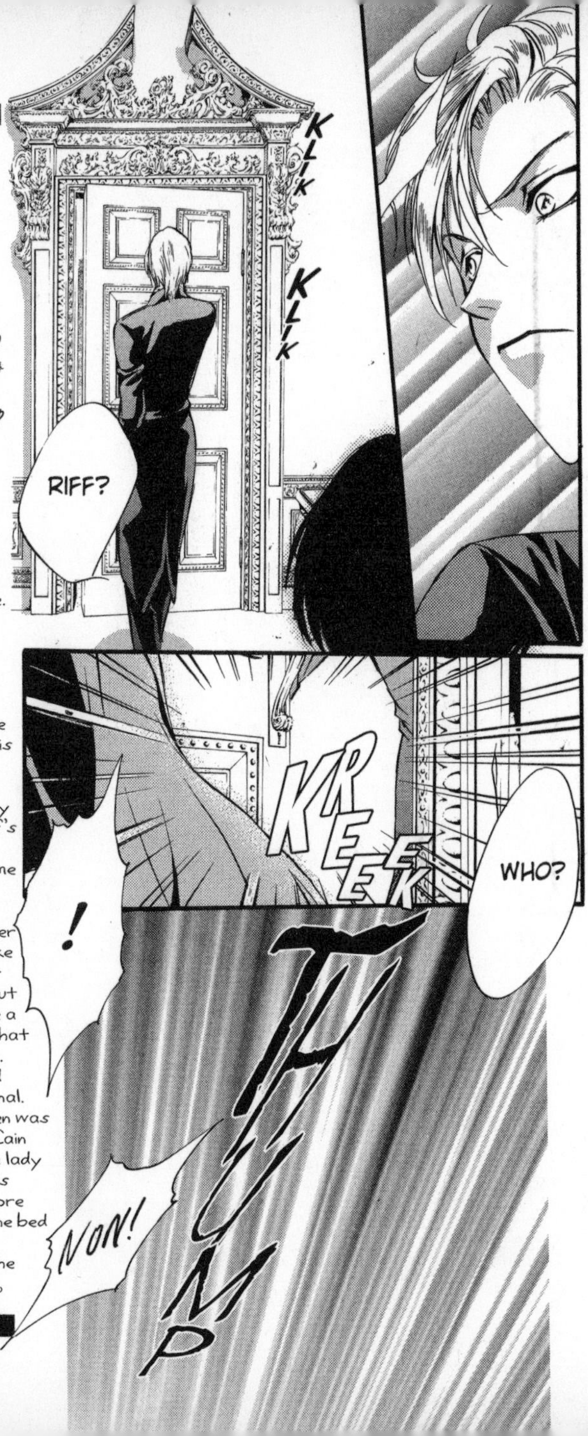
KLIK
KLIK
RIFF?
KREEEK
WHO?
!
THUMP
NON!

Black Sheep.

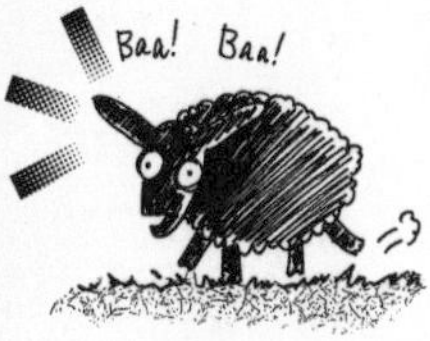
Baa! Baa!

Baa, baa, black sheep
Have you any wool?
Yes, sir, yes, sir,
Three bags full: ~

I was told that this poem was actually a comment on the wool tax laws at the time. Apparently, sheep have a 1/100 chance of turning out black due to genetic mutations. I myself think black sheep are rather beautiful. This time I had a specific schedule in mind and planned to do a story about Cain's and Riff's past in chapter 4. I didn't want first-time readers to wonder about the scars on Cain's back in Chapter 1, so I decided to make the room look darker with screen tones. But one reader wrote me a letter pointing out that there were no scars. Please rest assured that it was intentional. The lighting back then was fairly dark so that Cain could get it on with a lady without her seeing his scars. And right before daylight he leaves the bed before it gets light outside. No, I guess he isn't a very nice man, is he?

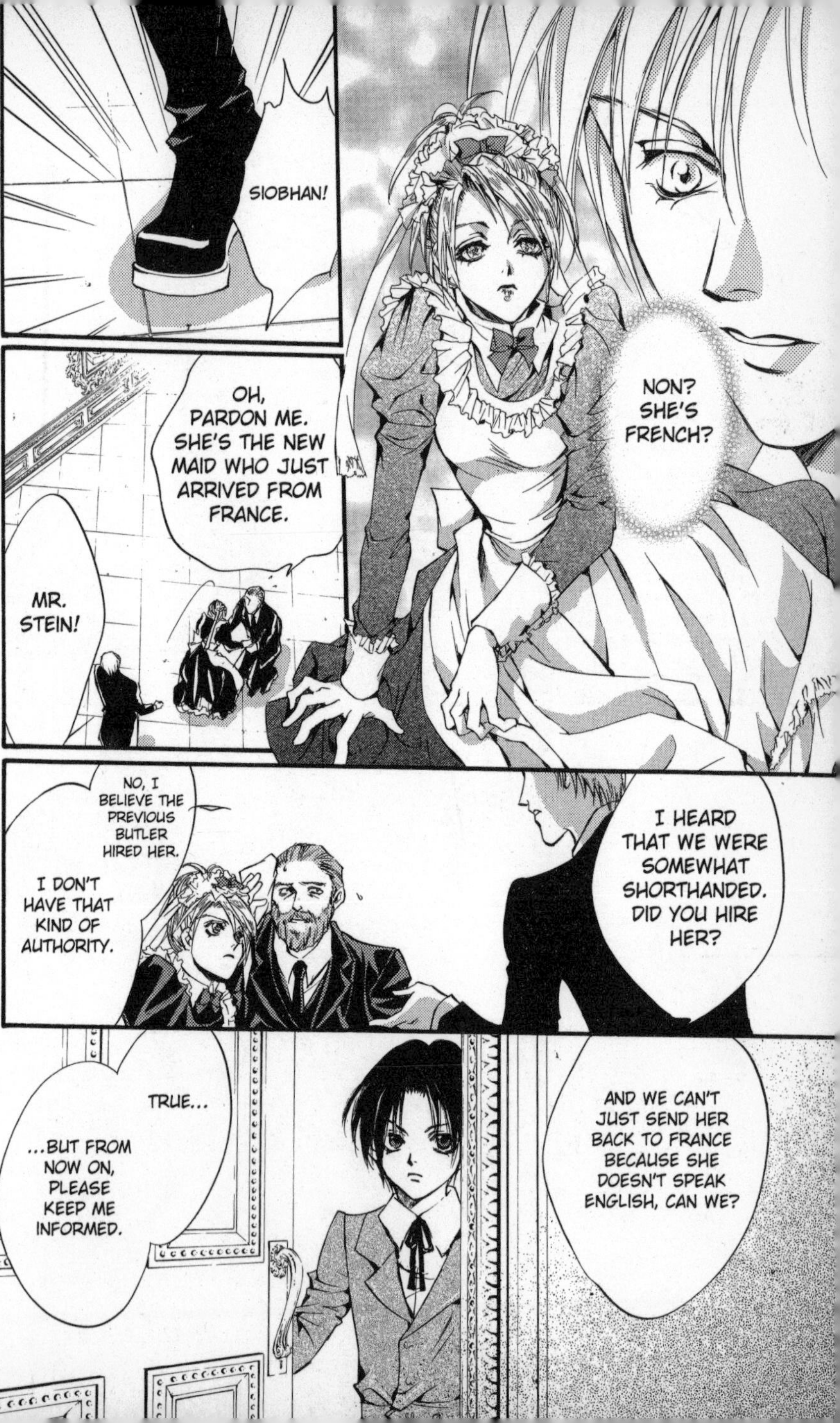
NON? SHE'S FRENCH?
SIOBHAN!
OH, PARDON ME. SHE'S THE NEW MAID WHO JUST ARRIVED FROM FRANCE.
MR. STEIN!
I HEARD THAT WE WERE SOMEWHAT SHORTHANDED. DID YOU HIRE HER?
NO, I BELIEVE THE PREVIOUS BUTLER HIRED HER.
I DON'T HAVE THAT KIND OF AUTHORITY.
AND WE CAN'T JUST SEND HER BACK TO FRANCE BECAUSE SHE DOESN'T SPEAK ENGLISH, CAN WE?
TRUE...
...BUT FROM NOW ON, PLEASE KEEP ME INFORMED.

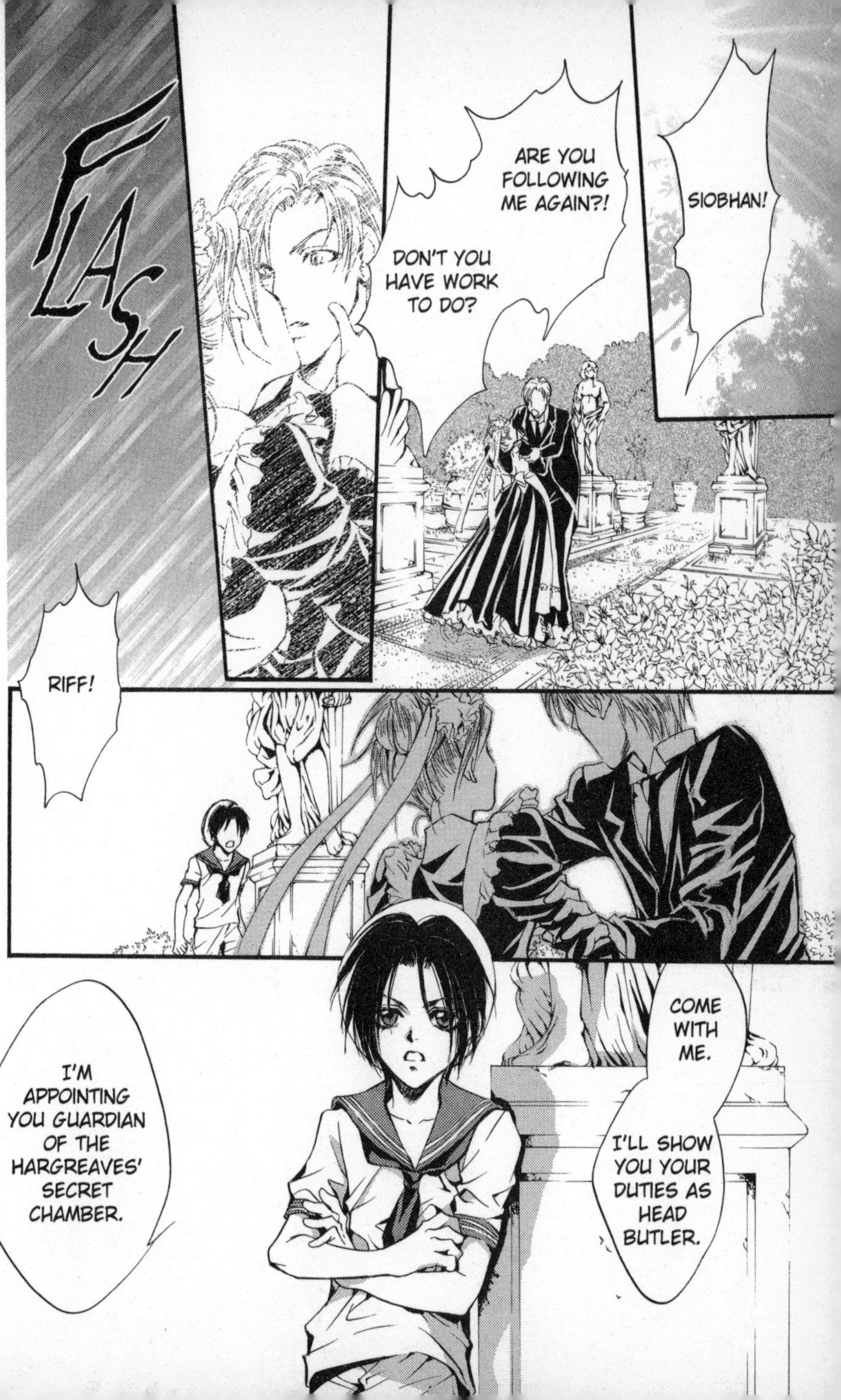
SIOBHAN!
ARE YOU FOLLOWING ME AGAIN?!
DON'T YOU HAVE WORK TO DO?
FLASH
RIFF!
COME WITH ME.
I'LL SHOW YOU YOUR DUTIES AS HEAD BUTLER.
I'M APPOINTING YOU GUARDIAN OF THE HARGREAVES' SECRET CHAMBER.

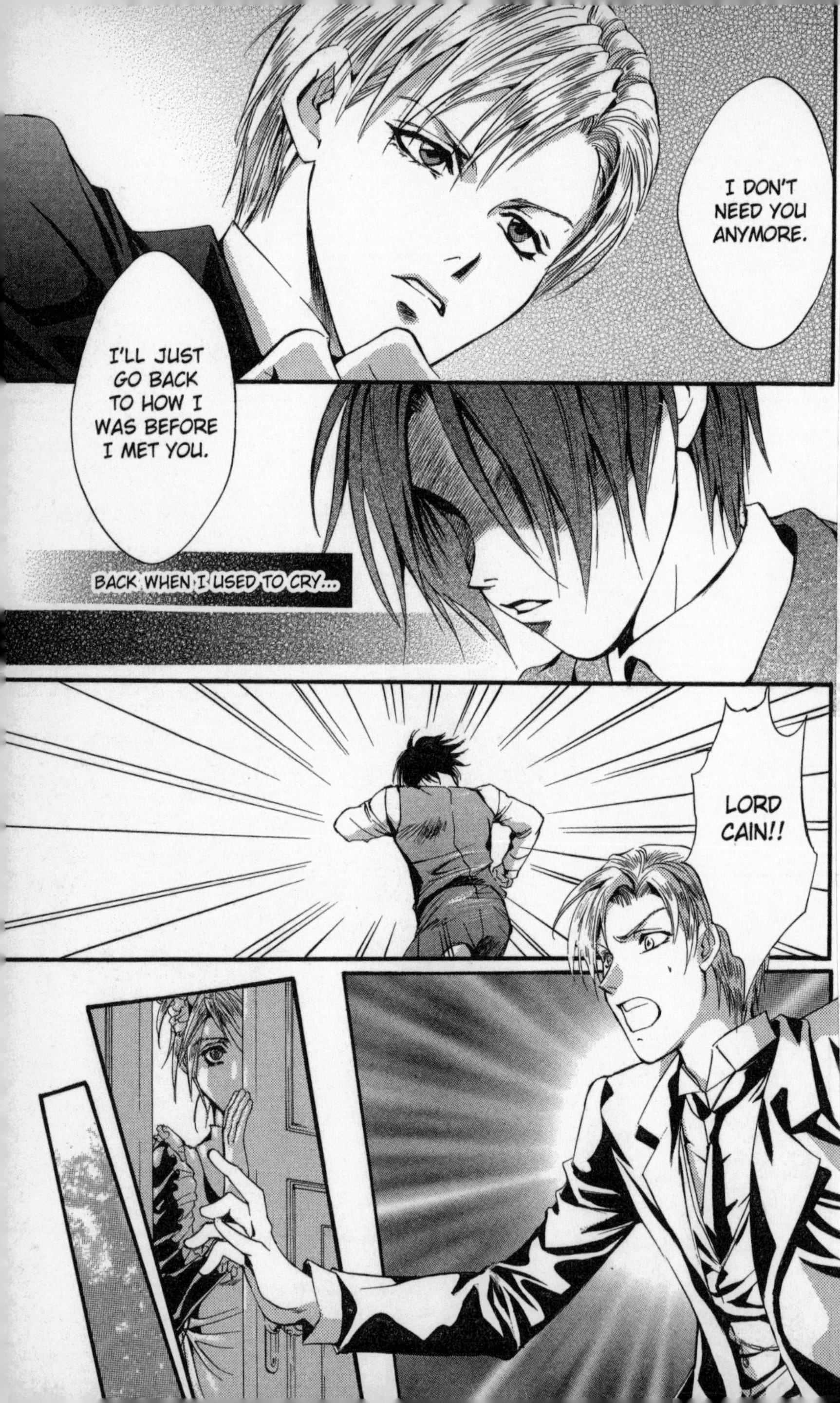
I DON'T NEED YOU ANYMORE.
I'LL JUST GO BACK TO HOW I WAS BEFORE I MET YOU.
BACK WHEN I USED TO CRY...
LORD CAIN!!

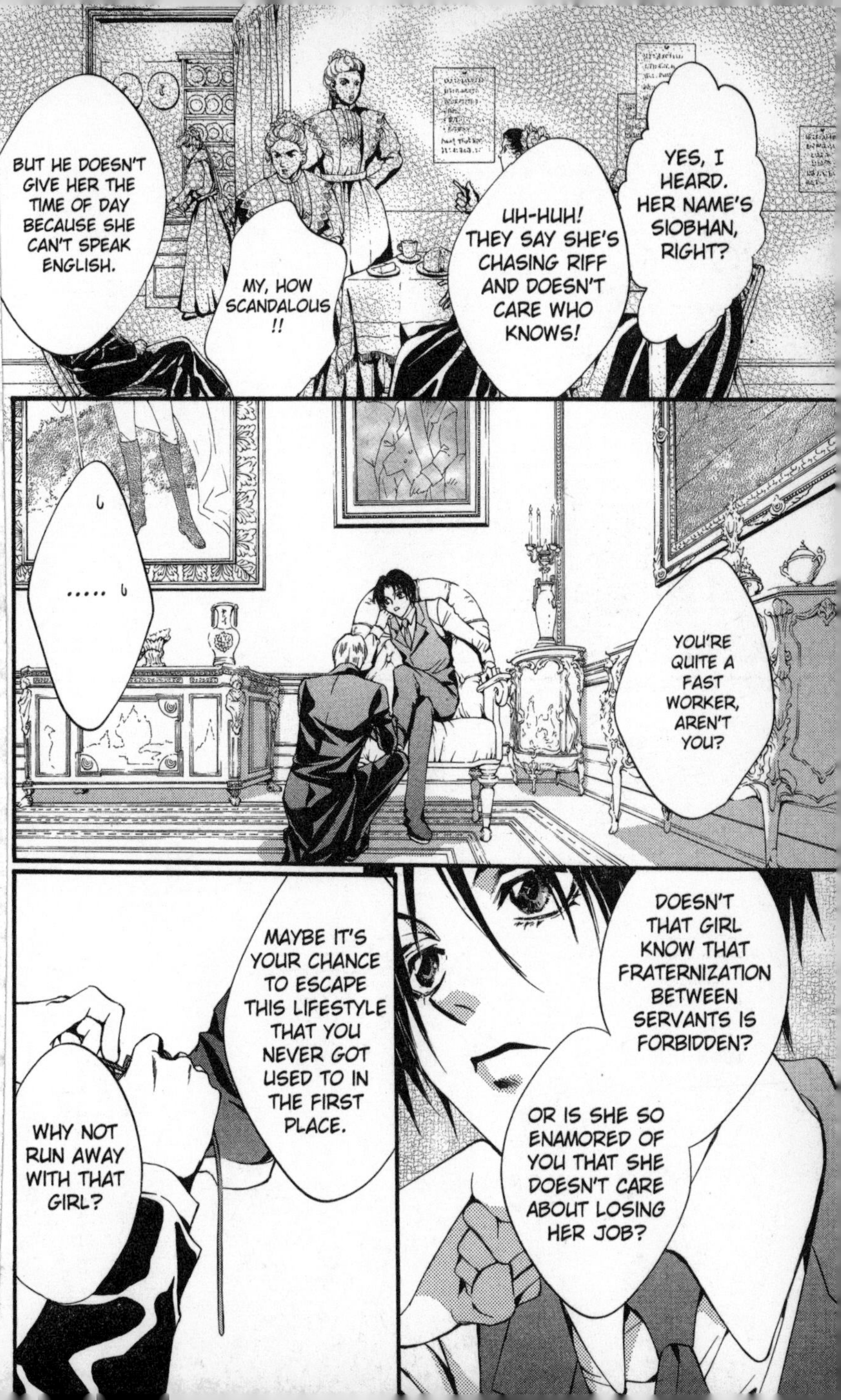
YES, I HEARD. HER NAME'S SIOBHAN, RIGHT?
UH-HUH! THEY SAY SHE'S CHASING RIFF AND DOESN'T CARE WHO KNOWS!
MY, HOW SCANDALOUS !!
BUT HE DOESN'T GIVE HER THE TIME OF DAY BECAUSE SHE CAN'T SPEAK ENGLISH.
YOU'RE QUITE A FAST WORKER, AREN'T YOU?
.....
DOESN'T THAT GIRL KNOW THAT FRATERNIZATION BETWEEN SERVANTS IS FORBIDDEN?
OR IS SHE SO ENAMORED OF YOU THAT SHE DOESN'T CARE ABOUT LOSING HER JOB?
MAYBE IT'S YOUR CHANCE TO ESCAPE THIS LIFESTYLE THAT YOU NEVER GOT USED TO IN THE FIRST PLACE.
WHY NOT RUN AWAY WITH THAT GIRL?

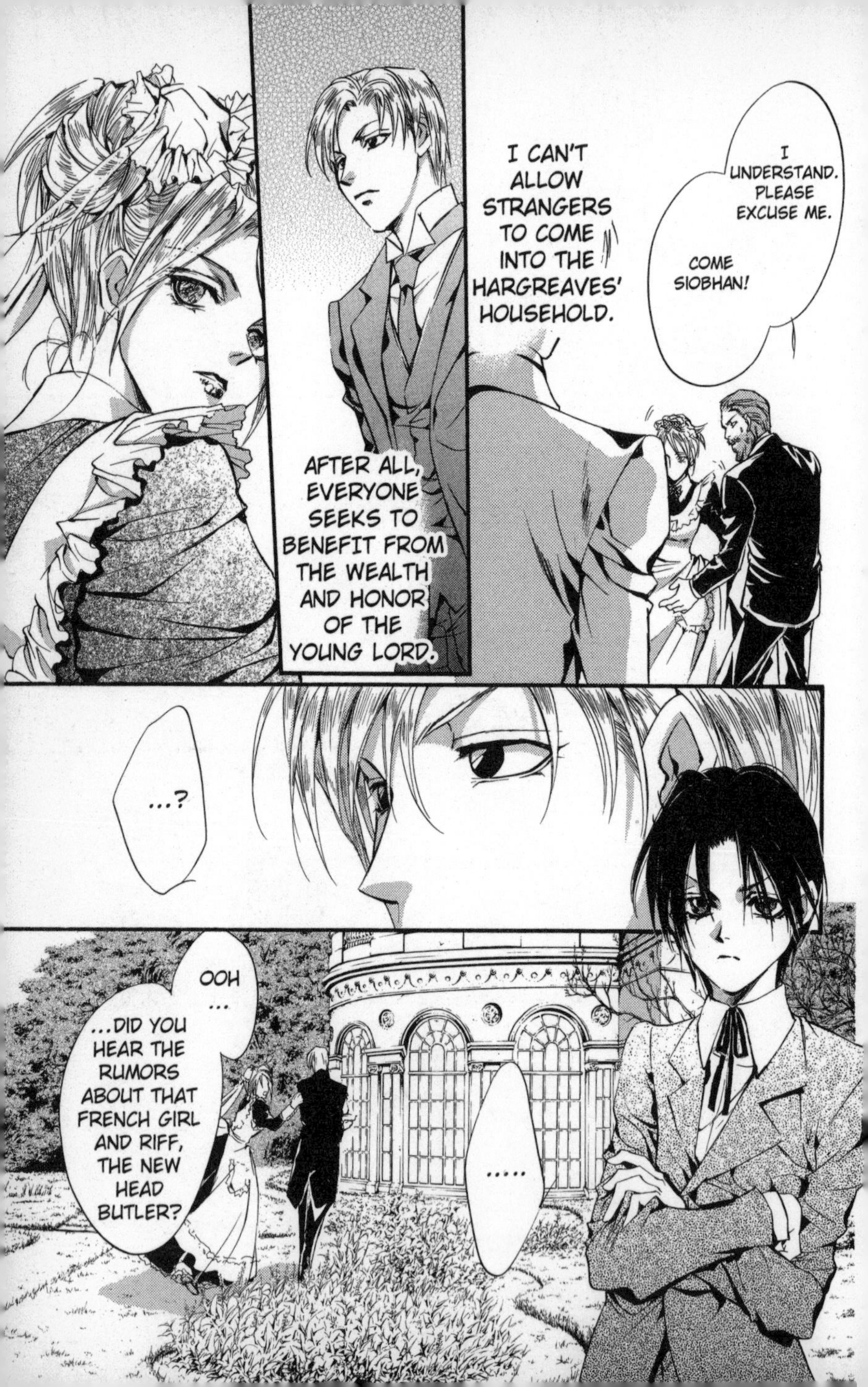
I UNDERSTAND. PLEASE EXCUSE ME.
COME SIOBHAN!
I CAN'T ALLOW STRANGERS TO COME INTO THE HARGREAVES' HOUSEHOLD.
AFTER ALL, EVERYONE SEEKS TO BENEFIT FROM THE WEALTH AND HONOR OF THE YOUNG LORD.
...?
.....
OOH ...
...DID YOU HEAR THE RUMORS ABOUT THAT FRENCH GIRL AND RIFF, THE NEW HEAD BUTLER?

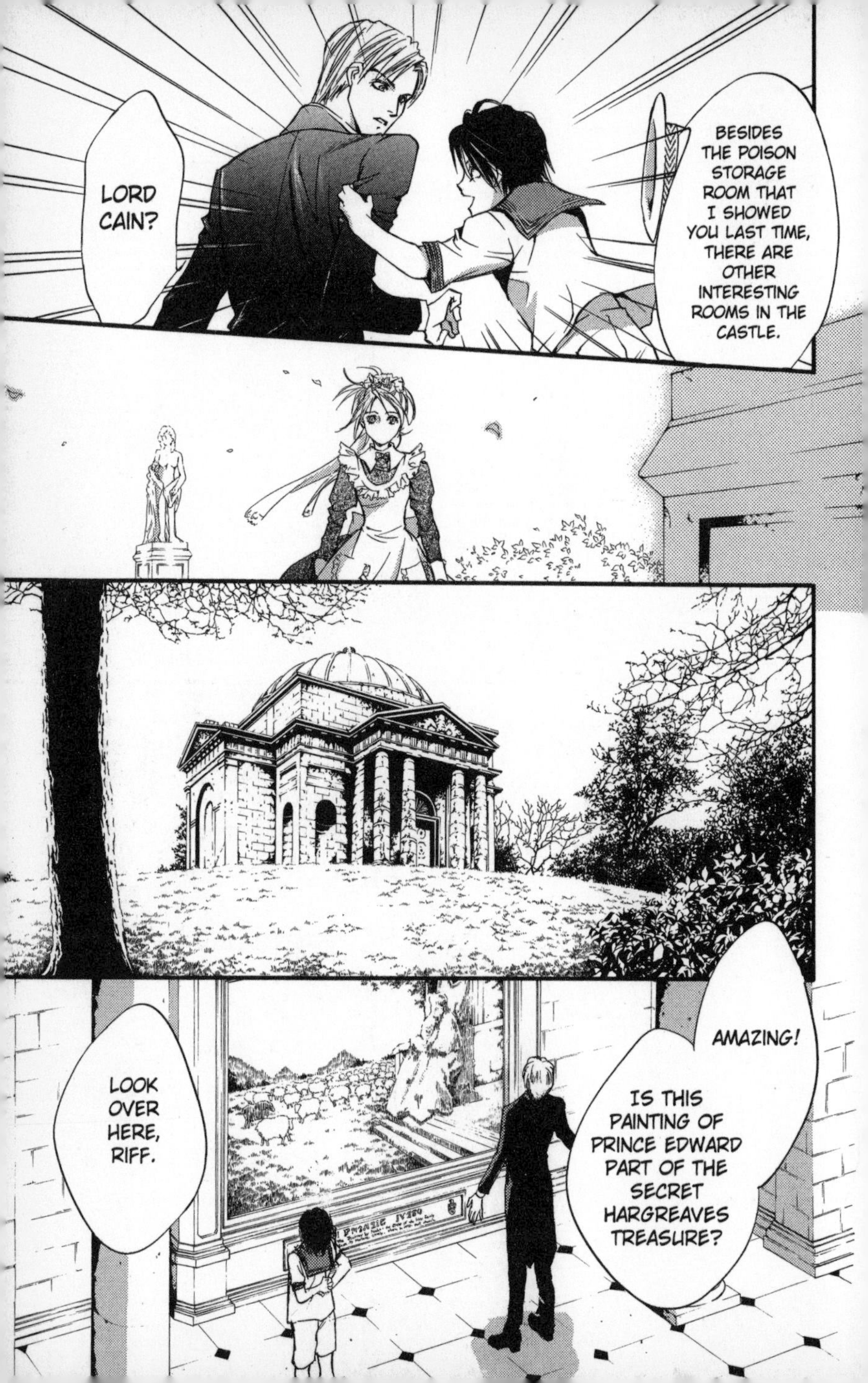
BESIDES THE POISON STORAGE ROOM THAT I SHOWED YOU LAST TIME, THERE ARE OTHER INTERESTING ROOMS IN THE CASTLE.
LORD CAIN?
AMAZING!
IS THIS PAINTING OF PRINCE EDWARD PART OF THE SECRET HARGREAVES TREASURE?
LOOK OVER HERE, RIFF.

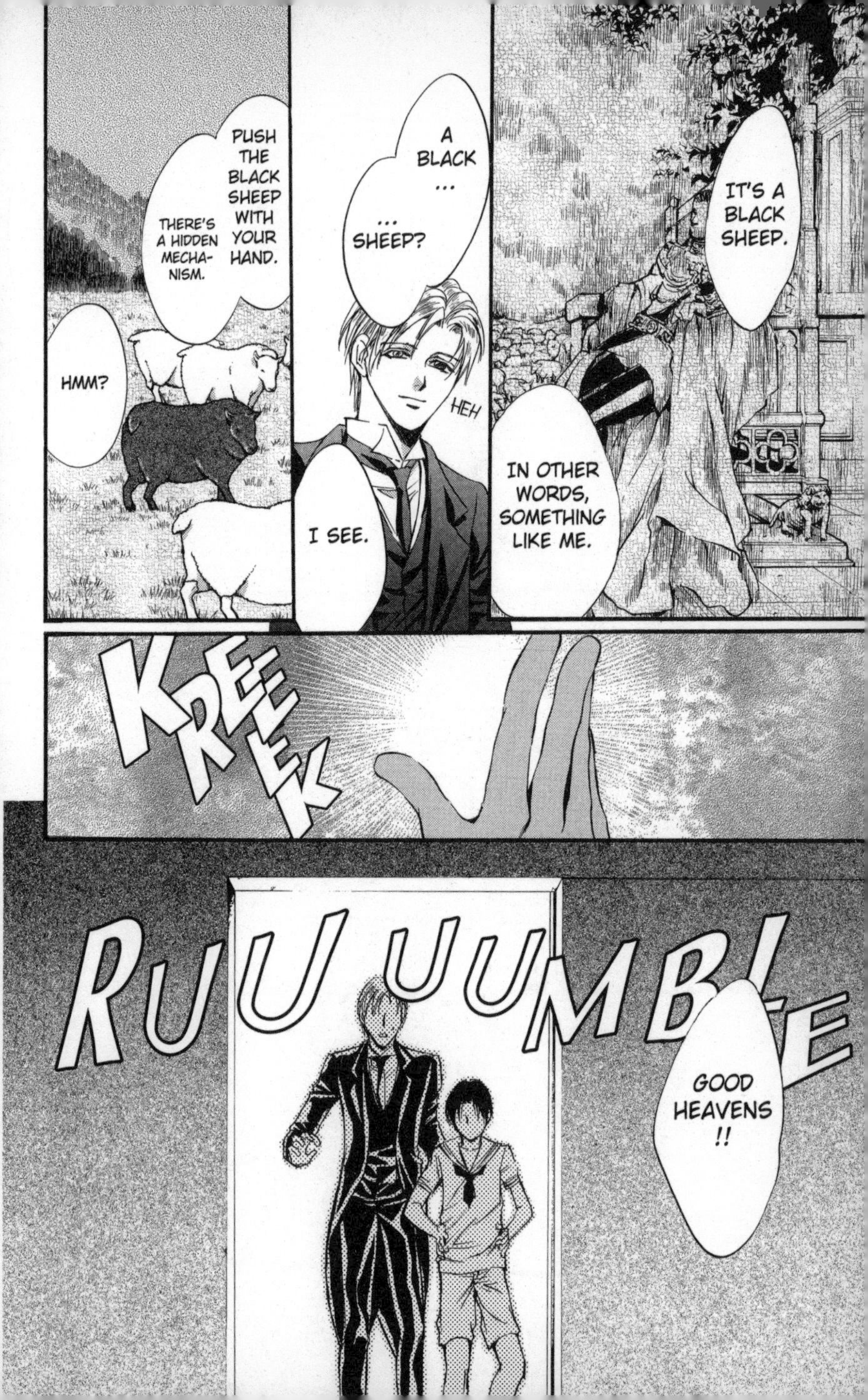
IT'S A BLACK SHEEP.
IN OTHER WORDS, SOMETHING LIKE ME.
A BLACK ...
... SHEEP?
HEH
I SEE.
PUSH THE BLACK SHEEP WITH YOUR HAND.
THERE'S A HIDDEN MECHANISM.
HMM?
KREEEK
RUUUUMBLE
GOOD HEAVENS !!

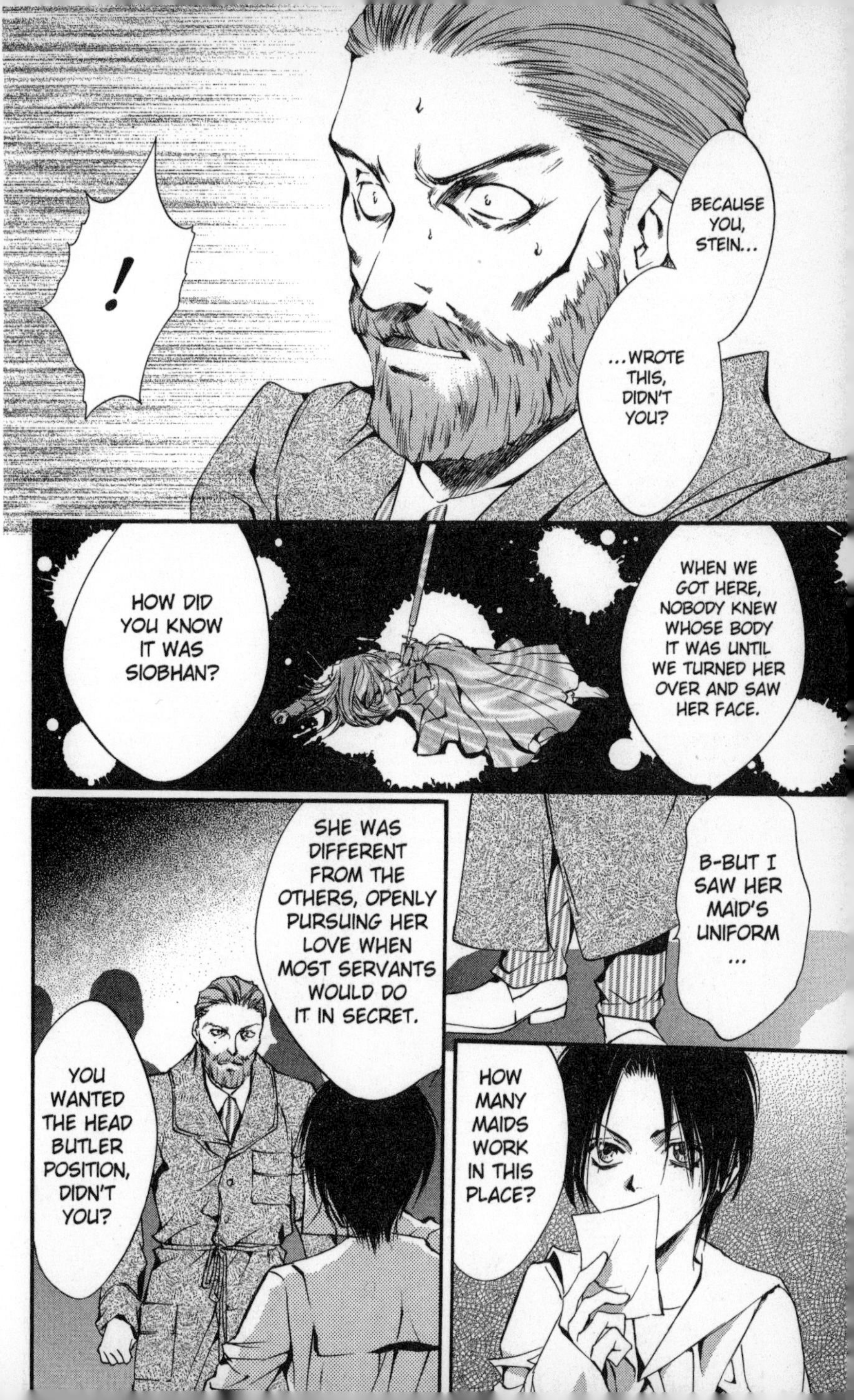
BECAUSE YOU, STEIN...
...WROTE THIS, DIDN'T YOU?
!
WHEN WE GOT HERE, NOBODY KNEW WHOSE BODY IT WAS UNTIL WE TURNED HER OVER AND SAW HER FACE.
HOW DID YOU KNOW IT WAS SIOBHAN?
B-BUT I SAW HER MAID'S UNIFORM ...
HOW MANY MAIDS WORK IN THIS PLACE?
SHE WAS DIFFERENT FROM THE OTHERS, OPENLY PURSUING HER LOVE WHEN MOST SERVANTS WOULD DO IT IN SECRET.
YOU WANTED THE HEAD BUTLER POSITION, DIDN'T YOU?

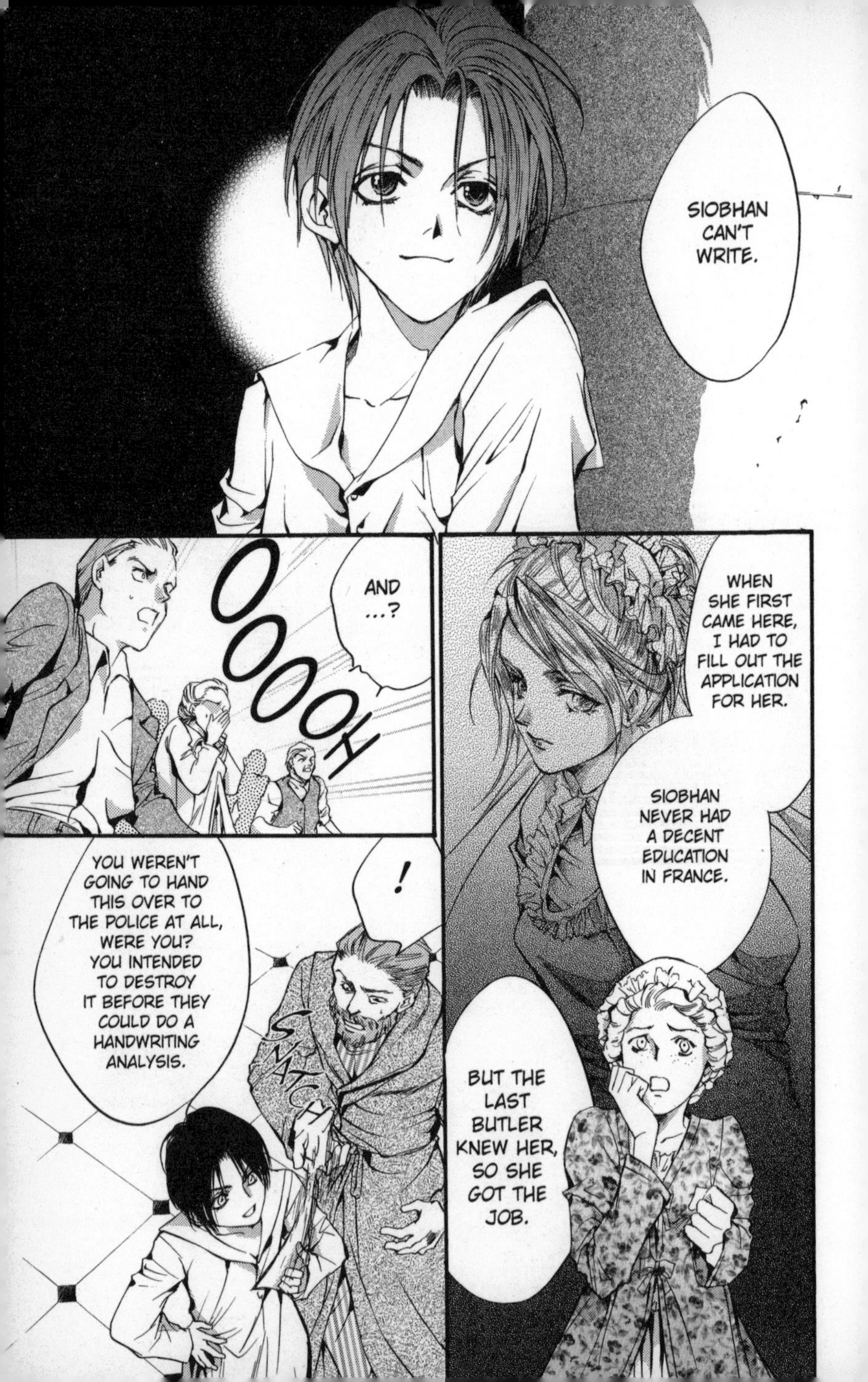
SIOBHAN CAN'T WRITE.
OOOOOH
AND ...?
WHEN SHE FIRST CAME HERE, I HAD TO FILL OUT THE APPLICATION FOR HER.
SIOBHAN NEVER HAD A DECENT EDUCATION IN FRANCE.
BUT THE LAST BUTLER KNEW HER, SO SHE GOT THE JOB.
!
YOU WEREN'T GOING TO HAND THIS OVER TO THE POLICE AT ALL, WERE YOU? YOU INTENDED TO DESTROY IT BEFORE THEY COULD DO A HANDWRITING ANALYSIS.
SNATCH

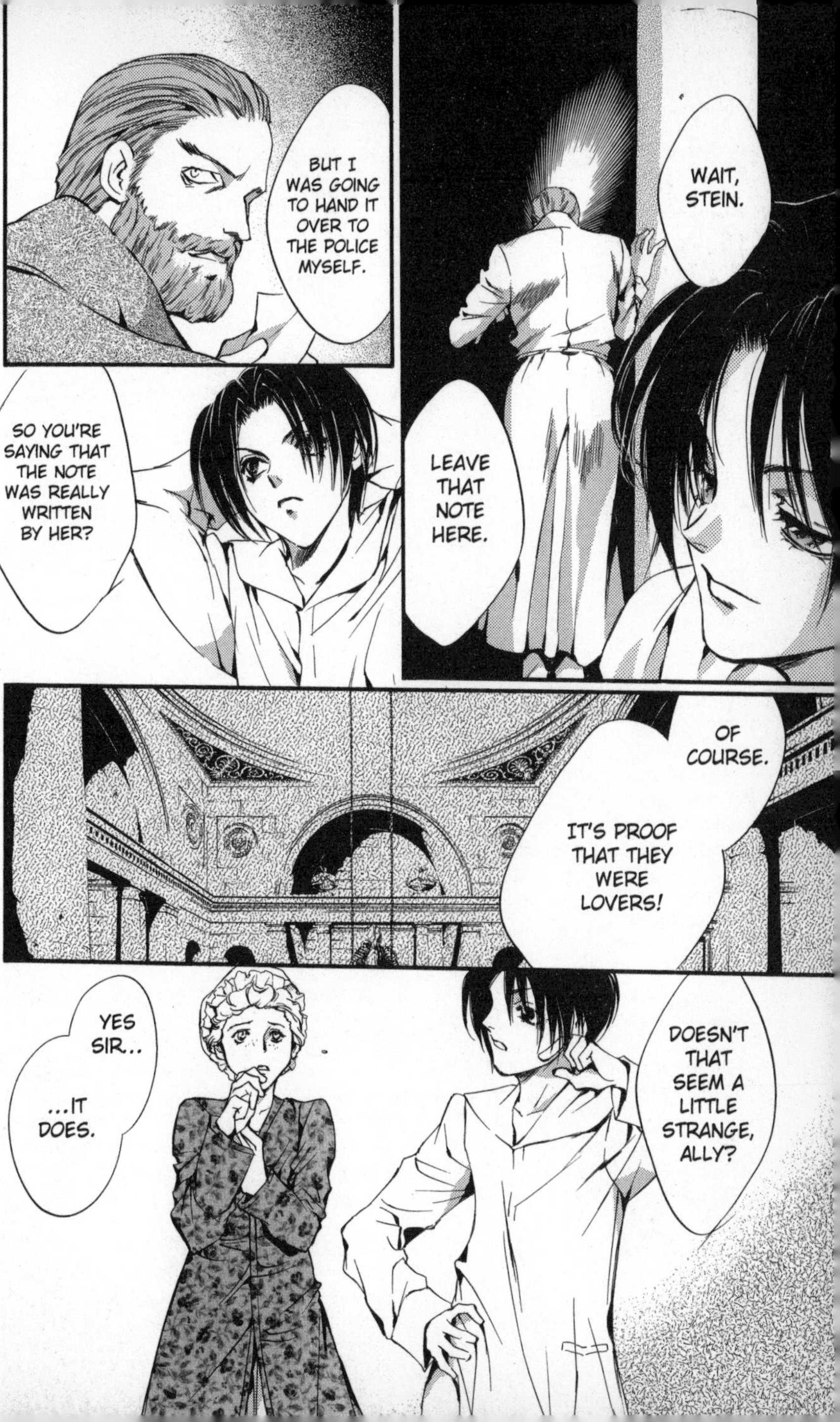
WAIT, STEIN.
LEAVE THAT NOTE HERE.
BUT I WAS GOING TO HAND IT OVER TO THE POLICE MYSELF.
SO YOU'RE SAYING THAT THE NOTE WAS REALLY WRITTEN BY HER?
OF COURSE.
IT'S PROOF THAT THEY WERE LOVERS!
DOESN'T THAT SEEM A LITTLE STRANGE, ALLY?
YES SIR...
...IT DOES.

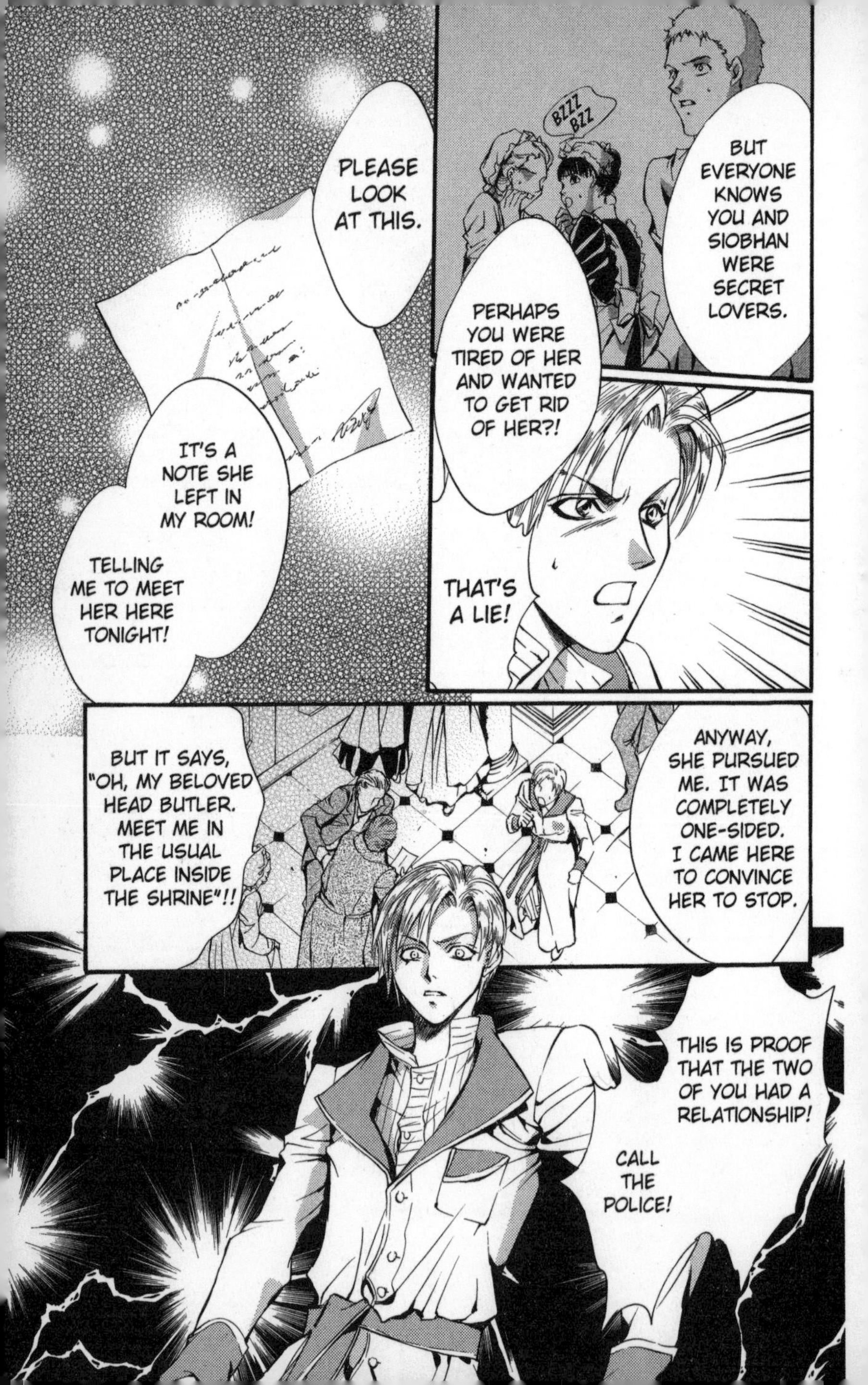
BUT EVERYONE KNOWS YOU AND SIOBHAN WERE SECRET LOVERS.
BZZZ BZZ
PERHAPS YOU WERE TIRED OF HER AND WANTED TO GET RID OF HER?!
THAT'S A LIE!
PLEASE LOOK AT THIS.
IT'S A NOTE SHE LEFT IN MY ROOM!
TELLING ME TO MEET HER HERE TONIGHT!
ANYWAY, SHE PURSUED ME. IT WAS COMPLETELY ONE-SIDED. I CAME HERE TO CONVINCE HER TO STOP.
BUT IT SAYS, "OH, MY BELOVED HEAD BUTLER. MEET ME IN THE USUAL PLACE INSIDE THE SHRINE"!!
THIS IS PROOF THAT THE TWO OF YOU HAD A RELATIONSHIP!
CALL THE POLICE!

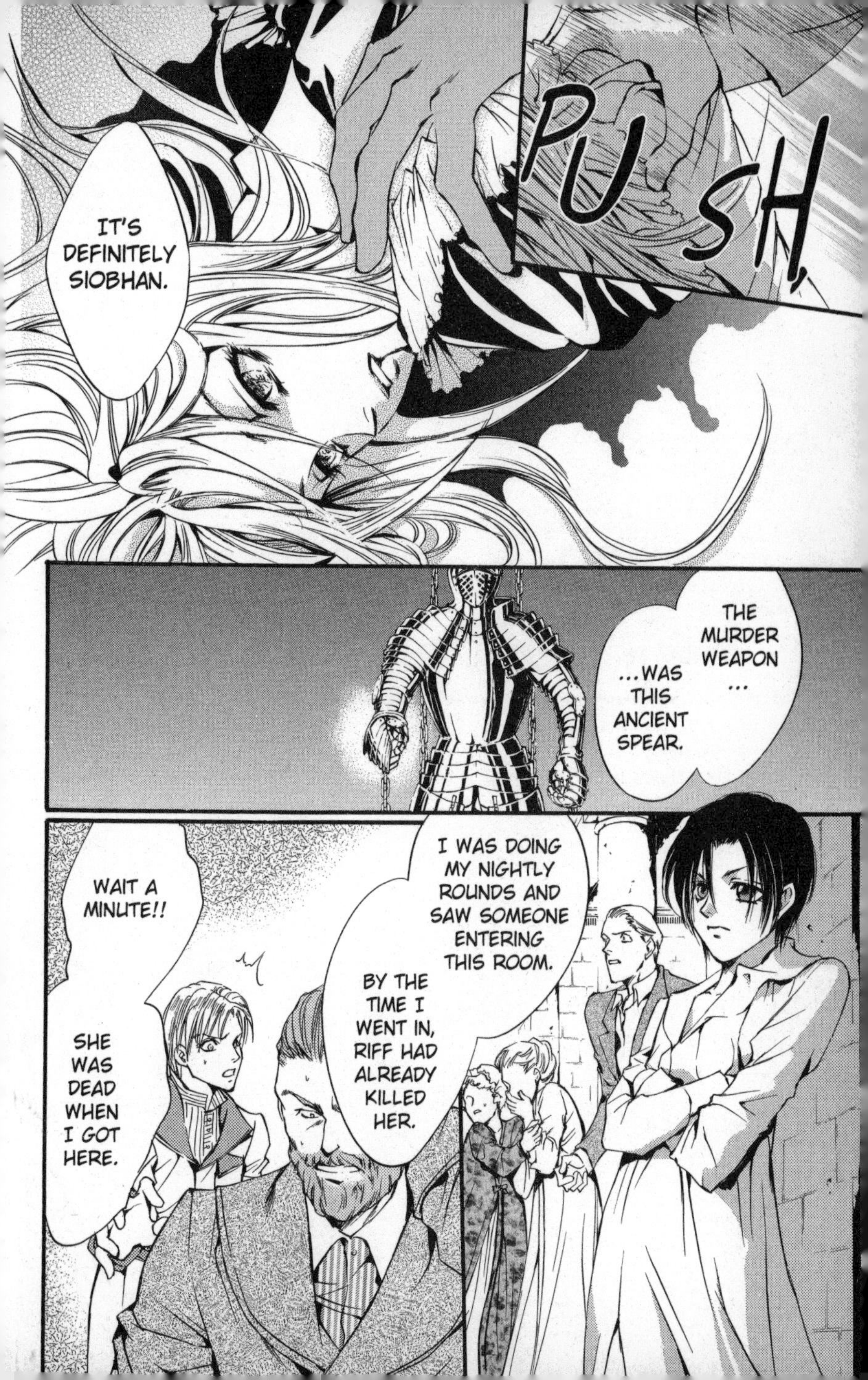
PUSH
IT'S DEFINITELY SIOBHAN.
THE MURDER WEAPON...
...WAS THIS ANCIENT SPEAR.
I WAS DOING MY NIGHTLY ROUNDS AND SAW SOMEONE ENTERING THIS ROOM.
BY THE TIME I WENT IN, RIFF HAD ALREADY KILLED HER.
WAIT A MINUTE!!
SHE WAS DEAD WHEN I GOT HERE.

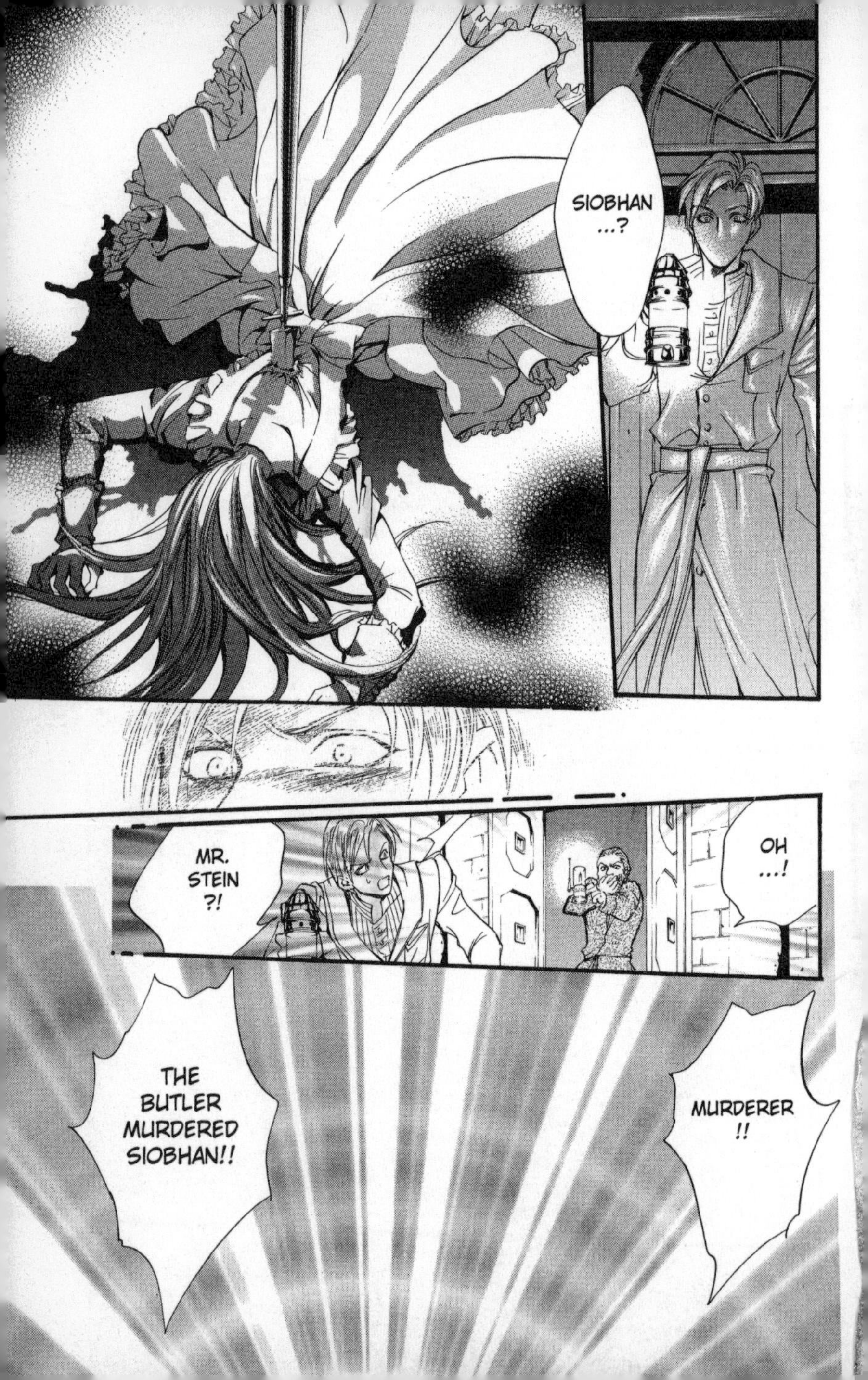
SIOBHAN ...?
OH ...!
MR. STEIN ?!
MURDERER !!
THE BUTLER MURDERED SIOBHAN!!

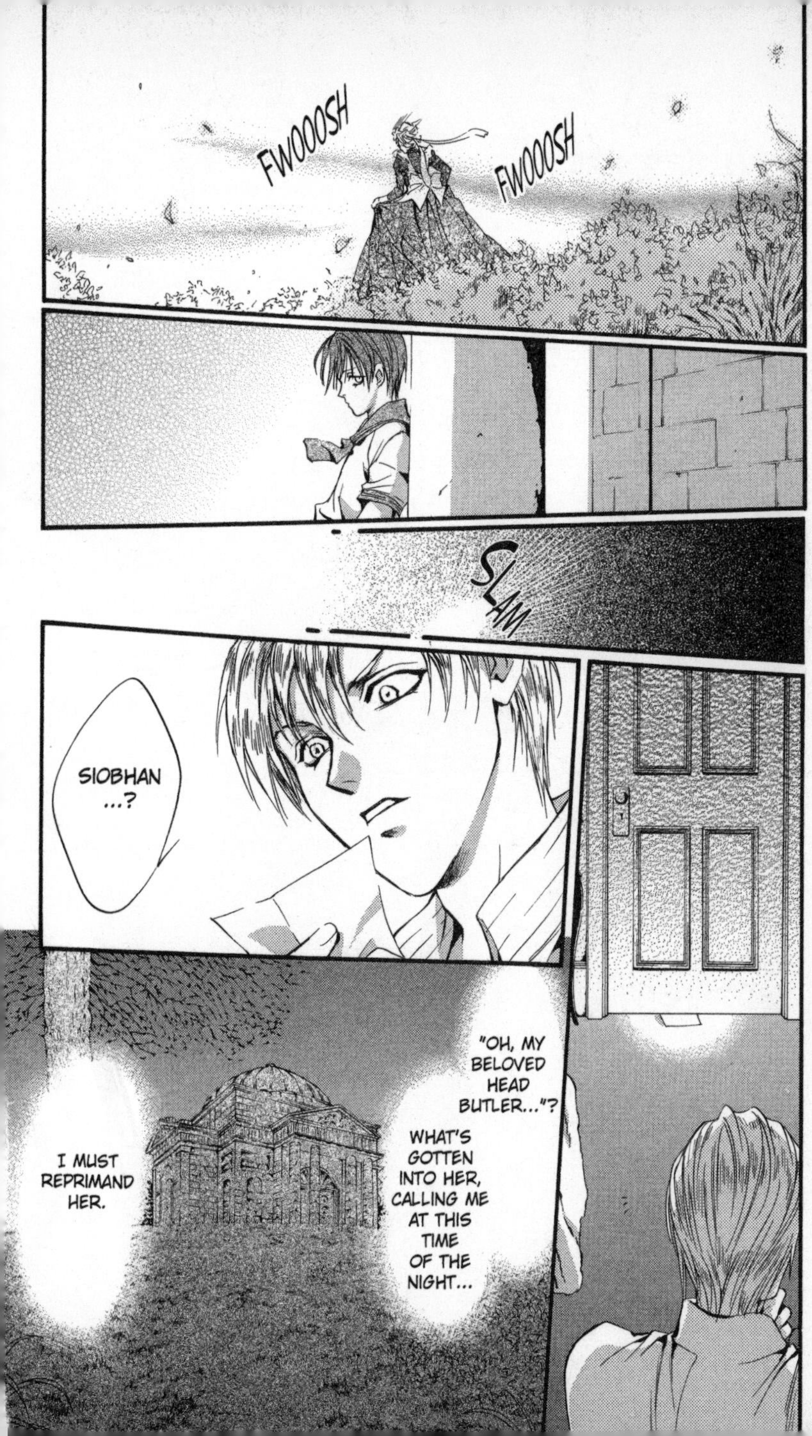
FWOOOSH
FWOOOSH
SLAM
SIOBHAN ...?
"OH, MY BELOVED HEAD BUTLER..."?
WHAT'S GOTTEN INTO HER, CALLING ME AT THIS TIME OF THE NIGHT...
I MUST REPRIMAND HER.

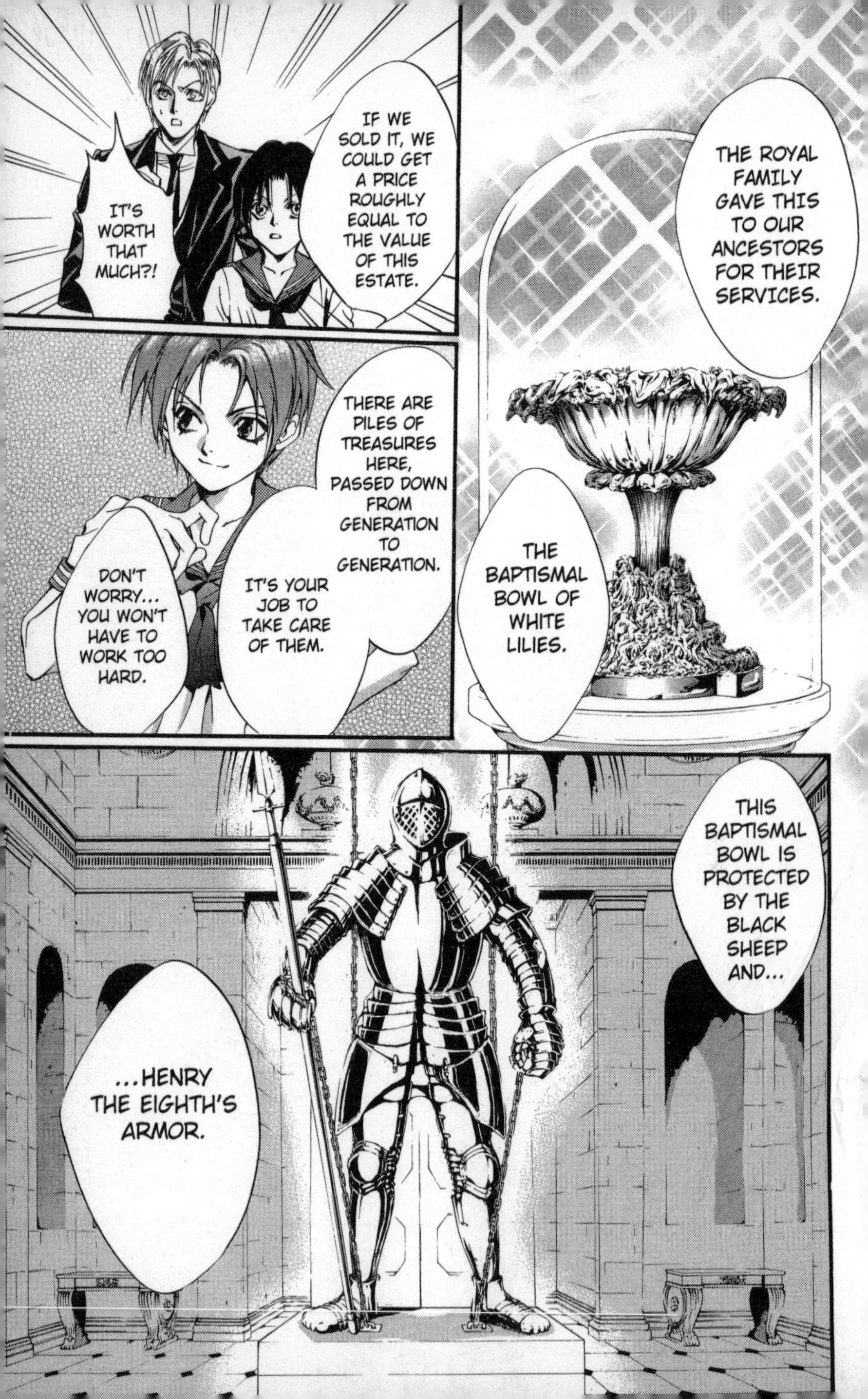
THE ROYAL FAMILY GAVE THIS TO OUR ANCESTORS FOR THEIR SERVICES.
THE BAPTISMAL BOWL OF WHITE LILIES.
IF WE SOLD IT, WE COULD GET A PRICE ROUGHLY EQUAL TO THE VALUE OF THIS ESTATE.
IT'S WORTH THAT MUCH?!
THERE ARE PILES OF TREASURES HERE, PASSED DOWN FROM GENERATION TO GENERATION.
IT'S YOUR JOB TO TAKE CARE OF THEM.
DON'T WORRY... YOU WON'T HAVE TO WORK TOO HARD.
THIS BAPTISMAL BOWL IS PROTECTED BY THE BLACK SHEEP AND...
...HENRY THE EIGHTH'S ARMOR.

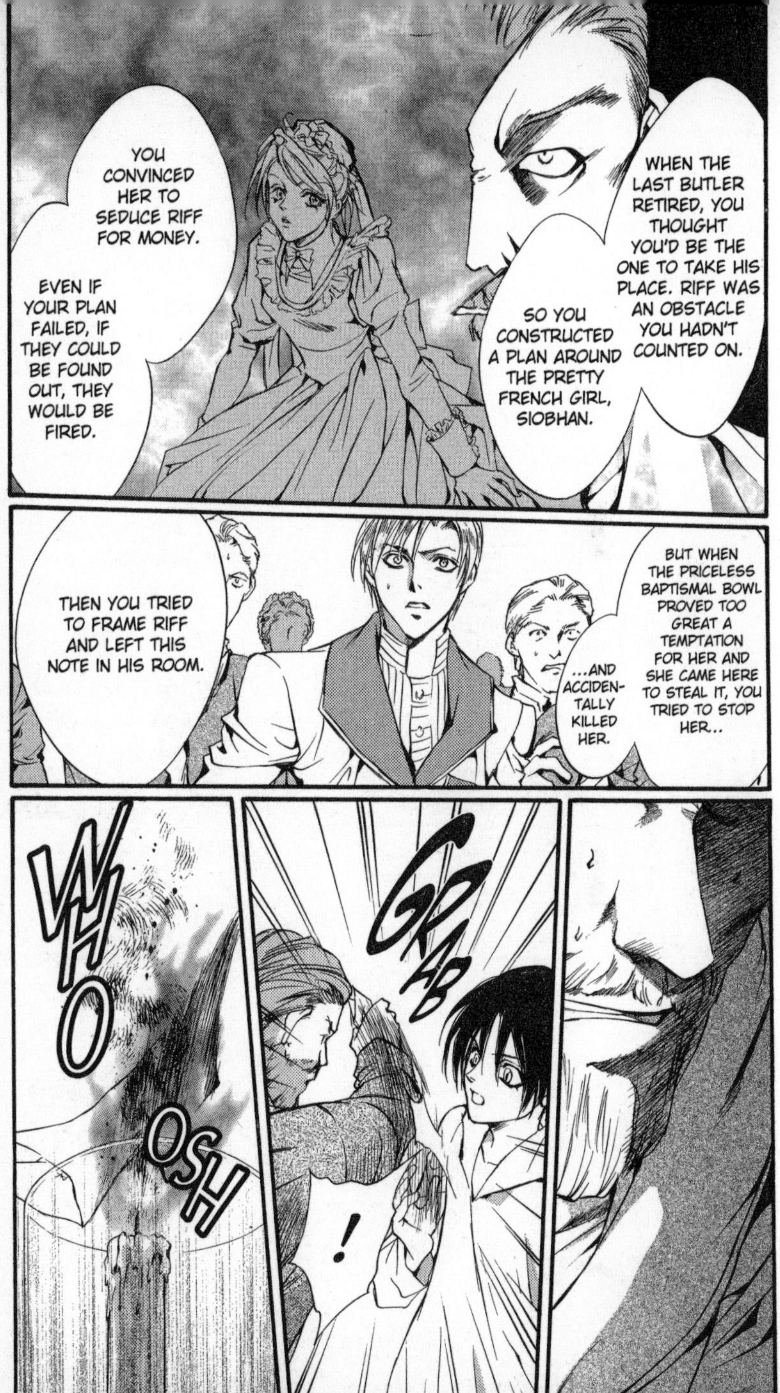
WHEN THE LAST BUTLER RETIRED, YOU THOUGHT YOU'D BE THE ONE TO TAKE HIS PLACE. RIFF WAS AN OBSTACLE YOU HADN'T COUNTED ON.
SO YOU CONSTRUCTED A PLAN AROUND THE PRETTY FRENCH GIRL, SIOBHAN.
YOU CONVINCED HER TO SEDUCE RIFF FOR MONEY.
EVEN IF YOUR PLAN FAILED, IF THEY COULD BE FOUND OUT, THEY WOULD BE FIRED.
BUT WHEN THE PRICELESS BAPTISMAL BOWL PROVED TOO GREAT A TEMPTATION FOR HER AND SHE CAME HERE TO STEAL IT, YOU TRIED TO STOP HER...
...AND ACCIDENTALLY KILLED HER.
THEN YOU TRIED TO FRAME RIFF AND LEFT THIS NOTE IN HIS ROOM.
GRAB
!
WHOOSH

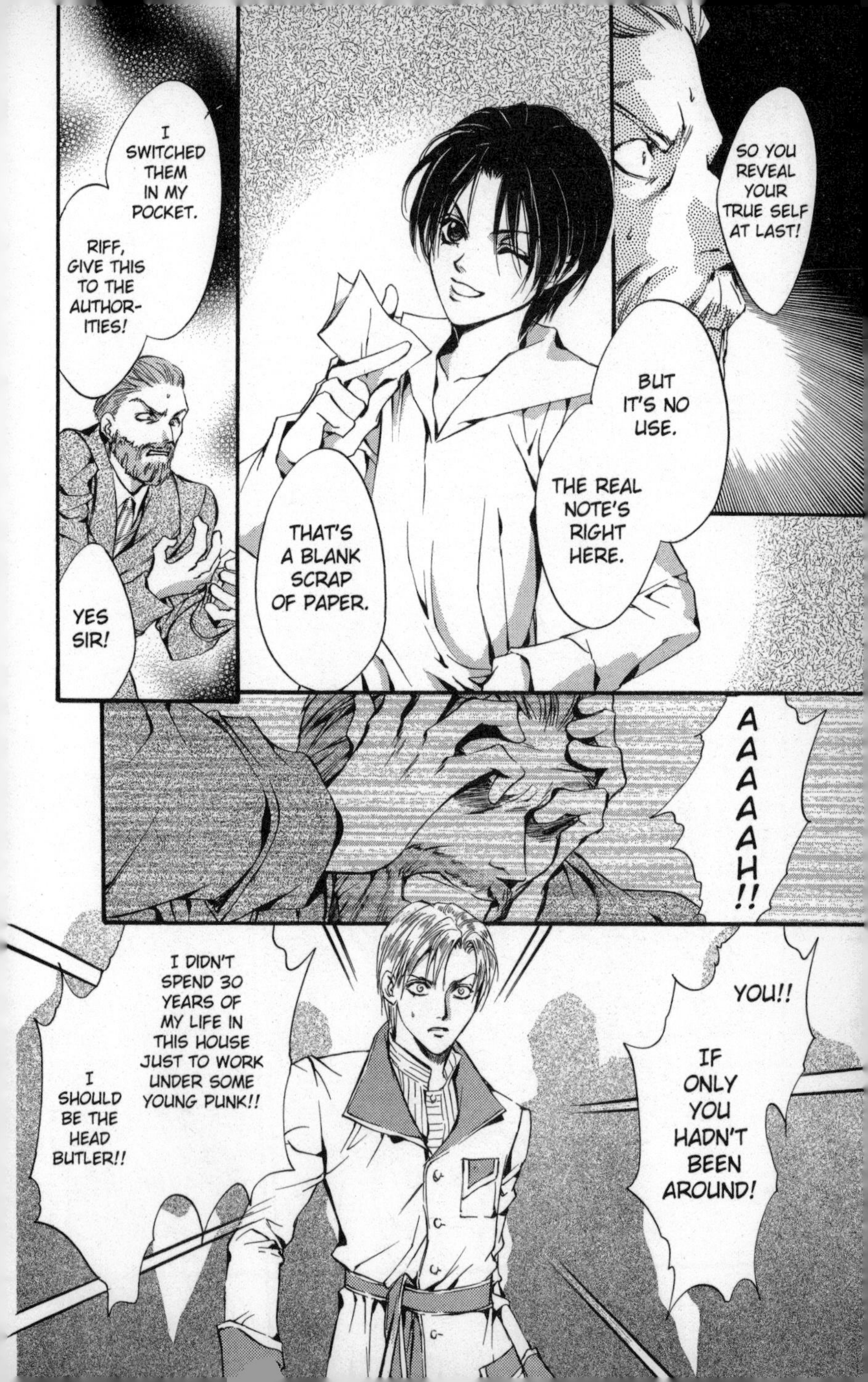
SO YOU REVEAL YOUR TRUE SELF AT LAST!
BUT IT'S NO USE.
THE REAL NOTE'S RIGHT HERE.
THAT'S A BLANK SCRAP OF PAPER.
I SWITCHED THEM IN MY POCKET.
RIFF, GIVE THIS TO THE AUTHOR-ITIES!
YES SIR!
AAAAAAH!!
YOU!!
IF ONLY YOU HADN'T BEEN AROUND!
I DIDN'T SPEND 30 YEARS OF MY LIFE IN THIS HOUSE JUST TO WORK UNDER SOME YOUNG PUNK!!
I SHOULD BE THE HEAD BUTLER!!

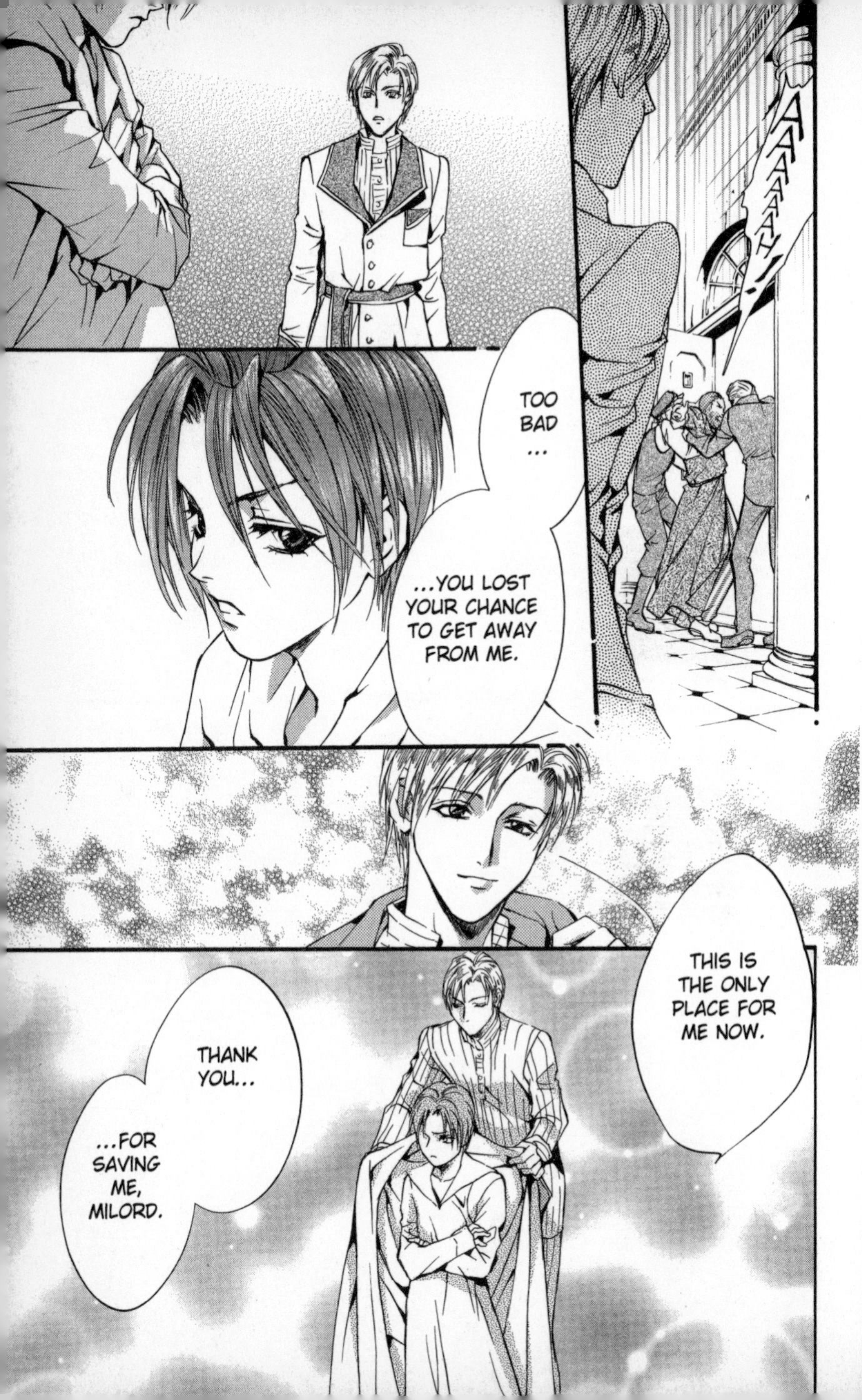
AAAAAAH!
TOO BAD...
...YOU LOST YOUR CHANCE TO GET AWAY FROM ME.
THIS IS THE ONLY PLACE FOR ME NOW.
THANK YOU...
...FOR SAVING ME, MILORD.

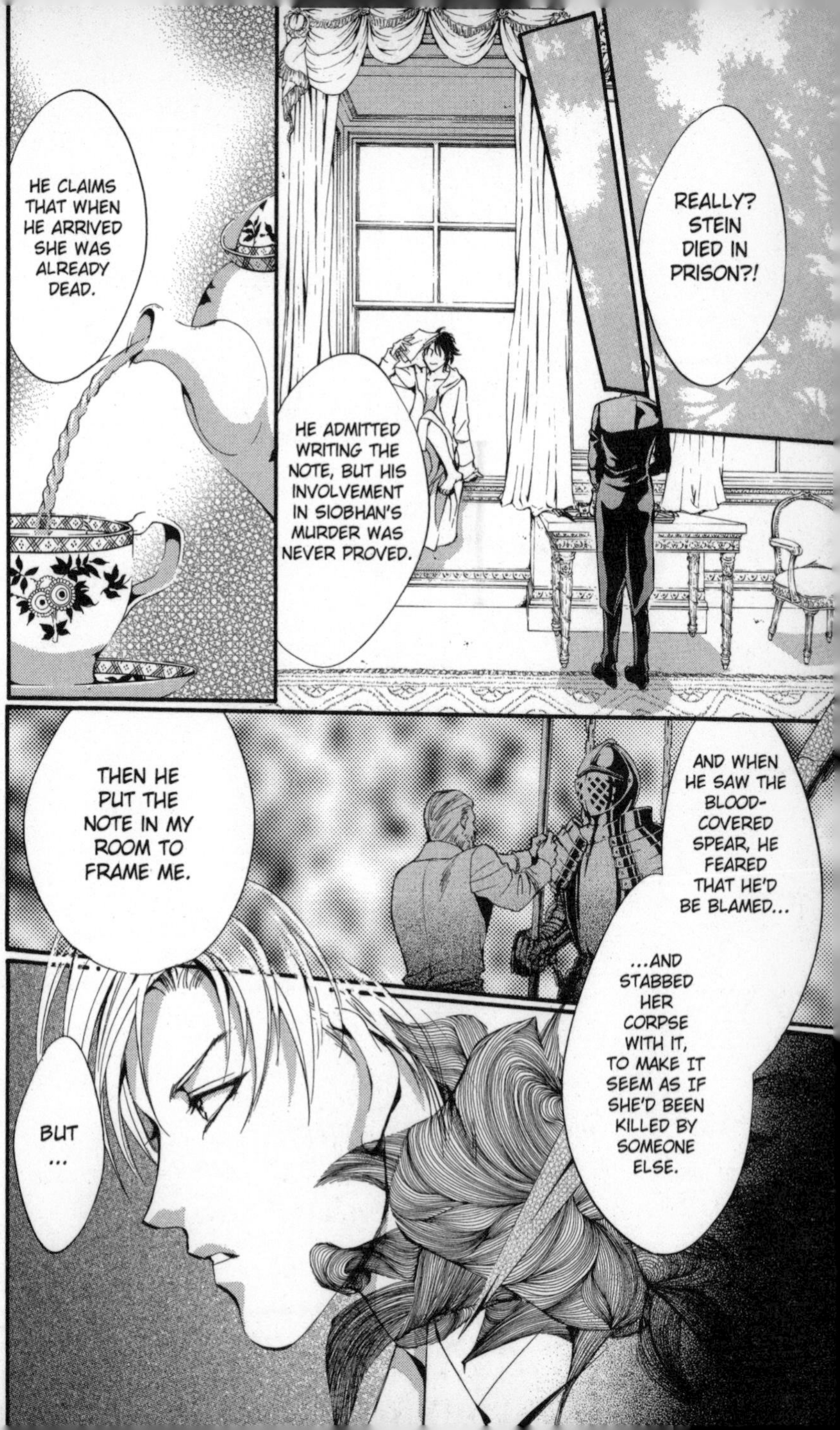
REALLY? STEIN DIED IN PRISON?!
HE ADMITTED WRITING THE NOTE, BUT HIS INVOLVEMENT IN SIOBHAN'S MURDER WAS NEVER PROVED.
HE CLAIMS THAT WHEN HE ARRIVED SHE WAS ALREADY DEAD.
AND WHEN HE SAW THE BLOOD-COVERED SPEAR, HE FEARED THAT HE'D BE BLAMED...
...AND STABBED HER CORPSE WITH IT, TO MAKE IT SEEM AS IF SHE'D BEEN KILLED BY SOMEONE ELSE.
THEN HE PUT THE NOTE IN MY ROOM TO FRAME ME.
BUT ...

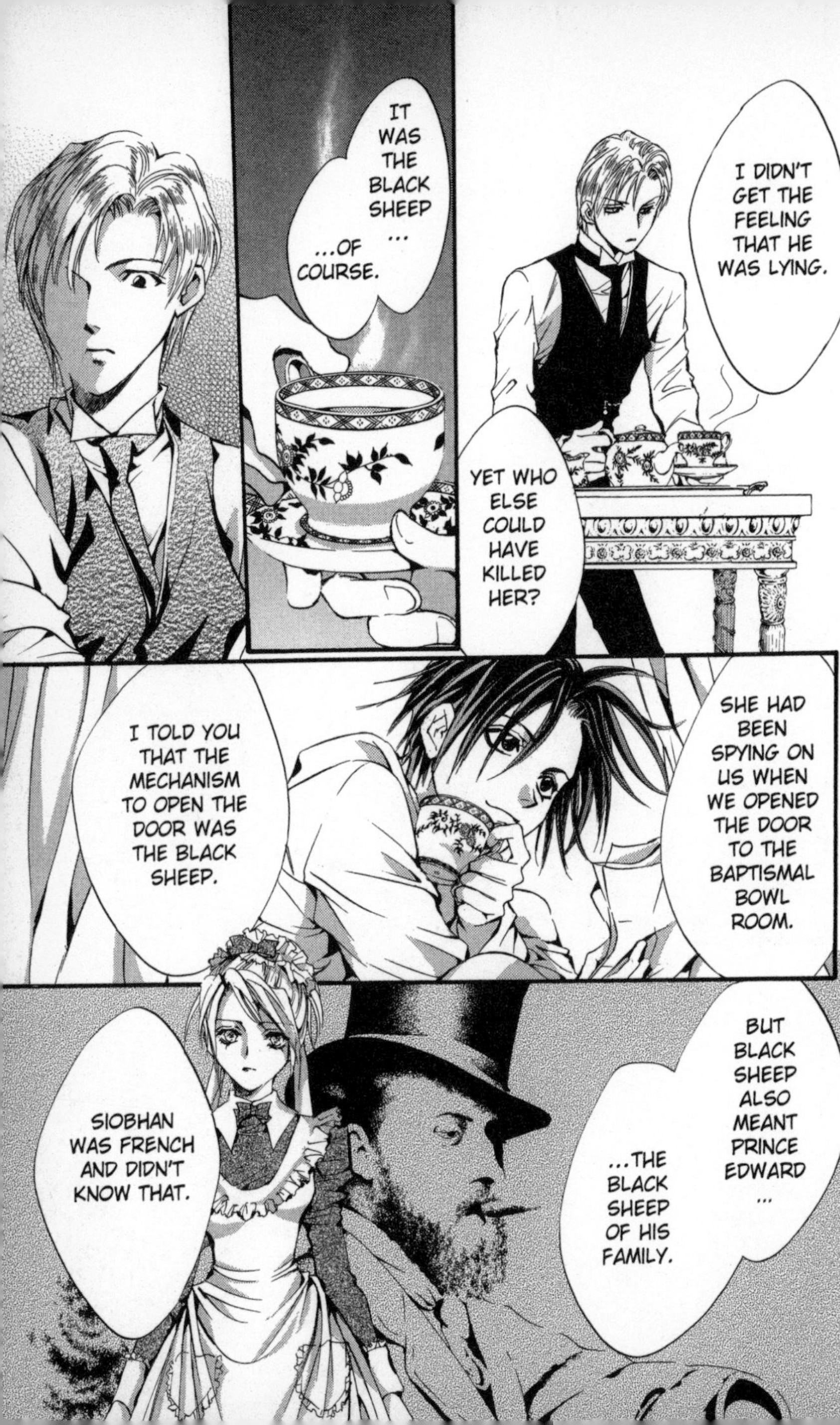

I DIDN'T GET THE FEELING THAT HE WAS LYING.
YET WHO ELSE COULD HAVE KILLED HER?
IT WAS THE BLACK SHEEP ...
...OF COURSE.
SHE HAD BEEN SPYING ON US WHEN WE OPENED THE DOOR TO THE BAPTISMAL BOWL ROOM.
I TOLD YOU THAT THE MECHANISM TO OPEN THE DOOR WAS THE BLACK SHEEP.
BUT BLACK SHEEP ALSO MEANT PRINCE EDWARD ...
...THE BLACK SHEEP OF HIS FAMILY.
SIOBHAN WAS FRENCH AND DIDN'T KNOW THAT.

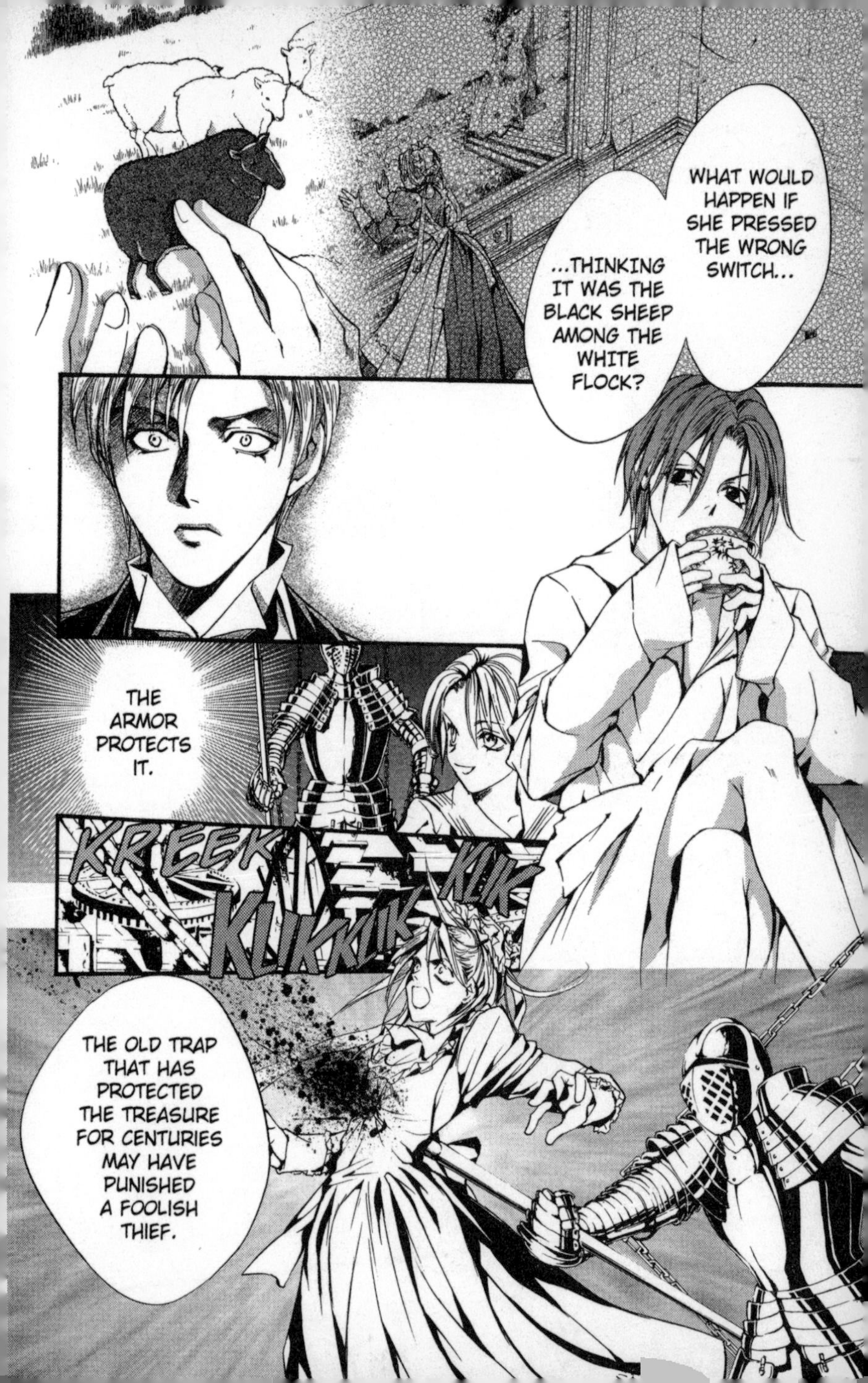
WHAT WOULD HAPPEN IF SHE PRESSED THE WRONG SWITCH...
...THINKING IT WAS THE BLACK SHEEP AMONG THE WHITE FLOCK?
THE ARMOR PROTECTS IT.
KREEK
KLIK
KLIKKLIK
THE OLD TRAP THAT HAS PROTECTED THE TREASURE FOR CENTURIES MAY HAVE PUNISHED A FOOLISH THIEF.

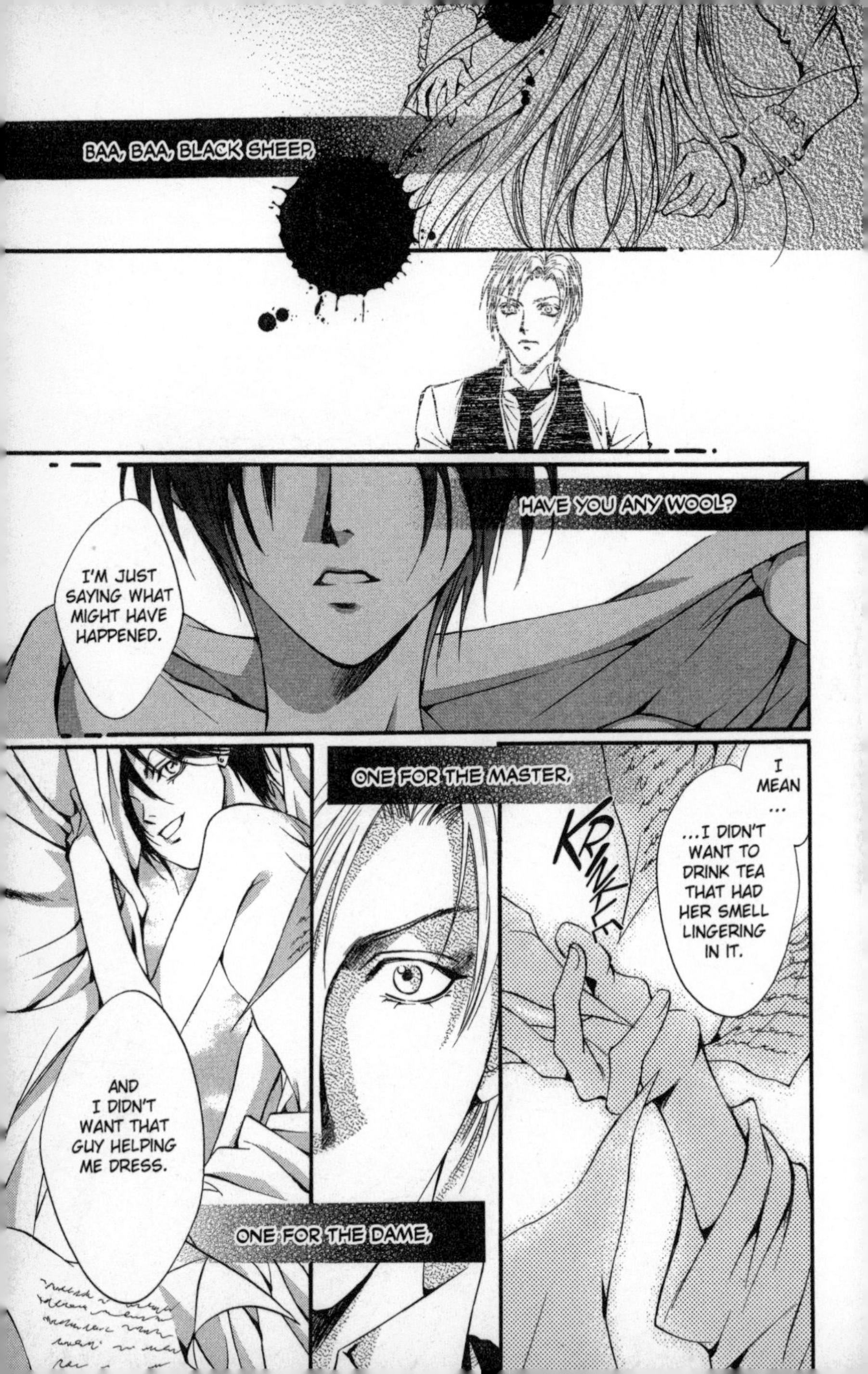
BAA, BAA, BLACK SHEEP,
HAVE YOU ANY WOOL?
I'M JUST SAYING WHAT MIGHT HAVE HAPPENED.
I MEAN ...
...I DIDN'T WANT TO DRINK TEA THAT HAD HER SMELL LINGERING IN IT.
KRINKLE
ONE FOR THE MASTER,
AND I DIDN'T WANT THAT GUY HELPING ME DRESS.
ONE FOR THE DAME,

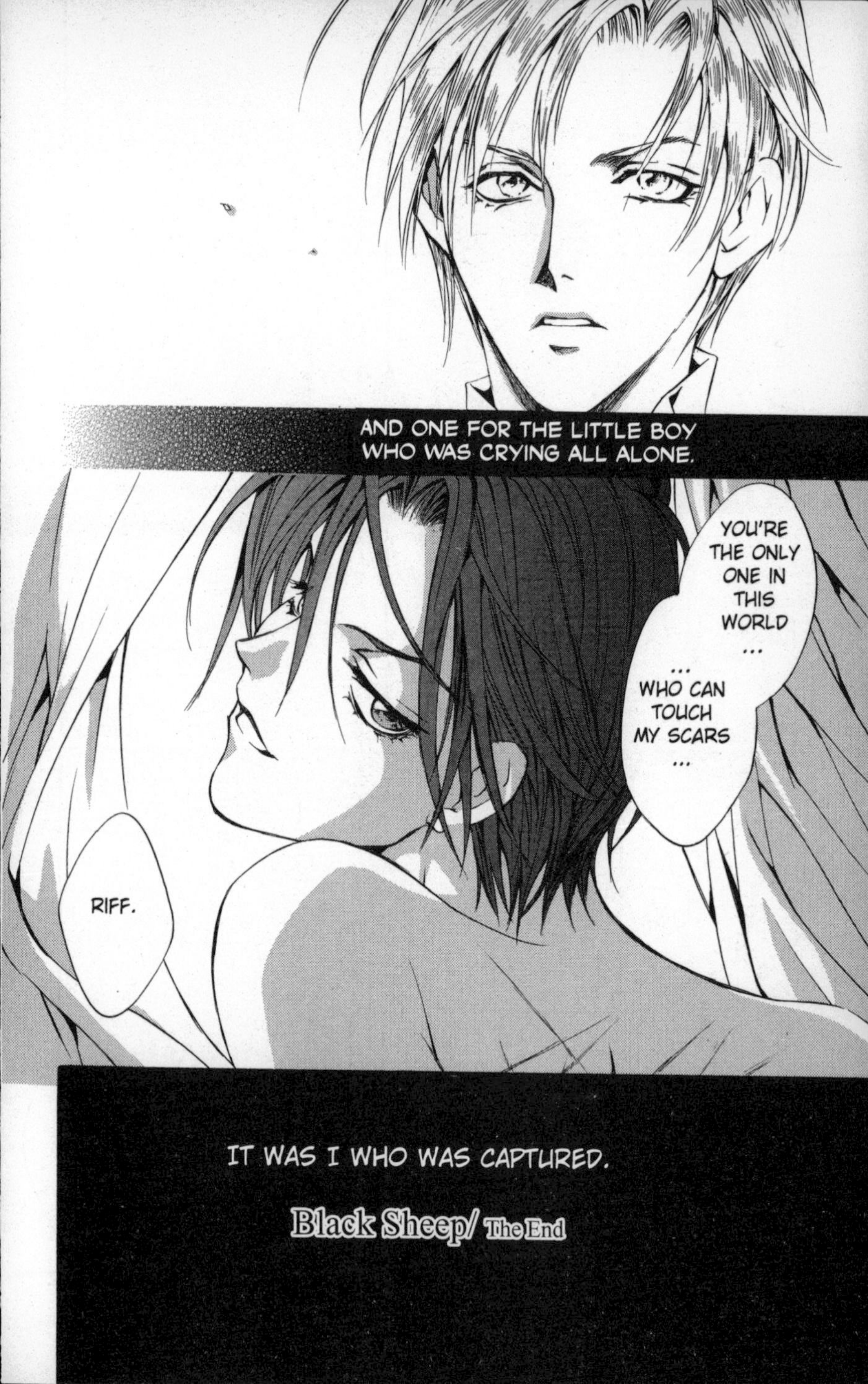
AND ONE FOR THE LITTLE BOY WHO WAS CRYING ALL ALONE.
YOU'RE THE ONLY ONE IN THIS WORLD ... ... WHO CAN TOUCH MY SCARS ...
RIFF.
IT WAS I WHO WAS CAPTURED.
Black Sheep/ The End

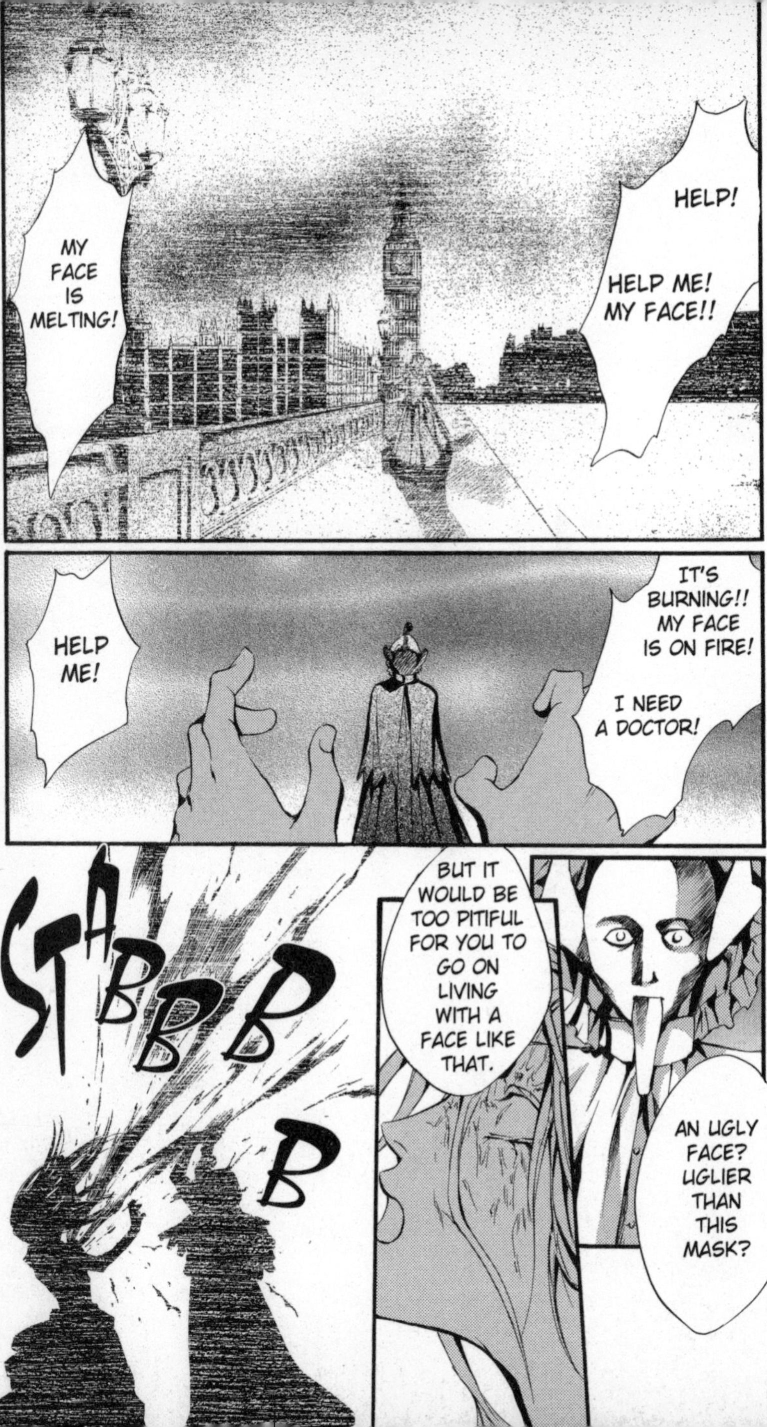
HELP!
HELP ME! MY FACE!!
MY FACE IS MELTING!
IT'S BURNING!! MY FACE IS ON FIRE!
I NEED A DOCTOR!
HELP ME!
BUT IT WOULD BE TOO PITIFUL FOR YOU TO GO ON LIVING WITH A FACE LIKE THAT.
AN UGLY FACE? UGLIER THAN THIS MASK?
STABBBB
B

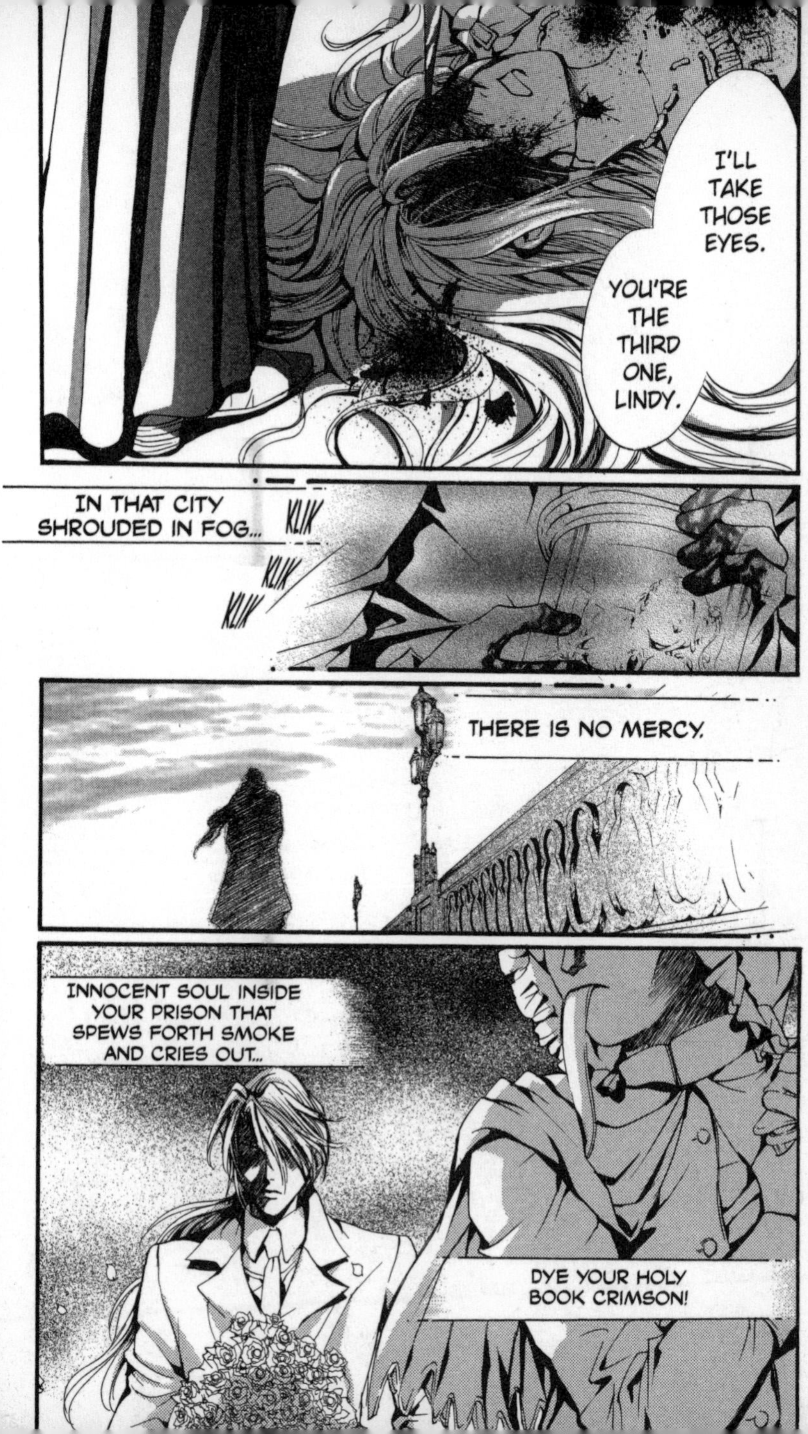
I'LL TAKE THOSE EYES.
YOU'RE THE THIRD ONE, LINDY.
KLIK
KLIK
KLIK
IN THAT CITY SHROUDED IN FOG...
THERE IS NO MERCY.
INNOCENT SOUL INSIDE YOUR PRISON THAT SPEWS FORTH SMOKE AND CRIES OUT...
DYE YOUR HOLY BOOK CRIMSON!

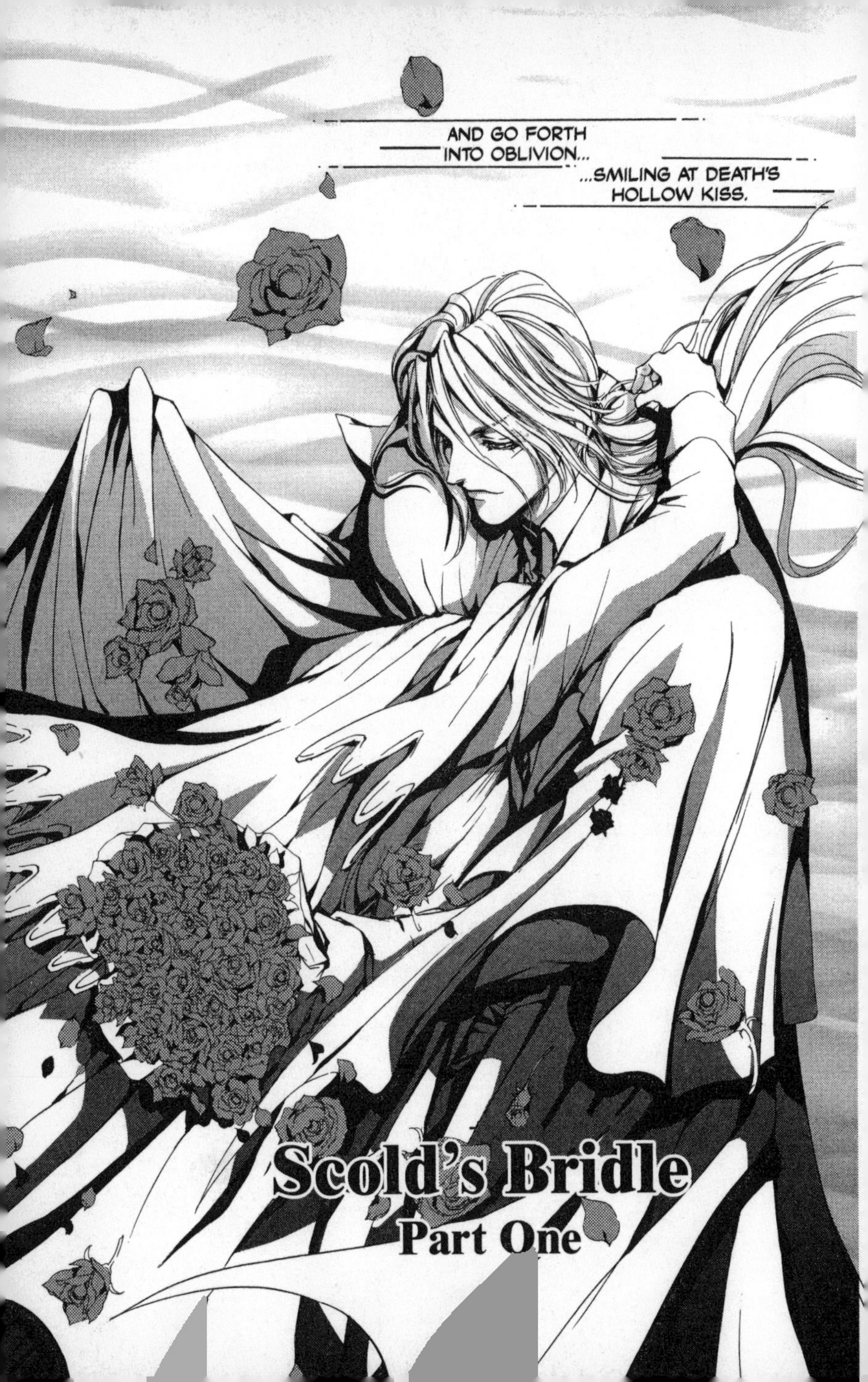
AND GO FORTH INTO OBLIVION...
...SMILING AT DEATH'S HOLLOW KISS.
Scold's Bridle
Part One

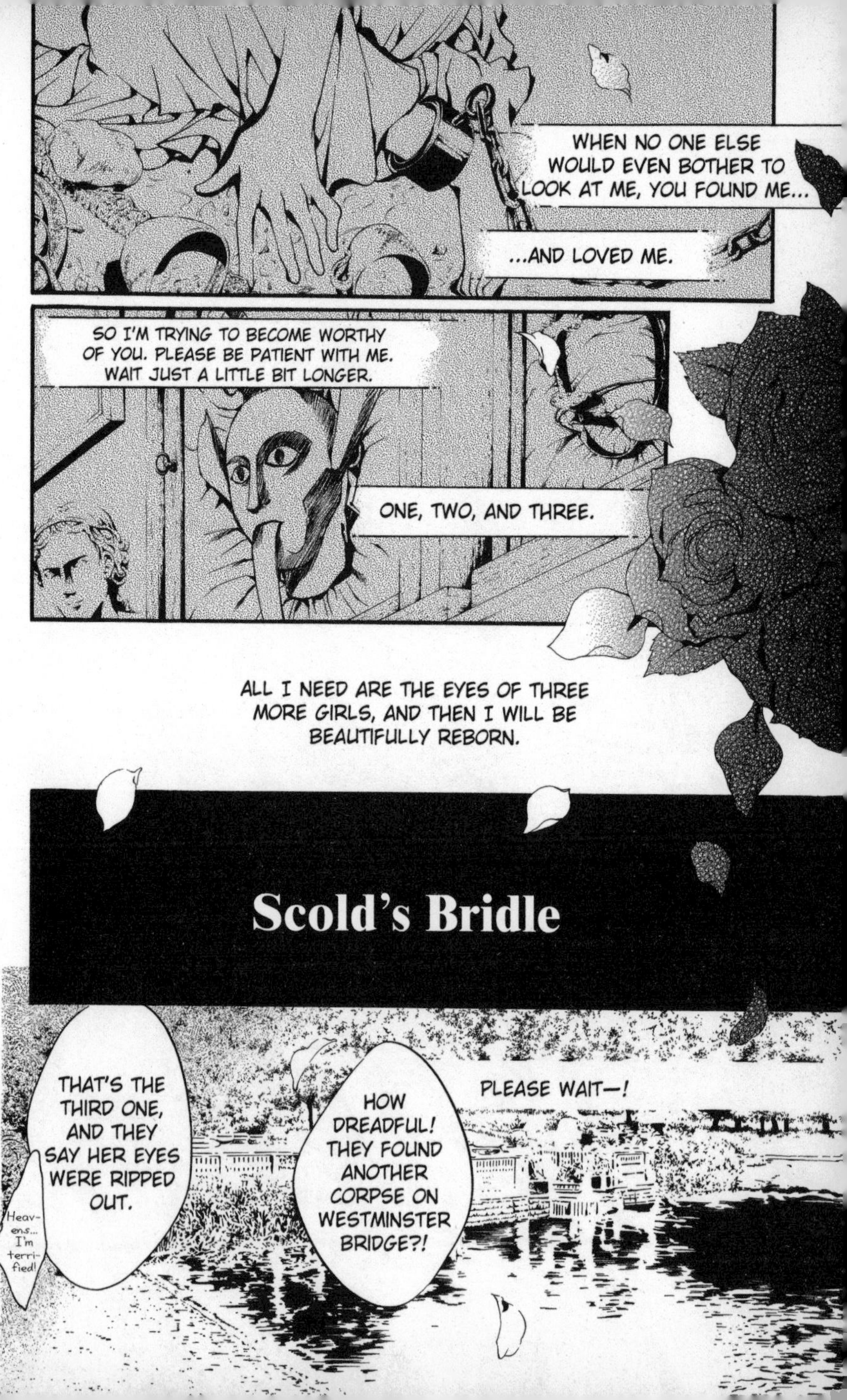
WHEN NO ONE ELSE WOULD EVEN BOTHER TO LOOK AT ME, YOU FOUND ME...
...AND LOVED ME.
SO I'M TRYING TO BECOME WORTHY OF YOU. PLEASE BE PATIENT WITH ME. WAIT JUST A LITTLE BIT LONGER.
ONE, TWO, AND THREE.
ALL I NEED ARE THE EYES OF THREE MORE GIRLS, AND THEN I WILL BE BEAUTIFULLY REBORN.
Scold's Bridle
PLEASE WAIT—!
HOW DREADFUL! THEY FOUND ANOTHER CORPSE ON WESTMINSTER BRIDGE?!
THAT'S THE THIRD ONE, AND THEY SAY HER EYES WERE RIPPED OUT.
Heavens... I'm terrified!

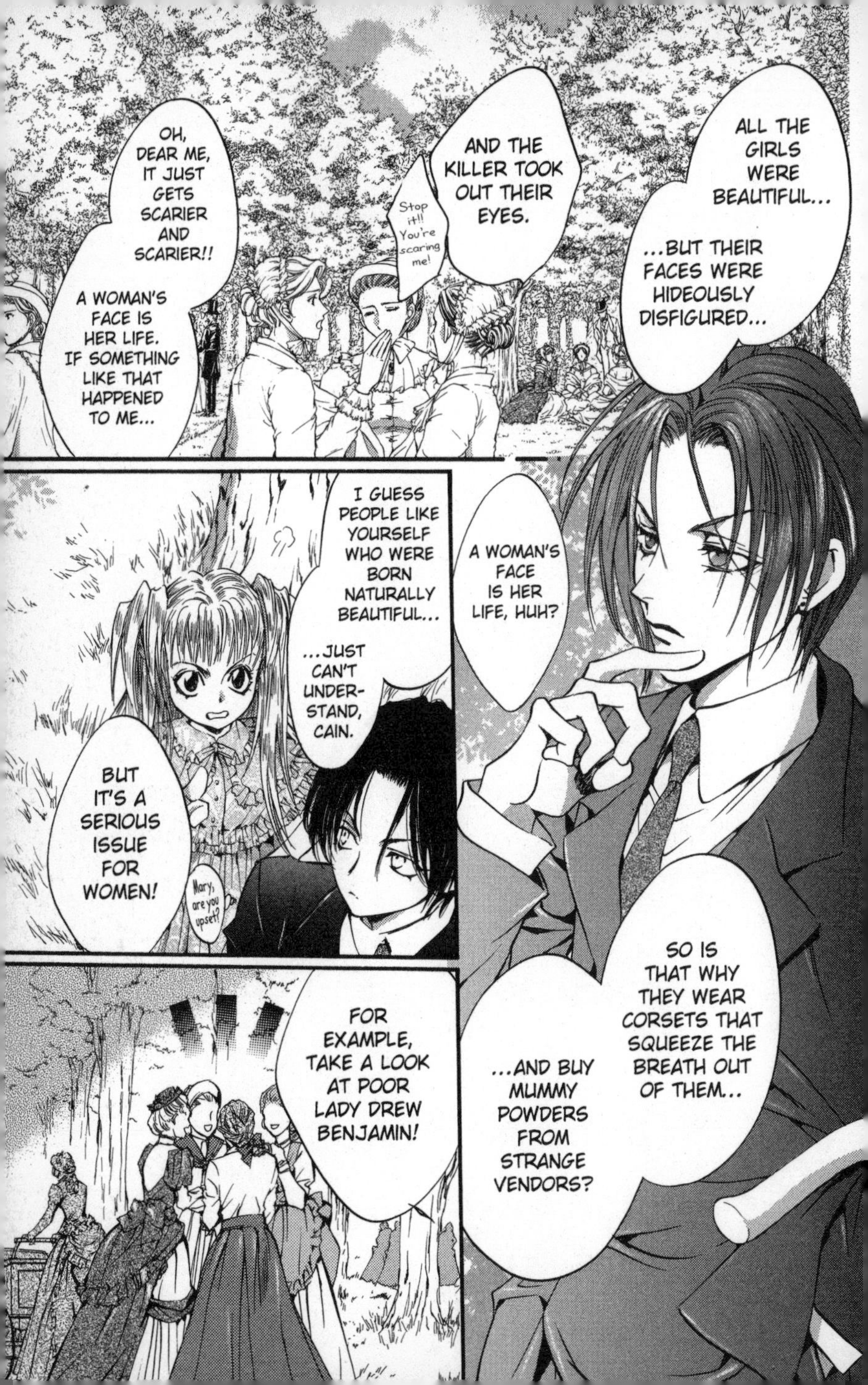
ALL THE GIRLS WERE BEAUTIFUL...
...BUT THEIR FACES WERE HIDEOUSLY DISFIGURED...
AND THE KILLER TOOK OUT THEIR EYES.
Stop it!! You're scaring me!
OH, DEAR ME, IT JUST GETS SCARIER AND SCARIER!!
A WOMAN'S FACE IS HER LIFE. IF SOMETHING LIKE THAT HAPPENED TO ME...
A WOMAN'S FACE IS HER LIFE, HUH?
SO IS THAT WHY THEY WEAR CORSETS THAT SQUEEZE THE BREATH OUT OF THEM...
...AND BUY MUMMY POWDERS FROM STRANGE VENDORS?
I GUESS PEOPLE LIKE YOURSELF WHO WERE BORN NATURALLY BEAUTIFUL...
...JUST CAN'T UNDER-STAND, CAIN.
BUT IT'S A SERIOUS ISSUE FOR WOMEN!
Mary, are you upset?
FOR EXAMPLE, TAKE A LOOK AT POOR LADY DREW BENJAMIN!

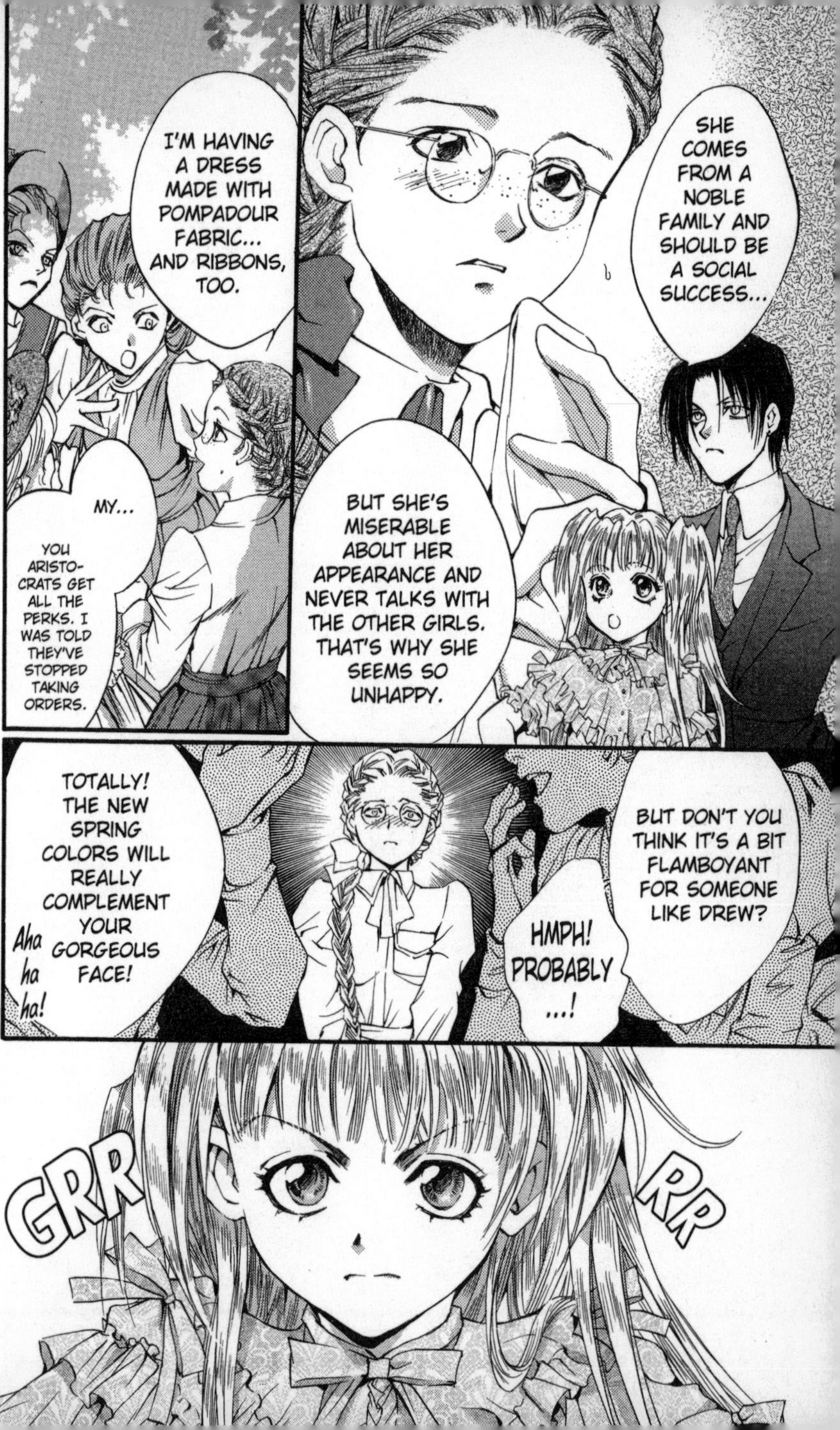
SHE COMES FROM A NOBLE FAMILY AND SHOULD BE A SOCIAL SUCCESS...
BUT SHE'S MISERABLE ABOUT HER APPEARANCE AND NEVER TALKS WITH THE OTHER GIRLS. THAT'S WHY SHE SEEMS SO UNHAPPY.
I'M HAVING A DRESS MADE WITH POMPADOUR FABRIC... AND RIBBONS, TOO.
MY...
YOU ARISTO-CRATS GET ALL THE PERKS. I WAS TOLD THEY'VE STOPPED TAKING ORDERS.
BUT DON'T YOU THINK IT'S A BIT FLAMBOYANT FOR SOMEONE LIKE DREW?
HMPH! PROBABLY ...!
TOTALLY! THE NEW SPRING COLORS WILL REALLY COMPLEMENT YOUR GORGEOUS FACE!
Aha ha ha!
GRR
RR

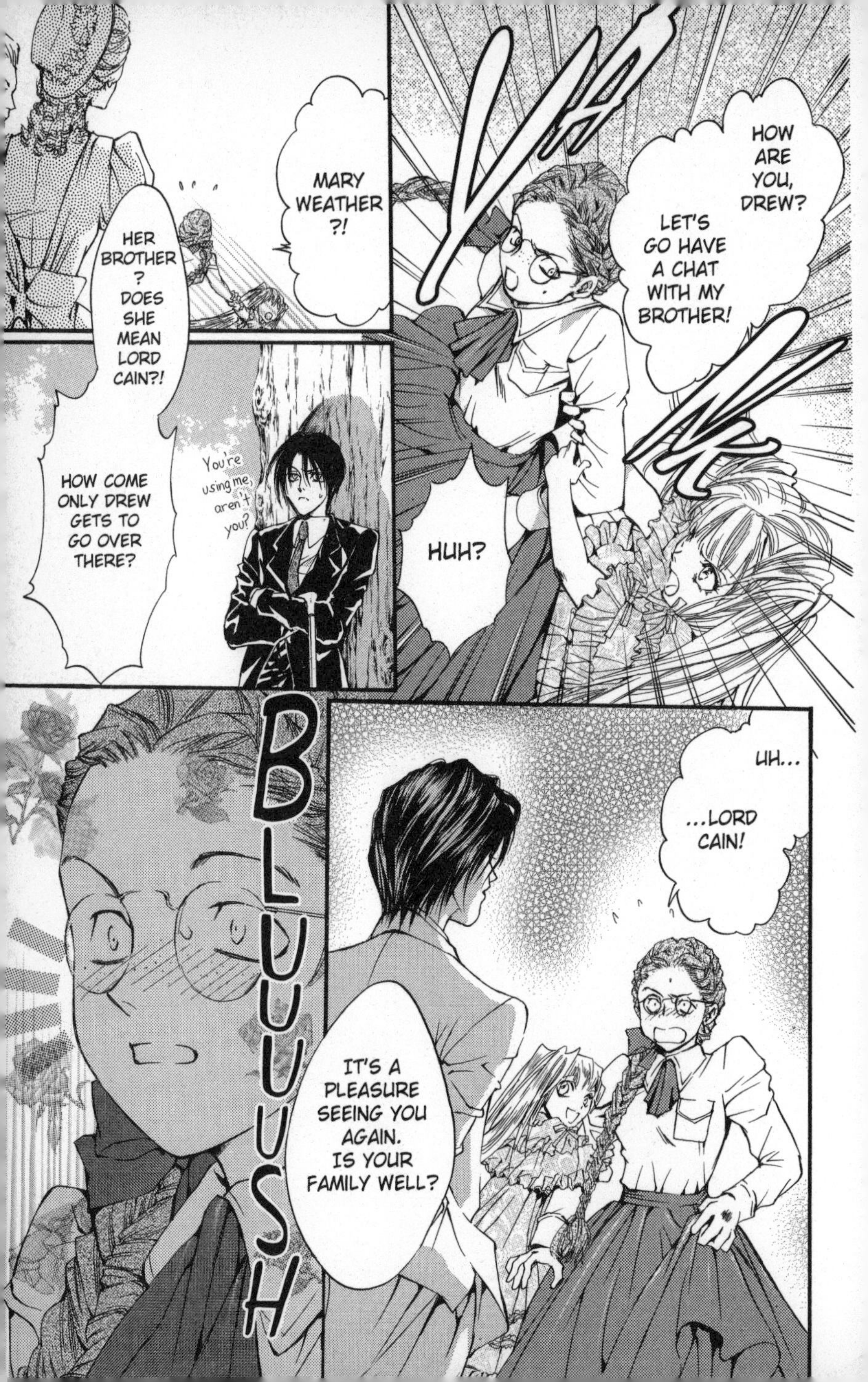
YA
HOW ARE YOU, DREW?
LET'S GO HAVE A CHAT WITH MY BROTHER!
NK
HUH?
MARY WEATHER ?!
HER BROTHER ? DOES SHE MEAN LORD CAIN?!
HOW COME ONLY DREW GETS TO GO OVER THERE?
You're using me, aren't you?
UH...
...LORD CAIN!
IT'S A PLEASURE SEEING YOU AGAIN. IS YOUR FAMILY WELL?
BLUUUUUSH

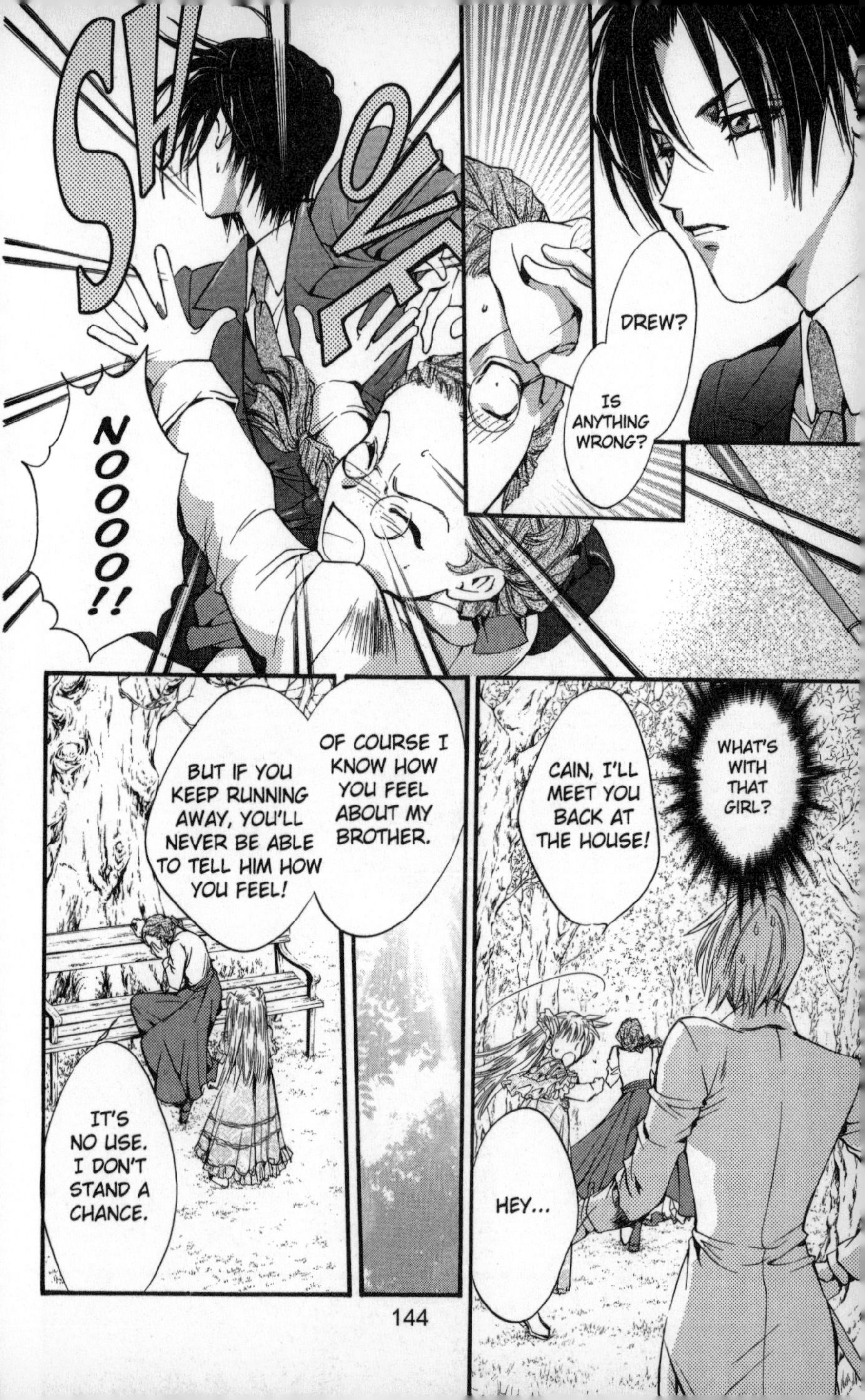
DREW?
IS ANYTHING WRONG?
SHOVE
NOOOOO!!
WHAT'S WITH THAT GIRL?
CAIN, I'LL MEET YOU BACK AT THE HOUSE!
HEY...
OF COURSE I KNOW HOW YOU FEEL ABOUT MY BROTHER.
BUT IF YOU KEEP RUNNING AWAY, YOU'LL NEVER BE ABLE TO TELL HIM HOW YOU FEEL!
IT'S NO USE. I DON'T STAND A CHANCE.

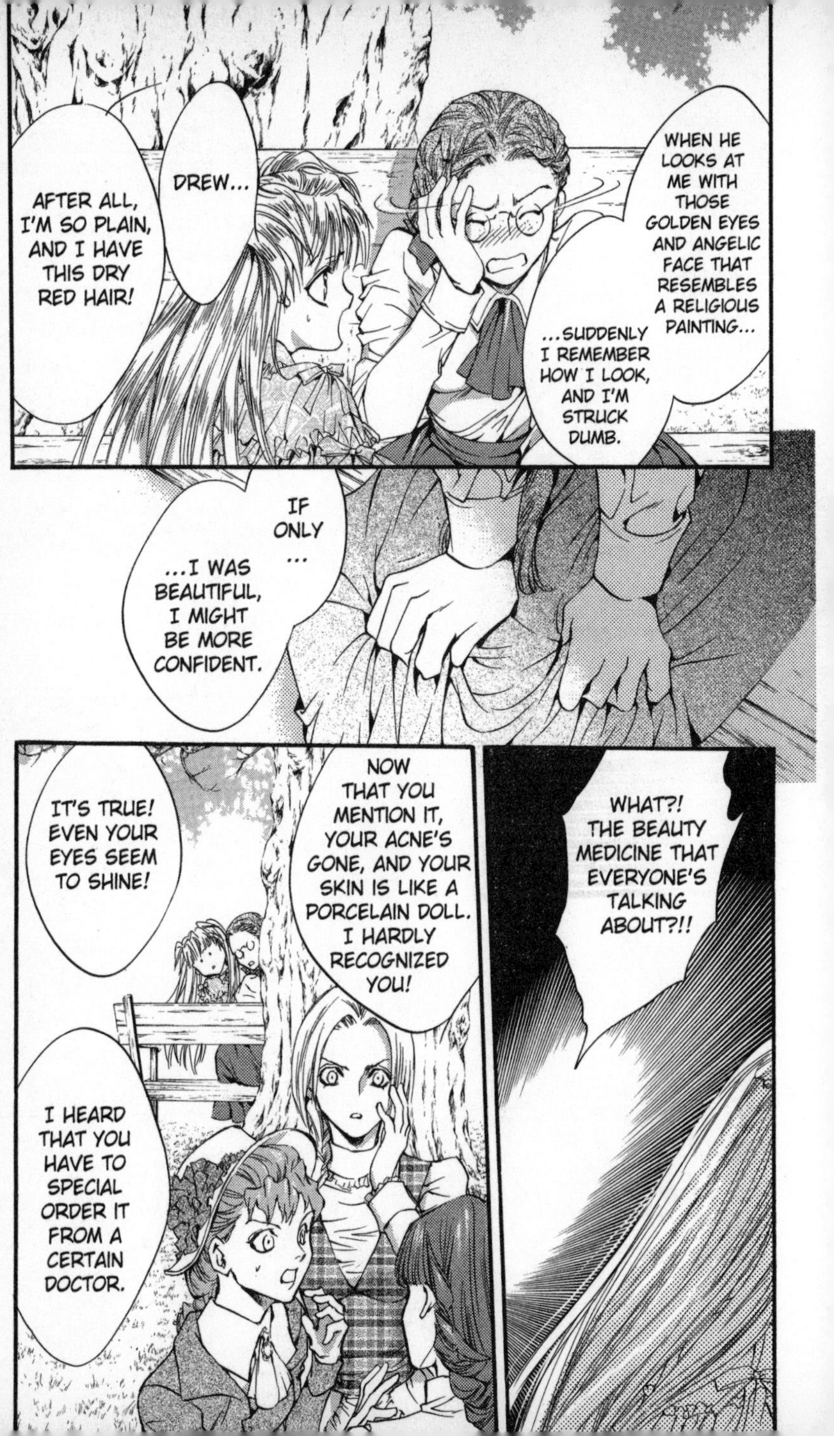
WHEN HE LOOKS AT ME WITH THOSE GOLDEN EYES AND ANGELIC FACE THAT RESEMBLES A RELIGIOUS PAINTING...
...SUDDENLY I REMEMBER HOW I LOOK, AND I'M STRUCK DUMB.
DREW...
AFTER ALL, I'M SO PLAIN, AND I HAVE THIS DRY RED HAIR!
IF ONLY...
...I WAS BEAUTIFUL, I MIGHT BE MORE CONFIDENT.
WHAT?! THE BEAUTY MEDICINE THAT EVERYONE'S TALKING ABOUT?!!
NOW THAT YOU MENTION IT, YOUR ACNE'S GONE, AND YOUR SKIN IS LIKE A PORCELAIN DOLL. I HARDLY RECOGNIZED YOU!
IT'S TRUE! EVEN YOUR EYES SEEM TO SHINE!
I HEARD THAT YOU HAVE TO SPECIAL ORDER IT FROM A CERTAIN DOCTOR.

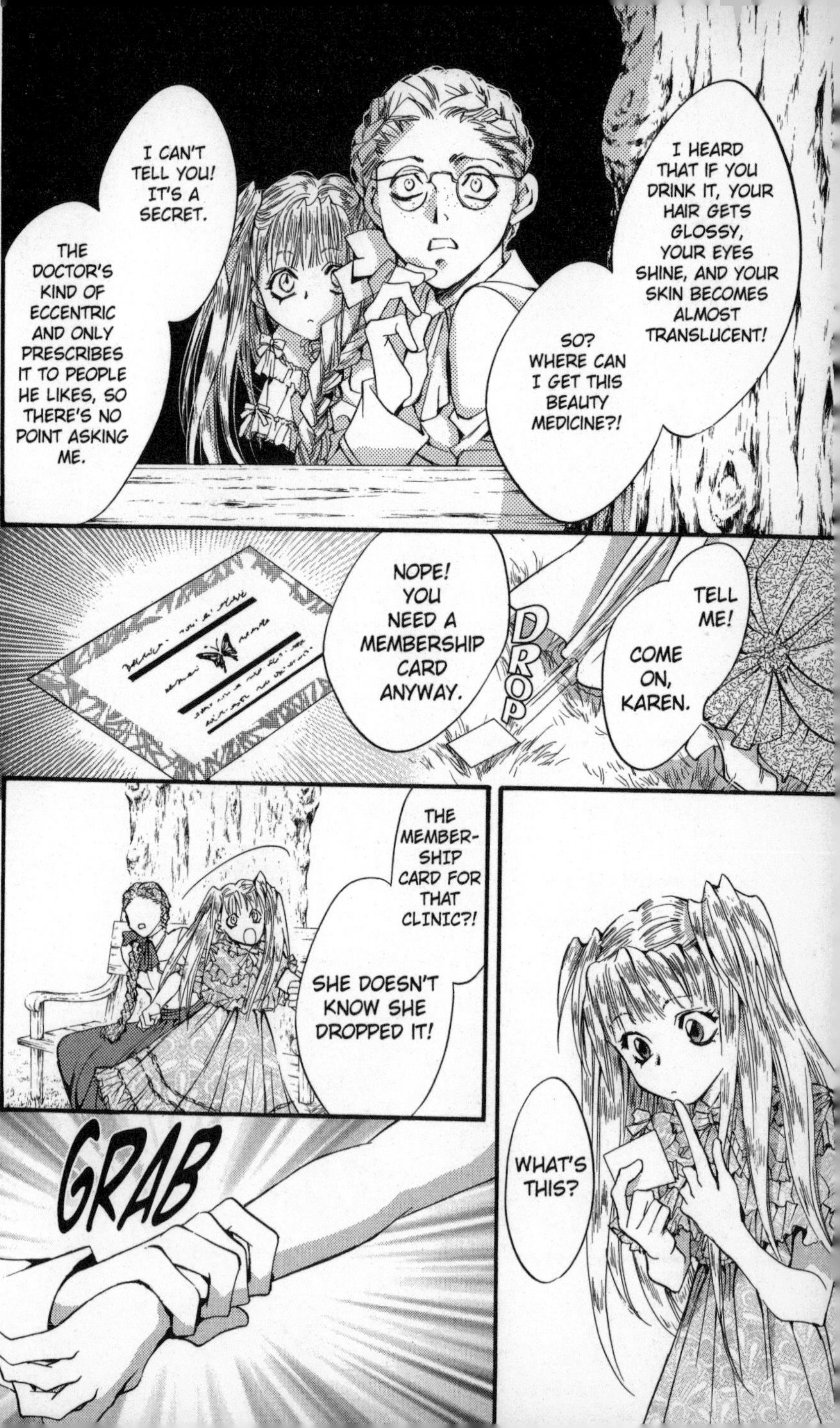
I HEARD THAT IF YOU DRINK IT, YOUR HAIR GETS GLOSSY, YOUR EYES SHINE, AND YOUR SKIN BECOMES ALMOST TRANSLUCENT!
SO? WHERE CAN I GET THIS BEAUTY MEDICINE?!
I CAN'T TELL YOU! IT'S A SECRET.
THE DOCTOR'S KIND OF ECCENTRIC AND ONLY PRESCRIBES IT TO PEOPLE HE LIKES, SO THERE'S NO POINT ASKING ME.
TELL ME!
COME ON, KAREN.
DROP
NOPE! YOU NEED A MEMBERSHIP CARD ANYWAY.
WHAT'S THIS?
THE MEMBERSHIP CARD FOR THAT CLINIC?!
SHE DOESN'T KNOW SHE DROPPED IT!
GRAB

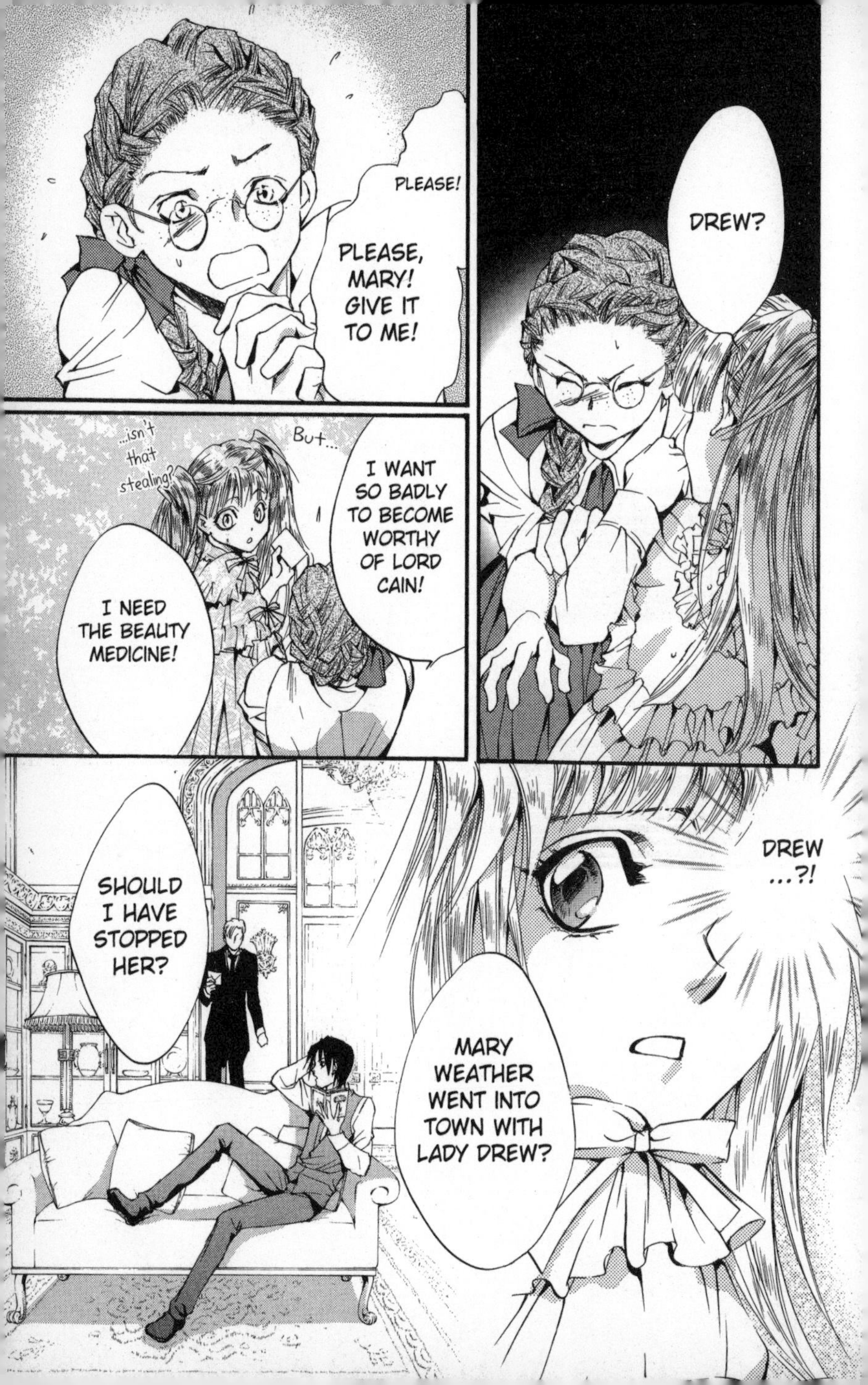
DREW?
PLEASE!
PLEASE, MARY! GIVE IT TO ME!
I WANT SO BADLY TO BECOME WORTHY OF LORD CAIN!
But...
...isn't that stealing?
I NEED THE BEAUTY MEDICINE!
DREW ...?!
MARY WEATHER WENT INTO TOWN WITH LADY DREW?
SHOULD I HAVE STOPPED HER?

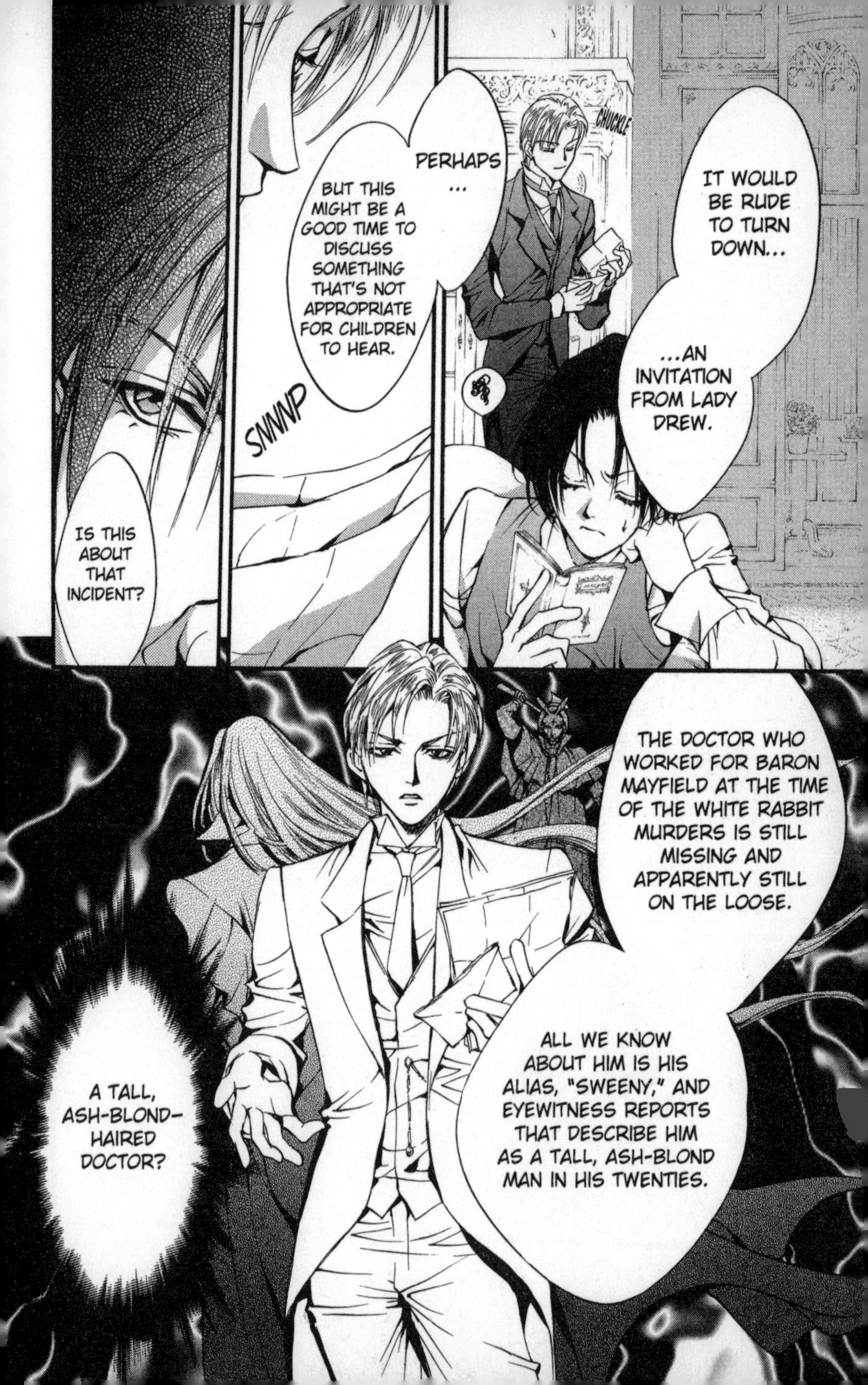

IT WOULD BE RUDE TO TURN DOWN...
CHUCKLE
...AN INVITATION FROM LADY DREW.
PERHAPS...
BUT THIS MIGHT BE A GOOD TIME TO DISCUSS SOMETHING THAT'S NOT APPROPRIATE FOR CHILDREN TO HEAR.
SNNNP
IS THIS ABOUT THAT INCIDENT?
THE DOCTOR WHO WORKED FOR BARON MAYFIELD AT THE TIME OF THE WHITE RABBIT MURDERS IS STILL MISSING AND APPARENTLY STILL ON THE LOOSE.
ALL WE KNOW ABOUT HIM IS HIS ALIAS, "SWEENY," AND EYEWITNESS REPORTS THAT DESCRIBE HIM AS A TALL, ASH-BLOND MAN IN HIS TWENTIES.
A TALL, ASH-BLOND-HAIRED DOCTOR?

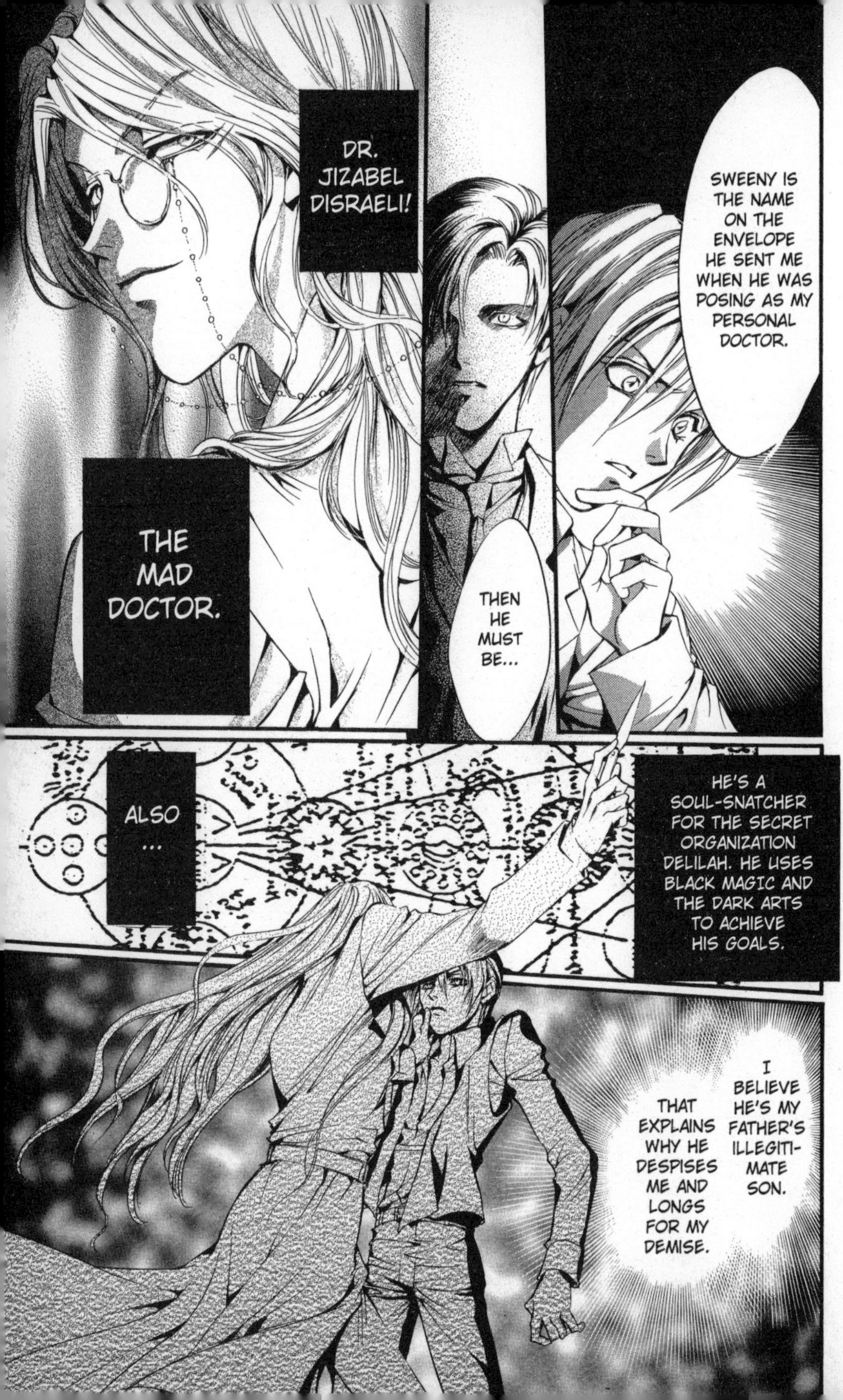
SWEENY IS THE NAME ON THE ENVELOPE HE SENT ME WHEN HE WAS POSING AS MY PERSONAL DOCTOR.
THEN HE MUST BE...
DR. JIZABEL DISRAELI!
THE MAD DOCTOR.
HE'S A SOUL-SNATCHER FOR THE SECRET ORGANIZATION DELILAH. HE USES BLACK MAGIC AND THE DARK ARTS TO ACHIEVE HIS GOALS.
ALSO ...
I BELIEVE HE'S MY FATHER'S ILLEGITI-MATE SON.
THAT EXPLAINS WHY HE DESPISES ME AND LONGS FOR MY DEMISE.

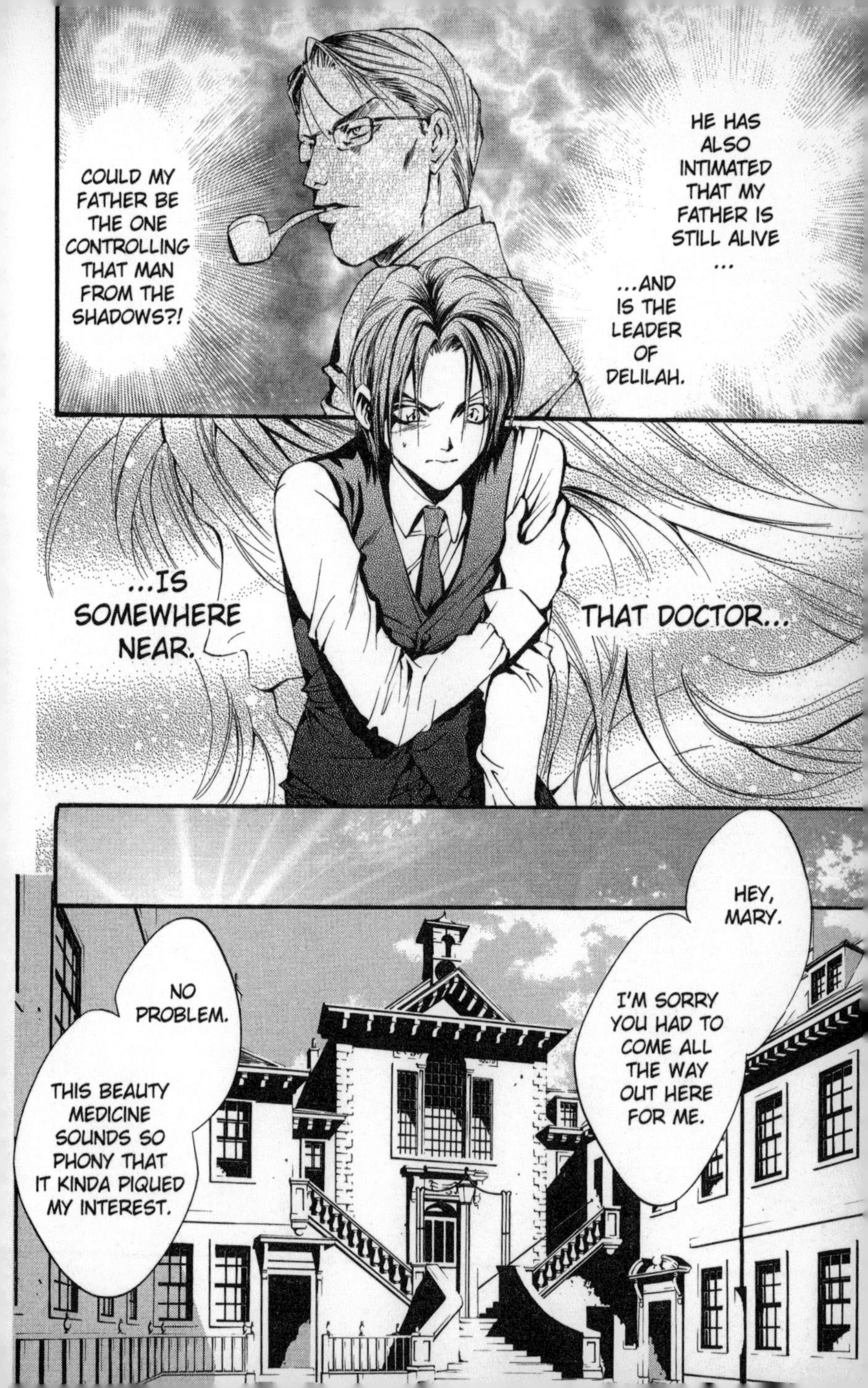
HE HAS ALSO INTIMATED THAT MY FATHER IS STILL ALIVE ...
...AND IS THE LEADER OF DELILAH.
COULD MY FATHER BE THE ONE CONTROLLING THAT MAN FROM THE SHADOWS?!
THAT DOCTOR...
...IS SOMEWHERE NEAR.
HEY, MARY.
I'M SORRY YOU HAD TO COME ALL THE WAY OUT HERE FOR ME.
NO PROBLEM.
THIS BEAUTY MEDICINE SOUNDS SO PHONY THAT IT KINDA PIQUED MY INTEREST.

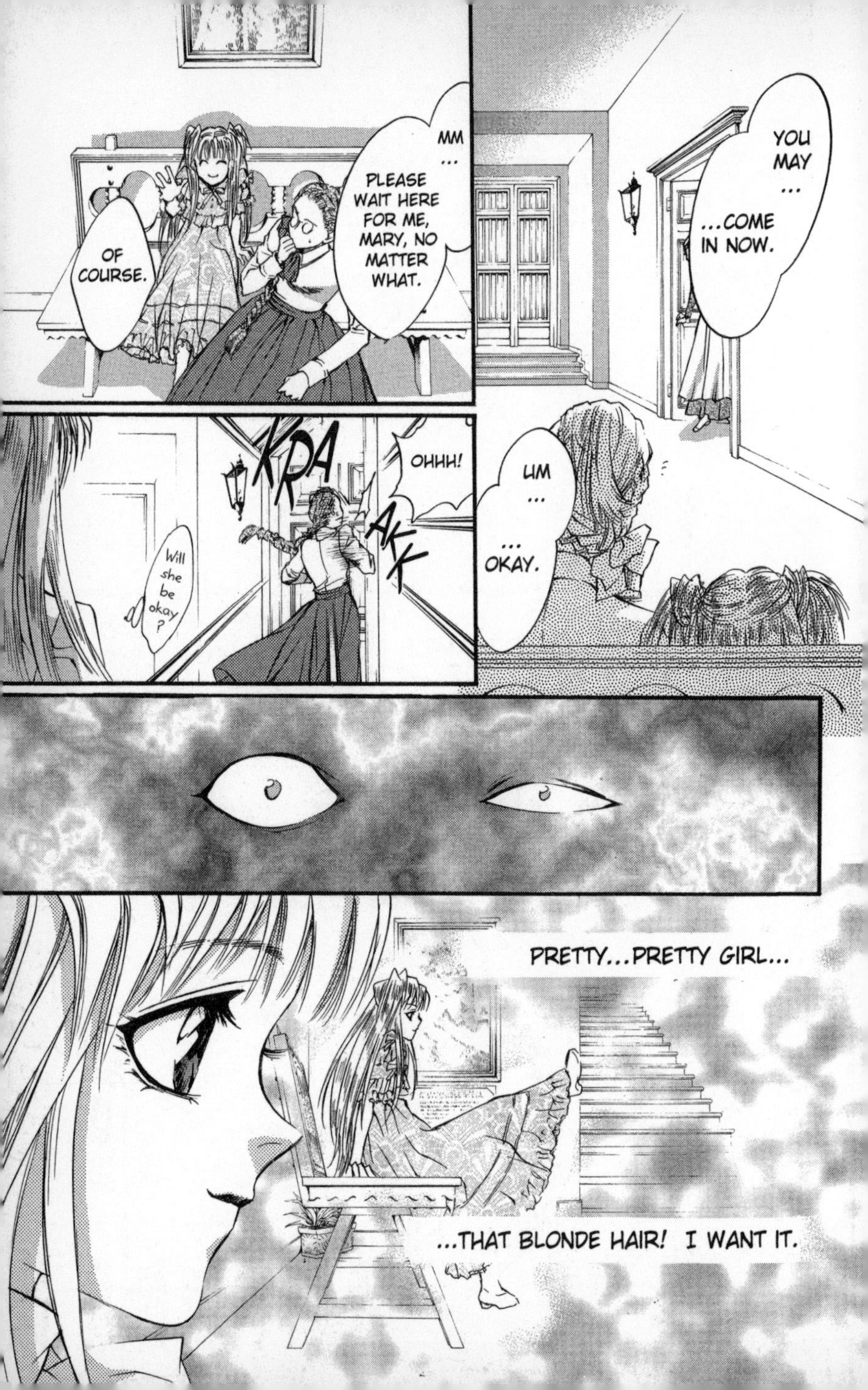

YOU MAY ...
...COME IN NOW.
UM ...
... OKAY.
MM ... PLEASE WAIT HERE FOR ME, MARY, NO MATTER WHAT.
OF COURSE.
OHHH!
KRA AKK
Will she be okay?
PRETTY...PRETTY GIRL...
...THAT BLONDE HAIR! I WANT IT.

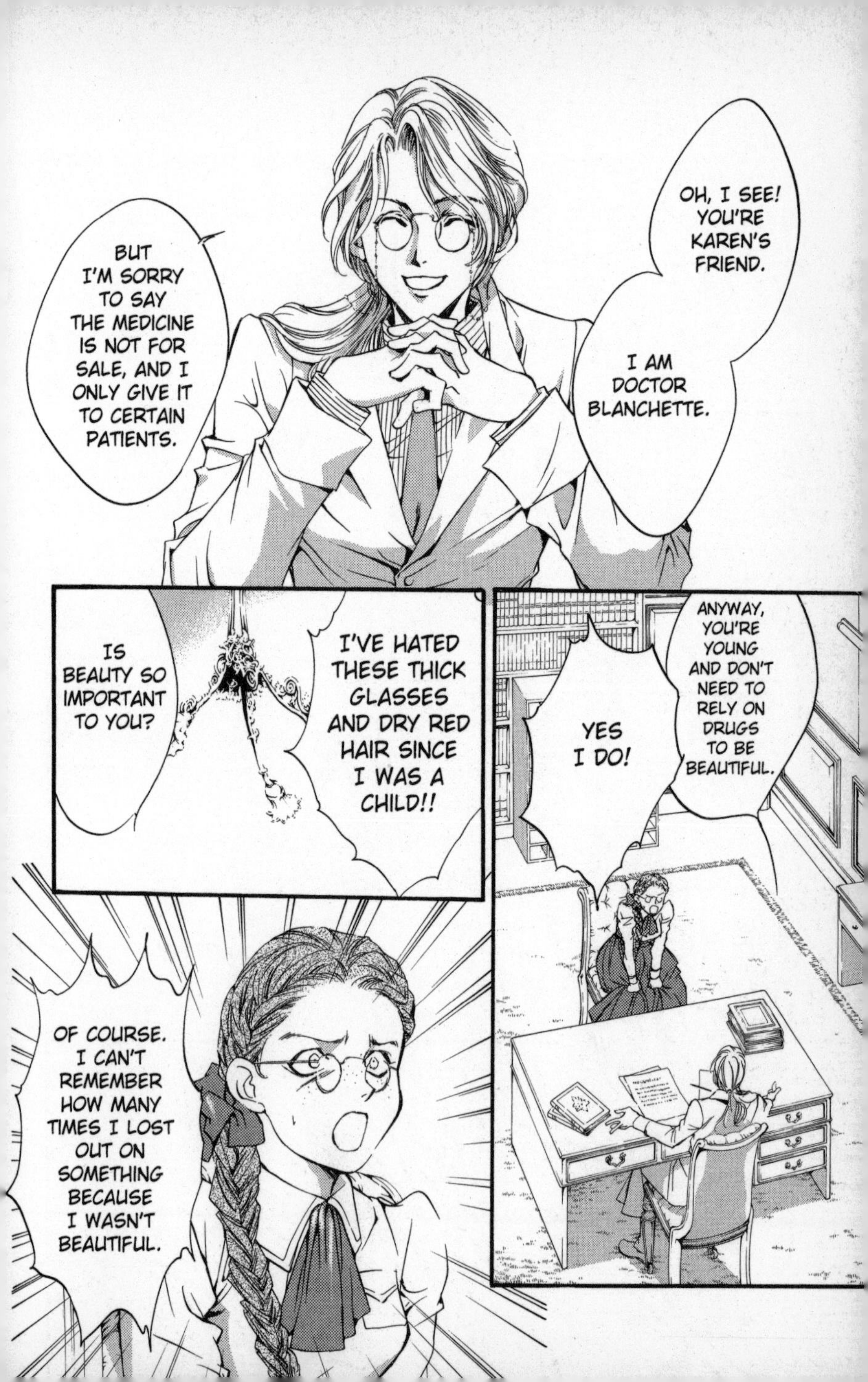
OH, I SEE! YOU'RE KAREN'S FRIEND.
I AM DOCTOR BLANCHETTE.
BUT I'M SORRY TO SAY THE MEDICINE IS NOT FOR SALE, AND I ONLY GIVE IT TO CERTAIN PATIENTS.
ANYWAY, YOU'RE YOUNG AND DON'T NEED TO RELY ON DRUGS TO BE BEAUTIFUL.
YES I DO!
I'VE HATED THESE THICK GLASSES AND DRY RED HAIR SINCE I WAS A CHILD!!
IS BEAUTY SO IMPORTANT TO YOU?
OF COURSE. I CAN'T REMEMBER HOW MANY TIMES I LOST OUT ON SOMETHING BECAUSE I WASN'T BEAUTIFUL.

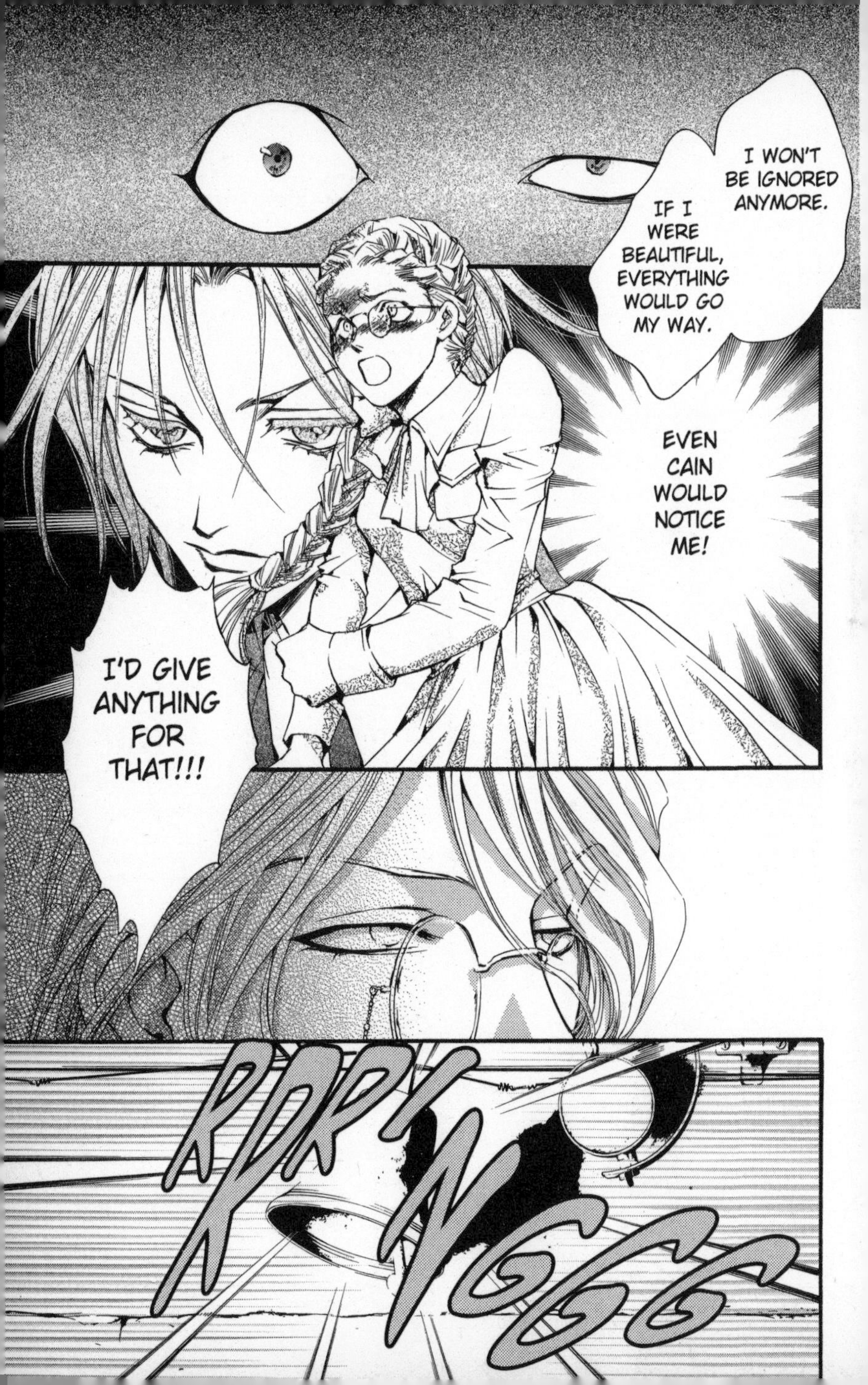
I WON'T BE IGNORED ANYMORE.
IF I WERE BEAUTIFUL, EVERYTHING WOULD GO MY WAY.
EVEN CAIN WOULD NOTICE ME!
I'D GIVE ANYTHING FOR THAT!!!
RRRINGGG

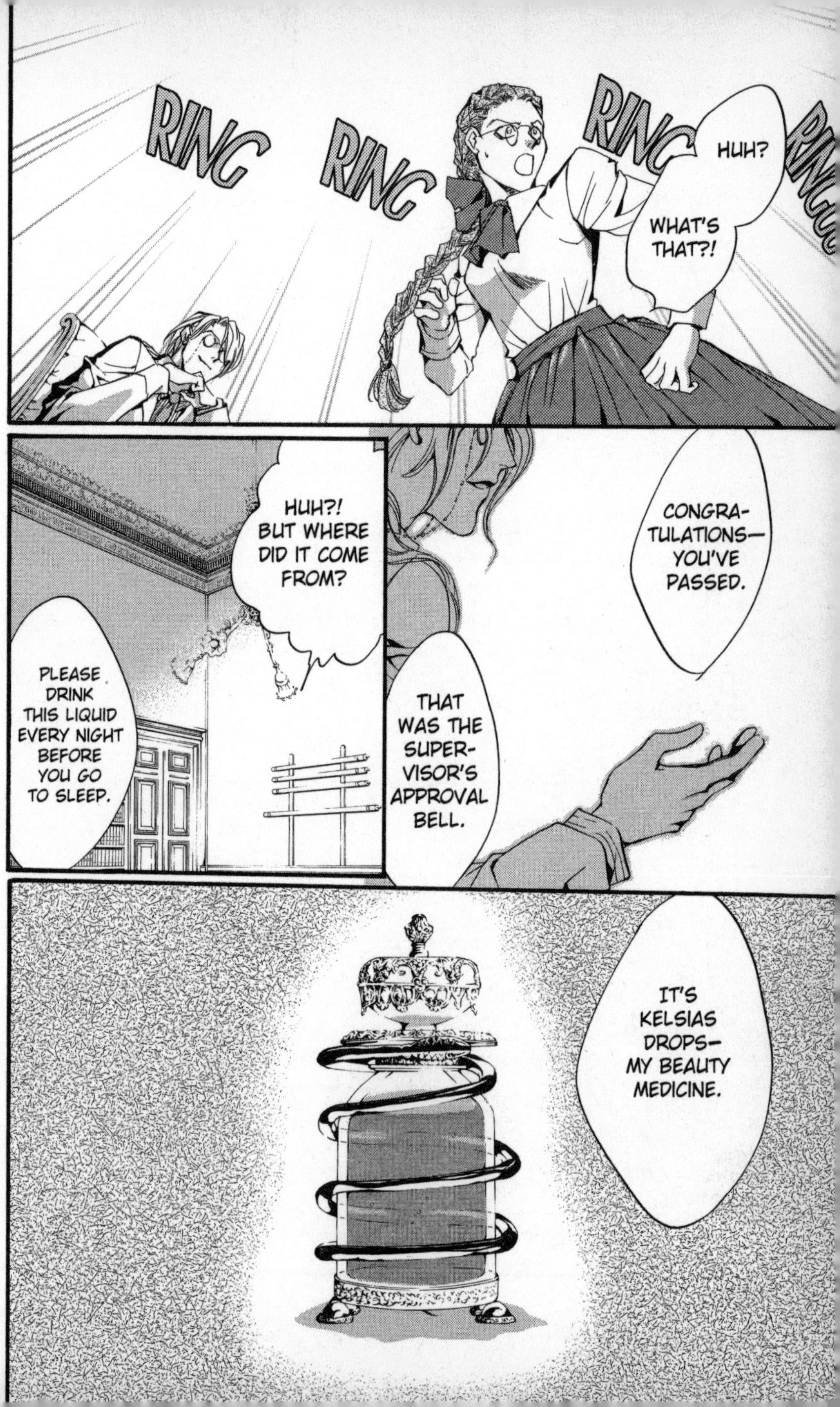
RINGG
RING
RING
RING
HUH?
WHAT'S THAT?!
CONGRA-TULATIONS—YOU'VE PASSED.
THAT WAS THE SUPER-VISOR'S APPROVAL BELL.
HUH?! BUT WHERE DID IT COME FROM?
PLEASE DRINK THIS LIQUID EVERY NIGHT BEFORE YOU GO TO SLEEP.
IT'S KELSIAS DROPS—MY BEAUTY MEDICINE.

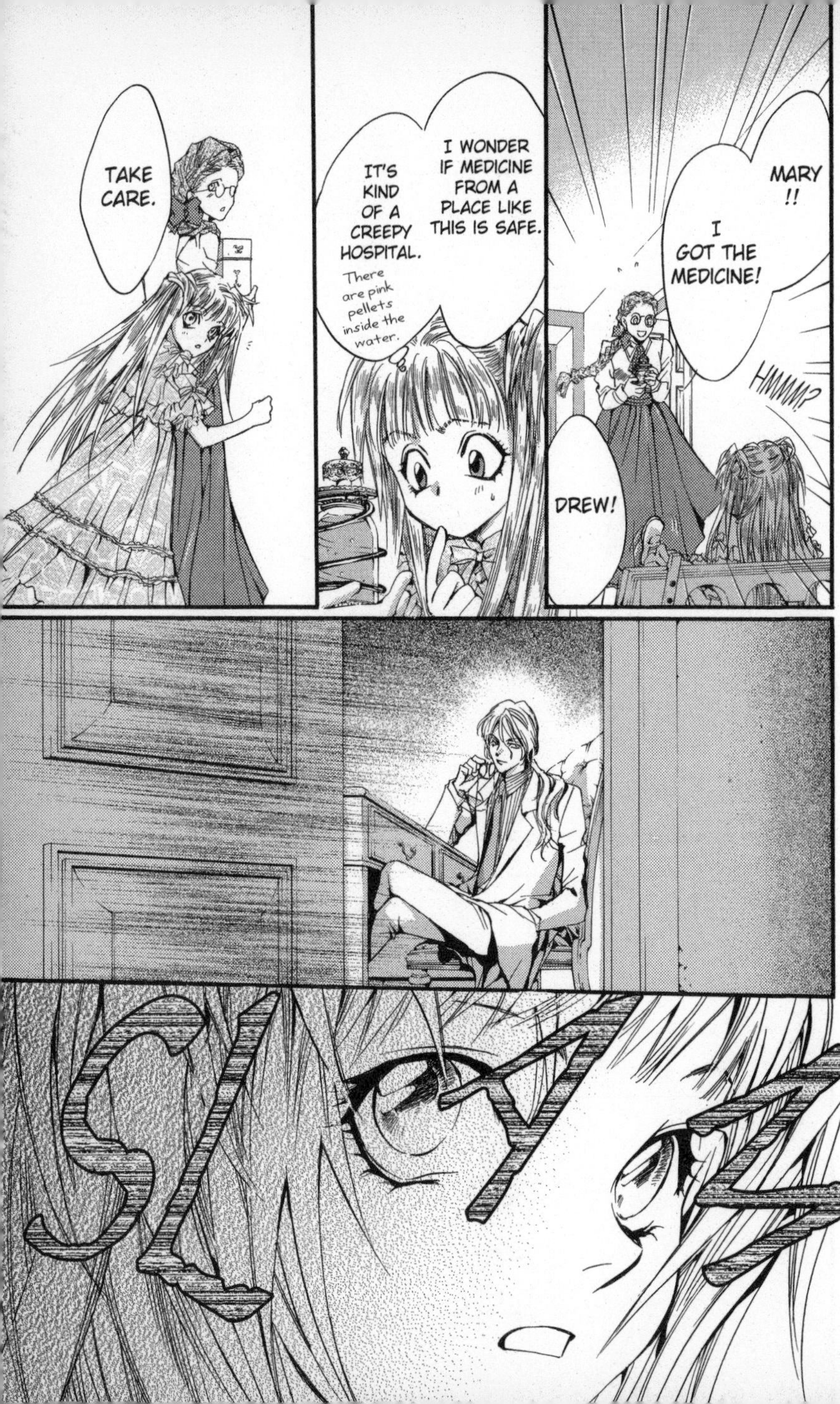
MARY!!
I GOT THE MEDICINE!
HMMM?
DREW!
I WONDER IF MEDICINE FROM A PLACE LIKE THIS IS SAFE.
IT'S KIND OF A CREEPY HOSPITAL.
There are pink pellets inside the water.
TAKE CARE.

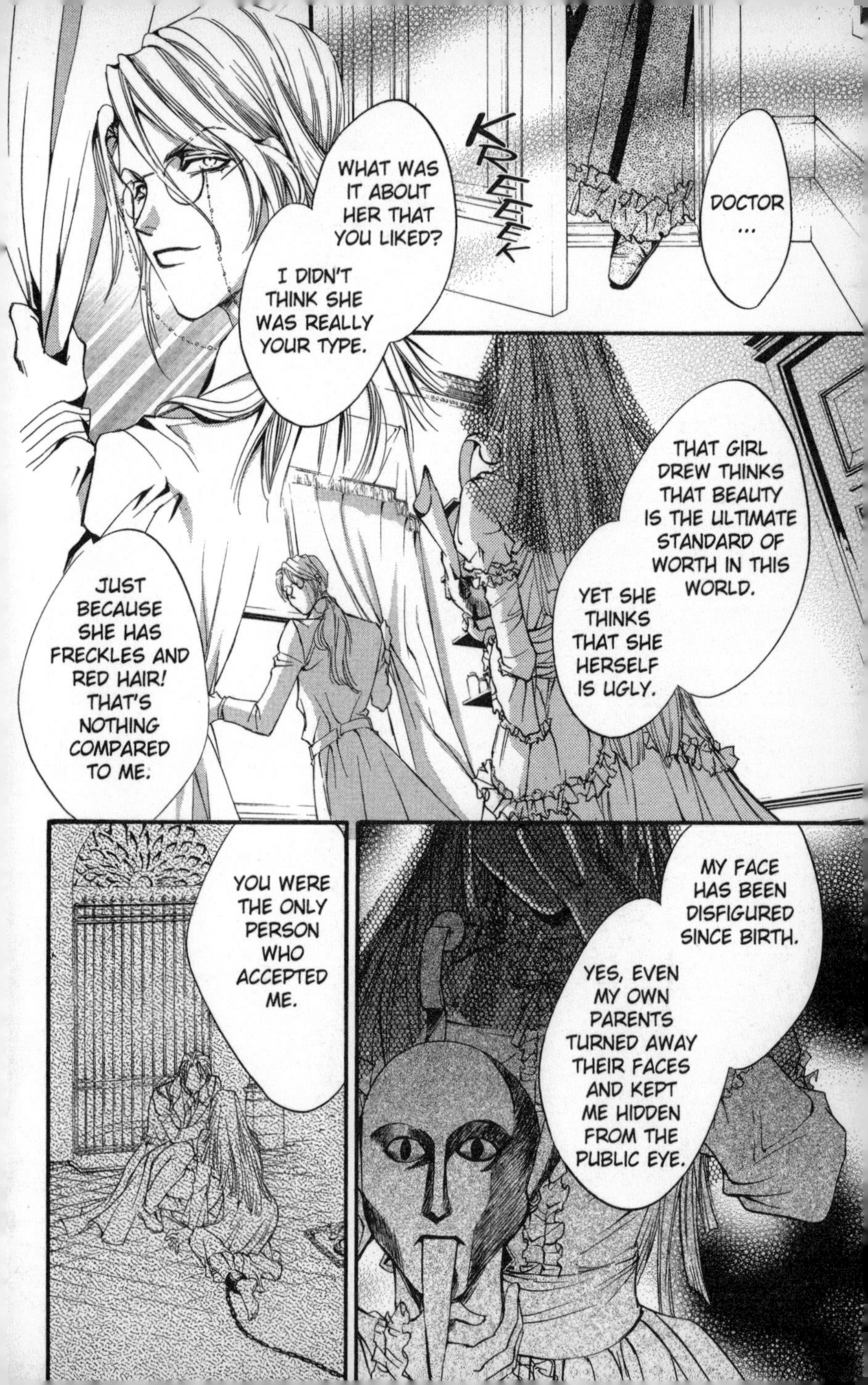
DOCTOR ...
KREEEK
WHAT WAS IT ABOUT HER THAT YOU LIKED?
I DIDN'T THINK SHE WAS REALLY YOUR TYPE.
THAT GIRL DREW THINKS THAT BEAUTY IS THE ULTIMATE STANDARD OF WORTH IN THIS WORLD.
YET SHE THINKS THAT SHE HERSELF IS UGLY.
JUST BECAUSE SHE HAS FRECKLES AND RED HAIR! THAT'S NOTHING COMPARED TO ME.
MY FACE HAS BEEN DISFIGURED SINCE BIRTH.
YES, EVEN MY OWN PARENTS TURNED AWAY THEIR FACES AND KEPT ME HIDDEN FROM THE PUBLIC EYE.
YOU WERE THE ONLY PERSON WHO ACCEPTED ME.

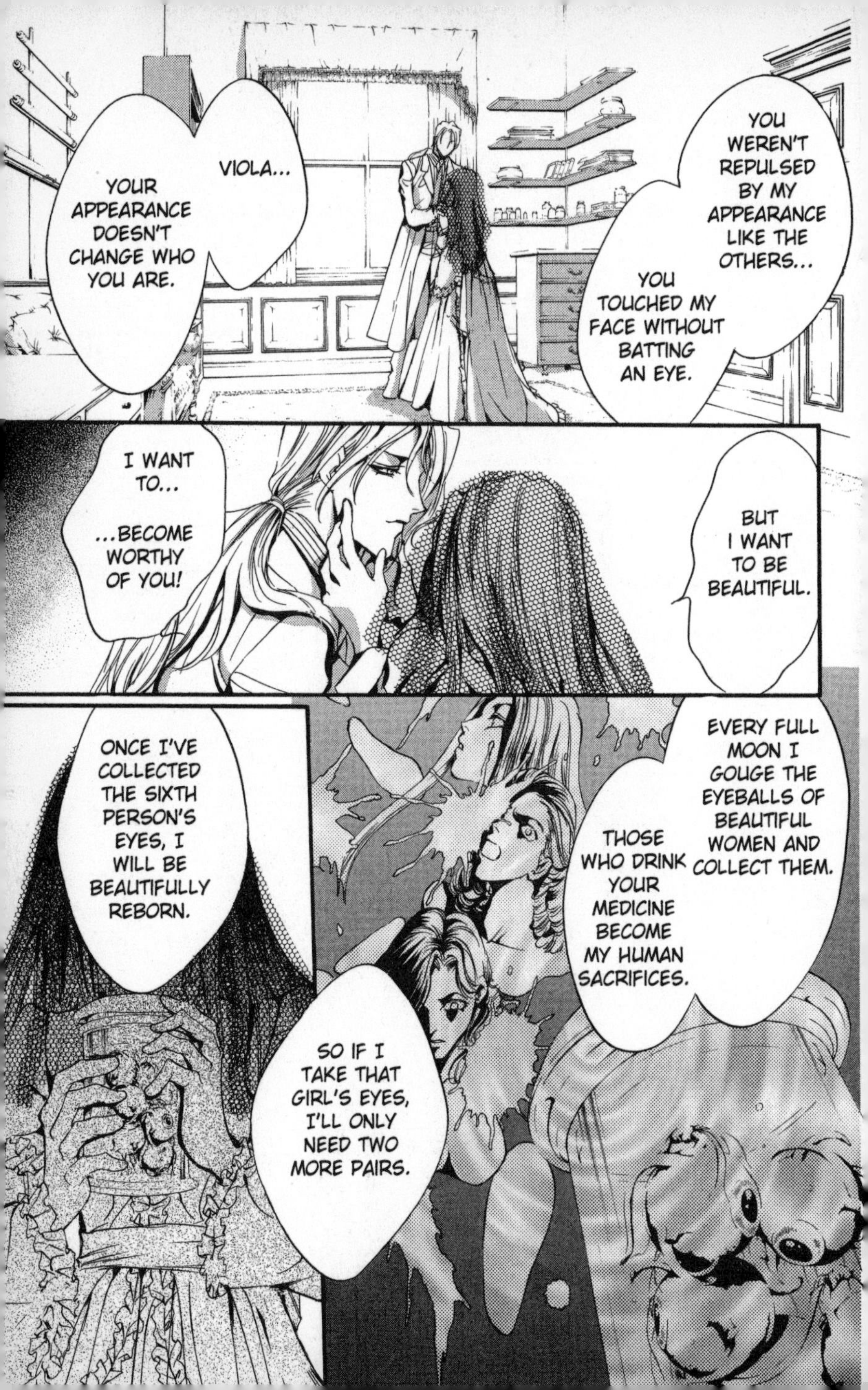
YOU WEREN'T REPULSED BY MY APPEARANCE LIKE THE OTHERS...
YOU TOUCHED MY FACE WITHOUT BATTING AN EYE.
VIOLA...
YOUR APPEARANCE DOESN'T CHANGE WHO YOU ARE.
BUT I WANT TO BE BEAUTIFUL.
I WANT TO...
...BECOME WORTHY OF YOU!
EVERY FULL MOON I GOUGE THE EYEBALLS OF BEAUTIFUL WOMEN AND COLLECT THEM.
THOSE WHO DRINK YOUR MEDICINE BECOME MY HUMAN SACRIFICES.
SO IF I TAKE THAT GIRL'S EYES, I'LL ONLY NEED TWO MORE PAIRS.
ONCE I'VE COLLECTED THE SIXTH PERSON'S EYES, I WILL BE BEAUTIFULLY REBORN.

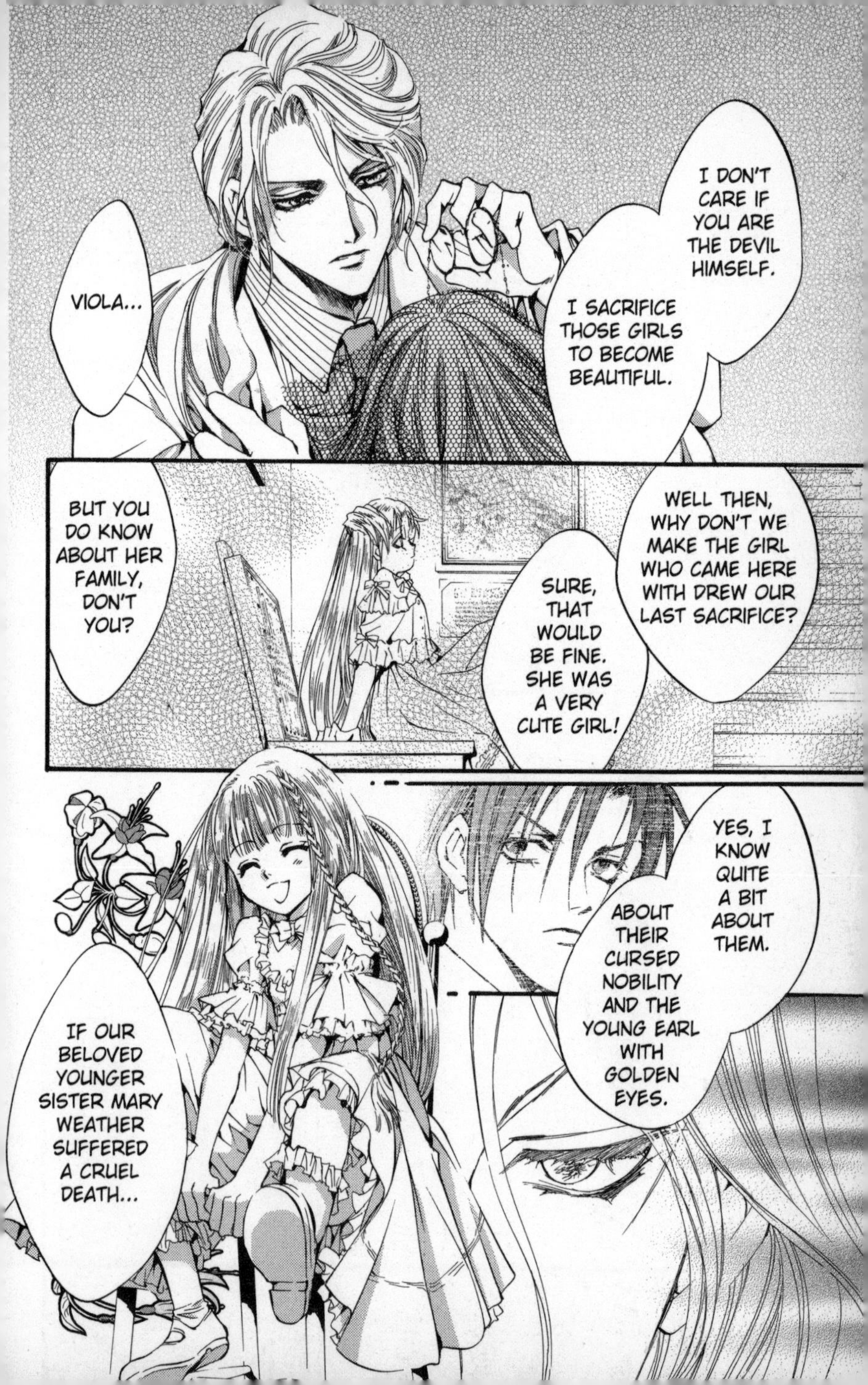
I DON'T CARE IF YOU ARE THE DEVIL HIMSELF.
I SACRIFICE THOSE GIRLS TO BECOME BEAUTIFUL.
VIOLA...
WELL THEN, WHY DON'T WE MAKE THE GIRL WHO CAME HERE WITH DREW OUR LAST SACRIFICE?
SURE, THAT WOULD BE FINE. SHE WAS A VERY CUTE GIRL!
BUT YOU DO KNOW ABOUT HER FAMILY, DON'T YOU?
YES, I KNOW QUITE A BIT ABOUT THEM.
ABOUT THEIR CURSED NOBILITY AND THE YOUNG EARL WITH GOLDEN EYES.
IF OUR BELOVED YOUNGER SISTER MARY WEATHER SUFFERED A CRUEL DEATH...

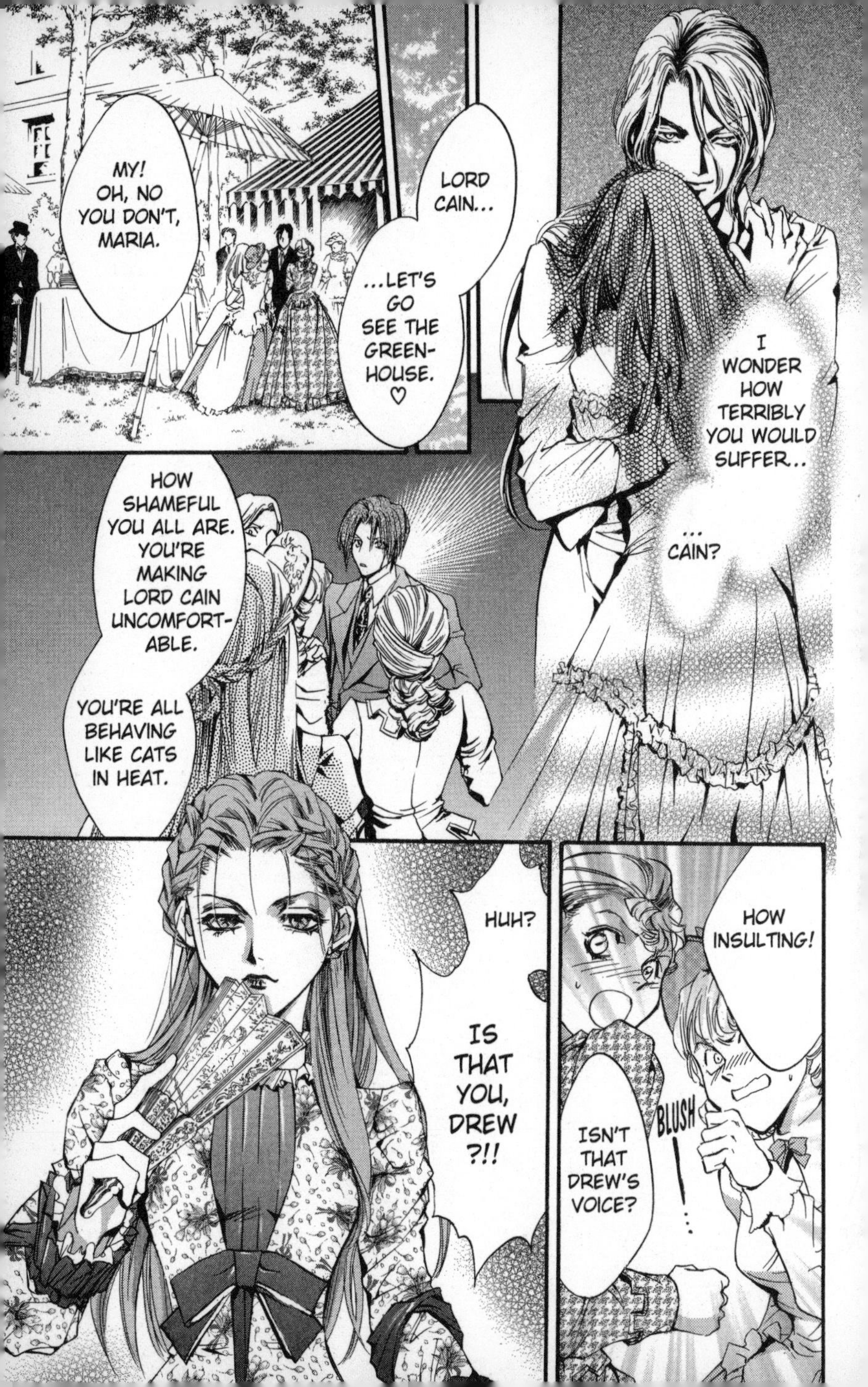
I WONDER HOW TERRIBLY YOU WOULD SUFFER...
...CAIN?
LORD CAIN...
...LET'S GO SEE THE GREEN-HOUSE. ♡
MY! OH, NO YOU DON'T, MARIA.
HOW SHAMEFUL YOU ALL ARE. YOU'RE MAKING LORD CAIN UNCOMFORT-ABLE.
YOU'RE ALL BEHAVING LIKE CATS IN HEAT.
HOW INSULTING!
BLUSH
...
ISN'T THAT DREW'S VOICE?
HUH?
IS THAT YOU, DREW?!!

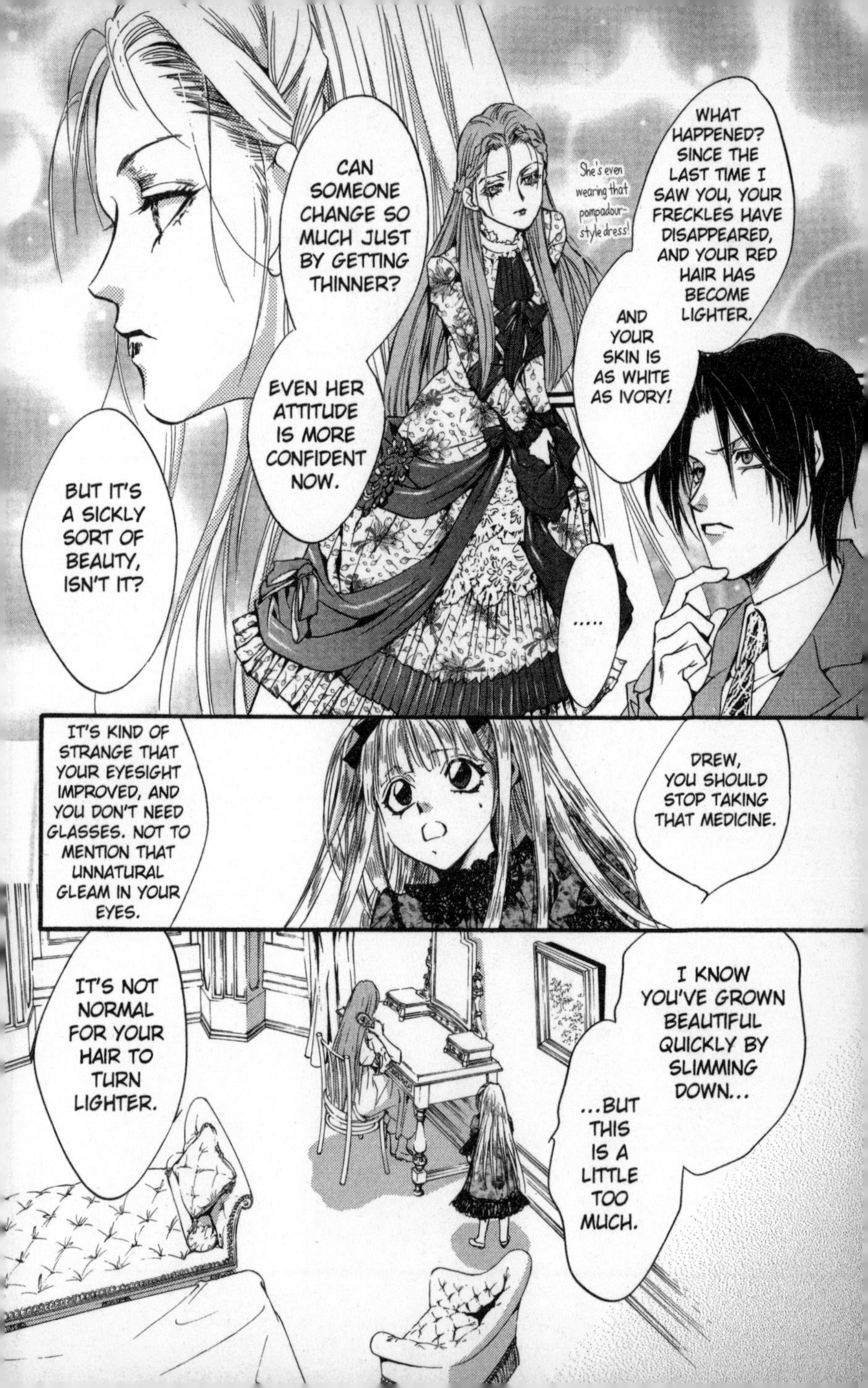
WHAT HAPPENED? SINCE THE LAST TIME I SAW YOU, YOUR FRECKLES HAVE DISAPPEARED, AND YOUR RED HAIR HAS BECOME LIGHTER.
She's even wearing that pompadour-style dress!
AND YOUR SKIN IS AS WHITE AS IVORY!
CAN SOMEONE CHANGE SO MUCH JUST BY GETTING THINNER?
EVEN HER ATTITUDE IS MORE CONFIDENT NOW.
.....
BUT IT'S A SICKLY SORT OF BEAUTY, ISN'T IT?
DREW, YOU SHOULD STOP TAKING THAT MEDICINE.
IT'S KIND OF STRANGE THAT YOUR EYESIGHT IMPROVED, AND YOU DON'T NEED GLASSES. NOT TO MENTION THAT UNNATURAL GLEAM IN YOUR EYES.
I KNOW YOU'VE GROWN BEAUTIFUL QUICKLY BY SLIMMING DOWN...
...BUT THIS IS A LITTLE TOO MUCH.
IT'S NOT NORMAL FOR YOUR HAIR TO TURN LIGHTER.

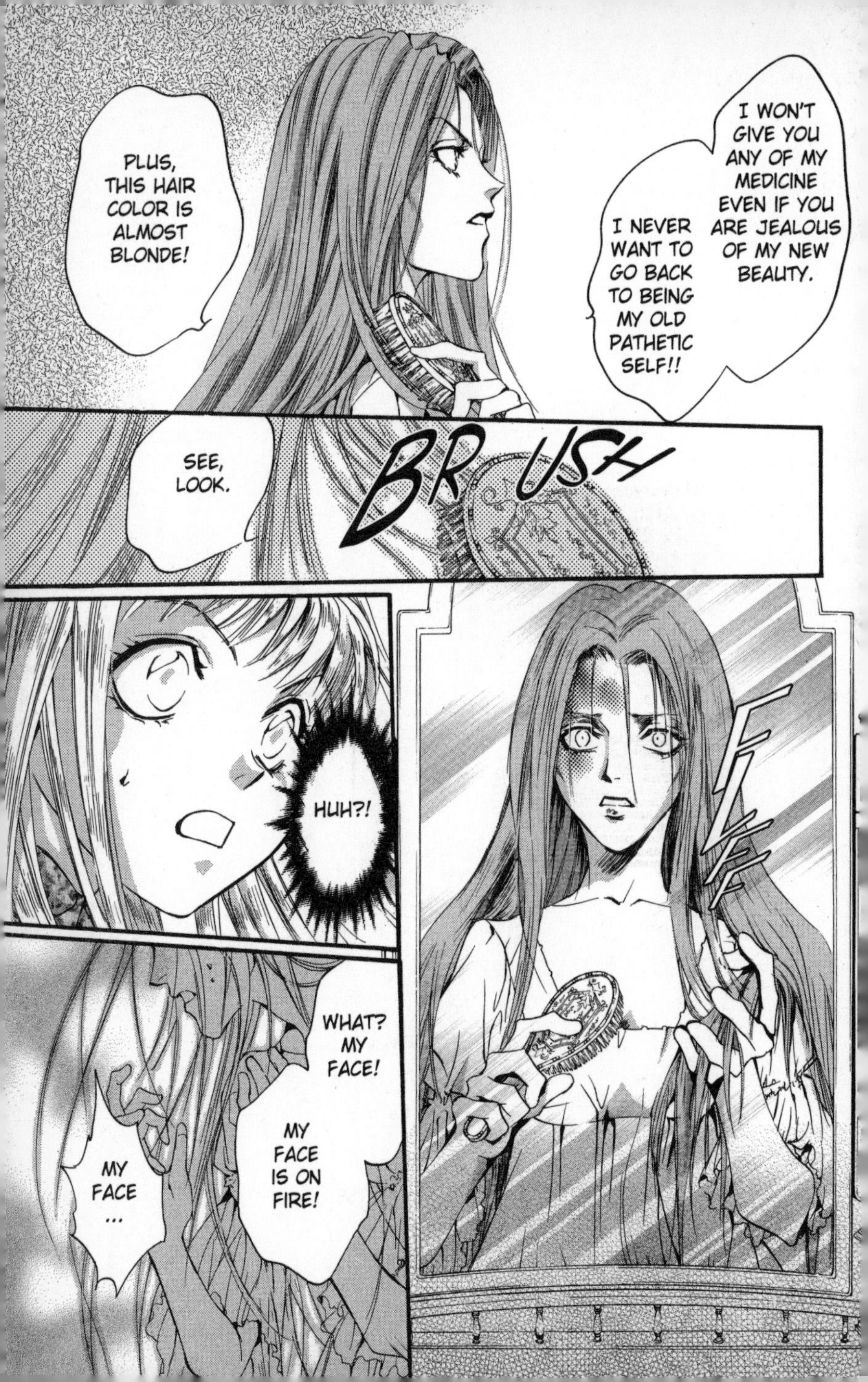
I WON'T GIVE YOU ANY OF MY MEDICINE EVEN IF YOU ARE JEALOUS OF MY NEW BEAUTY.
I NEVER WANT TO GO BACK TO BEING MY OLD PATHETIC SELF!!
PLUS, THIS HAIR COLOR IS ALMOST BLONDE!
BRUSH
SEE, LOOK.
HUH?!
WHAT? MY FACE!
MY FACE IS ON FIRE!
MY FACE ...

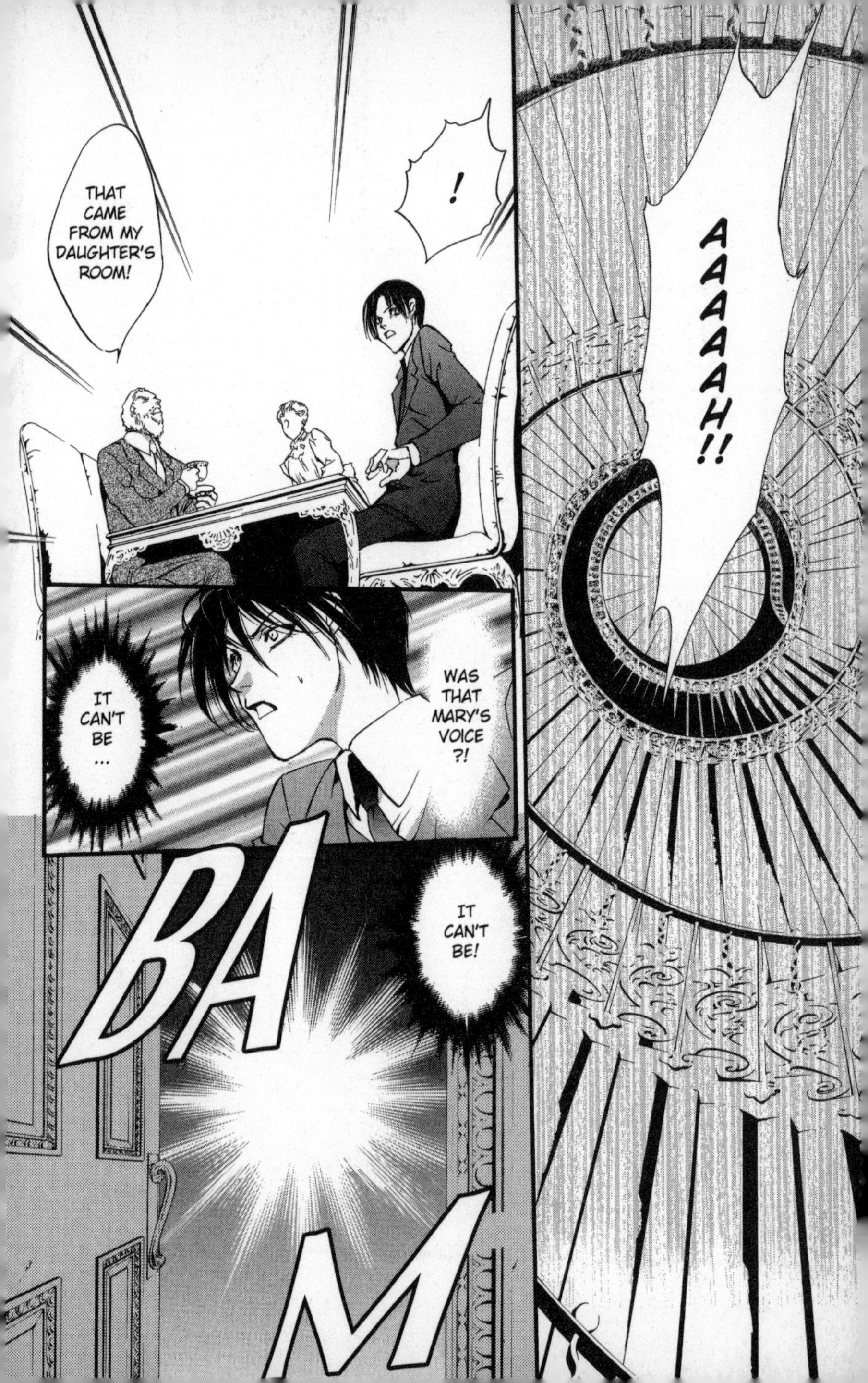
AAAAAH!!
!
THAT CAME FROM MY DAUGHTER'S ROOM!
WAS THAT MARY'S VOICE ?!
IT CAN'T BE ...
IT CAN'T BE!
BAM

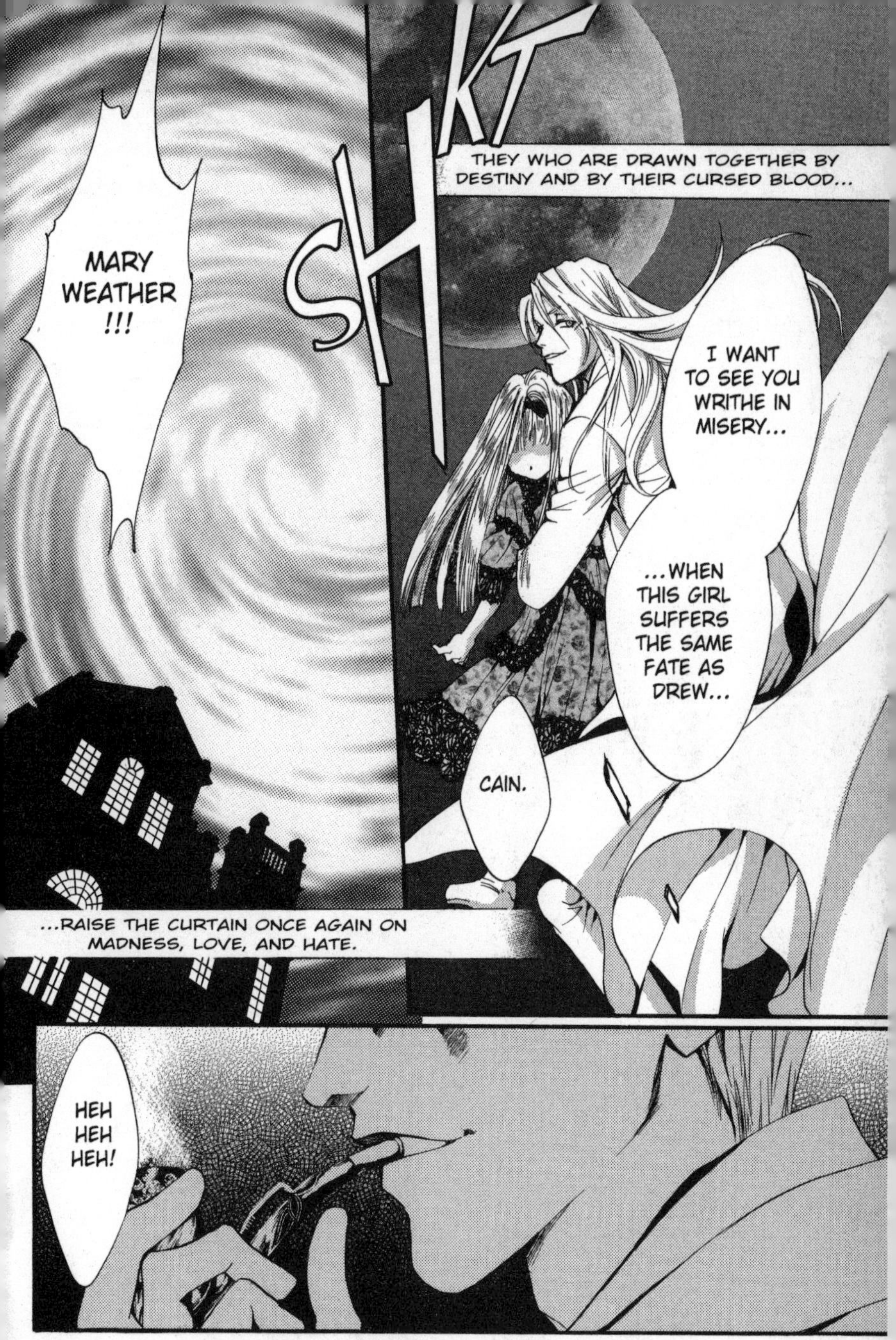
SHKT
THEY WHO ARE DRAWN TOGETHER BY DESTINY AND BY THEIR CURSED BLOOD...
I WANT TO SEE YOU WRITHE IN MISERY...
...WHEN THIS GIRL SUFFERS THE SAME FATE AS DREW...
CAIN.
MARY WEATHER !!!
...RAISE THE CURTAIN ONCE AGAIN ON MADNESS, LOVE, AND HATE.
HEH HEH HEH!

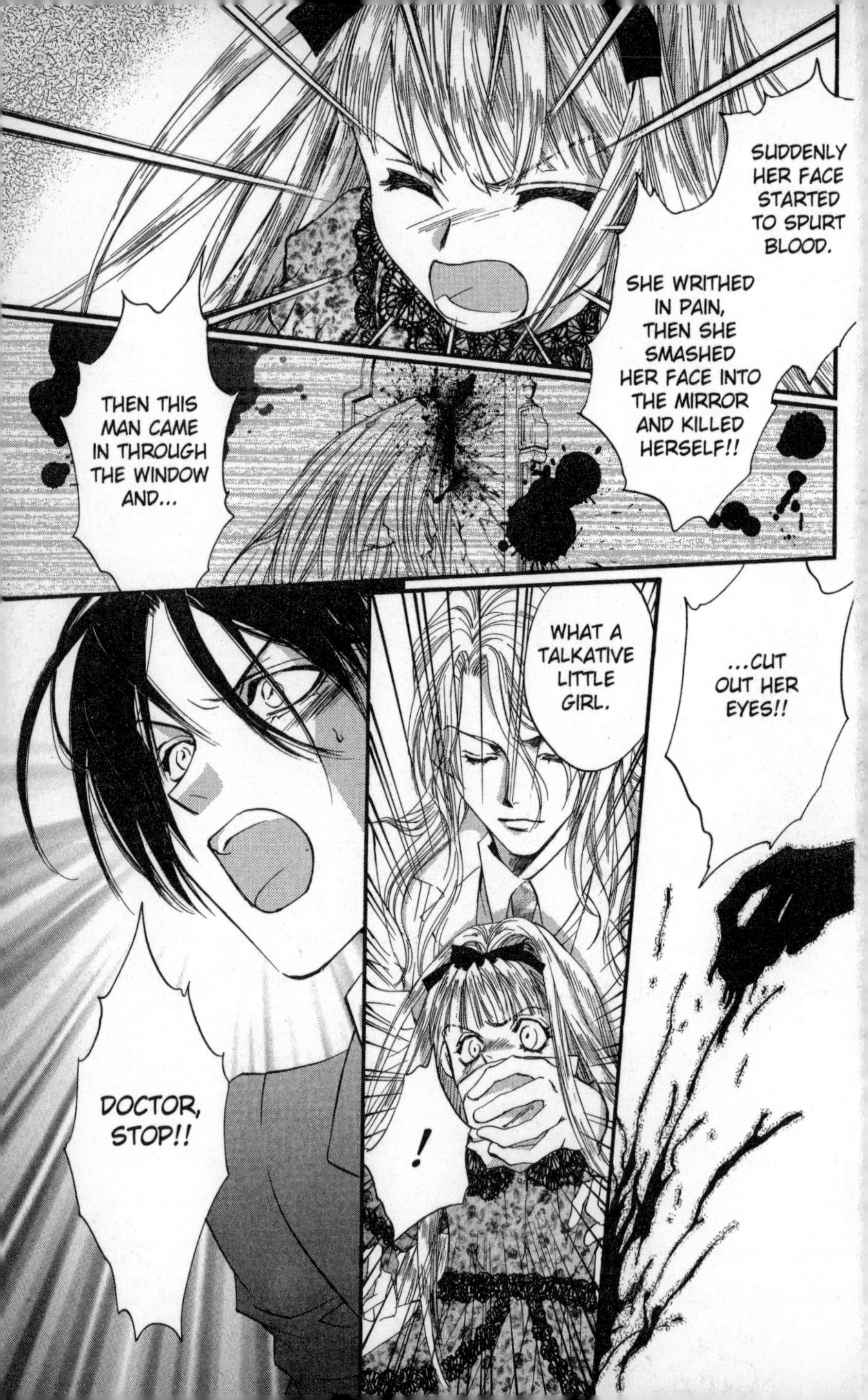
SUDDENLY HER FACE STARTED TO SPURT BLOOD.
SHE WRITHED IN PAIN, THEN SHE SMASHED HER FACE INTO THE MIRROR AND KILLED HERSELF!!
THEN THIS MAN CAME IN THROUGH THE WINDOW AND...
...CUT OUT HER EYES!!
WHAT A TALKATIVE LITTLE GIRL.
!
DOCTOR, STOP!!

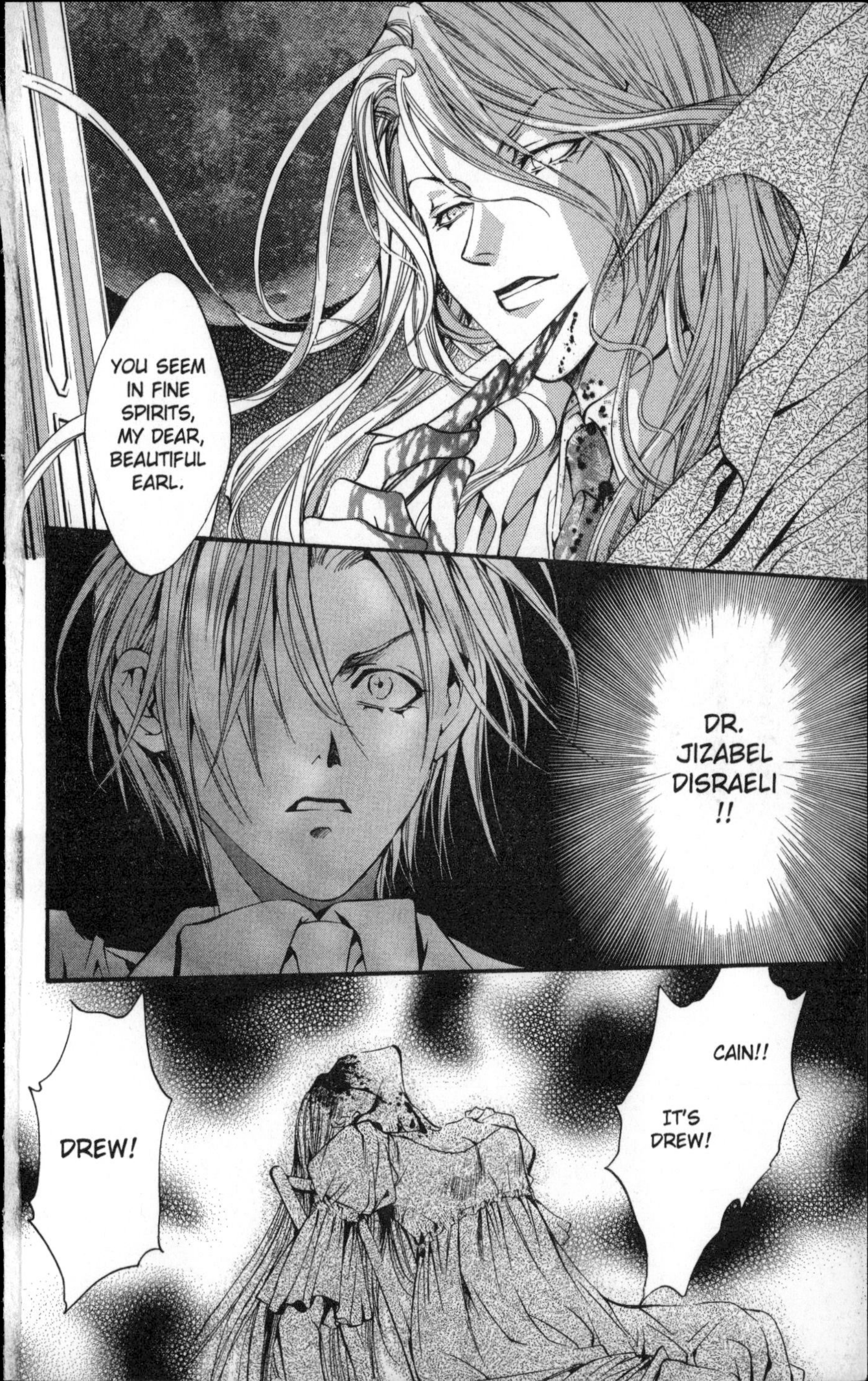
YOU SEEM IN FINE SPIRITS, MY DEAR, BEAUTIFUL EARL.
DR. JIZABEL DISRAELI !!
CAIN!!
IT'S DREW!
DREW!

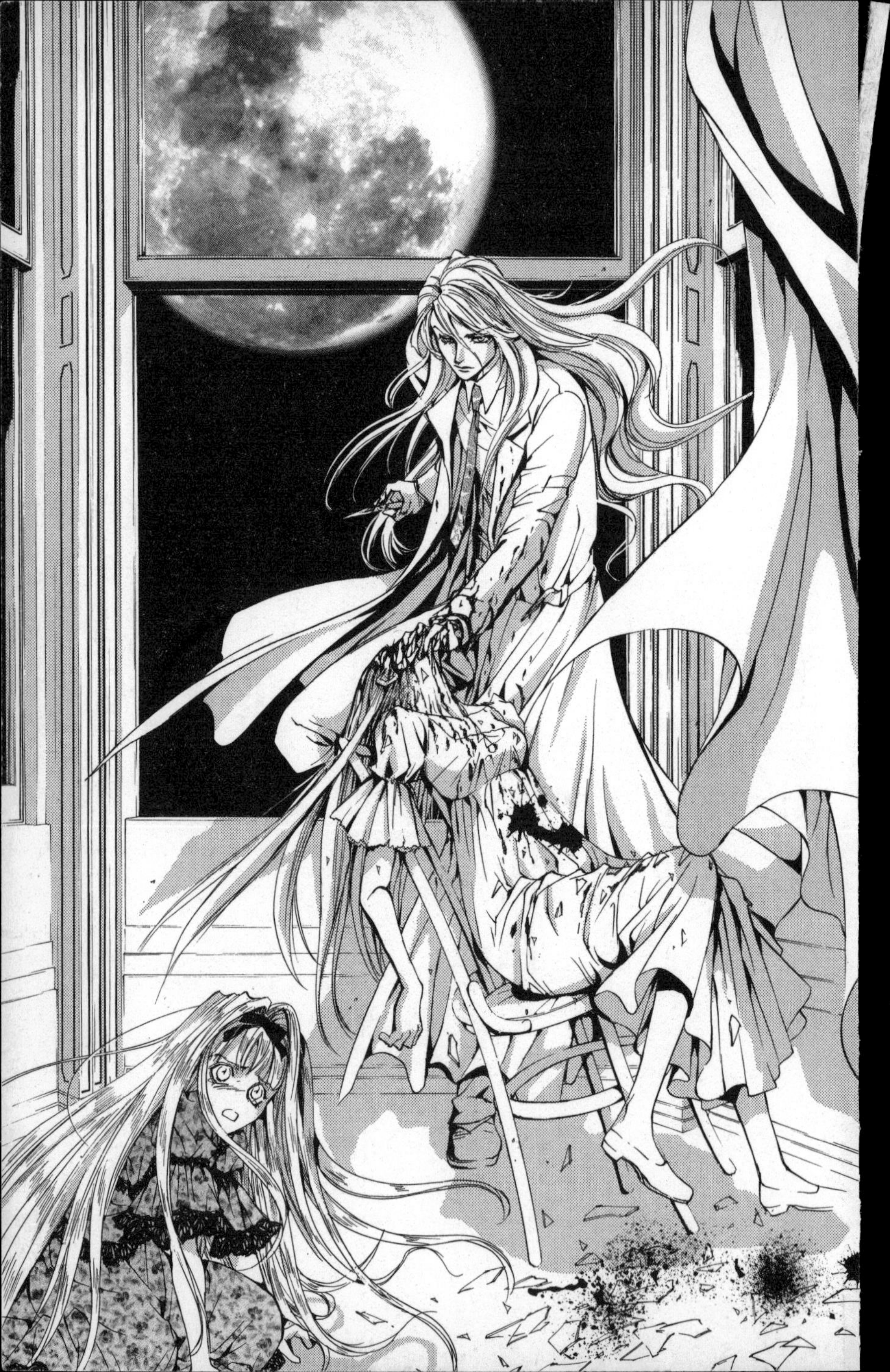

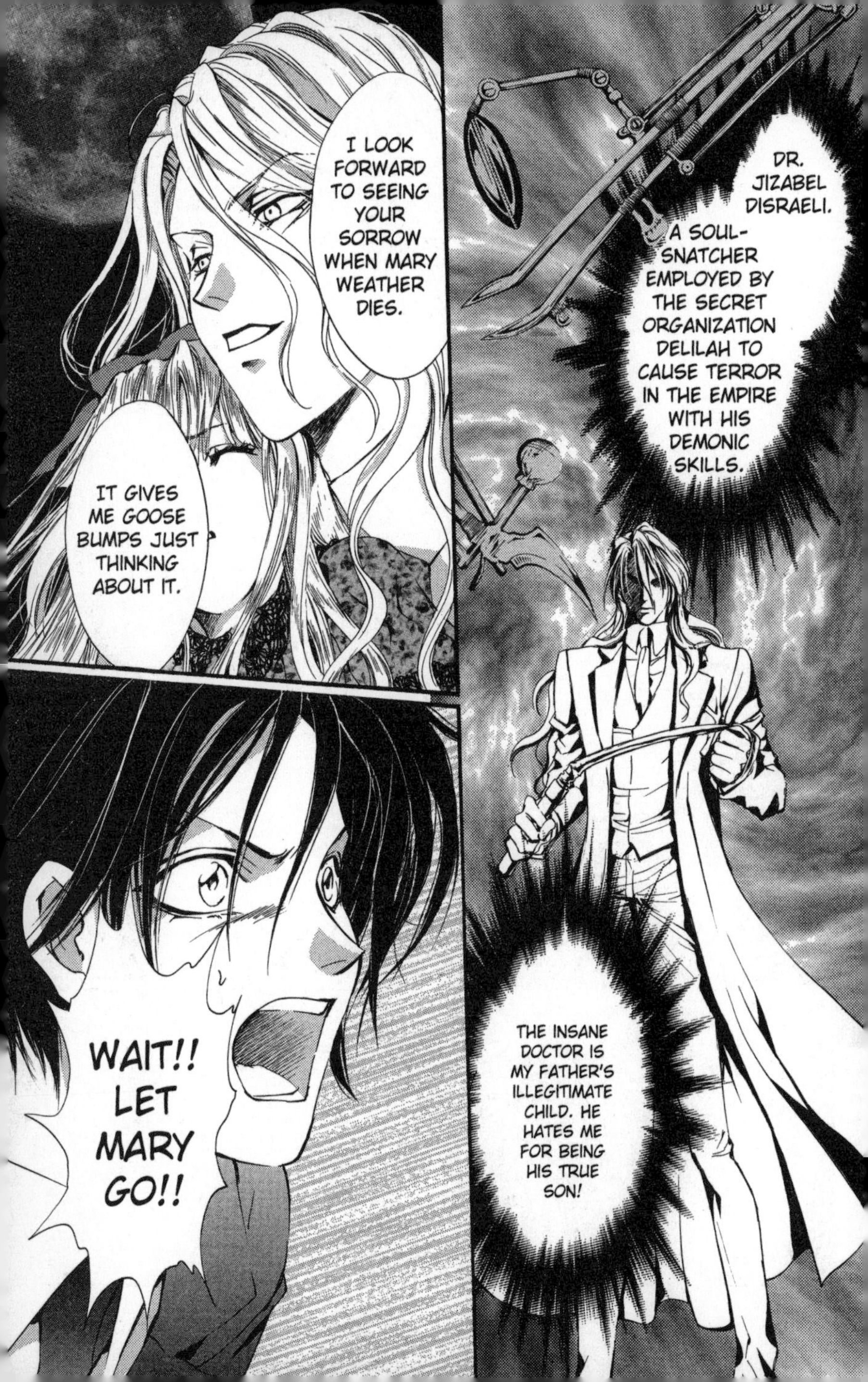
DR. JIZABEL DISRAELI.
A SOUL-SNATCHER EMPLOYED BY THE SECRET ORGANIZATION DELILAH TO CAUSE TERROR IN THE EMPIRE WITH HIS DEMONIC SKILLS.
THE INSANE DOCTOR IS MY FATHER'S ILLEGITIMATE CHILD. HE HATES ME FOR BEING HIS TRUE SON!
I LOOK FORWARD TO SEEING YOUR SORROW WHEN MARY WEATHER DIES.
IT GIVES ME GOOSE BUMPS JUST THINKING ABOUT IT.
WAIT!! LET MARY GO!!

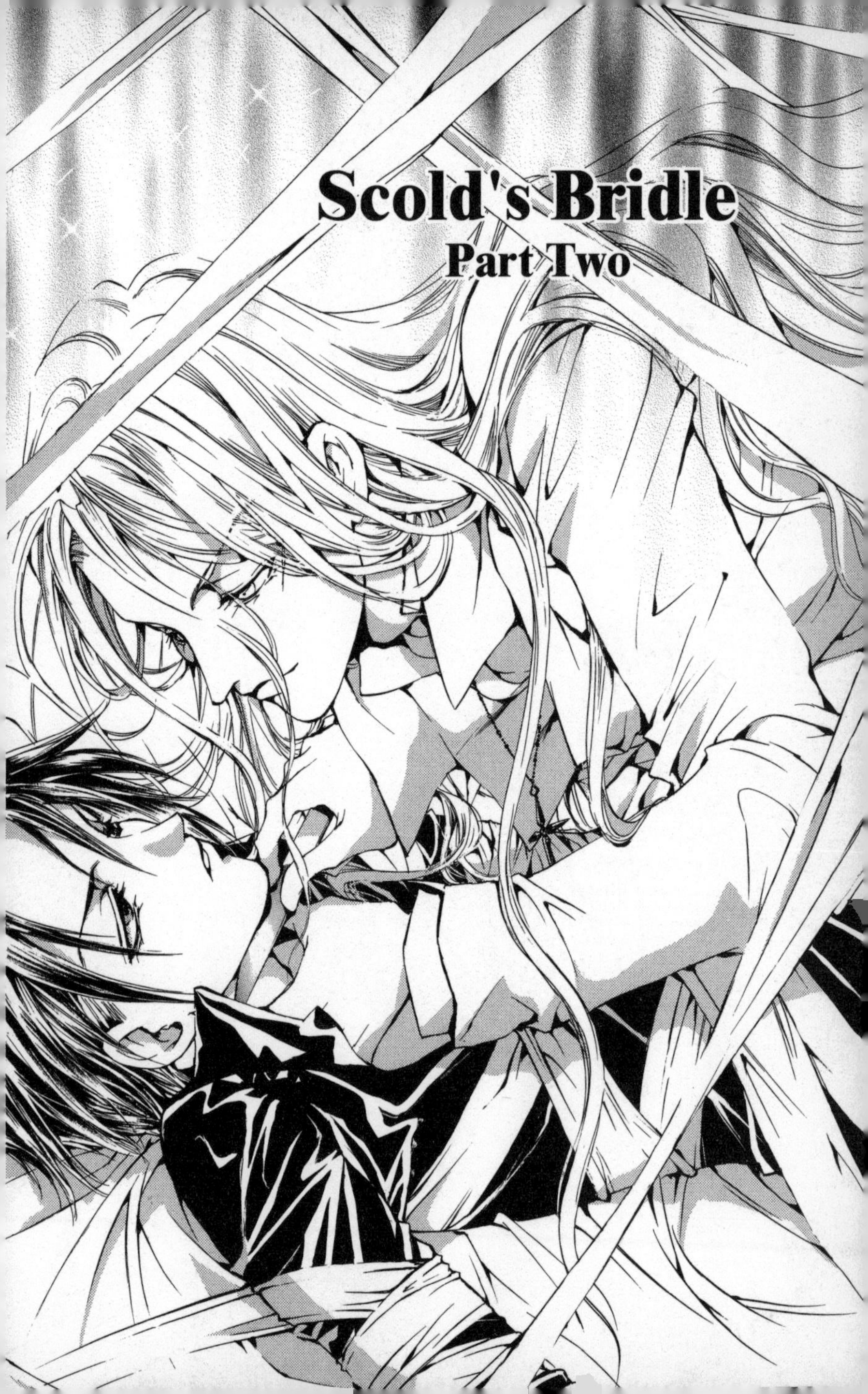
Scold's Bridle
Part Two

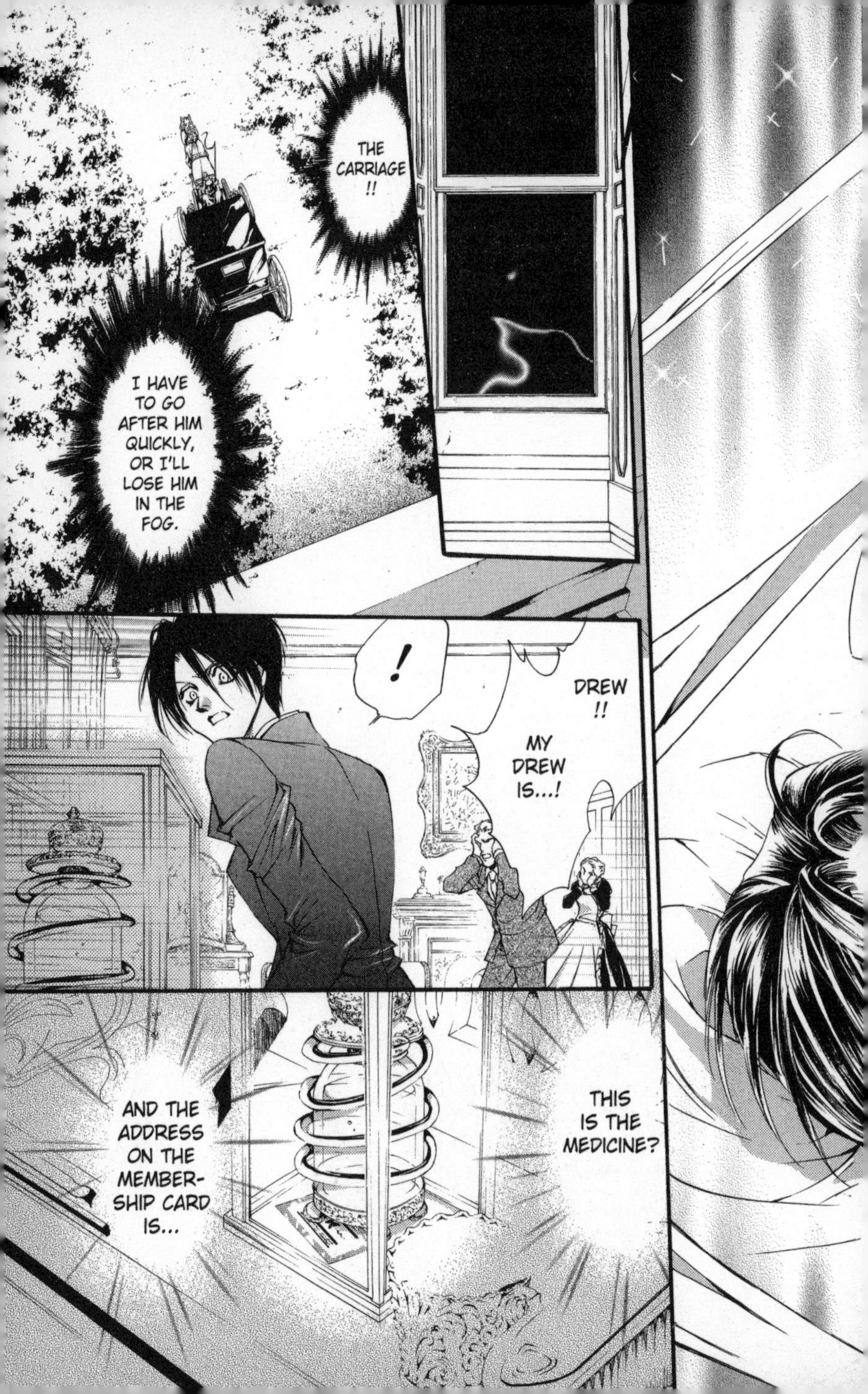
THE CARRIAGE !!
I HAVE TO GO AFTER HIM QUICKLY, OR I'LL LOSE HIM IN THE FOG.
DREW !!
MY DREW IS...!
!
THIS IS THE MEDICINE?
AND THE ADDRESS ON THE MEMBER-SHIP CARD IS...

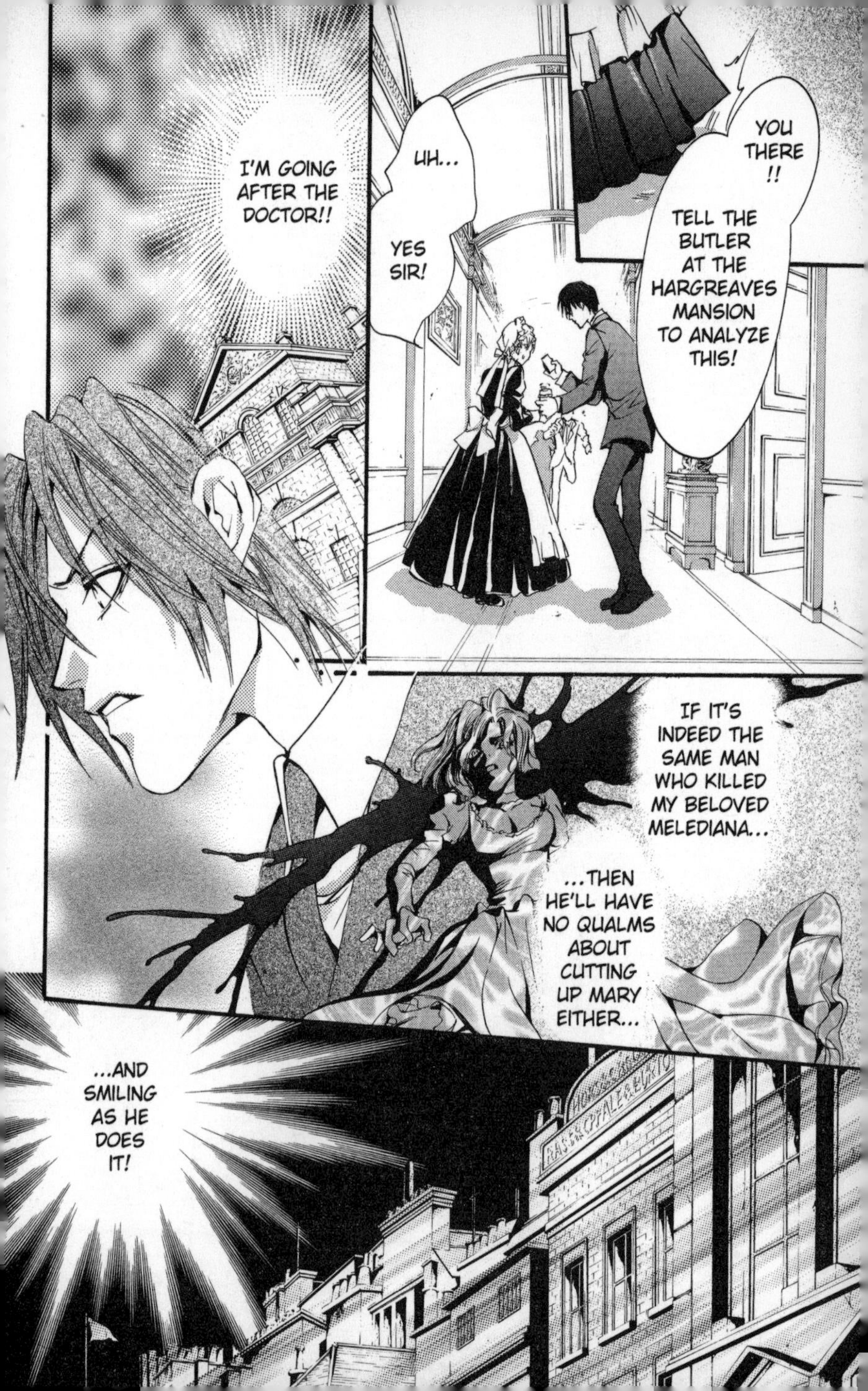
YOU THERE!!
TELL THE BUTLER AT THE HARGREAVES MANSION TO ANALYZE THIS!
UH...
YES SIR!
IF IT'S INDEED THE SAME MAN WHO KILLED MY BELOVED MELEDIANA...
...THEN HE'LL HAVE NO QUALMS ABOUT CUTTING UP MARY EITHER...
I'M GOING AFTER THE DOCTOR!!
...AND SMILING AS HE DOES IT!

Medieval torture masks.

Oddly, many of them are humorous.

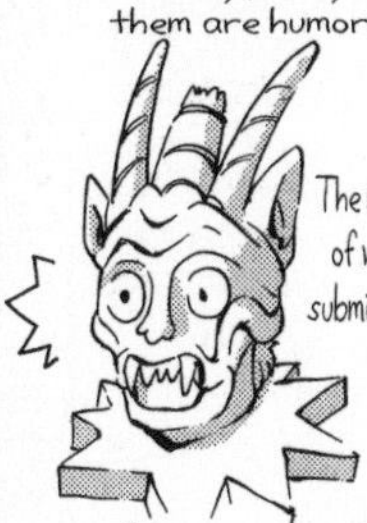

The mask of wife submission.

↑ Wooden collar. Also known as the nagging wife's mask. Apparently they come in all different shapes.

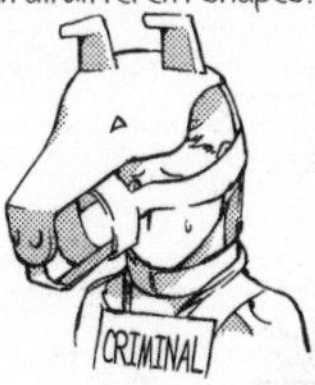

CRIMINAL

Pig-shaped?

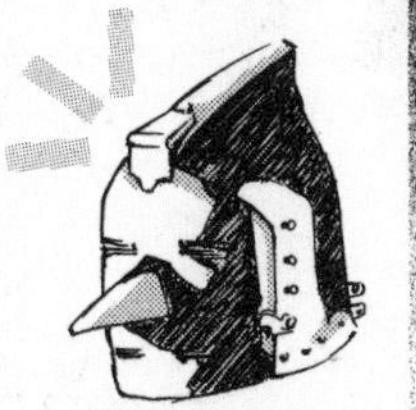

This one is an executioner's mask, so it's different from the masks above.

The face is cute.

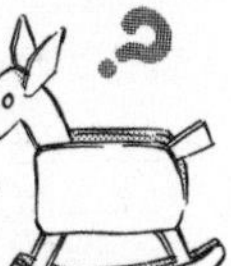

There's also one called the Mule. It looks like a rocking horse, but you have to sit on it in front of spectators. Books on torture sure are scary!

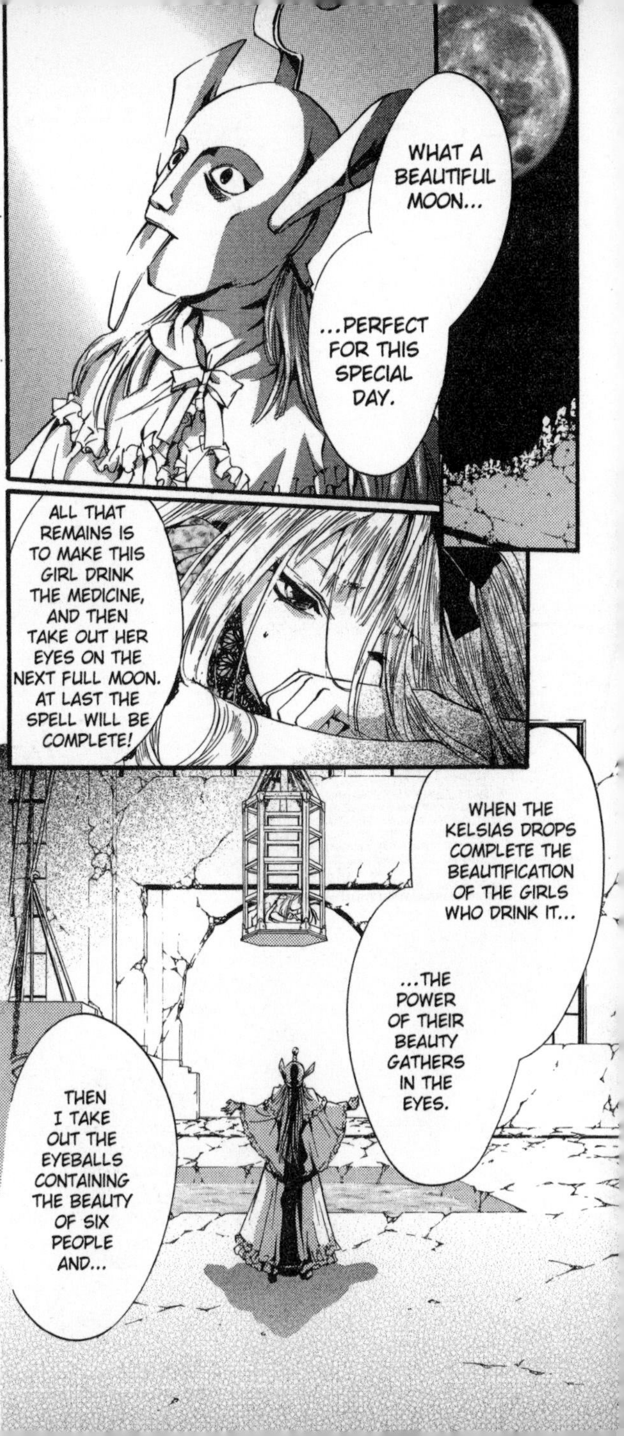

WHAT A BEAUTIFUL MOON...
...PERFECT FOR THIS SPECIAL DAY.
ALL THAT REMAINS IS TO MAKE THIS GIRL DRINK THE MEDICINE, AND THEN TAKE OUT HER EYES ON THE NEXT FULL MOON. AT LAST THE SPELL WILL BE COMPLETE!
WHEN THE KELSIAS DROPS COMPLETE THE BEAUTIFICATION OF THE GIRLS WHO DRINK IT...
...THE POWER OF THEIR BEAUTY GATHERS IN THE EYES.
THEN I TAKE OUT THE EYEBALLS CONTAINING THE BEAUTY OF SIX PEOPLE AND...

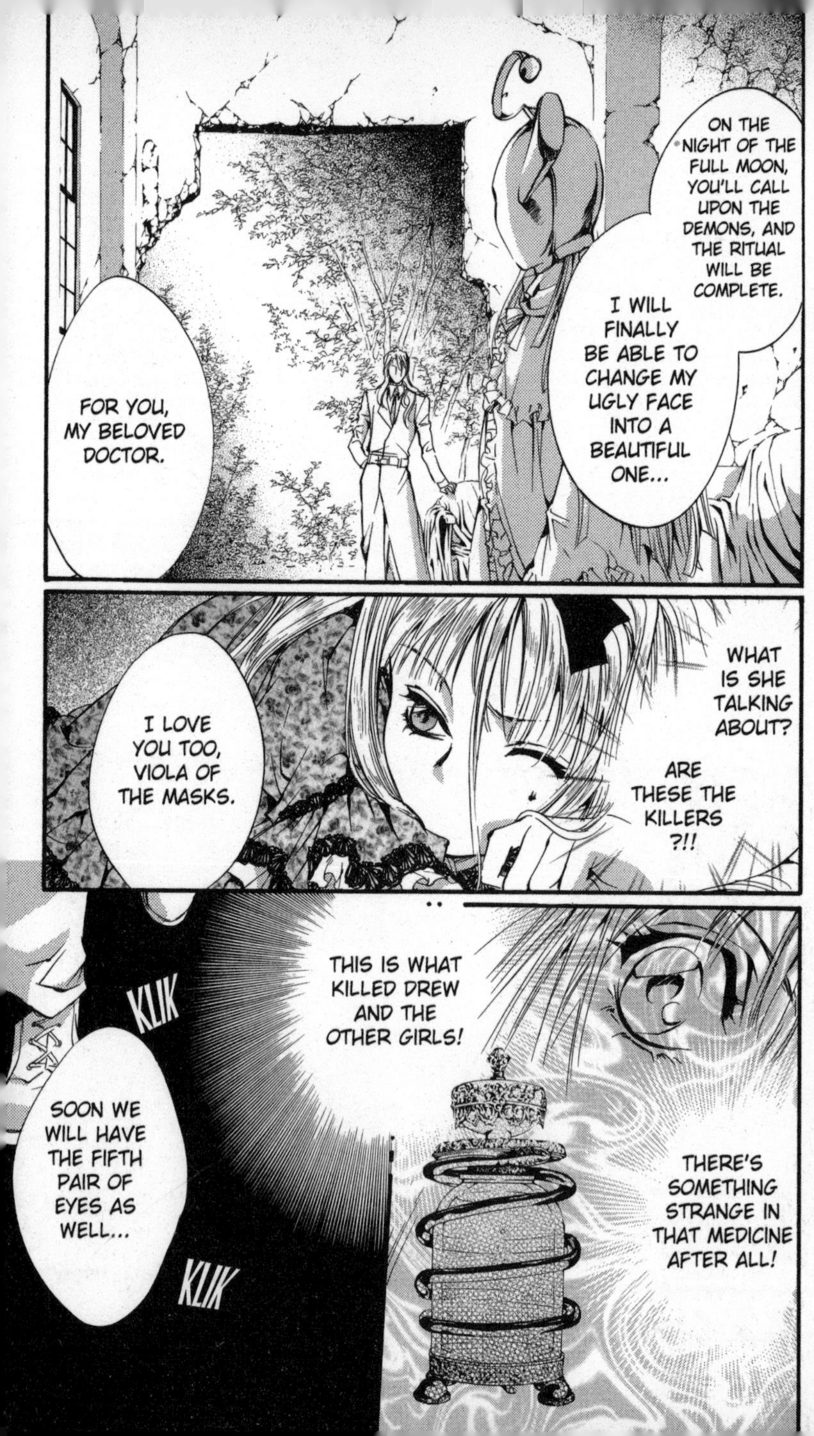
ON THE NIGHT OF THE FULL MOON, YOU'LL CALL UPON THE DEMONS, AND THE RITUAL WILL BE COMPLETE.
I WILL FINALLY BE ABLE TO CHANGE MY UGLY FACE INTO A BEAUTIFUL ONE...
FOR YOU, MY BELOVED DOCTOR.
WHAT IS SHE TALKING ABOUT?
ARE THESE THE KILLERS ?!!
I LOVE YOU TOO, VIOLA OF THE MASKS.
THIS IS WHAT KILLED DREW AND THE OTHER GIRLS!
THERE'S SOMETHING STRANGE IN THAT MEDICINE AFTER ALL!
KLIK
SOON WE WILL HAVE THE FIFTH PAIR OF EYES AS WELL...
KLIK

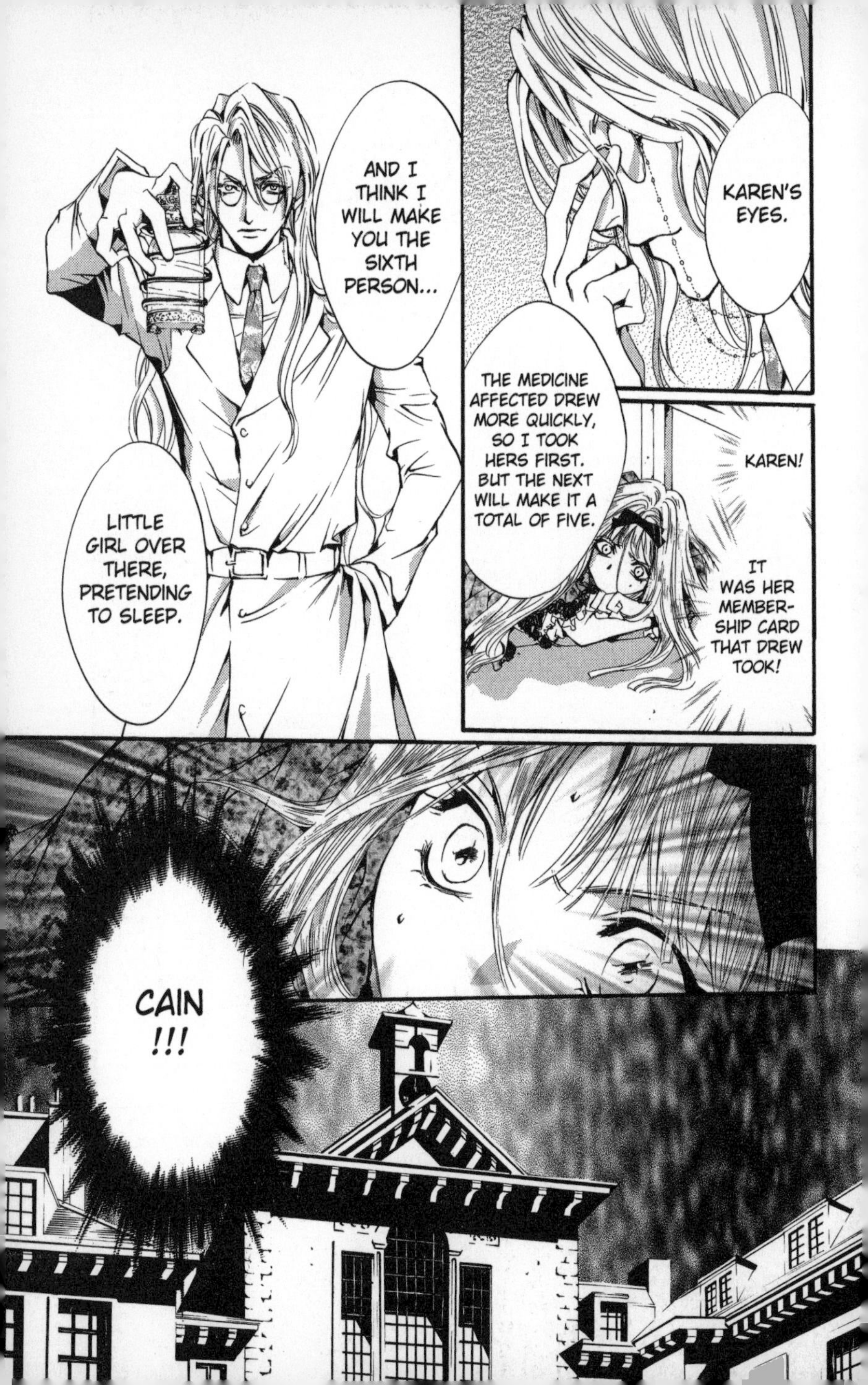
KAREN'S EYES.
THE MEDICINE AFFECTED DREW MORE QUICKLY, SO I TOOK HERS FIRST. BUT THE NEXT WILL MAKE IT A TOTAL OF FIVE.
KAREN!
IT WAS HER MEMBER-SHIP CARD THAT DREW TOOK!
AND I THINK I WILL MAKE YOU THE SIXTH PERSON...
LITTLE GIRL OVER THERE, PRETENDING TO SLEEP.
CAIN !!!

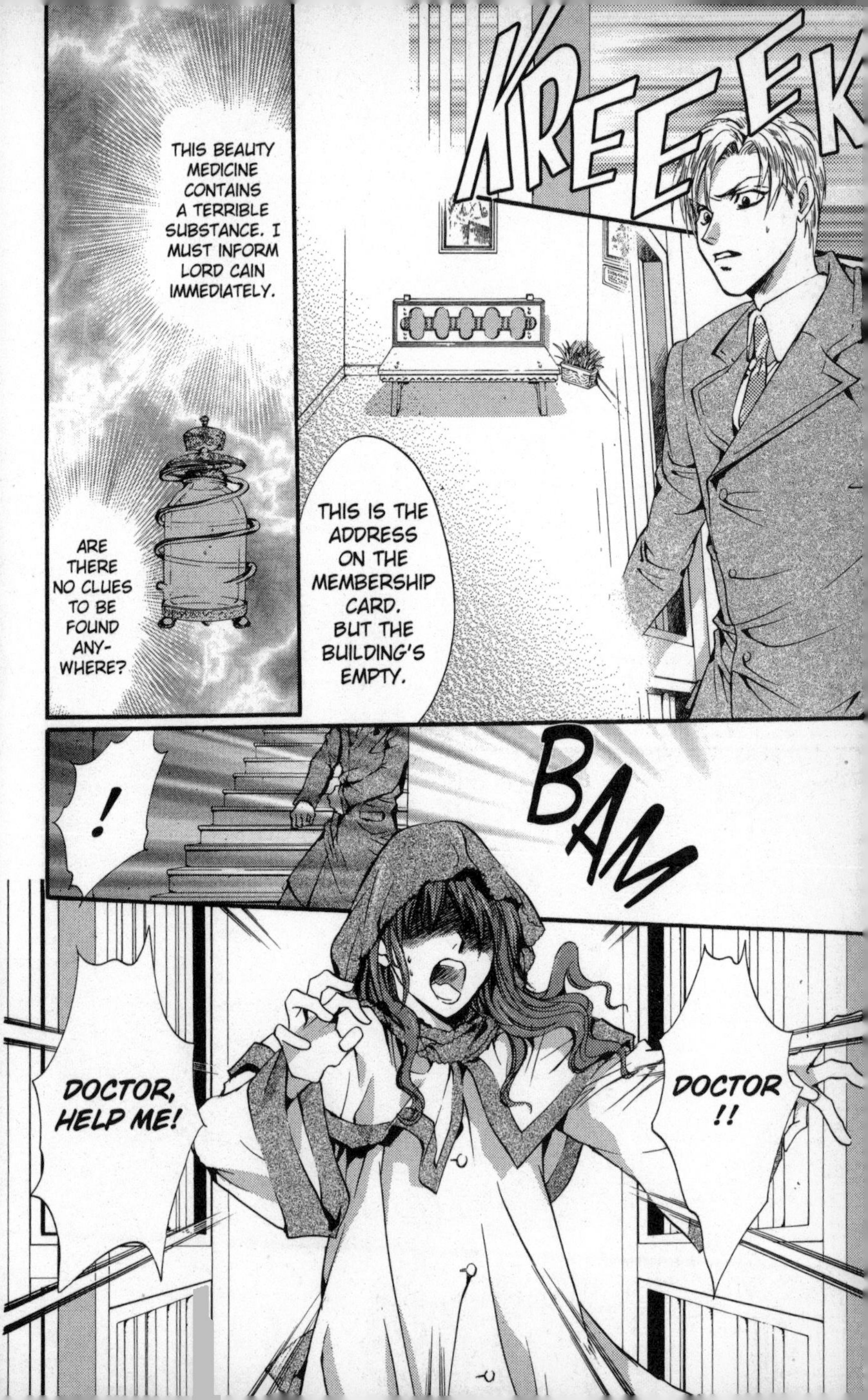
KREE-EK
THIS IS THE ADDRESS ON THE MEMBERSHIP CARD. BUT THE BUILDING'S EMPTY.
THIS BEAUTY MEDICINE CONTAINS A TERRIBLE SUBSTANCE. I MUST INFORM LORD CAIN IMMEDIATELY.
ARE THERE NO CLUES TO BE FOUND ANY-WHERE?
!
BAM
DOCTOR !!
DOCTOR, HELP ME!

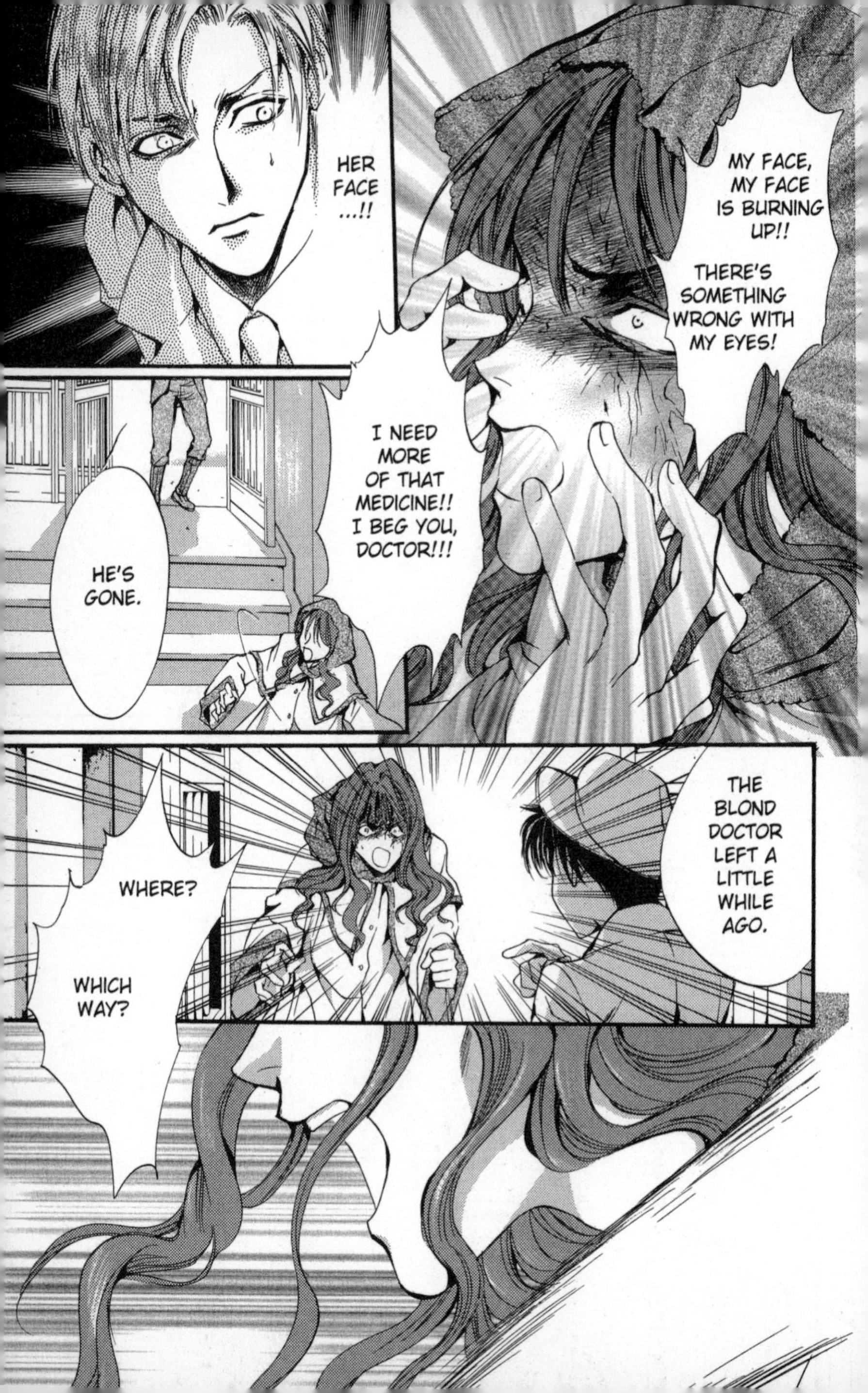
MY FACE, MY FACE IS BURNING UP!!
THERE'S SOMETHING WRONG WITH MY EYES!
I NEED MORE OF THAT MEDICINE!! I BEG YOU, DOCTOR!!!
HER FACE ...!!
HE'S GONE.
THE BLOND DOCTOR LEFT A LITTLE WHILE AGO.
WHERE?
WHICH WAY?

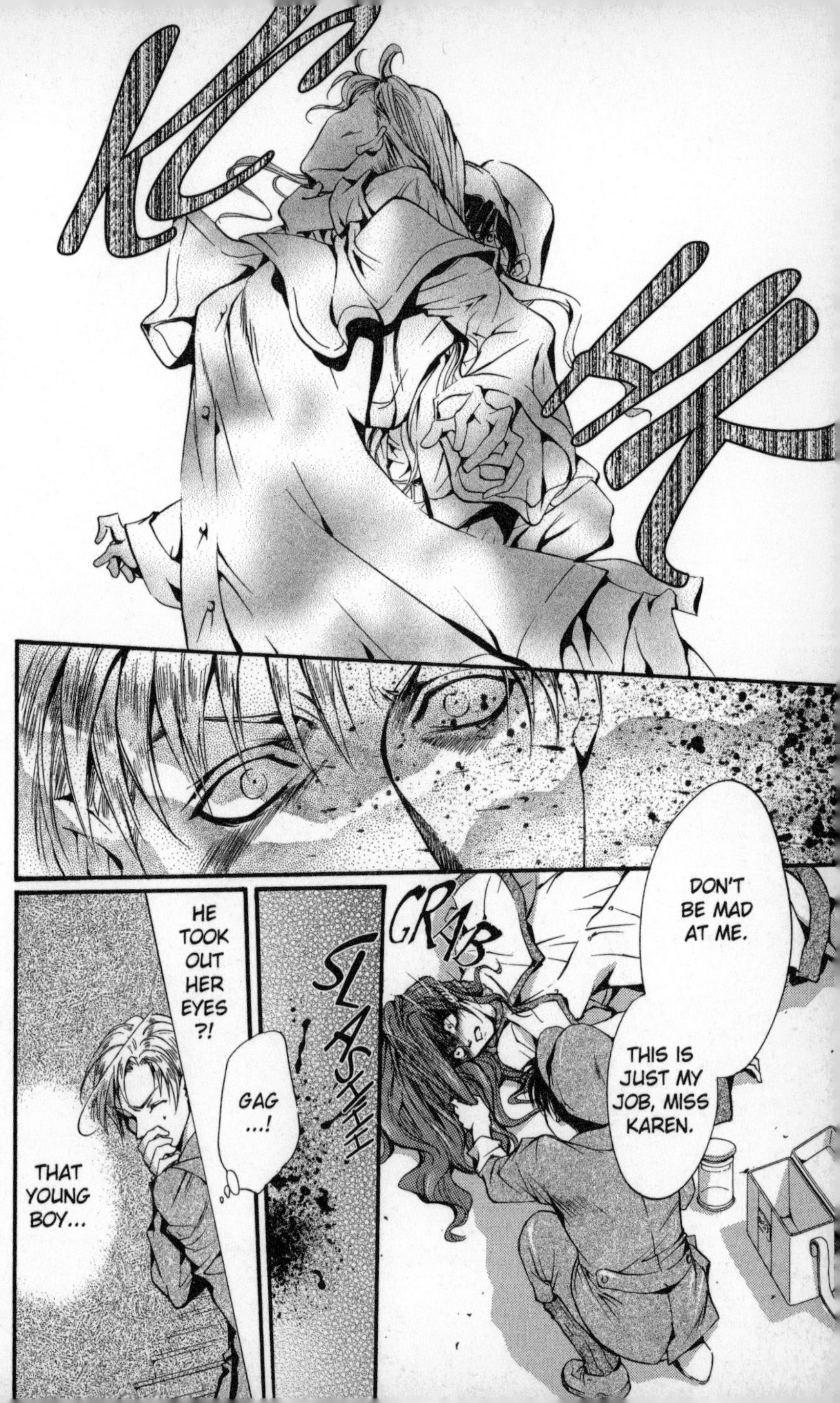
DON'T BE MAD AT ME.
THIS IS JUST MY JOB, MISS KAREN.
GRAB
SLASHHH
HE TOOK OUT HER EYES?!
GAG...!
THAT YOUNG BOY...

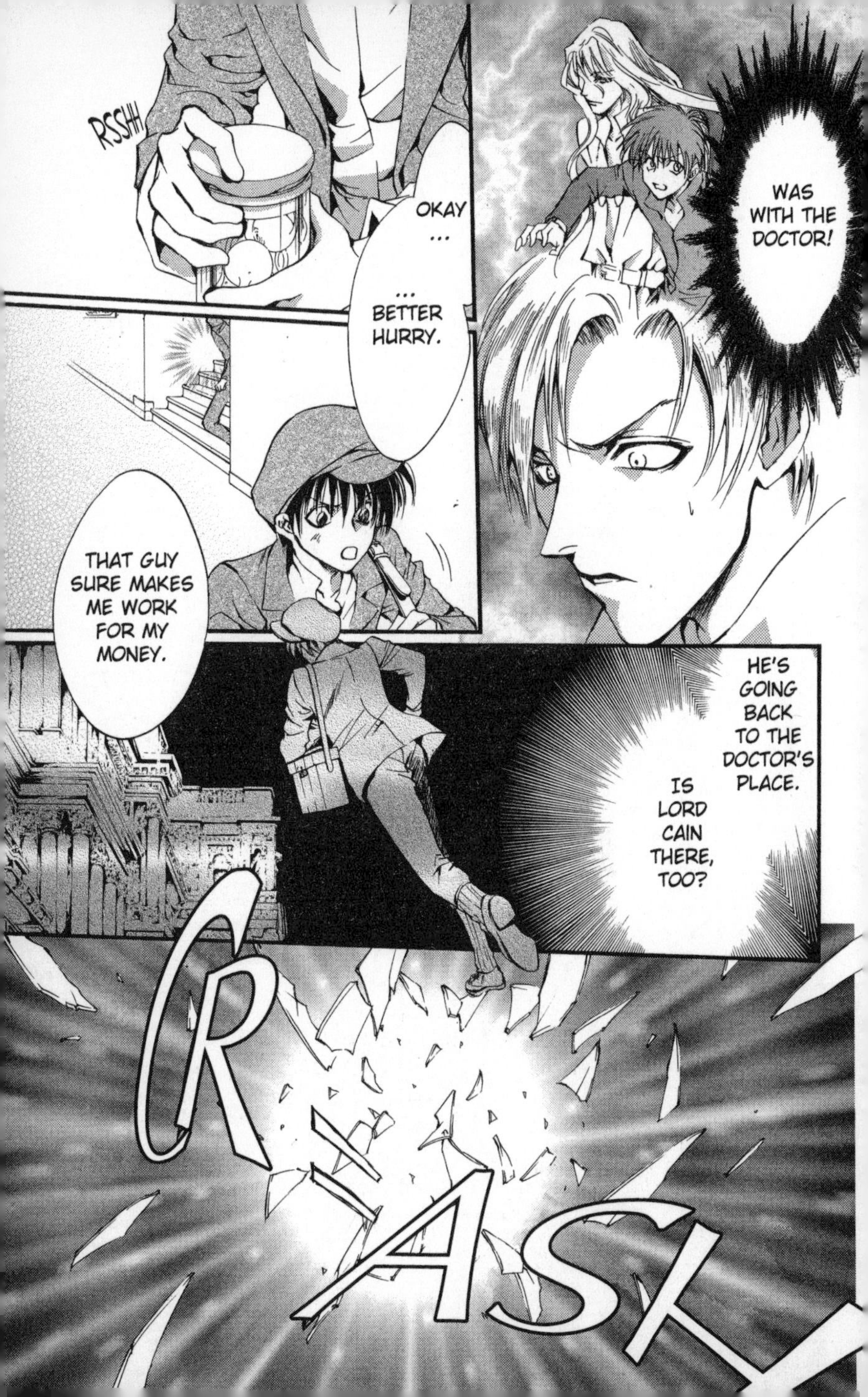
WAS WITH THE DOCTOR!
RSSHH
OKAY ...
... BETTER HURRY.
THAT GUY SURE MAKES ME WORK FOR MY MONEY.
HE'S GOING BACK TO THE DOCTOR'S PLACE.
IS LORD CAIN THERE, TOO?
CRASH

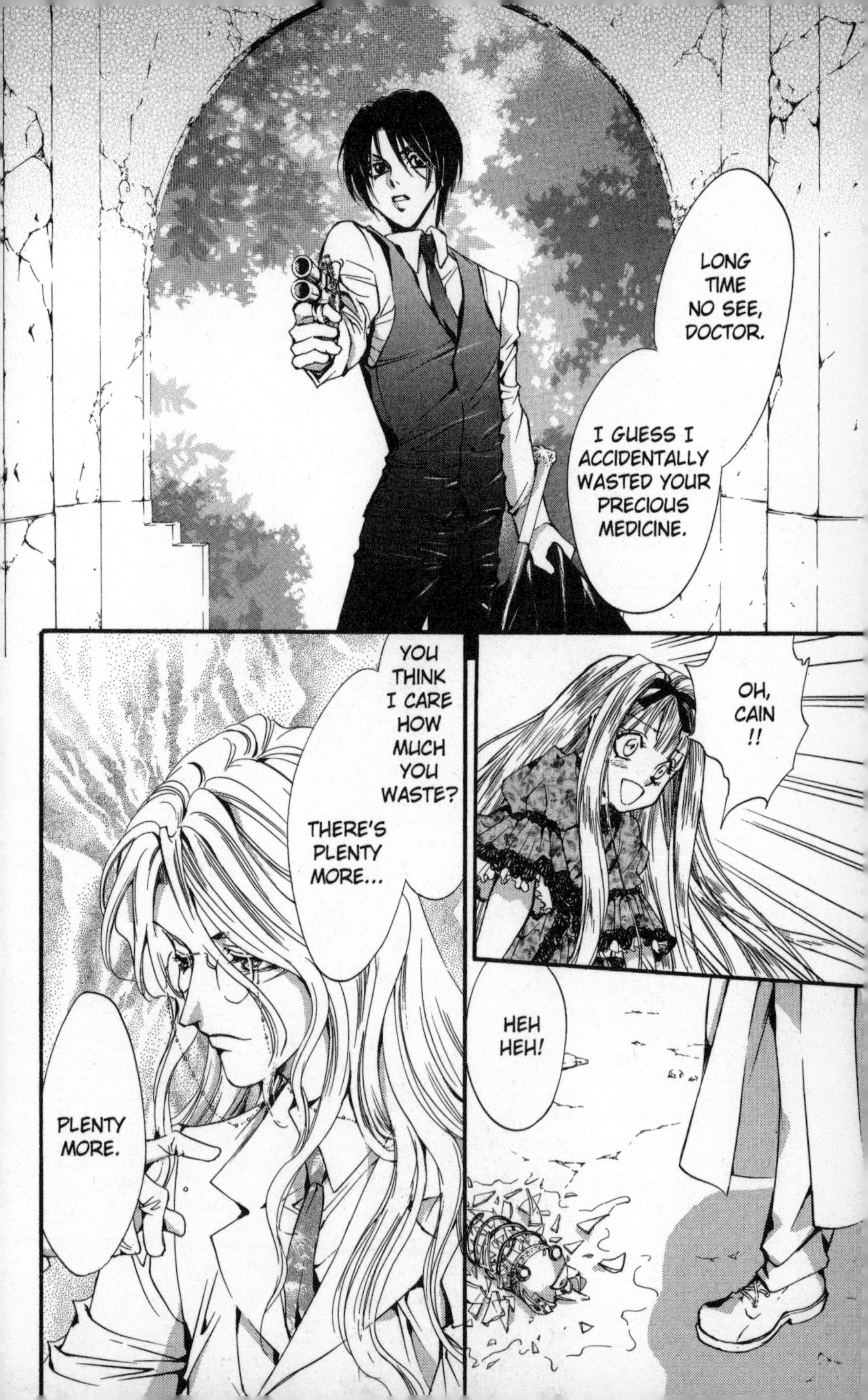
LONG TIME NO SEE, DOCTOR.
I GUESS I ACCIDENTALLY WASTED YOUR PRECIOUS MEDICINE.
OH, CAIN !!
HEH HEH!
YOU THINK I CARE HOW MUCH YOU WASTE?
THERE'S PLENTY MORE...
PLENTY MORE.

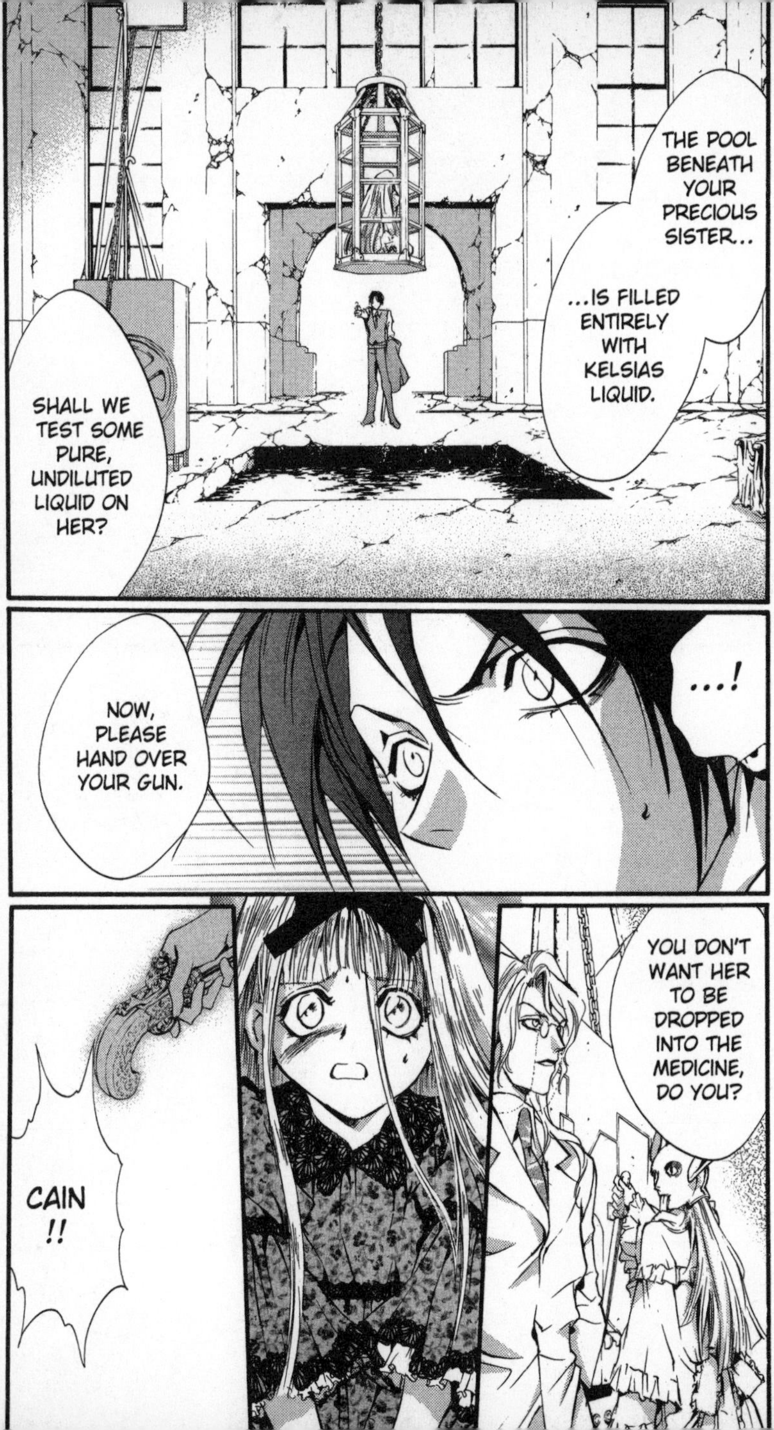
THE POOL BENEATH YOUR PRECIOUS SISTER...
...IS FILLED ENTIRELY WITH KELSIAS LIQUID.
SHALL WE TEST SOME PURE, UNDILUTED LIQUID ON HER?
...!
NOW, PLEASE HAND OVER YOUR GUN.
YOU DON'T WANT HER TO BE DROPPED INTO THE MEDICINE, DO YOU?
CAIN !!

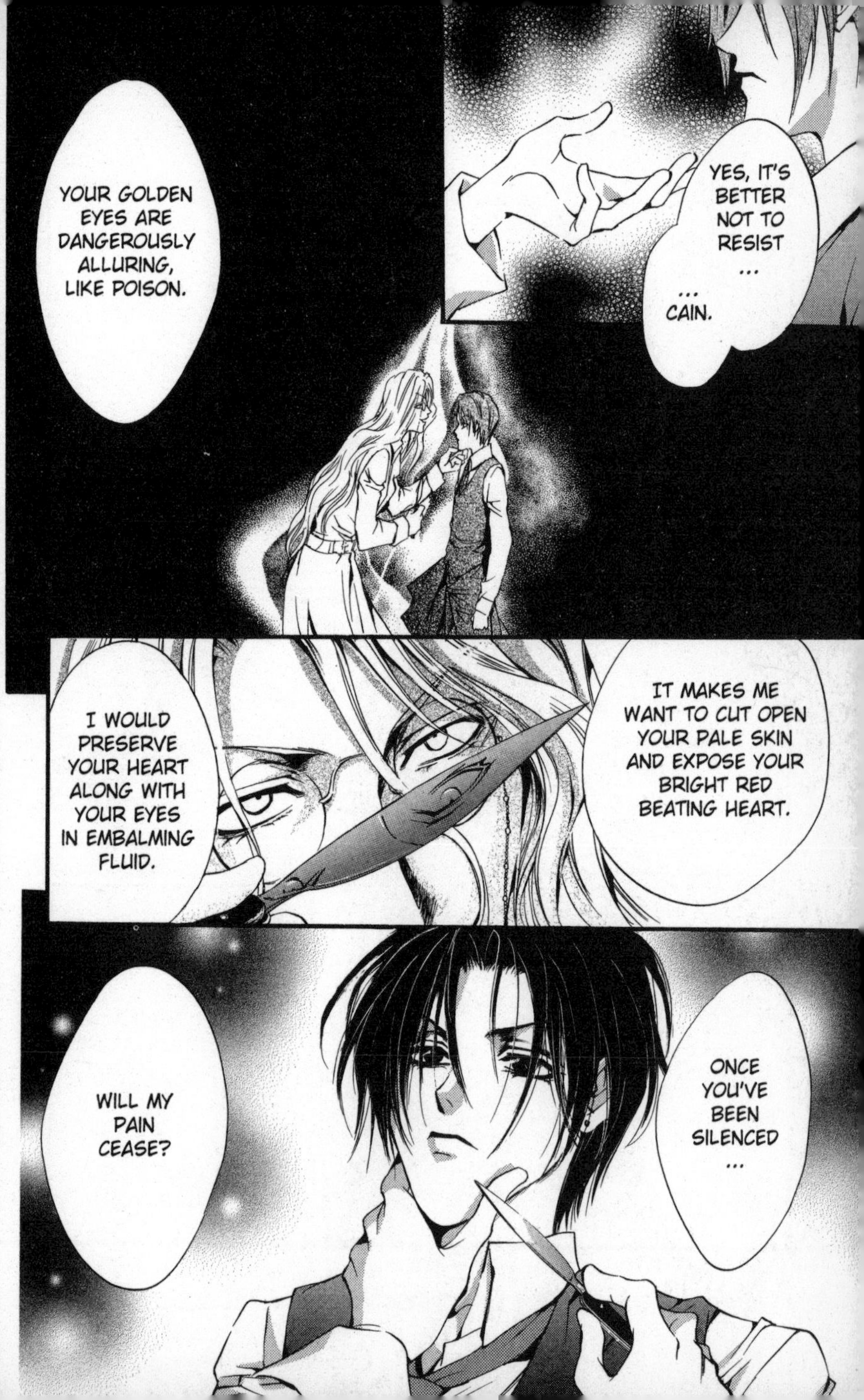
YES, IT'S BETTER NOT TO RESIST ... ... CAIN.
YOUR GOLDEN EYES ARE DANGEROUSLY ALLURING, LIKE POISON.
IT MAKES ME WANT TO CUT OPEN YOUR PALE SKIN AND EXPOSE YOUR BRIGHT RED BEATING HEART.
I WOULD PRESERVE YOUR HEART ALONG WITH YOUR EYES IN EMBALMING FLUID.
ONCE YOU'VE BEEN SILENCED ...
WILL MY PAIN CEASE?

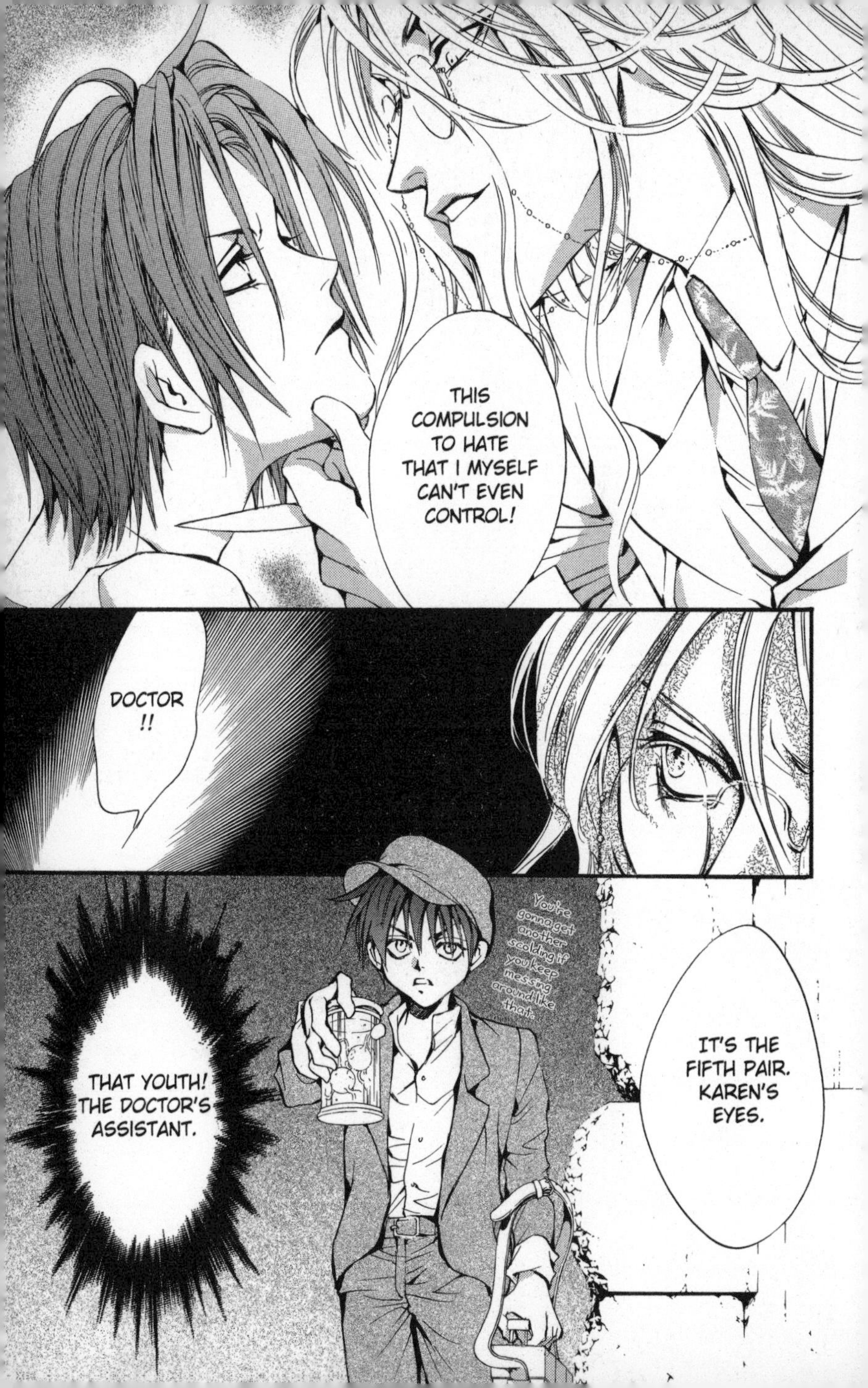
THIS COMPULSION TO HATE THAT I MYSELF CAN'T EVEN CONTROL!
DOCTOR !!
IT'S THE FIFTH PAIR. KAREN'S EYES.
You're gonna get another scolding if you keep messing around like that.
THAT YOUTH! THE DOCTOR'S ASSISTANT.

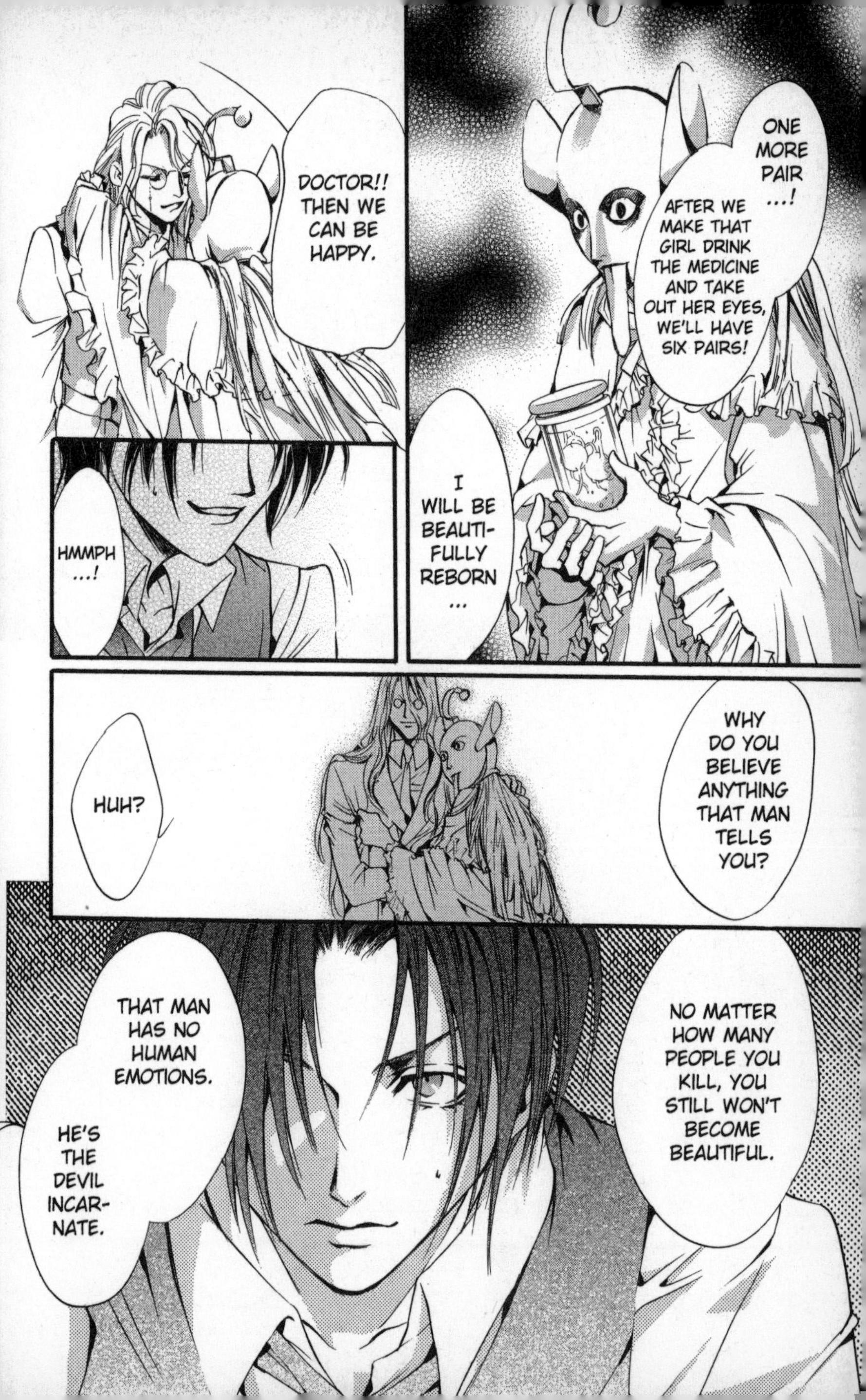
ONE MORE PAIR ...!
AFTER WE MAKE THAT GIRL DRINK THE MEDICINE AND TAKE OUT HER EYES, WE'LL HAVE SIX PAIRS!
I WILL BE BEAUTIFULLY REBORN ...
DOCTOR!! THEN WE CAN BE HAPPY.
HMMPH ...!
WHY DO YOU BELIEVE ANYTHING THAT MAN TELLS YOU?
HUH?
NO MATTER HOW MANY PEOPLE YOU KILL, YOU STILL WON'T BECOME BEAUTIFUL.
THAT MAN HAS NO HUMAN EMOTIONS.
HE'S THE DEVIL INCARNATE.

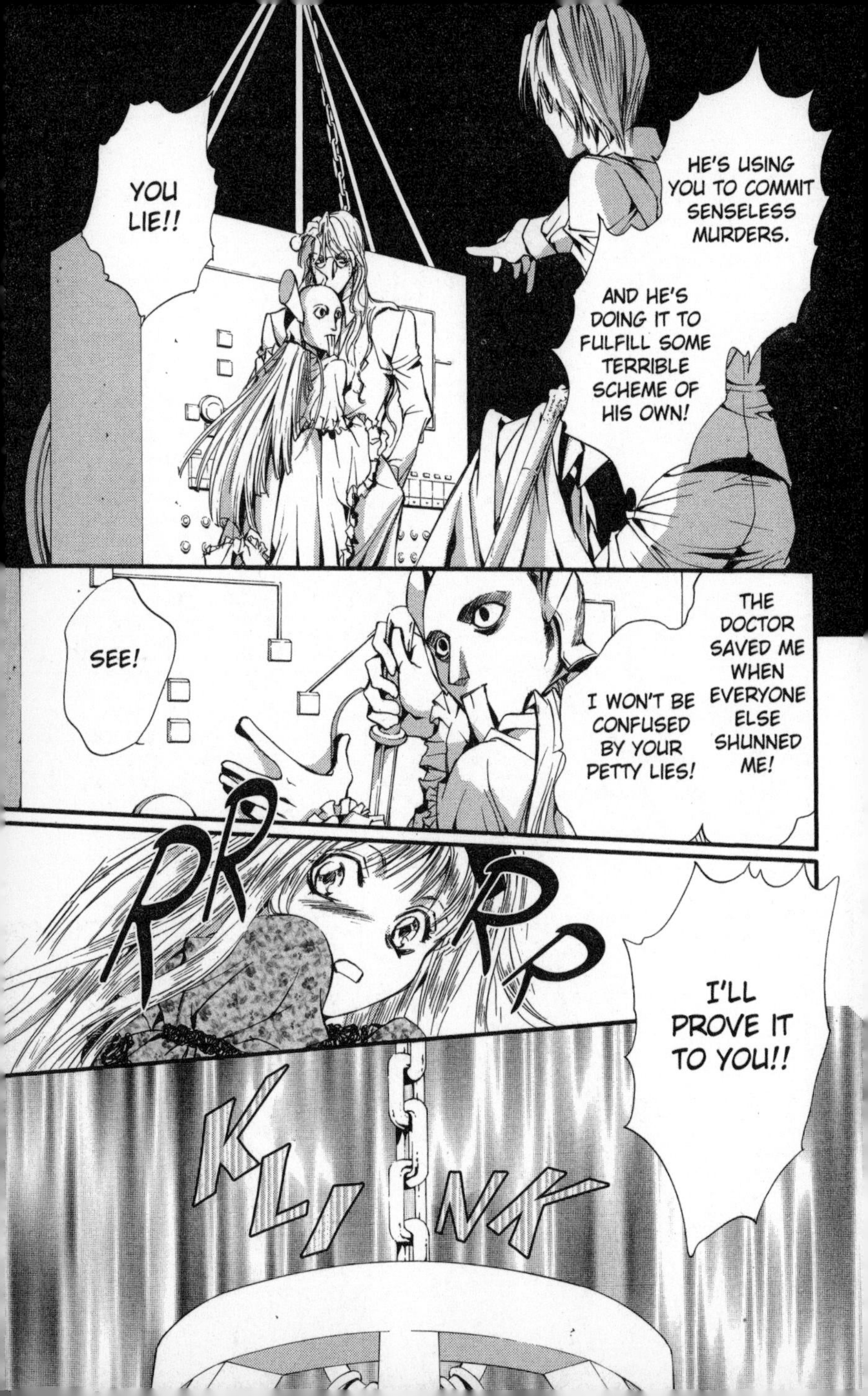
HE'S USING YOU TO COMMIT SENSELESS MURDERS.
AND HE'S DOING IT TO FULFILL SOME TERRIBLE SCHEME OF HIS OWN!
YOU LIE!!
THE DOCTOR SAVED ME WHEN EVERYONE ELSE SHUNNED ME!
I WON'T BE CONFUSED BY YOUR PETTY LIES!
SEE!
RRRR
I'LL PROVE IT TO YOU!!
KLINK

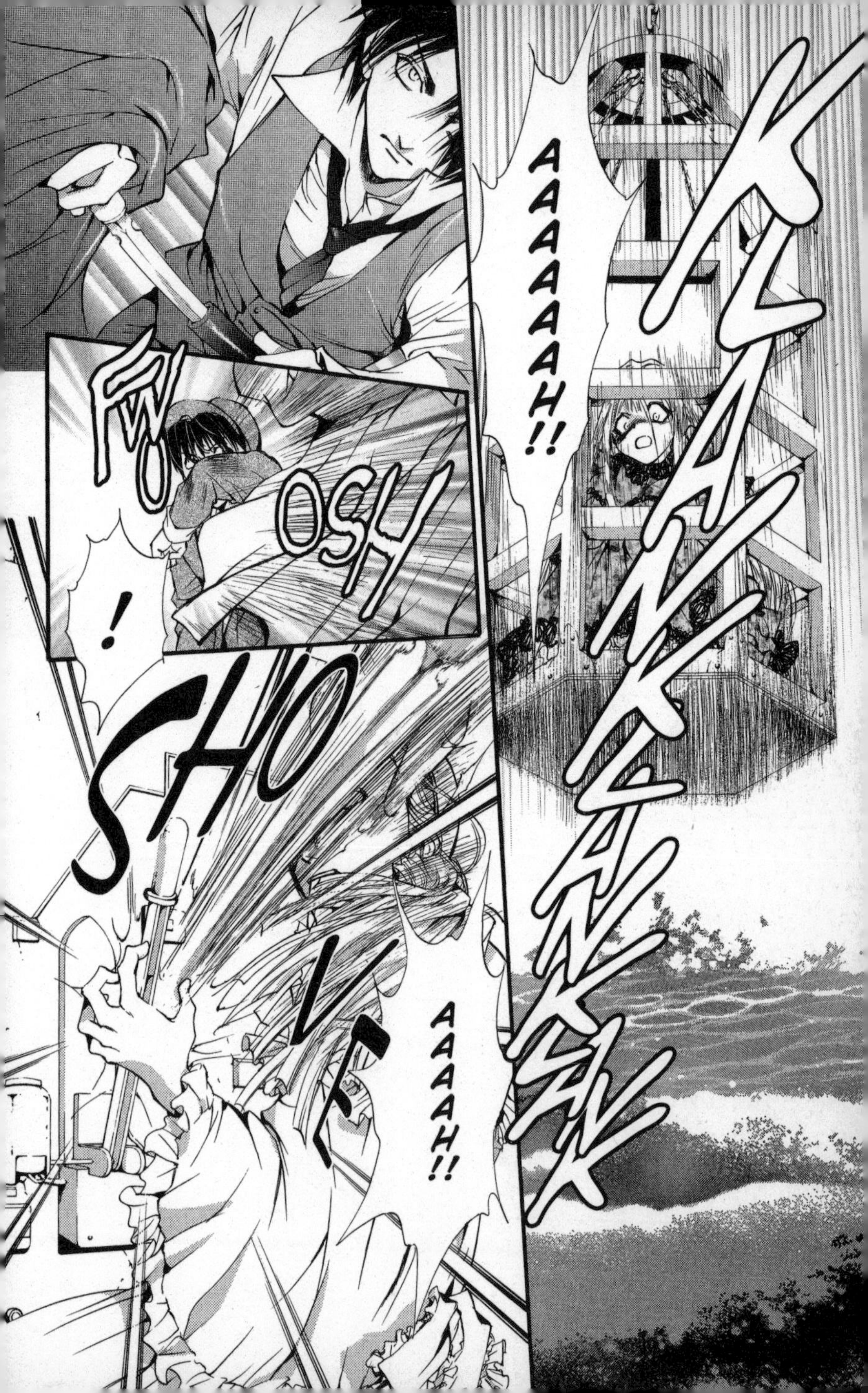
KLANKLANKLANK
AAAAAAAAAH!!
FWOOSH
!
SHOOV
AAAAAH!!

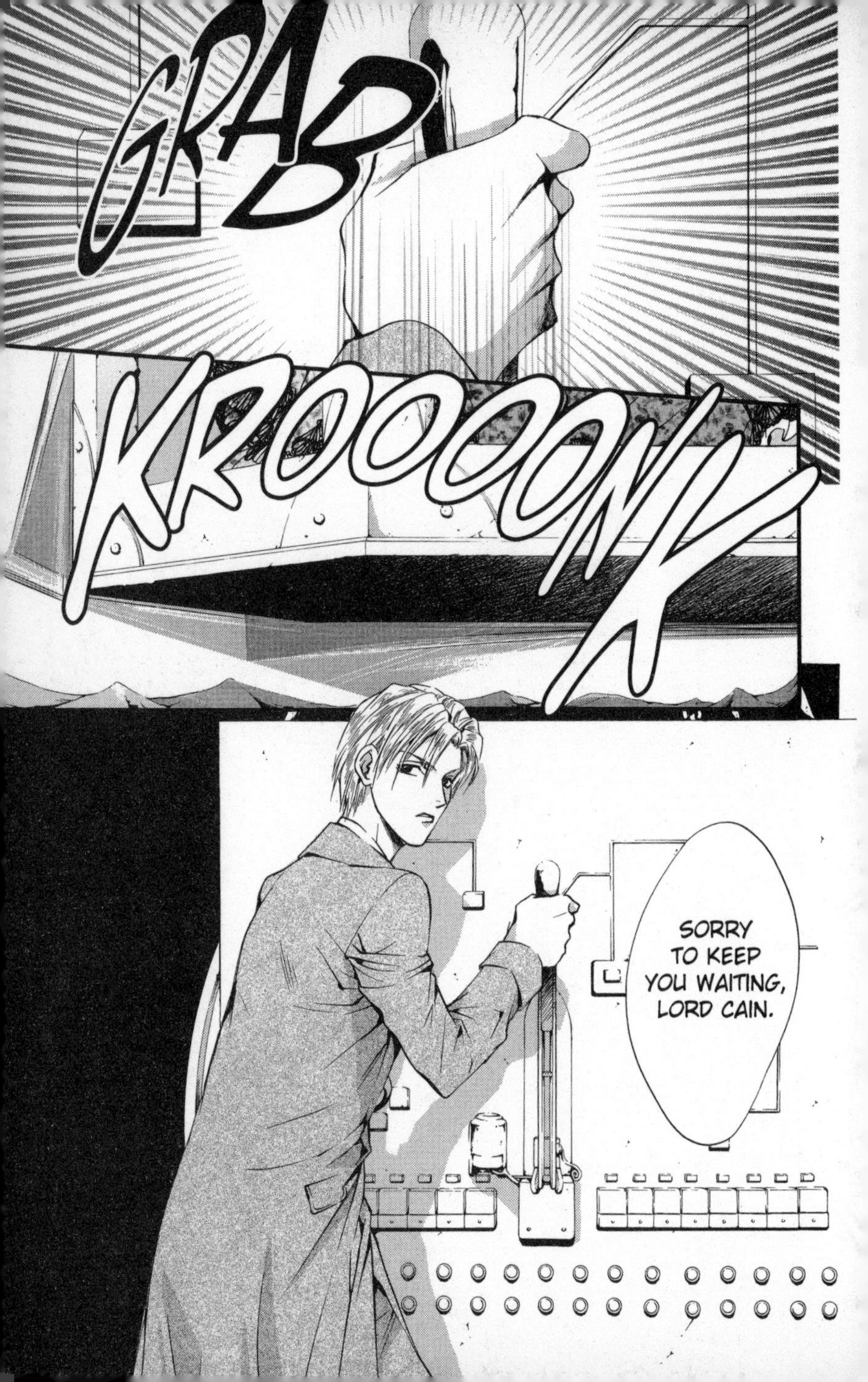
GRAB
KROOOONK
SORRY TO KEEP YOU WAITING, LORD CAIN.

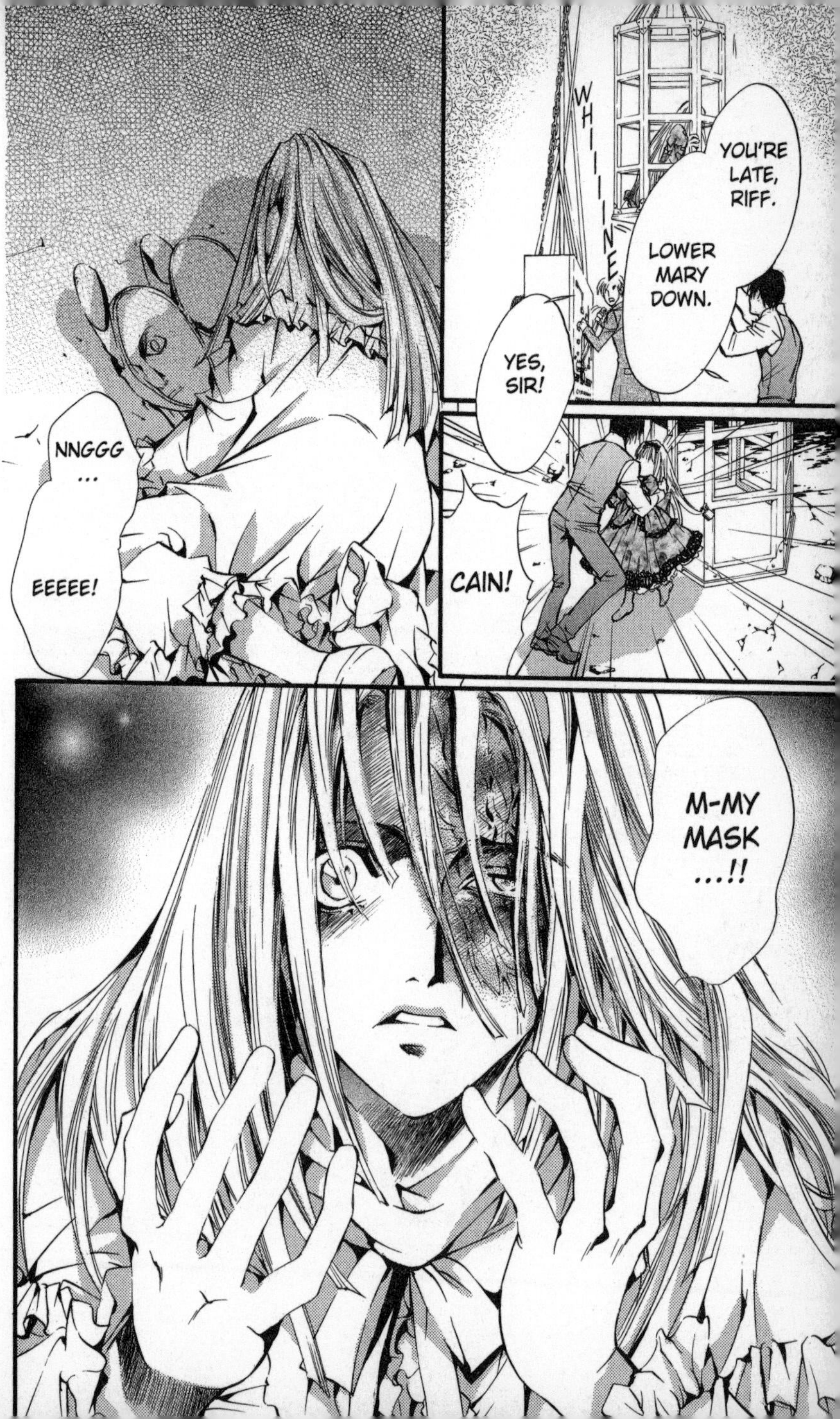
YOU'RE LATE, RIFF.
LOWER MARY DOWN.
WHIIIINE
YES, SIR!
CAIN!
NNGGG ...
EEEEE!
M-MY MASK ...!!

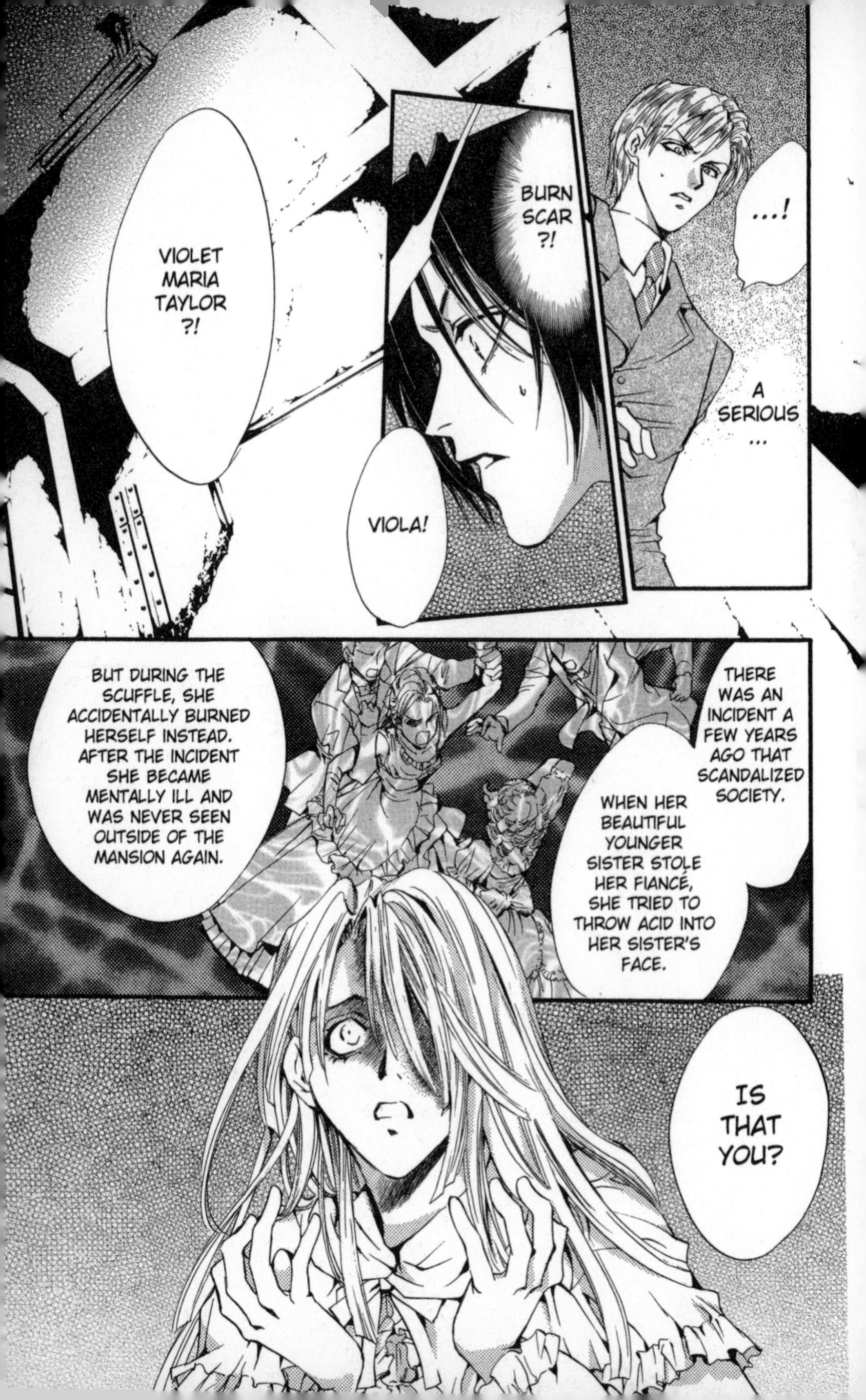
...!
A SERIOUS ...
BURN SCAR ?!
VIOLA!
VIOLET MARIA TAYLOR ?!
THERE WAS AN INCIDENT A FEW YEARS AGO THAT SCANDALIZED SOCIETY.
WHEN HER BEAUTIFUL YOUNGER SISTER STOLE HER FIANCÉ, SHE TRIED TO THROW ACID INTO HER SISTER'S FACE.
BUT DURING THE SCUFFLE, SHE ACCIDENTALLY BURNED HERSELF INSTEAD. AFTER THE INCIDENT SHE BECAME MENTALLY ILL AND WAS NEVER SEEN OUTSIDE OF THE MANSION AGAIN.
IS THAT YOU?

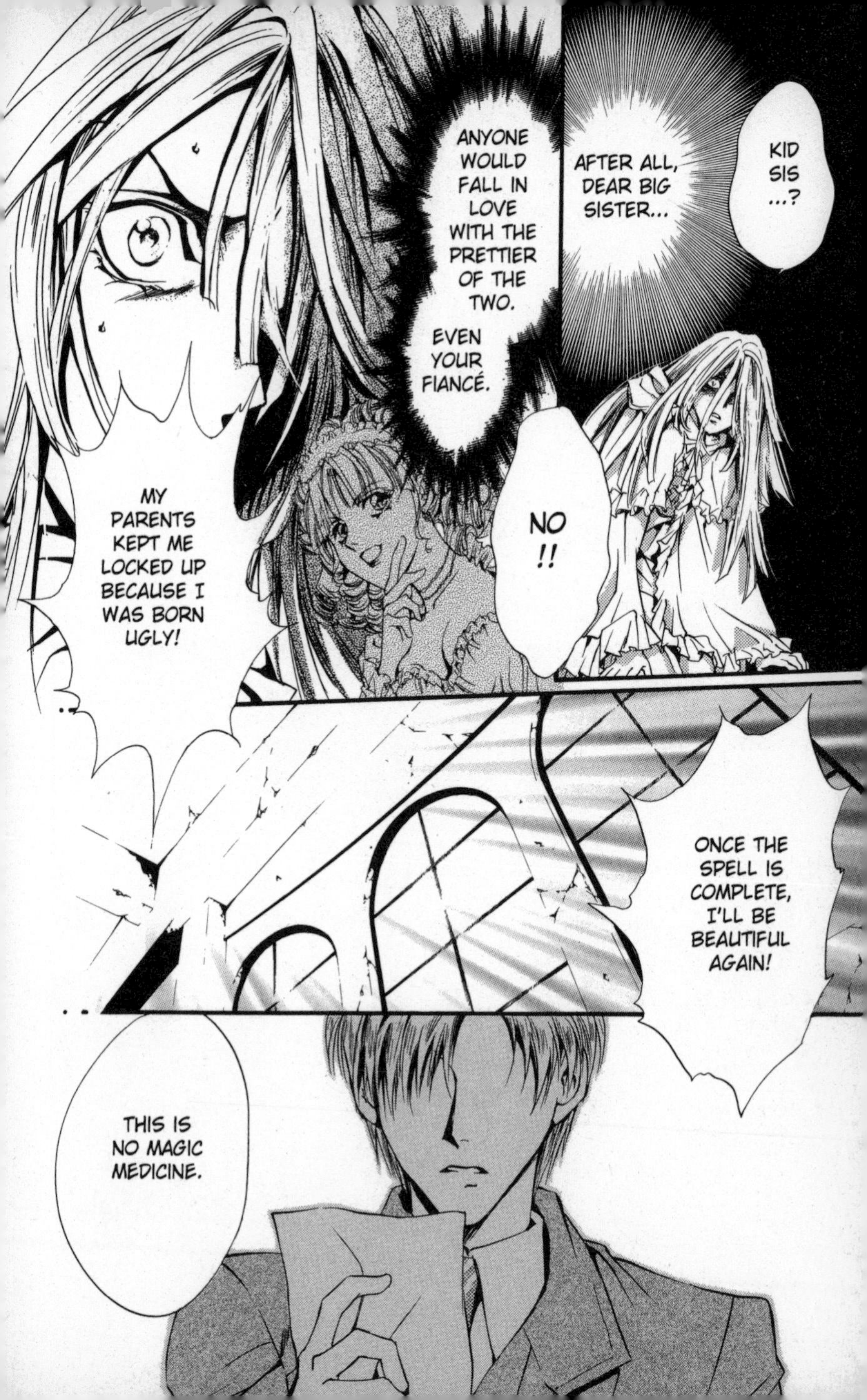
KID SIS ...?
AFTER ALL, DEAR BIG SISTER...
ANYONE WOULD FALL IN LOVE WITH THE PRETTIER OF THE TWO.
EVEN YOUR FIANCÉ.
NO !!
MY PARENTS KEPT ME LOCKED UP BECAUSE I WAS BORN UGLY!
ONCE THE SPELL IS COMPLETE, I'LL BE BEAUTIFUL AGAIN!
THIS IS NO MAGIC MEDICINE.

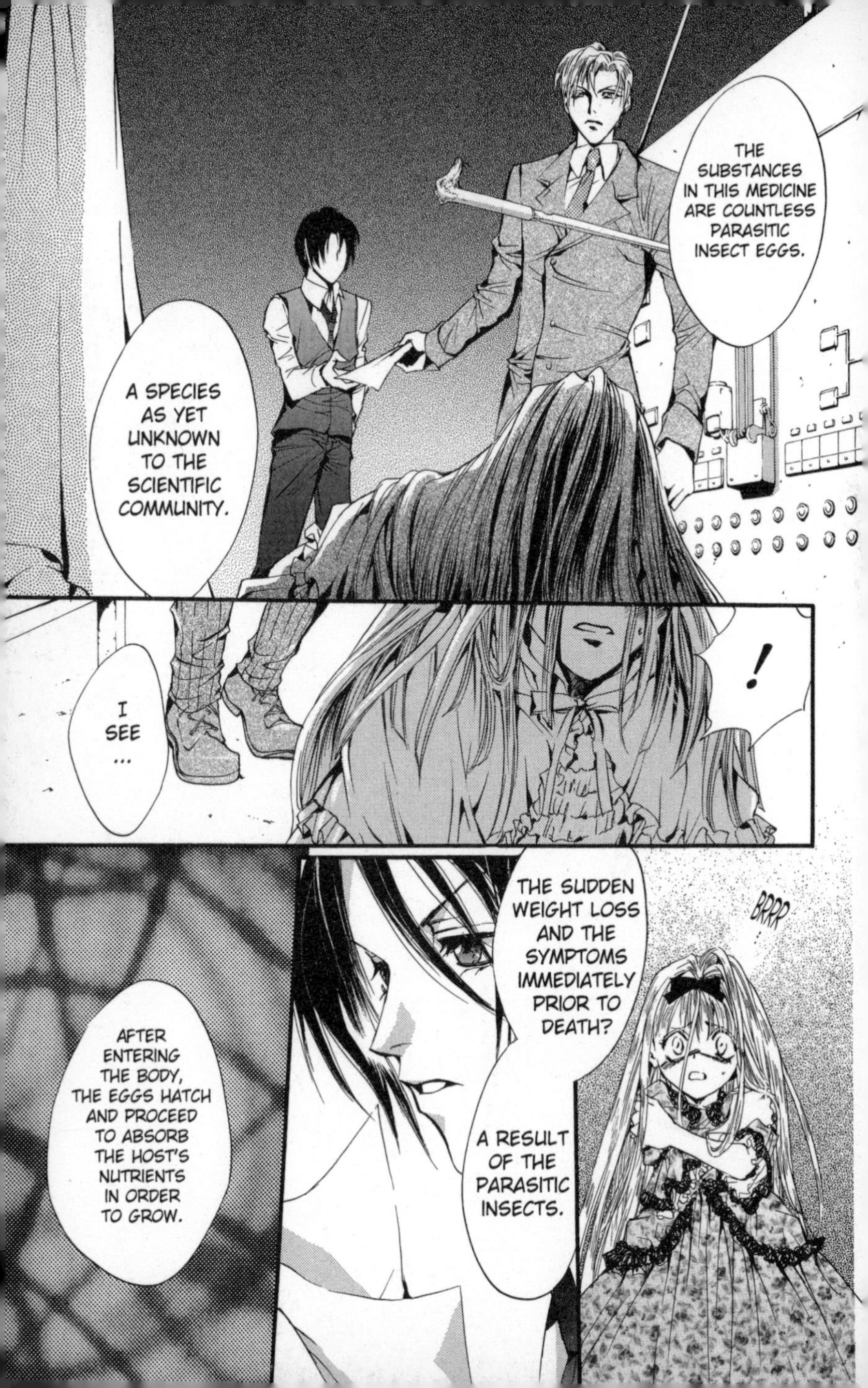
THE SUBSTANCES IN THIS MEDICINE ARE COUNTLESS PARASITIC INSECT EGGS.
A SPECIES AS YET UNKNOWN TO THE SCIENTIFIC COMMUNITY.
!
I SEE ...
BRRR
THE SUDDEN WEIGHT LOSS AND THE SYMPTOMS IMMEDIATELY PRIOR TO DEATH?
A RESULT OF THE PARASITIC INSECTS.
AFTER ENTERING THE BODY, THE EGGS HATCH AND PROCEED TO ABSORB THE HOST'S NUTRIENTS IN ORDER TO GROW.

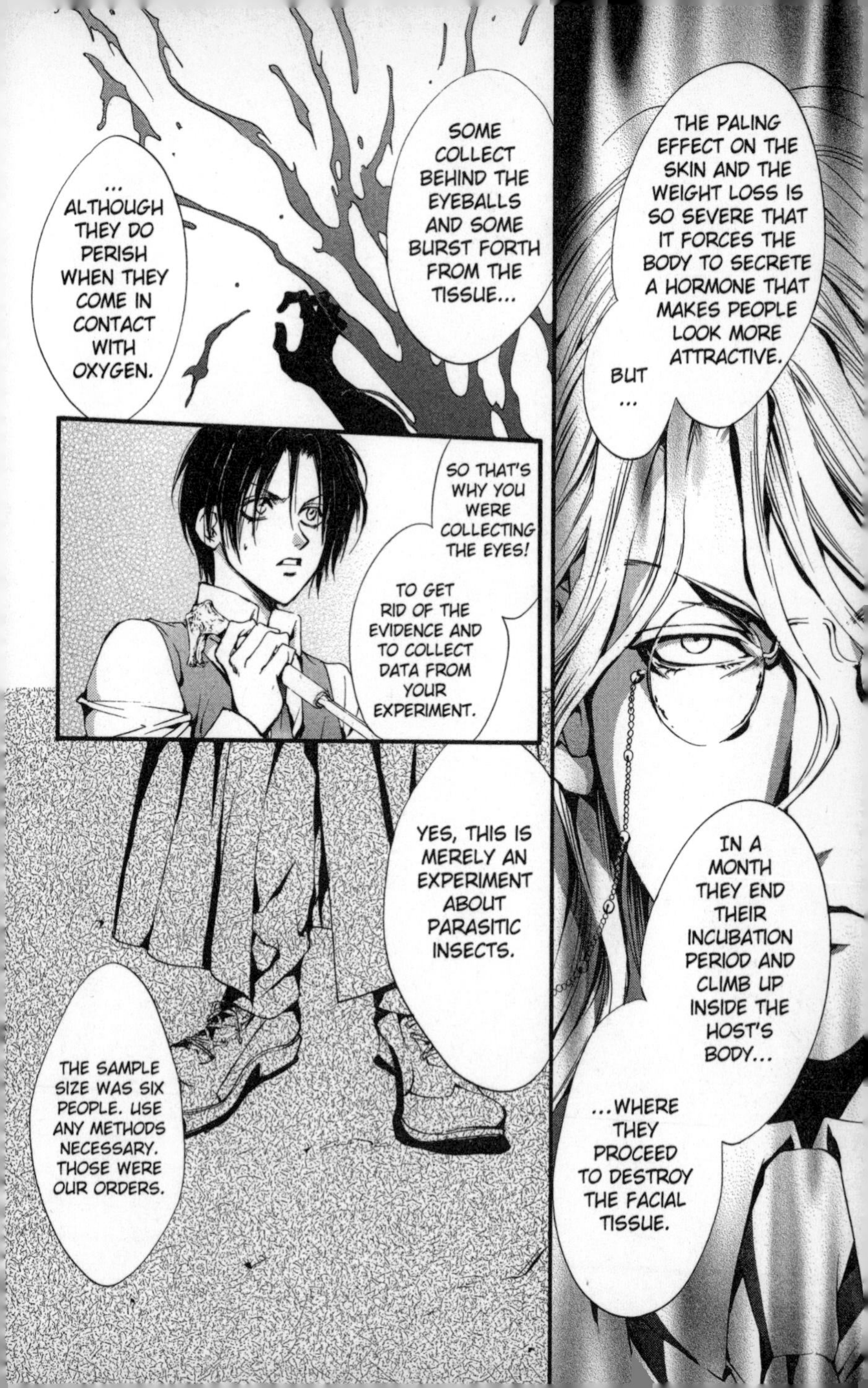
THE PALING EFFECT ON THE SKIN AND THE WEIGHT LOSS IS SO SEVERE THAT IT FORCES THE BODY TO SECRETE A HORMONE THAT MAKES PEOPLE LOOK MORE ATTRACTIVE.
BUT ...
IN A MONTH THEY END THEIR INCUBATION PERIOD AND CLIMB UP INSIDE THE HOST'S BODY...
...WHERE THEY PROCEED TO DESTROY THE FACIAL TISSUE.
SOME COLLECT BEHIND THE EYEBALLS AND SOME BURST FORTH FROM THE TISSUE...
... ALTHOUGH THEY DO PERISH WHEN THEY COME IN CONTACT WITH OXYGEN.
SO THAT'S WHY YOU WERE COLLECTING THE EYES!
TO GET RID OF THE EVIDENCE AND TO COLLECT DATA FROM YOUR EXPERIMENT.
YES, THIS IS MERELY AN EXPERIMENT ABOUT PARASITIC INSECTS.
THE SAMPLE SIZE WAS SIX PEOPLE. USE ANY METHODS NECESSARY. THOSE WERE OUR ORDERS.

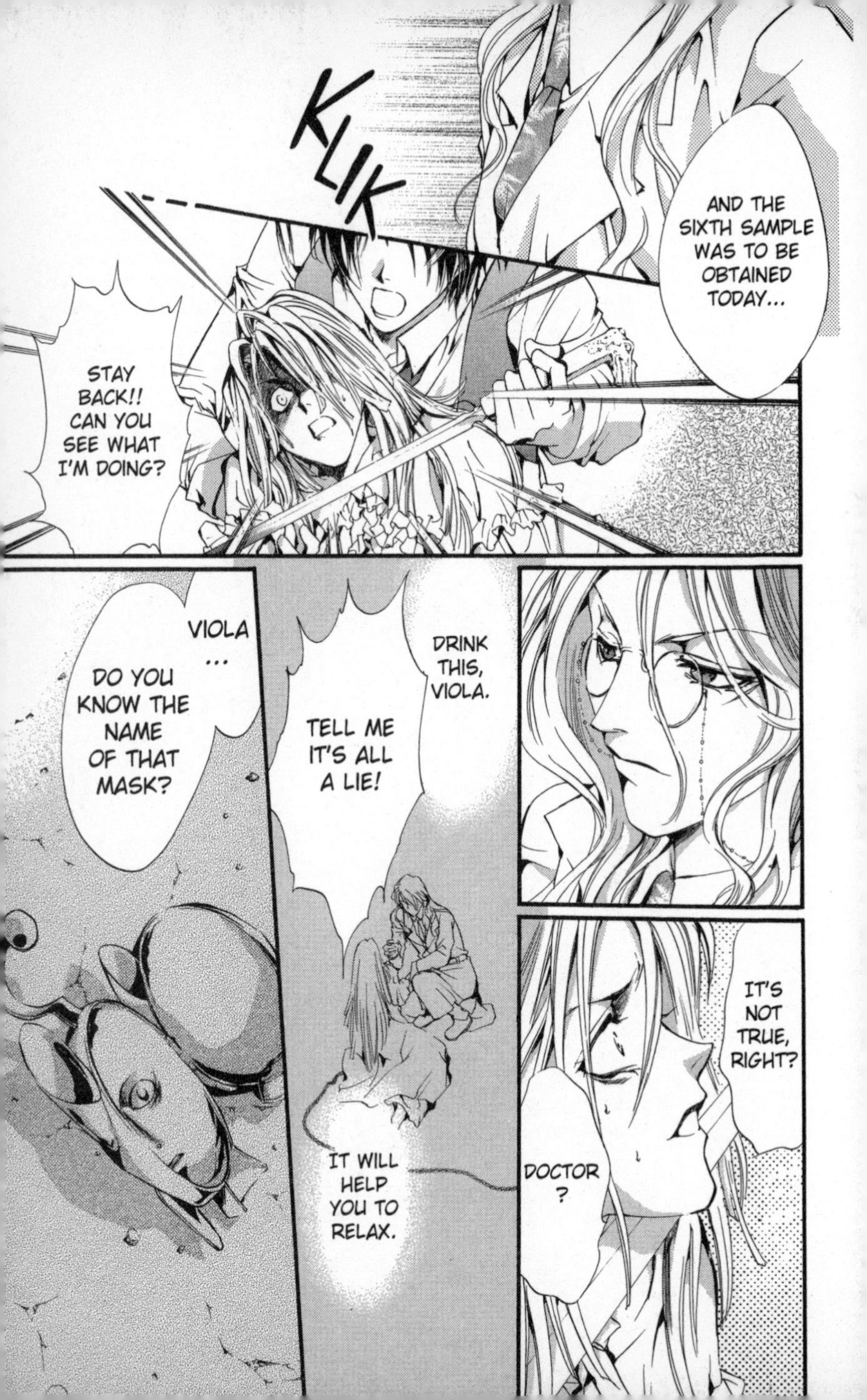
AND THE SIXTH SAMPLE WAS TO BE OBTAINED TODAY...
KLIK
STAY BACK!! CAN YOU SEE WHAT I'M DOING?
IT'S NOT TRUE, RIGHT?
DOCTOR?
DRINK THIS, VIOLA.
TELL ME IT'S ALL A LIE!
IT WILL HELP YOU TO RELAX.
VIOLA...
DO YOU KNOW THE NAME OF THAT MASK?

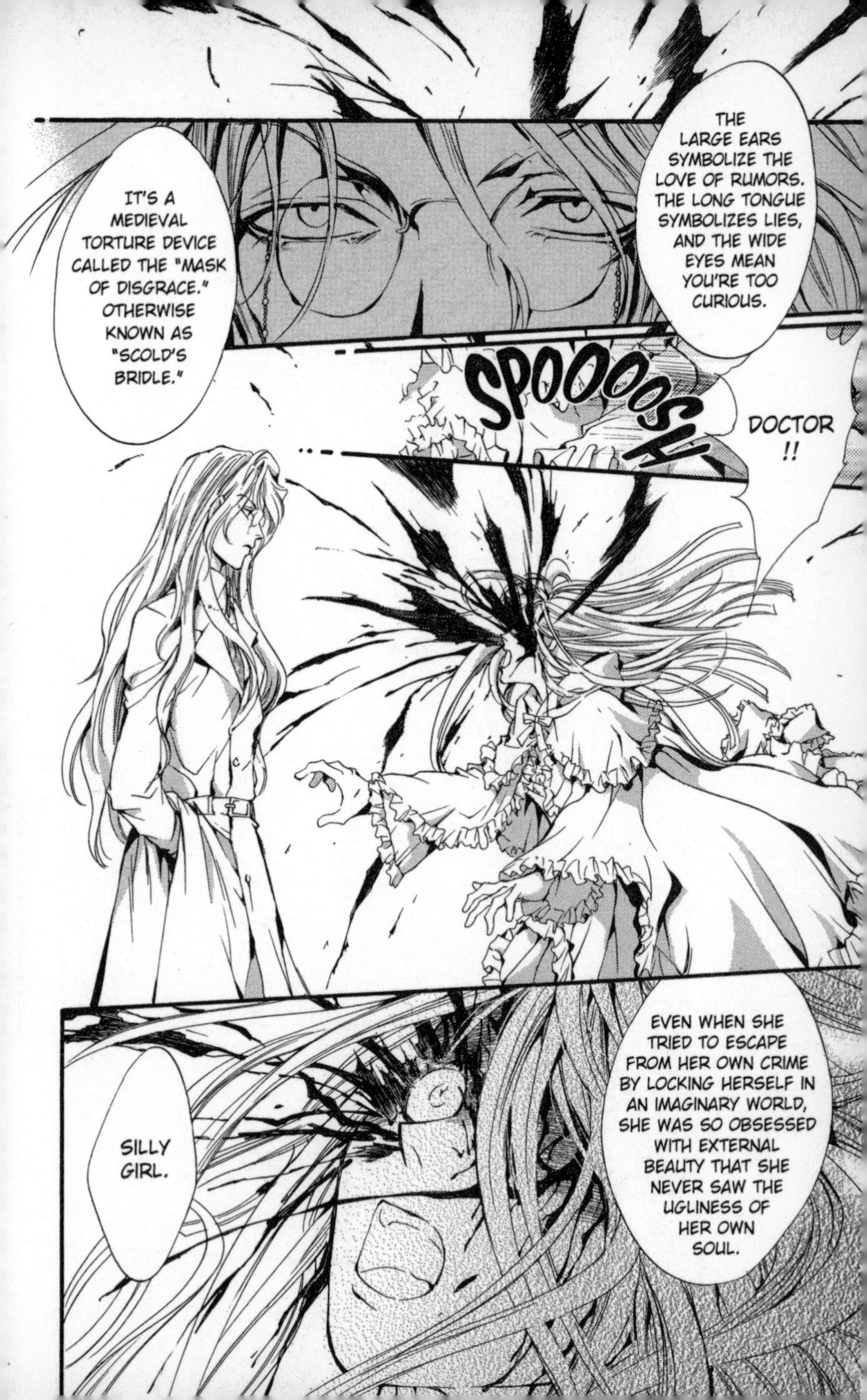
THE LARGE EARS SYMBOLIZE THE LOVE OF RUMORS. THE LONG TONGUE SYMBOLIZES LIES, AND THE WIDE EYES MEAN YOU'RE TOO CURIOUS.
IT'S A MEDIEVAL TORTURE DEVICE CALLED THE "MASK OF DISGRACE." OTHERWISE KNOWN AS "SCOLD'S BRIDLE."
DOCTOR !!
SPOOOOSH
EVEN WHEN SHE TRIED TO ESCAPE FROM HER OWN CRIME BY LOCKING HERSELF IN AN IMAGINARY WORLD, SHE WAS SO OBSESSED WITH EXTERNAL BEAUTY THAT SHE NEVER SAW THE UGLINESS OF HER OWN SOUL.
SILLY GIRL.

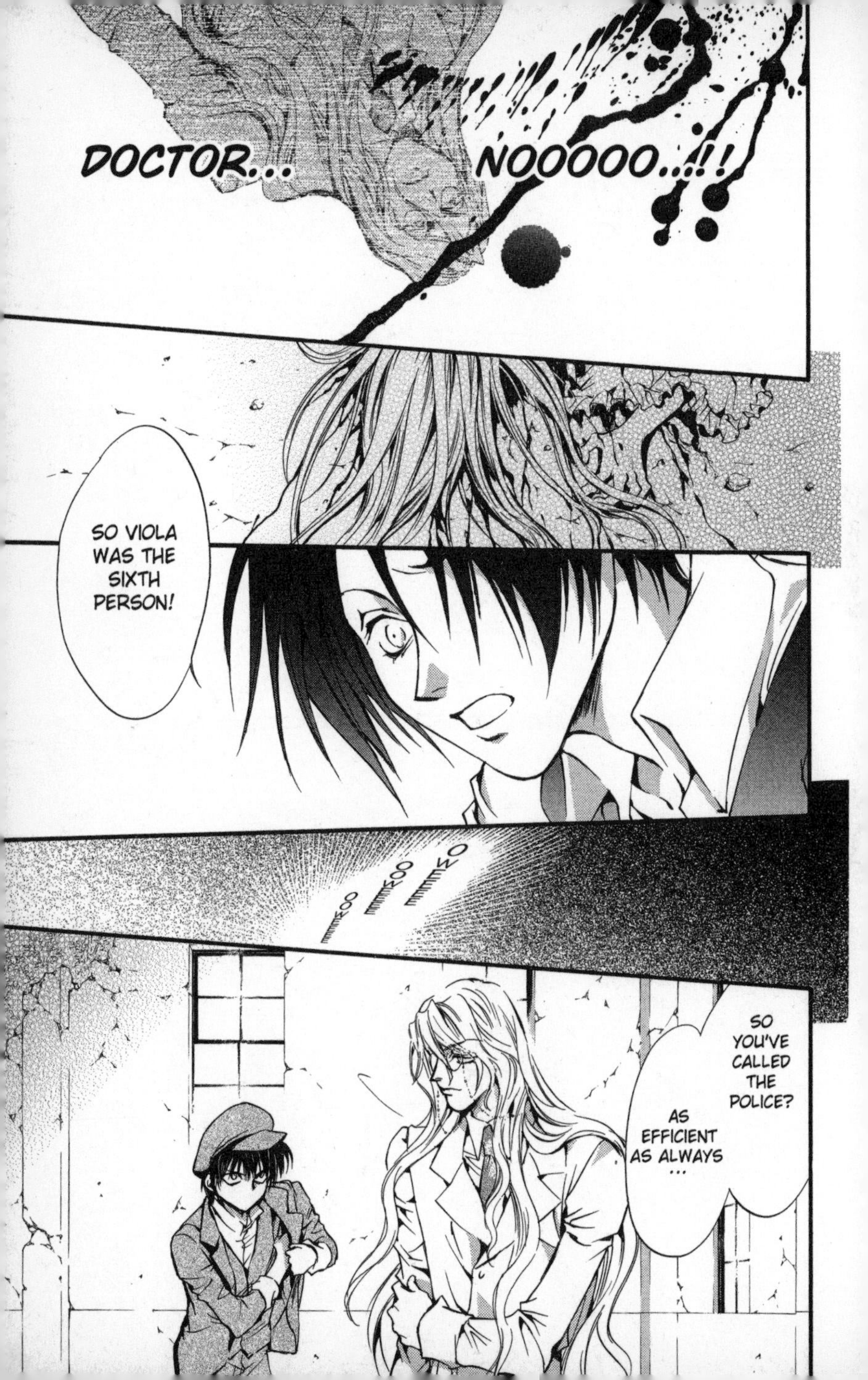
NOOOOO...!!
DOCTOR...
SO VIOLA WAS THE SIXTH PERSON!
OWEEE
OWEEE
OWEEE
SO YOU'VE CALLED THE POLICE?
AS EFFICIENT AS ALWAYS ...

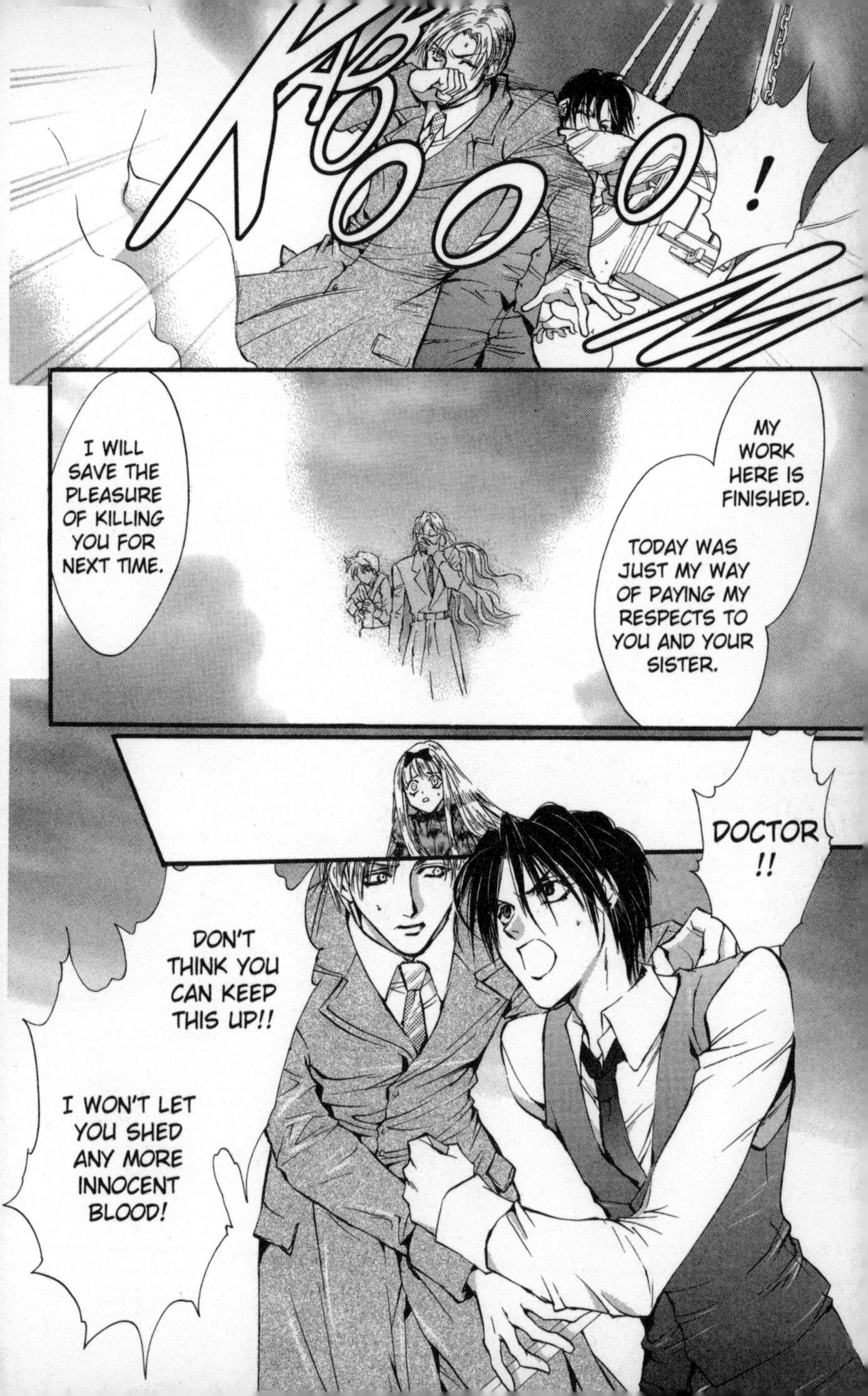
KABOOOOOM!
MY WORK HERE IS FINISHED.
TODAY WAS JUST MY WAY OF PAYING MY RESPECTS TO YOU AND YOUR SISTER.
I WILL SAVE THE PLEASURE OF KILLING YOU FOR NEXT TIME.
DOCTOR!!
DON'T THINK YOU CAN KEEP THIS UP!!
I WON'T LET YOU SHED ANY MORE INNOCENT BLOOD!

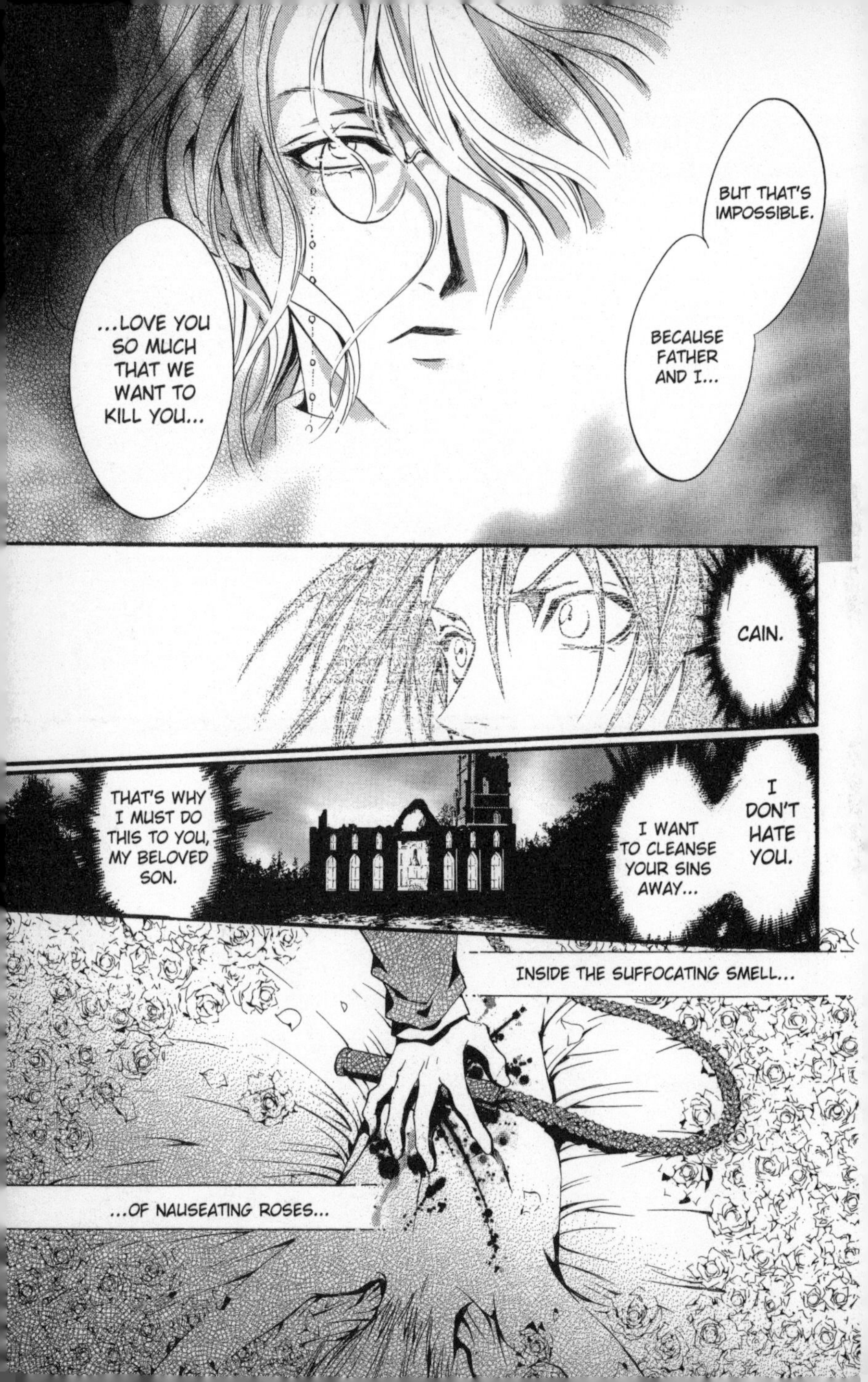
BUT THAT'S IMPOSSIBLE.
BECAUSE FATHER AND I...
...LOVE YOU SO MUCH THAT WE WANT TO KILL YOU...
CAIN.
I DON'T HATE YOU.
I WANT TO CLEANSE YOUR SINS AWAY...
THAT'S WHY I MUST DO THIS TO YOU, MY BELOVED SON.
INSIDE THE SUFFOCATING SMELL...
...OF NAUSEATING ROSES...

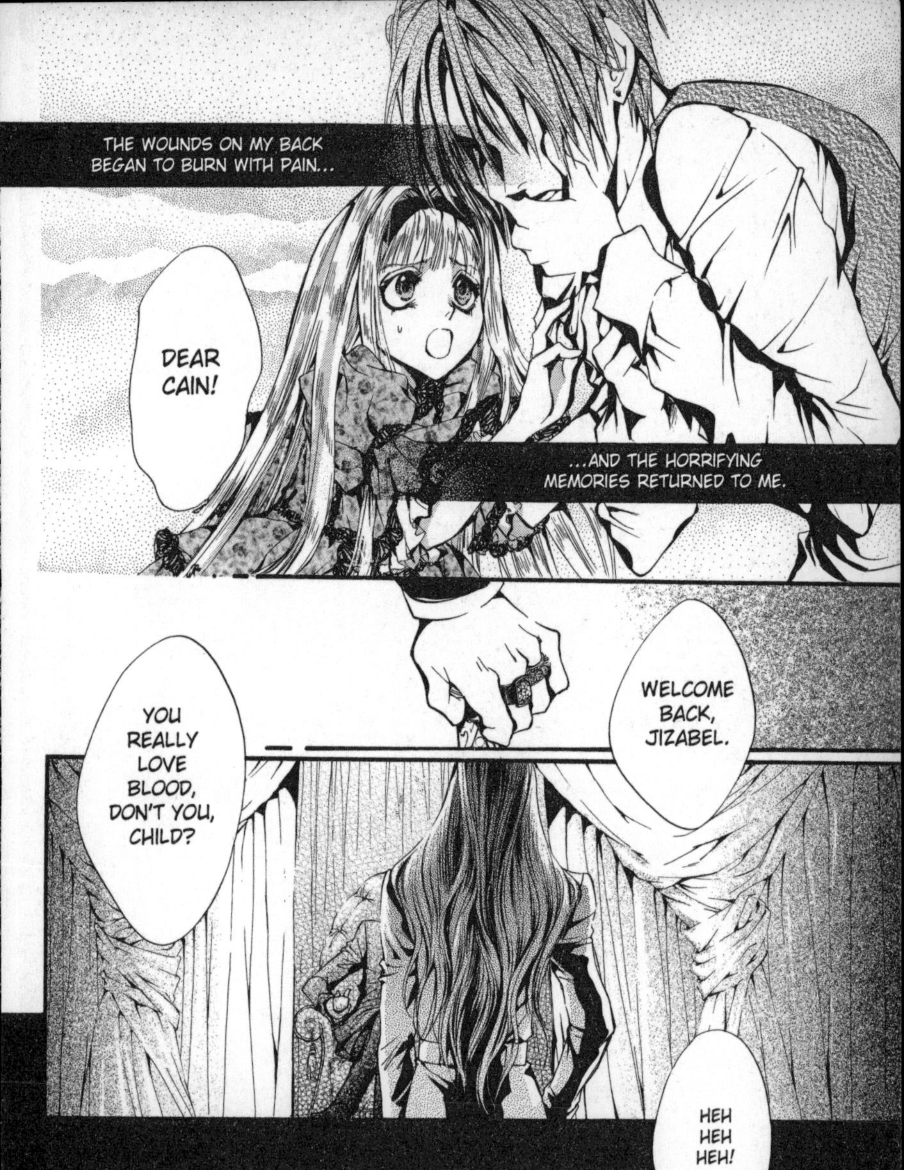
THE WOUNDS ON MY BACK BEGAN TO BURN WITH PAIN...
DEAR CAIN!
...AND THE HORRIFYING MEMORIES RETURNED TO ME.
WELCOME BACK, JIZABEL.
YOU REALLY LOVE BLOOD, DON'T YOU, CHILD?
HEH HEH HEH!
And that's all…?
Scold's Bridle/ The End

LET'S GO TO THE MEADOWS.

CAIN, WHO DID NOT LOOK BACK AT THE OFFERINGS,
KILLED HIS BROTHER ABEL.

CAIN, THE BLOOD OF YOUR DEAD BROTHER CRIES OUT FROM
BENEATH THE GROUND. YOU'VE BEEN CURSED BY THE GROUND THAT
YOU'VE BLEMISHED AND FORCED TO ROAM THE LAND FOREVER.

BUT NOW SOMEONE WILL TRY TO TAKE MY LIFE.

CAIN, THEN I WILL UNLEASH A PUNISHMENT OF REVENGE
SEVEN TIMES GREATER TO THAT PERSON, SO THAT
YOU WILL NOT BE KILLED.

CAIN BECAME A WANDERER OF THE WORLD.

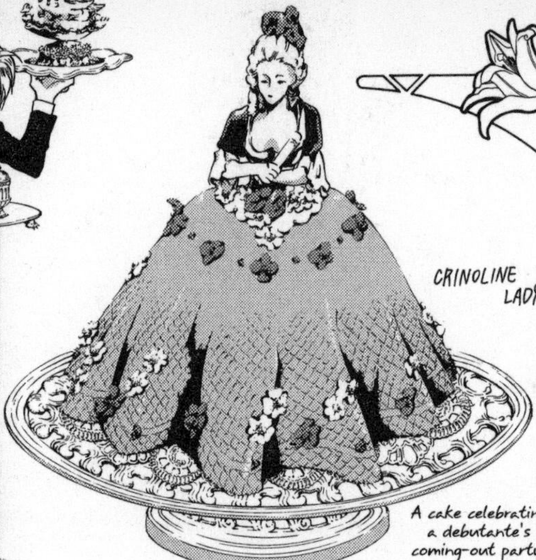

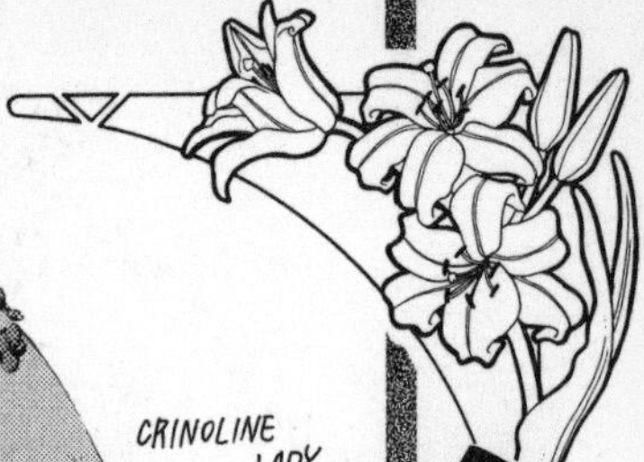

CRINOLINE LADY.

A cake celebrating a debutante's coming-out party.

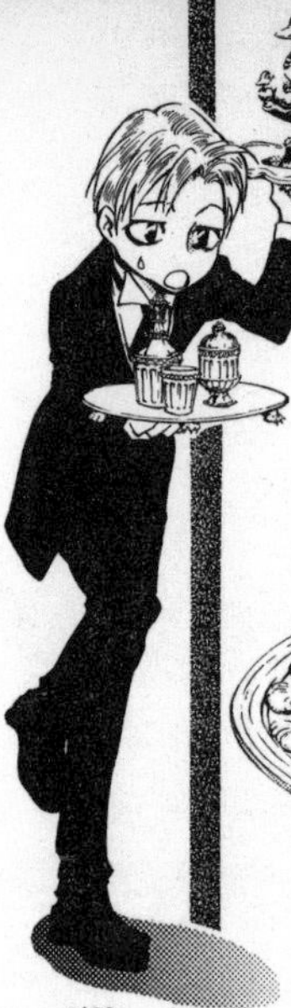

Riff

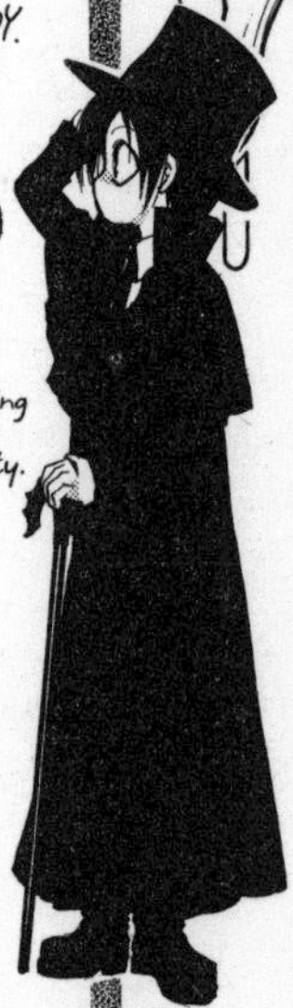

Cain

I want to thank all the returning readers and all the new ones as well. This series starring Cain, the Earl of Poison, was a separate project, published in a magazine before this. So there's a lag time of about six to seven years since it started, and as a result, those who were reading it back then are probably all over the age of 20 by now. (A new manga artist just told me that she used to read it back in elementary school. Aaah, the flow of time!) That's why I'm slightly perplexed at how most readers are probably reading this series for the first time. In an attempt to make it easier for readers to come back, I've included some past episodes. I re-introduced the characters in order and shortened the narrations. Now, thanks to all of you, the series has been a big hit since its publication. Thank you very much. Also, to all the people who read the first Cain series, sorry to keep you waiting. My drawing style has changed quite a bit from the previous series. Cain's and Mary's hair lengths have changed as well, but the story's plotline is the same as before.

◆

I would like to learn from your letters, so it would please me very much if you would send me your comments! If you can, please tell me about your favorite character and episode. (In Godchild.)

Address: Viz Media
295 Bay St.
San Francisco, CA 94133
Attn: Godchild Favorite Character

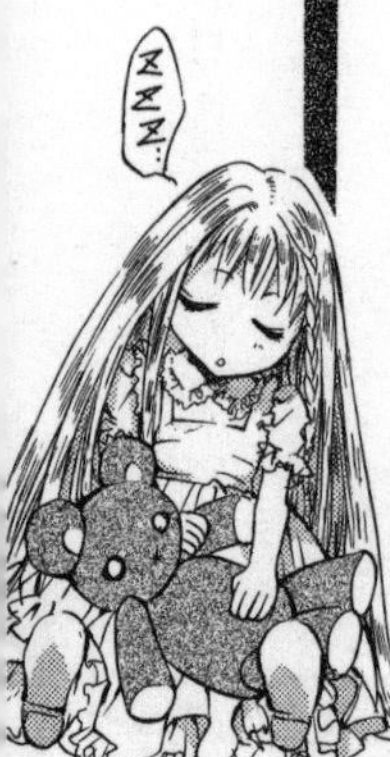
MMM...

Marie

Dr. Disraeli ♥

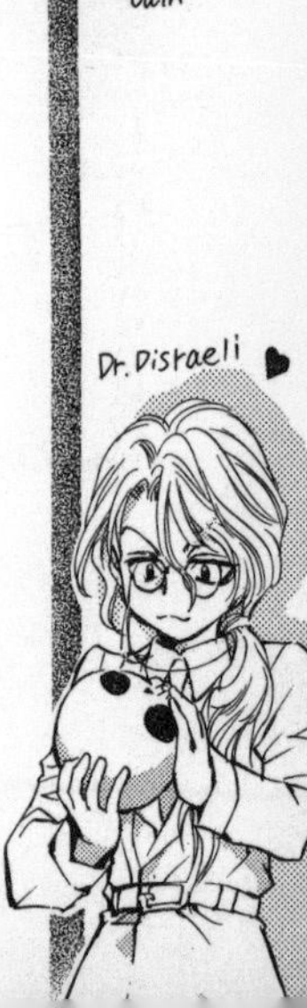

Greater London Traveler Log

Not really quite all that, but...

I went to London to do research for this new series! I thought I'd be going to some unusual locations, but I ended up going to all the normal tourist spots: the Tower of London, Windsor Castle, Thames River, Westminster Abbey, Big Ben, the British Museum, and Hyde Park. Next time I'd like to see Stonehenge and Eaton School, too. I was a little disappointed that I didn't get to drink any really delicious tea, but the food was pretty good. I bought a lot of reference books and took a ton of pictures. But the British Empire is full of mysteries, and there is so much that I still don't know about its long history. I went there in October, so it was really cold!! Next time I'd like to go during the summer, when there's lots of beautiful greenery. It was a very nice place. I want to go again!!

See you again in Volume 2!

2001/07/5.
Kaori Yuki
XXX

Epilogue/ The End

Creator: Kaori Yuki

Date of Birth: December 18

Blood Type: B

Major Works: *Angel Sanctuary*
and *The Cain Saga*

Kaori Yuki was born in Tokyo and started drawing at a very early age. Following her debut work *Natsufuku no Erie* (Ellie in Summer Clothes) in the Japanese magazine *Bessatsu Hana to Yume* (1987), she wrote a compelling series of short stories: *Zankoku na Douwatachi* (Cruel Fairy Tales), *Neji* (Screw), and *Sareki Ôkoku* (Gravel Kingdom).

As proven by her best-selling series *Angel Sanctuary* and *The Cain Saga*, her celebrated body of work has etched an indelible mark on the gothic comics genre. She likes mysteries and British films, and is a fan of the movie *Dead Poets Society* and the show *Twin Peaks*.

GODCHILD, vol. 1
The Shojo Beat Manga Edition

This manga volume contains material that was originally published in English
in *Shojo Beat* magazine, July - August 2005 issues.

STORY & ART BY KAORI YUKI

English Adaptation/Trina Robbins
Translation/Akira Watanabe
Touch-up Art & Lettering/James Gaubatz
Design/Courtney Utt
Editors/Michelle Pangilinan & Joel Enos

Editor in Chief, Books/Alvin Lu
Editor in Chief, Magazines/Marc Weidenbaum
VP of Publishing Licensing/Rika Inouye
VP of Sales/Gonzalo Ferreyra
Sr. VP of Marketing/Liza Coppola
Publisher/Hyoe Narita

God Child by Kaori Yuki © Kaori Yuki 2001. All rights reserved. First published in Japan in 2001
by HAKUSENSHA, Inc., Tokyo. English language translation rights in America and Canada arranged
with HAKUSENSHA, Inc., Tokyo. The Godchild logo is a trademark of VIZ Media, LLC.
The stories, characters and incidents mentioned in this publication are entirely fictional.

Printed in Canada

Published by VIZ Media, LLC
P.O. Box 77010
San Francisco, CA 94107

Shojo Beat Manga Edition
10 9 8 7 6 5
First printing, March 2006
Fifth printing, August 2007

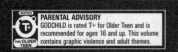

PARENTAL ADVISORY
GODCHILD is rated T+ for Older Teen and is
recommended for ages 16 and up. This volume
contains graphic violence and adult themes.

store.viz.com

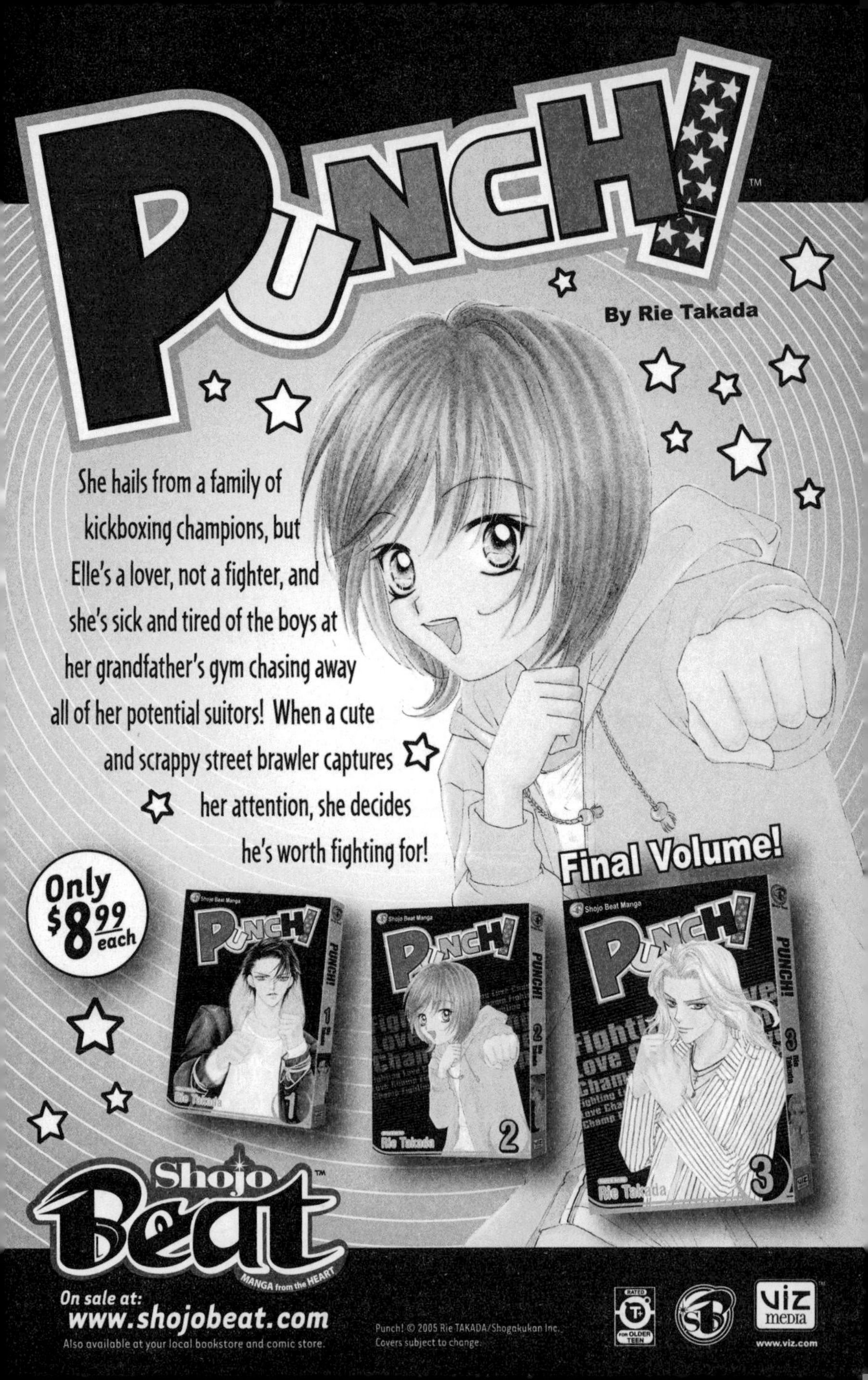
PUNCH!™
By Rie Takada
She hails from a family of kickboxing champions, but Elle's a lover, not a fighter, and she's sick and tired of the boys at her grandfather's gym chasing away all of her potential suitors! When a cute and scrappy street brawler captures her attention, she decides he's worth fighting for!
Only $8.99 each
Final Volume!
Shojo Beat™
MANGA from the HEART
On sale at:
www.shojobeat.com
Also available at your local bookstore and comic store.
Punch! © 2005 Rie TAKADA/Shogakukan Inc.
Covers subject to change.
RATED T+ FOR OLDER TEEN
VIZ media
www.viz.com

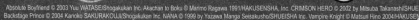